Family Living

Family Living

1961 Edition

EVELYN MILLIS DUVALL, Ph.D. _-1906_
Family Life Consultant

Edited by Dora S. Lewis
Chairman, Department of Home Economics
Hunter College, New York City

The Macmillan Company: New York

Introduction

The Educational Department of The Macmillan Company now makes available a series of five textbooks for the Home Economics Department. Central in this series is this edition of *Family Living*. It has been completely rewritten to meet the need of senior-high-school students for instruction which makes a significant contribution to education for responsible personal and family living.

The author, eminent in the field of family education, has carefully selected subject matter and experiences to prepare young people for taking increasing responsibility for their own development, for facing life frankly, for thinking and acting with integrity in all human relationships, focusing specifically on relationships with parents, siblings, and friends. They are encouraged to set life goals and to move toward them, to develop basic respect for themselves and others, to clarify their values in regard to family life and to consider the purposes, attitudes, and behavior patterns for dating, courtship, and an engagement period which will be effective preparation for marriage.

Choosing a marriage partner realistically, anticipating situations that are apt to arise in marriage, and ways of meeting these situations intelligently are discussed. Realizing that students look forward to parenthood and formulate some bases for understanding the needs of children, *Family Living* emphasizes family development and the interdependence of families and communities. These are aspects of education that all secondary schools are challenged to make available to students of both sexes before high-school graduation.

It is anticipated, therefore, that *Family Living* will be widely used in whatever department of the high school these aspects of family education are developed. Certainly all departments of home economics will find it indispensable.

The first book of The Macmillan Company series of five for departments of home economics, *Tomorrow's Homemaker*, was written with the needs of junior-high-school students in focus. It provides content for a general introductory course. Each of the four senior-high-school books deals comprehensively with specific areas of home economics. *Housing and Home Manage-*

ment presents the home in the community as the setting for the life of the family, the selection, arrangement, and use of furnishings and equipment, and encourages the development of skills needed to extend resources and to achieve the goal of a well-managed home. *Clothing Construction and Wardrobe Planning* helps students to appraise clothing needs and wants, to develop good taste and the ability to buy wisely, and directs experiences in constructing garments. *Family Meals and Hospitality* gives guides to good nutrition at different cost levels in line with advances in nutrition knowledge and new developments in good products. It emphasizes the social aspects of skillful and creative food management.

Each book in the series encourages students (1) to think critically and to apply principles of science, art, economics, and human relationships to problems of personal and home living; (2) to make decisions and choices in the light of values important to family and community living; (3) to learn to work competently in the home by developing essential homemaking skills; and (4) to make long-range plans based on thoughtful consideration of what life can be if the newer knowledge of the many resources now available to them is used with purpose and understanding.

Young people are more than ever determined to make their marriages a success. The authors and editors of The Macmillan Series for Home Economics believe that each of their books will contribute significantly to the development of the competences that are basic to them for this success in personal and family living.

DORA S. LEWIS

Preface

Family life education in the high schools has become generally accepted since the first edition of *Family Living* appeared in 1950. Until then, exploratory programs proved their worth in forward-looking schools in many communities. Now secondary schools with no emphasis on personal and family living are the exception.

Converging forces from several directions have thrust a focus on family living into the curriculum: (1) student demand for this subject matter so central to their present and future well-being; (2) public faith in education as a constructive approach to such growing problems as youthful indiscretions, exclusive dating, going steady, young marriages, and failing families; (3) teacher readiness, reflecting increased emphasis on family life education by teacher-training institutions and family life workshops and institutes now available across the country; (4) administrative awareness that, even in the Space Age, a relatively small percentage of students will be needed as scientists, whereas practically all must function as family members now and tomorrow as home builders; and (5) text coverage incorporating the growing body of objective research, maturing concepts, and ongoing values in an academically substantial field of study:

Human development is the central theme of this text. Persons are seen as growing in their abilities to understand themselves and others, to handle many situations with increasing competence, and to make decisions in terms of the lasting values of life. Young people are helped to see their own maturation as persons, along with their parents' continued growth within the context of family development through the years.

Student interest is the point of departure for each topic throughout the text. As family life consultant, the author has for many years worked closely with hundreds of thousands of high-school students and their teachers in various types of family living programs. In each situation the questions students raised for discussion were analyzed for content and correlated by age, grade, sex, and region. The universal nature of the major questions that come up whenever young people articulate their real concerns is clear. It is this central core of student interest that forms the basis for the body of this text.

Functionality is the philosophy of education upon which this text is based. In each area of study, results of research, clinical findings, statistical evidence, and major concepts are focused upon the questions that young people themselves are asking. Fallacies and folklore are exposed to the floodlights of scientifically established reality. Students are helped to weigh the evidence, to envisage various consequences of the several available possibilities, and to make decisions in terms of the present and future well-being of themselves and others.

Boys and girls together or separately can find themselves at home in these pages. Mixed classes are becoming increasingly accepted in the many areas of family living common to both sexes. In schools where home economics classes are restricted to girls, the materials are equally relevant.

Updating and upgrading make this basically a new book. A wealth of new material from many sources appearing within the past decade enrich and enliven the content. Beyond this all-inclusive updating has been a general upgrading of the text to meet the higher level of sophistication of today's high-school students. Family life education itself has matured over the past decade, requiring at every grade more substantial theory and research foundation than once was expected.

One unit or six can be the area of study. Each unit is complete in itself, and, with the others, provides the basis for a full year's course. The six units of the text advance from the individual's consideration of himself as a growing personality to his relationships with others within his family and his own age group, through his interest in the processes that lead to successful marriage, his concern for the development and guidance of children, and finally to his growing awareness of the larger aspects of American family life. Although these units are arranged from the simpler to the more advanced in content and developmental readiness, it is quite possible to start with any given unit for which a particular class is most clearly ready and work backward and forward through the text.

Modern teaching methods of proven effectiveness are introduced throughout. Suggested activities at the close of each chapter are designed both for individual study and group work, offering variety and challenge to assignments in each area of study. Student polls, simple research investigations, panel discussions, guided trips, action projects, interview reports, book reviews, research analysis, self-evaluation devices, tests, and development appraisers, role-playing, group dynamics, audio-visual aids of many kinds, and consultations with significant individuals outside the classroom are specifically described at the points where such methods would be most appropriate. Readings include not only the most relevant materials designed especially for high-school students, but also those primary sources that alert students find stimulating—all annotated for ready reference.

Family use of this text is widely reported. Mothers tell of asking their daughters to share their copies of *Family Living* with younger brothers and sisters. Fathers report their interest in these materials that were not part of their education only a brief generation ago. Young wives use the book as a ready reference in everyday living. This fourth dimension of family living through time is the most gratifying of all. For learning to live fully as a person among others is not achieved upon the successful completion of a unit or a course of study. It is beyond school that *Family Living* gets its most severe test—in the homes of tomorrow.

EVELYN MILLIS DUVALL

Contents

Max Tharpe from Monkmeyer

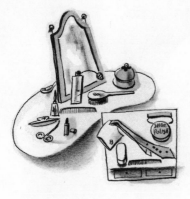

I

What Makes You—You
Your Development as a Teen-Ager
How Mature Are You?
What It Takes to Grow On

Your Growing Personality

Bloom from Monkmeyer

Chapter 1

What Makes You—You

Who are you? You say your name and address, but what do they mean? You know what family you have come from, and yet that is not all of you. You list your connections and still know that you have an individuality beyond them. All of this tells something about you, but it is only a small part of who you are and what you are becoming.

What do you see when you look in a mirror? You are first of all a boy or a girl. You are big or not so big for your age. You see a smile or a frown. You may be attractive, but still you may see room for improvement. You may gain a feeling of confidence from what you see, or you may be haunted by a sense of inadequacy. You may catch a glimpse of the way others see you and have seen you through the years.

Many, many influences have helped to make you you. What are these influences? How have they affected your development? What are the ways in which you have reacted to the pressures and opportunities that have surrounded you since before you were born? The answers to such questions as these help you understand yourself as you are now, and give you some idea of the direction in which you are developing.

You are in the process of becoming. Your past lies behind you and can be changed only in the ways you now think and feel about it. Your present is an immediate challenge. Your future depends upon how well you can take advantage of what you are and what you have in order to grow into the kind of person you have the capacity for becoming.

You are not completely self-made. Nor are you the helpless product of forces beyond your control. Both what you are and may become depend upon your interaction with life within and around you. The most important influence on what you are and what you will be is YOU—your perceptions about yourself now, your understanding of who you are, and your aspirations as to what you want to become.

3

What You Started With

Have you ever seen your baby pictures? Perhaps at some time or other your mother has shown you some of these first pictures of you. Maybe she said, "You were such a pretty baby!" Or perhaps your folks laugh and remind you that when you were small you were the homeliest little rascal they had ever seen. Whichever their verdict on your early beauty, you know and they know that it was not very important. The quality that made you the kind of baby whose picture adorns a camera company's advertisement is of little value later on when compared to the other qualities you may have had back there at the beginning.

Boy or Girl. Whether you were born a boy or a girl has naturally made a difference in your development. The way your mother cared for you indicated her feeling about having a boy or a girl. The way your father played with you reflected how he felt about having a son or a daughter. Your toys showed what your parents (and the neighbors) thought proper for boys, or girls, to play with. The hour of your bedtime, the distance from home you could range, the extent to which you were allowed to fight your own battles, the language you were allowed to use, the ways in which you had to help around the house, and a hundred other things, were all different from what they would have been had you been born a member of the other sex.[1]

Most important of all is the way you feel about being what you are—a boy or a girl. If, as a girl, you are happy to be a girl and look forward to being a woman, you have made a good adjustment to your sex. But if you have always hated being a girl and wished you were a boy instead, sometimes even pretending that you were a boy, being a woman may be hard for you.

Though some boys, too, wish they belonged to the opposite sex, this problem is less common among them than among girls. The reason is that in this country, boys and men seem to have more advantages than girls and women. Boys born into all-girl families, however, may be brought up so much like their older sisters that they find it hard to be real boys. Other young people often make it harder by calling them "sissies" [2] or laughing at their efforts to be more masculine. Such a boy has a greater problem in developing into a man-like man than has the boy who has grown up with a loving, manly father to be like and a mother who likes having a real boy around the house.

[1] Two studies exploring sex differences in child training are: W. Allison Davis and Robert J. Havighurst, *Father of the Man* (Boston: Houghton Mifflin Company, 1947); and Robert R. Sears, Eleanor E. Maccoby, and Harry Levin, *Patterns of Child Rearing* (Evanston, Illinois: Row, Peterson, and Company, 1957).

[2] Helen L. Koch, "Sissiness and Tomboyishness in Relation to Sibling Characteristics," *Journal of Genetic Psychology*, Vol. 88 (1956), pp. 231–44.

The way you feel about the other sex you have learned, too. If, as a boy, you have been bossed and dominated by the women in your life, you may fear that some woman will always be trying "to put something over on you." But, if you have grown up enjoying the companionship of your mother and the other females around you, you may find joy in knowing, understanding, and loving the woman who will one day be your wife.

If, as a girl, you were brought up to feel that men are to be feared and kept at a distance as dangerous creatures, you will have a hard time attracting boy friends, and learning to enjoy and feel at ease with men. But, if as a girl, you have learned to like boys and to love the men in your life, to be glad when a boy notices you, and to enjoy his companionship without fear or guilt, you have a good start toward becoming a warm and appealing woman.

Playing one's sex role as our society expects it to be played is one of the most difficult adjustments any of us ever has to make. Being born a boy or a girl started you off on one of the two big forks in the road of life from the very beginning.

Your Individual Characteristics. "Am I normal?" you naturally wonder as you grow up. The answer is that most of us are amazingly all right. One of the miracles of life is that so many of us are so normal. Of course, all of us have some slight irregularities that we were born with: moles, little birthmarks, and other skin imperfections. Sometimes there is a harelip, or an abnormality of hand or foot, or a facial peculiarity that has been there from the beginning. Modern science is doing a great deal to correct many of these imperfections. But the big job is up to each of us. It is the way we feel about our peculiarities that makes the difference between a mature, able person and a timid, beaten spirit. The best approach is: *If it can be changed, change it; of not, live with it without shame.*

You inherited many of your individual characteristics from both your mother's and your father's side of the family. From all your ancestors, farther back than you can trace, you have inherited the particular combination of characteristics and tendencies that partly makes you what you are. Many of these inherited traits are already very familiar to you—the color of your skin and hair and whether your hair curls or not, for instance.

Some inherited traits may not show up for a long time. Your father's present tendency to baldness may have been set in him from the beginning. The tendency to live a long life seems to be inherited. Musical ability apparently comes down in families. Mathematical genius may have its beginnings in a good inheritance for this trait. The interesting thing about many of these characteristics is that they are very rarely the result of either inheritance or training alone, but rather of a combination of both.

Your Body: Born and Built. You inherited a certain kind of body. You may have a very efficient body system that utilizes its food well and gives you great vitality, or it may be that your body functions more slowly. Your re-sistance to certain diseases may be high or low. In physique you may tend to be tall or short, rounded or lean, muscular or not so strong. Research studies [3] indicate that there is some relationship between physique and temperament. There may be some truth in the popular observation that fat people are jolly and placid, while tall, lean people are often nervous. This relationship between physique and temperament, however, need not always be the same. It depends greatly on the person's attitudes and upon the use he makes of his endowment.

The physical tendencies with which you are born are at best only po-tentialities. With adequate nutrition, rest, exercise, and good care, your body will function near the peak of its ability. If you neglect or abuse it, you may be handicapped by ailments. Look upon your body with respect and apprecia-tion, guard its health as a precious heritage, and the chances are that it will serve you well.

History is full of men who have built vigorous lives upon frail physiques. Theodore Roosevelt started out as a puny lad and became one of the most active men of his time. Franklin Delano Roosevelt became a world leader after being crippled by poliomyelitis. Helen Keller, both deaf and blind from babyhood on, learned to live a full life and is beloved and admired by people everywhere. Elizabeth Barrett Browning, an invalid for years, healed herself with her strong, vital love for her husband. Thousands of people all over the world have shown that, even on a frail physical base, life can be full and happy.

Using Your Special Abilities. The way you use your talents appears to be quite as important a factor in your development as what you started with. Take intellectual ability as an example. Intelligence is partly based on heredity. Other things being equal, bright people have bright children, and dull, feeble-minded parents have subnormal children. Studies at the University of Iowa,[4] however, show that this is not the whole story. When children whose parents are below average in intelligence are raised by normally intelligent people, they tend to develop IQ's closer to those of their foster parents than to those of their real parents! Many other studies show that all of us are born with more potential intelligence that we ever use. How much of our ability develops depends on our environment, our reaction to it, and our willingness to learn. The way you use and develop what you have is, in the final analysis, up to you.

There Is No One Else Just Like You. Nature has a rather wonderful way of seeing to it that each one of us is quite unlike anyone else. This difference is worked out through a system of *genes* (tiny packets of hereditary tendencies)

[3] W. H. Sheldon, S. S. Stevens, and W. P. Tucker, *The Varieties of Human Physique* (New York: Harper & Brothers, 1940); W. H. Sheldon and S. S. Stevens, *The Varieties of Temperament* (New York: Harper & Brothers, 1942).

[4] George Stoddard, *The Meaning of Intelligence* (New York: The Macmillan Com-pany, 1943).

Identical twins may look exactly alike, but they seldom are! Each boy has his own unique qualities, at least in personality. In these pictures we see also a striking example of the growth changes of teen-agers. At thirteen a boy is hardly more than a child; at seventeen, almost a man.

Look Magazine Photos

contained in the *chromosomes* (paired "color bodies" of the cell nucleus) in the germ cells.

Human beings the world over have the same number of chromosomes in every body cell. But the combinations of genes in different chromosomes differ in extraordinary ways. Your inherited qualities don't come *from* your parents, but, *through* them, from your other ancestors as well. Each of your parents carries within the reproductive system thousands of genes which have come down to them through the generations. These lend themselves to an endless variety of combinations.

In you, in turn, there appeared new combinations of traits drawn from the entire family stock. You may resemble your parents more than your grandparents and your grandparents more than your great-grandparents. But some traits or combinations of traits may reappear in you after skipping several generations of your family. It is all by chance. No one can control the combinations. Each new baby is a complete reshuffle of the characters present in the two life streams represented by its parents. Do you see why you are not just a "chip off the old block"? You are a unique being, to be discovered, developed, realized to the fullest, as the *you* that you can be.

What You Have Learned to Be

Do not let anyone tell you that you are just like your Uncle Jim. You did not inherit his laziness, or his temper, or his shyness, or his tendency to get along well with people. If you have any of these characteristics, it is because you have learned them yourself. Most of the ways in which you behave you have learned. Even the way you talk was learned. You were born with potentialities for speech, but the inheritance of language stopped there. Even if you had had a grandmother who spoke fluent French, you would still have to learn it for yourself. Of course it might be easier if you had lived with her as a child and learned to ask for favors in French, but it would still have been you who had to do the learning. So it is with shyness and friendliness. These are learned characteristics. Temper, moodiness, sulkiness, fears, anxieties, optimism, all these are learned as you grow up.

The big difference between us and the lower animals is our ability to think and to learn. It is this adaptability that makes it possible for us to keep on growing, changing, and learning, as long as we live.

Your Place in the Family

One of the important influences in your life is your order of birth into your family. Just what difference it makes being the oldest, the youngest, a middle, or an only child in a given family, is hard to determine. Many studies on the effect of position in the family have shed some light on this interesting point.

Oldest, Youngest, or In-Between. If you are a first-born child, you had your parents all to yourself for a while. When you were small, your parents were younger than they were when your brothers and sisters came along. They may have been poorer than they were later. Since your parents had not had children before you, they may have been a little more concerned and insecure about you in your early life than about your brothers or sisters at the same stage. They may have been stricter with you than with the others. Several recent studies indicate that oldest children do not confide in their mothers, kiss their mothers, or feel indulged by their parents as often as do youngest children.

Jealousy is not a pretty word. Yet studies of children have shown that when a new baby comes into the family, the older child is very often jealous of the newcomer. An analysis [5] of many of these pieces of research suggests that this is an experience comparable to being jilted. Feelings of jealousy and injured pride, a loss of confidence in one's understanding of one's world, and the necessity of readapting to the new situation all tumble in upon one. It is therefore not surprising that first children often become jealous of the new baby, hostile to their parents, and feel considerable rivalry toward the younger children in the family.

On the other hand, the oldest child is bigger, stronger, and more skilled for many years while the younger children are growing up. He is the model for the others to follow. He carries responsibility for the younger ones, and often acts in the place of the parent.

Just how the oldest child is affected by all this depends to a great extent upon how he feels about himself, his parents, and his world. If you are an oldest child, it might be interesting for you to think through the advantages of your position in the family as you have experienced it.

The "baby of the family" holds a position that varies considerably with the size of the family. If you are the youngest of six or eight children, yours is quite a different position from that of the youngest in a family of three. Studies support the popular opinion that the youngest child is often closer to the parents than the older children. Youngest children seem to profit by the teaching and experience of their older brothers and sisters, for they come out relatively better in intelligence and are less likely to be problem children, according to some of the studies. Yet, on the whole, they do not seem to be as good marriage risks as are oldest children.

The effect of being the youngest child in the family is not at all clearly outlined by the research that has been done so far. We can suppose that one of the reasons why findings are often contradictory is that children differ, families differ, and the way they react upon each other brings about enormous variation.

Some studies say that middle children may not be as close to their parents as are either the oldest or the youngest children. Whether this makes for fewer problems of untying apron strings in growing up we do not know.

[5] Jessie Bernard, *American Family Behavior* (New York: Harper & Brothers, 1942), Chap. 13.

Middle children never have their parents all to themselves. So perhaps they are less likely to be intensely jealous than are oldest children. Usually the middle child is "the baby" for only a little while and so misses the full advantages and disadvantages of being youngest. Middle children grow up in a household with other children and are not dominated by an entirely adult world. There are both assets and liabilities to being an in-betweener, depending upon individual circumstances.

Each Child in the Family Has to Be Different. You may have marveled at how different brothers and sisters in the same family often are. Many a mother of several children can assure you that each one of her children is like no other she ever had. At the University of Pennsylvania studies [6] have been made of families with six or more living children. At least eight personality types have been found among the children in large families: (1) the responsible one; (2) the sociable one; (3) the socially ambitious "social butterfly"; (4) the studious one; (5) the self-centered "lone-wolf"; (6) the irresponsible one; (7) the sickly one; and (8) the "spoiled" one.

Such a variety can hardly have been caused by chance. There is evidence that children in the same family are different because each child *has to be himself* a distinctly different person from his brothers or sisters.

Being an Only Child—Privilege or Problem? You may possibly feel that being an only child is a misfortune. Yet studies tend to show that only children are superior in school grades, health habits, initiative, dominance, self-sufficiency, self-control, dependability, co-operation, work habits, moral knowledge, and courtesy. The only child stacks up equally well with other children both as a mixer and in physical well-being. Since the only children studied usually came from comfortably well-off families, their superiority may be largely one of economic advantage. There is enough evidence, however, to convince us that no one need be unhappy about being an only child or feel justified in making too much of the position one way or the other.

Your Family's Influence on You

Good, poor, or indifferent, your home has left its mark on you. To a considerable extent, you are what your home has taught you to be. Putting it in another way, your home influences have been important building blocks in your personality.

Your Health and Well-Being. For some years now evidence has been piling up indicating that healthy children come from homes providing adequate nutrition, good medical care, and healthful habits. On the other hand, children from homes in which nutrition and medical care have been neglected grow up shorter, underweight, and in poorer health.

[6] James H. S. Bossard and Eleanor S. Boll, *The Large Family System* (Philadelphia: University of Pennsylvania Press, 1956).

"She certainly is at home."

Cartoon courtesy of Better Homes & Gardens magazine

Your Ability and Interests. Intelligence as we measure it today is largely a product of stimulating environment at home: books to read; varied conversation to participate in; educated friends to enjoy; and an atmosphere that encourages intelligent questions and fosters mental growth.

A very important study of identical twins reared apart [7] showed that while the physical traits of such a pair tend to remain similar even though each member is raised in a different environment, characteristics of personality and intelligence often vary considerably between the two.

Our families are a part of us not only through the genes, but also through their influence upon our early learnings and experiences.

Your Self-Confidence. Your opinion of yourself may not be a real measure of your ability. It quite often reflects some early experiences you have had at home that made you feel either adequate or inadequate.

[7] H. H. Newman, F. N. Freeman, and K. J. Holzinger, *Twins: A Study of Heredity and Environment* (Chicago: University of Chicago Press, 1937).

Louella tells of how she suffered as a child because her family commented so often about how square her face was. Even today she undergoes agonies when shopping for a hat, because the hat-shop mirrors reflect for her those square lines so over-emphasized when she was young. Whenever she can, she turns her head so that only her profile will show. Other people hardly noticed the shape of her face, but Louella's self-confidence still suffers because of the fuss her family made over it.

Eloise beguiles with her eyes. When she was a little girl, her father used to take her on his lap and tell her how beautiful her big, blue eyes were. She can remember holding her eyes wide open whenever he looked her way, so that he would keep noticing them. Today, although she is a grown woman, it still buoys her up to know she has nice eyes. Whenever someone comes along whom she wants to impress, she keeps her eyes wide open, confident that they will exert the power they always used to.

Children who have been rejected by their parents when they were young may have difficulty in regaining their self-confidence. Mothers who do not really love their children may neglect them, or they may be too severe or too solicitous, but in any case the children suffer. Probably many of us feel rejected at times. None of us can always be the center of attention, even in our families. If we feel rejected when we really are not, we only make life more unhappy for ourselves than necessary. People who have learned the happy faculty of thinking of others brood less often about their own difficulties and suffer less real and imagined neglect.

Your Growing Independence. Your ability to live your own life, make your own decisions, and stand on your own feet has its roots in your early relationships with your parents. Some mothers keep too close to their children, baby them, supervise them too much. This kind of behavior is called "maternal over-protection." [8] Excessive mothering, for whatever reason, tends to keep a child too young for his age, prevents him from developing independence, and makes it difficult for him to grow up as an individual in his own right.

Some parents find it difficult to let their children go. The common reasons parents over-protect their children are: (1) the loss of one parent; (2) the separation of the parents for long periods of time; (3) the insecurity of the mother or the father as a person; (4) the persistence of older patterns of dependence; (5) fears and anxieties about the child's welfare; (6) too great a concern for the child, or guilt because of a lack of affection for him.

Homes that foster the independent maturity of their children encourage growing youth to make their own choices, to participate in family decisions,

---

[8] One extensive study is reported in David M. Levy, M.D., *Maternal Overprotection* (New York: Columbia University Press, 1943).

to venture forth into new areas with encouragement, and to break away from home ties without losing the affection and support of their parents.

Your Conception of Yourself. Your conception of yourself has its roots in your home. As a little child, your parents were the adults you knew best. You probably took them as models. It is common for girls to pattern themselves after their mothers and for boys to take after their fathers. Such imitation is not inherited in the sense that it is in the genes; rather it is learned through the child's identification of himself with his parents.

As children grow older, these early patterns are usually modified. Sometimes a child rejects a parent's way-of-life completely. But even such a reaction develops as the individual's response to his own growing conception of himself as different from his family.

Your education reflects your family. There is a relationship between the amount of education that children receive and the occupation of their fathers. Not only the amount, but also the *kind* of education is influenced by family interests. Musical parents tend to train their children musically. Mechanically expert fathers share with their sons both the tools and the know-how of their skills. A mother who is a good cook cultivates in her children a taste for good food, surrounds them with the operations, acquaints them with the ingredients, and sets in them the expectations of good cooking in a home. So it is with the many other skills, arts, and sciences that make up the total education of a person.

Your pattern of life was learned from your early experiences in your family. As you grow older, the details are modified, changed, and often drastically altered, but the original outlines remain in you. The more mature you become, the more able you will be to distinguish these basic aspects of your personality and to build intelligently on the real foundations of your own life.

Your Neighborhood Is a Part of You

There are some experts in diction who can tell just where a person has grown up by the way he talks. Professor Higgins in *Pygmalion* was such a man. Most of us bear many marks of our early neighborhood within our personalities; they may never be analyzed by a Professor Higgins, but they are there nevertheless.

Research in recent years has uncovered a rich mine of data that must be explored further, but which shows clearly that the place we grow up in is an important influence on what we are. Rural and city youth reflect the differences of their backgrounds. Foreign-born parents often bring up their children in a different way than do native-born Americans. Children on Beacon Hill in Boston are subject to a pattern of life different from that of youngsters growing up in Peoria, Illinois. *The Late George Apley* was amusing to many Americans who had not experienced the standards and values characteristic of so many New Englanders.

Regional and Social Differences. The North differs from the South, the East from the West, and the Middle West from all four of them in peculiarities of language, attitudes toward money, racial consciousness, certain religious forms, industrial development, and a host of other characteristics that influence the families in the region and affect the development of young people.

Other differences also appear in every community. The boy across the tracks may be just as good as the boy on the hill, but he is different, and he knows it. Scholars studying social class in recent years find that practically everyone recognizes that some people are "above" and others "below" them in community standing. Professor Warner summarizes some of the major facts about social classes in America in his booklet listed in your Readings.

Social status is more than a matter of being underprivileged or over-privileged. Differences between the various social classes are seen in many, many aspects of life such as occupation, level of aspiration, education completed, and the way children are reared. Professor Bronfenbrenner at Cornell University has recently summarized some fifteen different studies of the ways in which child-training practices across the country have differed in the major social classes through recent decades.[9]

In general over the past twenty-five years American middle-class mothers have become increasingly permissive in the feeding and toilet-training of their children. Even with children beyond the age of two, middle-class parents are more lenient about children's thumbsucking, toilet accidents, sex expression, and fighting. Working-class parents more often tend to use physical punishment in coping with their children, while middle-class fathers and mothers resort to reasoning, isolation, or appeal to the child's love by showing disappointment in his behavior. The general trend among middle-class parents has been to become increasingly more democratic and accepting in their relationships with their children.

The higher the social status of the mother, the more frequently she defines a good child as healthy, happy, and eager to learn—all conceptions related to the best development of the child.[10] Mothers in the lower social classes more often define a good child as one who keeps clean and neat, obeys and respects adults, and is a good worker. With such different concepts of

[9] Urie Bronfenbrenner, "Socialization and Social Class through Time and Space," in E. E. Maccoby, T. M. Newcomb, and E. L. Hartley, *Readings in Social Psychology* (New York: Henry Holt and Company, 1958), pp. 400–25.
[10] Evelyn Millis Duvall, "Conceptions of Parenthood," *The American Journal of Sociology*, Vol. 52 (November, 1946), pp. 194–203.

goodness, it is possible that even the things for which a child is praised or punished differ with social class. How the child, in turn, reacts depends upon his own view of himself.

What You Want to Become

The overall picture of your dreams and ambitions is a composite one which you have developed out of your many experiences so far. This picture acts as your drive and as your compass in life, giving you a sense of direction and purpose. It is colored by your opinions on what is worth fighting for, by your personal standards and values, and by the basis upon which you make each choice. It includes also, of course, your conscious and unconscious convictions about religion. This whole combination of feelings and ideas is sometimes called your philosophy of life.

Your sense of purpose grows as you grow. The more mature a person you become, the larger will be your purposes. The larger your goals, the finer a person you become. Your central purposes are always with you, selecting those elements of your world that you want to build on, ignoring aspects of life that lack meaning for you. A sense of direction is as necessary for you as a rudder for a ship. The difference is that your purposes change as you change, guiding yet guided by your growing mastery of yourself.

THE WAYS

To every man there openeth
A Way, and Ways, and a Way.
And the High Soul climbs the High Way,
And the Low Soul gropes the Low.
And in between, on the misty flats,
The rest drift to and fro.
But to every man there openeth
A High Way and Low.
And every man decideth
The Way his soul shall go.

John Oxenham

Summary

Abraham Lincoln is quoted as saying, "All that I am, I owe to my angel mother." Most of us do owe a great deal to our mothers and fathers. But even they are not the only important influences in our lives. Each of us is the product of a great many interrelated factors that have through the years become a part of us. A few of these influences have been discussed briefly and are summarized below. The way each person reacts to the influences in his life and adjusts to his own realities is perhaps the most important factor of all.

What Makes You—YOU

1. Being born a boy or a girl (and how you feel about it).
2. All that you inherited from all of your ancestors (and what you are doing with it).
3. Your place in your family (and how you are adjusting to it).
4. Your health (and what you are doing about it).
5. Your ability (and what you are making of it).
6. Your sense of self (and increasing your ability to be your best self).
7. Your place in society (and what you are doing about it).
8. Your values, dreams, convictions, philosophy of life, and religion.

Suggested Activities

Individual Study

1. With the help of a good book on heredity, such as Scheinfeld's *The New You and Heredity* (see Readings), chart the characteristics that are (a) almost entirely determined by heredity, such as eye color; (b) largely the result of learning, such as swimming ability; (c) a mixture of both heredity and learning. Which is the longest list? What ideas does this give you for building upon your own potentialities? Which of your own weaknesses must you accept? Which can you improve? What attitudes toward your strengths and weaknesses will be most helpful to your development as a person?

2. Collect clippings from newspaper columns, magazine articles, and short stories about characteristics of only children. To what extent do these popular ideas reflect the findings of research described in this chapter? What should this tell us about critical evaluation of the printed word? How different should we expect only children to be? Do we expect all only children to be alike? Why not? Write a paper on your observations of the problems and privileges of only children, perhaps using your clippings as a point of departure.

3. From cases you have known, stories you have read, or plays you have seen, list in your notebook some of the ways in which children are "babied" by their parents. Discuss in class *why* the parents may be behaving as they do in each case. Do young people always react the same way to too much parental control? What are some of the more frequent ways in which young people respond to over-protection? Which are the better ways? Why?

4. Make a double-column list of activities or kinds of behavior your community thinks proper only for boys and only for girls. It may start off something like the following. You and your classmates will be able to think of a much longer listing.

Girls Can	Boys Can
Polish their nails	Stay out later
Curl their hair	Shave their faces
Talk endearingly to each other	Use rough talk
Wear either skirts or slacks	Ask a girl for a date

5. Write your autobiography, including in it the more important influences in your own life. Include as many specific memories as you can, indicating how you felt about what happened. Tell about the things you used to be afraid of, what started these fears, and how you have overcome them. Mention the people you have most admired and why, and what they meant to you. Try to analyze the place you had in your parents' affection and your own mixed feelings toward them through the years. Do the same for your brothers and sisters, telling the jealousies, the rivalries, and the competition that you felt in relation to them. See if you can illustrate some of the ways your neighborhood has become a part of you. Conclude by stating as specifically as you can your own sense of purpose in terms of your ambitions and philosophy of life.

6. Write a letter to yourself to be opened when you graduate, listing what you hope you may do in the first five years out of high school. Put down your fears and questions as well as your dreams, hopes, and aspirations. When you have finished, show your letter, if you want to, to a trusted counselor or teacher. Talk over what you can do now to help make your dreams come true.

7. Talk over with your mother what she wanted to do when she was your age, and to what extent her aspirations have been realized. What helped, what hindered her? Get your father's point of view on what helped or hampered him in his development as a person as well as a breadwinner.

Group Activity

1. Arrange a showing of the film, A Desk for Billie (57 minutes; National Education Association, Washington, D. C.), and discuss how Billie surmounted the obstacles in her situation to go on and complete her education. Are your environmental handicaps greater than Billie's? How can you realize your ambitions?

2. Conduct a class poll of those who are youngest children in their families. Ask each one to discuss the position of the youngest in the family as he sees it. Compare agreements and disagreements. Remember that you will not get a complete consensus, since being youngest means different things to different people.

   Now do the same for (a) oldest children; (b) only children; (c) in-betweeners. Discuss the different ways the various individuals feel about their place in their own families.

3. Write on a piece of paper, without conferring with others, five things people praise you for doing. Have someone collect the papers and then choose two students to tabulate the results. How many different things are mentioned by the class? Which things are mentioned most frequently? Are some things mentioned by almost everyone? Which of the good things to do are mentioned by only one or two students? Can you think of why this may be? Would the things mentioned by students in a school in a different part of town be somewhat different? Do you have any way of finding out what these differences might be?

4. Act out, in a series of impromptu episodes, the way in which a person with a sense of purpose meets such familiar situations as (a) being offered a cigarette or a drink; (b) being invited to join the gang in a game of "chicken" on the highway; (c) deciding whether or not to go to college.

5. Ask an adult whom you all admire to speak to your class. Interview him (or her) as to when and why he chose his profession or vocation, what steps he took to prepare for his work, what obstacles he met, and how he overcame them. Encourage all the students to join in the questioning.

6. Have a class reading of the play, *Sunrise at Campobello* (New York: Random House, 1958), by Dore Schary.

Readings

MOORE, BERNICE MILLBURN, and LEAHY, DOROTHY M., *You and Your Family* (Boston: D. C. Heath and Company, 1953. This senior-high-school text gives you real insight into what makes you you. See especially Chapter 1, "You," and Chapter 5, "Human Beings Learn to Be Human."

NATIONAL FORUM FOUNDATION GUIDANCE STAFF, *Discovering Myself* (Chicago: National Forum Foundation, 1955). This book for senior-high-school students is written by a number of qualified guidance specialists to help young people understand themselves. The chapters are short and cover many specific questions.

SCHEINFELD, AMRAM, *The New You and Heredity* (Philadelphia: J. B. Lippincott Company, 1950). A book that tells in fascinating detail and with scientific accuracy the facts of human heredity of most vital importance in understanding yourself, your family, and your fellow human beings.

SMART, MOLLIE STEVENS and RUSSELL COOK, *Living in Families* (Boston: Houghton Mifflin Company, 1958). A useful senior-high book by a qualified husband-wife team. Chapter 7, "Your Personality Development," discusses such questions as how you became the person you are and what you can do about it.

WARNER, W. LLOYD and MILDRED HALL, *What You Should Know About Social Class* (Chicago: Science Research Associates, 1953). In this highly readable life-adjustment booklet, the Warners summarize a tremendous amount of scientific research about the part that social class plays in your life.

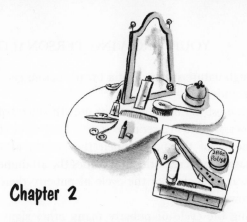

Chapter 2

Your Development as a Teen-Ager

The second decade of your life brings some of the most dramatic changes in your whole life. You enter your teens a child. You come out of them a young adult—almost ready to begin your life as a man or woman. This means that your development as a teen-ager is more than just an increase in height and weight. It involves the very special development that is called *maturation*—the process of attaining full development as a person.

Adolescent development and the process of maturation have been studied extensively in recent decades. Now you can have some idea of what happens as a young person grows up, when the various stages may be expected to come, how development differs among individuals, and what physical development means for your growing personality.

Physical Development

You do not develop at the same rate throughout life. Sometimes you grow very slowly, and during other periods you grow very rapidly. The chart given on page 20 shows the way the *velocity*, or speed, of growth changes from birth to twenty years of age. This is no one person's growth chart, but a general profile developed by Dr. Herbert Stolz at the University of California, from his studies of many young people over a period of years.

Notice that the velocity of growth decreases rapidly from birth to three years or so. As a baby you grew faster than you ever will again. By the time you were four or five, you began to level off in your growth velocity and grew at a fairly even rate for the next several years. Children in the first few grades of elementary school show a relatively uniform growth rate of about two per cent every six months.

Then, just before you began to spurt up in size, there was a period in which you almost stood still. The dip in the chart represents the slowing down of growth that marks the beginning of the cycle of puberty. Someone

19

has said that it is almost as though nature stopped for a breath before getting the great changes of adolescence under way.

The cycle of puberty is the most dramatic period of growth since baby-hood. It takes place over a number of years in a series of spurts. First comes the lengthening out of the long bones of the body. Then the growth of the muscles marks the filling-out phase of puberty. Still later comes the attainment of adult muscular strength. Toward the close of the cycle of puberty there is a noticeable slowing down of growth.

Changes at Puberty. During the cycle of puberty many other signs of physical maturing appear. A boy's voice begins to change to a deeper register, his beard grows, and mature characteristics develop. A girl gradually develops the form and functions characteristic of a woman.

Since all the glands of the body are changing over from childhood into maturity, it is not unusual for some of them to take some time in adjusting.

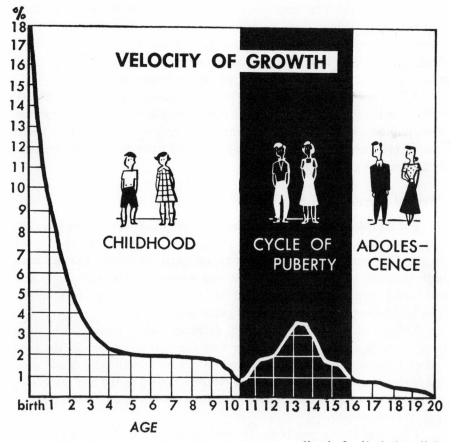

Chart by Graphics Institute, N. Y.
Adapted from Meck, The Personal-Social Development of Boys and Girls
with Implications for Secondary Education.

Certain slight physical irregularities are common during the teen years. The new adult functioning of the sweat glands makes body odors more noticeable. The oil glands of the body, especially of the scalp and face, may function overtime, causing oily hair and facial blemishes such as pimples and blackheads.

Good general hygiene, plenty of soap and water, and a well-balanced diet are usually sufficient to keep skin and hair problems under control until the body has settled down into the new regimes of adulthood. Worry over these temporary troubles, however, often causes more difficulty than the physical problems themselves. Therefore a good attitude toward yourself and these changes is more important than ever during the teen years.

Individual Differences in Physical Maturity. One of the most worrisome aspects of physical development in the teen years is the readily observed differences among individuals. You may have worried because your own physical maturation does not parallel that of others of your age. You probably have wondered why some teen-agers are so big for their age and others remain small for so long. You may be concerned because you are maturing more slowly or more rapidly than some of your friends.

The age at which boys and girls begin to mature varies considerably. Some begin the cycle of puberty as early as the ninth year. Others do not get started until the fourteenth year. Nor do all people complete the growth spurt at the same age. Some young people have reached the end of the puberal cycle in their fifteenth year. Others may be nineteen or twenty before they are completely mature physically. The length of the cycle also varies from individual to individual. Some boys dash through their growth spurt in a little over four years, while others take nearly eight years to complete the process.

There seems to be a relationship between nutrition and maturation. Well-nourished individuals grow up more rapidly and mature earlier than poorly nourished ones. Boys and girls who have had a tendency to be fat are slower to develop than others. In general, young people today mature earlier than their parents did, possibly because they have been better nourished.

Although individuals differ in the age at which they start, the age at which they finish, and the time it takes each to mature physically, all go through the same general changes. This sequence of growth can be seen as a timetable of development in which one station follows another in regular succession. Some people, like some trains, may linger between stations and move ahead slowly, while others rush through at express speed. Both local and express trains come out at the end of the line all right. So it is with teen-age growth. The time at which you start, or the rate at which you grow, is relatively unimportant. You grow at your own pace, and develop in your own way.

Girls Mature Earlier Than Boys. In general, girls mature physically a full year or two earlier than boys. The early puberal changes of girls are more dramatic and on the whole more intense than are the first puberal changes of boys. In time the boys catch up, and by the time high-school graduation comes along, most of them are considerably taller, bigger, and stronger than most of the girls.

Remember that these findings are based on group *averages*. An individual girl may be quite late in growing up, or a particular boy may start maturing quite early. But the general trend is for girls to undergo physical maturation at an earlier age than boys.

Interests Are Related to Physical Maturation. Your interests change as you grow older. The things that interest children are no longer absorbing later on. Age is only one factor in these changing interests. There is a close relationship between your interests and the level of your physical maturation. Let us illustrate from one of the research studies in which it was observed that girls of twelve or thirteen who have not begun to mature are still interested in little-girl things. They like comic books, bubble gum, group games, and playground activities, while girls of the *same age* who are more physically mature are interested in more grown-up things such as hair-dos, good grooming, shopping, love stories, and dates.

You see from these observations that the *developmental age* (or the stage of development achieved) is a better index of a person's maturity than chronological age. When individual differences are so great, it is relatively meaningless to talk about the interests of sixteen-year-olds, or to plan group activities as though being the same age meant having the same interests during the teen years. It makes much more sense to consider a given person's developmental age and his activities in relation to his particular readiness.

Developmental Tasks of Teen-Agers

Research in human development has shown that each individual continues to grow as a person all his life. The concept of the *developmental task* is a tool to use in shaping your own ideas of yourself and the people around you. This concept has emerged out of the scientific study of thousands of children, adolescents, and young and older adults in university centers, schools, and communities across the country. The seven chief points to know about the developmental-task concept are these:

1. Every growing person faces certain inevitable and urgent tasks in his own development.
2. He must accomplish each developmental task successfully before he can grow to the next level of his development.

3. No one else can accomplish his developmental tasks for him.
4. These growth responsibilities are so great and so demanding that they must take precedence over any outside pressures that may go counter to them.
5. Therefore, it is helpful for each individual to know about his own developmental tasks and to plan his life in such a way that he may accomplish them.
6. The extent to which you accomplish your own developmental tasks determines how fully and well you reach the next stage of maturity.
7. When you offer others encouragement and give them opportunities to accomplish their developmental tasks, you are helping to promote their growth.

Have you ever watched a baby work at learning some simple little skill? Have you ever realized that a baby must *work at the job of growing up* if he is ever to progress beyond babyhood?

To become a toddler, a baby must exercise his legs. He lies and kicks for long periods of time in his crib. He does not like to have you restrain his kicking. Before he can talk, he vocalizes to himself. He tries out many, many sounds, consonants, vowels, singly and in combinations. This kicking and vocalizing are all part of the developmental tasks which will enable him to grow out of babyhood into the next level of his development.

As a toddler, the baby has to get into things around the house. He must explore his world. He must find out how things feel, what is hard and what is soft, what hot, what cold, what heavy, and what light. Dresser drawers, pantry shelves, the flour bin, or the garbage pail—it is all the same to him. He is discovering his world. Others in the house who would help him with this developmental task protect their precious things from his fumbling fingers, but in every other way possible allow him freedom to grow through exploration.

Adults have their developmental tasks. Parents must practice letting their children go if they are to weather the untying of apron strings at adolescence. Middle-aged people must begin cutting down their strenuous activities if they are to adjust well to the slower pace of the later years. Even grandparents have developmental tasks at which they must work. In short, you have developmental tasks as long as you live. It is up to each person to understand these tasks at each period of his growth, make way for them, and work toward their accomplishment.

Teen-agers have especially important developmental tasks to perform if they are to become mature men and women. The responsibilities of growing up are many and complex. They involve adapting oneself to drastic physical transformations, adjusting oneself to the grown-up world, and developing the skills that make one an accepted and effective adult. Every teen-ager must face

The responsibility a teen-ager shows by his application to a part-time job will indicate his readiness to take on other responsibilities.

these developmental tasks and succeed in them if he is to achieve a mature personality.

Your essential developmental tasks as a teen-ager can be summarized as

1. Coming to terms with your changing body.
2. Getting along with others your age.
3. Establishing independence from your parents.
4. Achieving adult economic and social status.
5. Developing a satisfying sense of who you are.

Coming to Terms with Your Changing Body. As a teen-ager, you must learn to accept your own maturing body. Its size, shape, rate of growth, particular characteristics and functionings are yours to live with, adjust to, and make the best of. This may be difficult if you worry about the way your development differs from that of others your age. Differences are inevitable; whatever is happening in your development, it surely is not just like that of anyone else you know.

Some boys are slow developers, starting their growth spurt later than others of their age, remaining smaller than most of the other boys in their class, and finally reaching physical maturity after all the others of their age and grades. Late-maturing boys may worry about why they are not growing up as fast as others of their age. They may feel left behind in sports, in getting dates, and in attaining a sense of manhood. Such feelings are not unusual, but dwelling on them does not help the "little guy." A more constructive approach starts with a recognition that every individual has his own built-in timetable for development and that what is normal development for one person may not be for another. Instead of concentrating on what he can't do, many a "shorty" has found a place for himself in dramatics, in the school orchestra or band, in debating, or in scholastic achievement.

The early-blooming girl who matures before the others in her classroom may be somewhat embarrassed by her larger size and the obvious marks of maturity that set her apart from the other "children." Or the diminutive "little girl" may wonder why nothing seems to happen to her when all the other girls in her age group are rapidly turning into young women. Actually, both of these girls may be assured that they are perfectly normal even though their patterns of maturing do not parallel those of the majority of their age group. Each one matures happily as she comes to terms with her own changing body.

You are recognized by the way you look, the way you walk and hold yourself. You are reflected in the sound of your voice, your facial expressions and gestures. All these aspects of you can be attractive as you make a real attempt to accept and to develop your physical endowments to their best.

During adolescence, when the body is changing rapidly, a great deal of emphasis is placed on personal attractiveness. To be attractive, it is important for every boy to learn to be manly and to enjoy the privileges and responsibilities of his masculinity. Girls must learn the feminine role and feel positive about approaching womanhood if their adult lives are to be completely satisfying. Anything that makes a young person feel ashamed of his body hinders his accomplishment of this essential task. Anything that helps a boy or girl accept and adjust to his or her own body is growth-promoting.

Getting Along with Others Your Age. No one grows up in a vacuum. If you were Robinson Crusoe, your life might be harder in some ways, but in growing up it might be simpler than it is in the company of many other young people. Learning to cope with the complex and often conflicting demands of others takes a long while and considerable skill. Every young person matures not only in reference to his growing body, but also in relationship to his family, friends, and acquaintances. He must adjust not only to himself, but to others as individuals.

The fact that girls mature earlier than boys poses problems for young people of both sexes in our culture. You want the boy to take the lead in dating, dancing, and in other mixed activities. Yet, because boys mature more slowly, there are several years when girls are more ready and eager than boys for grown-up boy-girl associations. This is often apparent on a high-school dance floor. The girls want to dance and do so, even if it must be with each other. The boys hang back in a stag line or crowd into a corner, not quite mature enough to get into the mixed-group activity. It is usually the girl who teaches the boy to dance. She often must take the lead in arranging a date, in carrying on the conversation, and in the other skills involved in having fun together. Some boys do not like being "pushed around" by girls, while girls often complain that the boys in their grade are slow, dumb, silly, and otherwise awkward.

Schools tend to group young people by chronological age and academic achievement rather than by social development. Even social affairs are arranged by class and grade in most towns. So it is difficult for girls and boys with the same developmental interests to meet and know each other. There is a tendency for girls to date boys a year or two older, if they can. From the point of view of developmental differences, this trend might be more widely encouraged.

During junior- and senior-high school there is a strong desire to be like the others of one's own age. What the members of one's class and social group wear, believe, feel, and do becomes terribly important. This is understandable when you realize that teen-agers have to cast in their lot with their own generation. But it is complicated by the differing and changing standards of one's contemporaries. The behavior of young people varies according to the times of which they are a part, the community in which they live, and the level of social development that they have attained.

The social expectations of young people differ according to locality. Clothes that are appropriate in a high school in San Antonio would be strange in a Brooklyn classroom. "Slanguage" spoken in a big city school would not be understood in some rural communities. Standards of courtesy, morals, work, and play; attitudes toward money—all these vary from region to region, depending upon social and economic level, the size of the community, and the people who live there. Moving from one town to another may require many adjustments to a somewhat different culture, especially for teen-age people, for whom the approval of their group is so important.

What the others do depends a great deal on their level of social maturity. The ideal girl in the seventh grade may be a sedate little lady. But the same young people who in seventh grade approved such a girl may prefer, by ninth-grade, one who is enthusiastic, daring, and able to pep up a party. By twelfth-grade, the well-groomed, pretty girl has come into her own. One study shows that boys, too, are liked for differing reasons at various grade levels. According to this study, the ideal seventh-grade boy must be willing to take daring chances, be expert at games, and be generally boisterous. By ninth-grade the boys begin to admire social poise, good looks, and tidiness. At the twelfth-grade level, the boys admired are those who can assume leadership in sports, arts, and forum groups and who can meet adults on their level.

When high-school people list the things they worry about, they usually mention being left out, making social *faux pas*, being ridiculed, losing a boy friend or a girl friend, not being liked, and loneliness.

One poll of nearly a thousand high-school students asked the question, "What makes you happy?" The most frequent answer was, "Being with good friends." In the second place was, "Experiences with girl or boy friends." Other items with high ratings were also related to getting along with people of one's own age: participation in social events, going places, doing things, and school accomplishments.

Getting along with others of one's own age is not always easy. It takes time and experience to become socially competent. Many barriers both in yourself and in the world outside may frustrate and confuse your efforts. Dating, going steady, and choosing a mate, as well as your feelings of social adequacy, depend upon your success in these efforts.

The ability to get along with other people is gained through social experience. By practicing socially acceptable ways of doing things in all kinds of settings and situations, you improve your skills in successful interaction.

One of the hardest things for a teen-ager to do is to face social pressures with poise. Because the approval of other people is so important to them, it is hard for many young people to stand by their own principles. As teen-agers

A teen-ager who can make his friends feel at home and relaxed on informal as well as formal occasions is learning the art of getting along with others.

Sherwin-Williams Company

mature, they must learn to oppose group demands that conflict with their personal standards. As adults, they should be emancipated not only from the controls of their parents, but also from the whims of their contemporaries. This is what makes the difference between slavish obedience to fads and mature adjustment to the real demands of one's culture.

An individual has social poise when he moves smoothly among others, accepting and being accepted, yet never giving up his individuality. He can refuse an unwelcome invitation without offending. He can avoid an unpleasant situation without making a scene. He can stand up for what he believes to be right without being disagreeable. Mature social poise grows out of success in the developmental task of getting along with one's contemporaries.

Establishing Independence from Your Parents. Parents often complain that standards have certainly changed in the last generation, while many a son catches himself saying, or thinking, "Parents just don't understand. They are so old-fashioned." To some extent such a reaction is to be expected as young people strive to free themselves from parental control. To some extent, also, it is all too true. In many respects young people today live in a world quite different from the one in which their parents grew up. Both generations must learn to bridge the gap of changing times in order to reach a better understanding.

The teen years see the emergence of the young person from the control of his parents. Children must be protected by their parents. As they become adults, they must learn to stand upon their own feet and live their own lives. This shift takes place over many years, but most noticeably in the teens.

This does not mean leaving parents out entirely. Rather, it means establishing one's independence, while at the same time maintaining respect and affection for them. In action it looks something like this. The Joneses have a daughter named Mary. When Mary was growing up, she was known as the "Jones's little girl, Mary." Wherever she went, people recognized her as belonging to her parents. She was expected to obey her mother and her father completely and live by their decisions. Now that she is in her teens, she no longer wants to be so closely identified with her family, much as she still loves them. She prefers to be known as Mary Jones, and to be respected and considered as a person in her own right. She wants to make her own decisions, participate in family affairs as a full-fledged member, and build a life of her own outside the family.

Untying apron strings is rarely easy even in an understanding home. Parents find it hard to let their children go after taking care of them for so many years. New habits of living together have to be developed by both parents and teen-agers, and it takes time to perfect them. Teen-agers do not grow up all at once. In some situations they feel quite mature and want complete freedom. In others they may be quite inexpert and still want their parents' guidance. So parents and their teen-agers live on a sort of seesaw through the ups and downs of growing up.

Teen-agers often report that problems come up in their relationships with their parents. The Purdue Opinion Panel, in polling thousands of high-school students of both sexes from all sections of the country, tabulated many aspects of "the parent problem" as teen-agers see it.

The difficulties young people report having with their parents vary considerably. Some teen-agers have many problems and feel keenly about them.

"THE PARENT PROBLEM": TEENAGERS' VIEW [1]

Aspect of "The Parent Problem"	Per Cent of All Teenagers Reporting
1. Afraid to tell parents when I've done wrong	19%
2. Parents too strict about my going out at night	18
3. Parents too strict about family car	16
4. Family always worried about money	15
5. Parents too strict about dating	13
6. Parents nag about studying	13
7. Parents hate to admit I'm sometimes right	13
8. Parents interfere in my choice of friends	13
9. Parents too strict about dates on school nights	12
10. Wish parents would treat me like a grownup	12
11. Parents interfere with spending money I earn	11
12. Parents play favorites	10
13. Parents expect too much of me	9
14. Get no encouragement at home	9
15. Parents pry into private affairs	9
16. Parents won't let me make decisions	8
17. Parents won't respect my opinions	8
18. Parents don't trust me	8
19. Parents criticize me too much	8
20. Parents trying to decide my vocation	7
21. Want to gain confidence of my parents	7
22. Feel like leaving home	7
23. Parents won't let me do my own shopping	6
24. Parents object to my following fads	5
25. Parents disapprove of my social activities	5
26. Parents not interested in what I accomplish	5

[1] "The Parent Problem" as Teenagers See It. From H. H. Remmers and D. H. Radler, *The American Teenager* (Indianapolis: The Bobbs-Merrill Company, 1957), pp. 117–18. Copyright ©, 1957. Used by special permission of the publishers, The Bobbs-Merrill Company, Inc.

Others have fewer difficulties and work them out more harmoniously. The particular aspect which causes difficulty between a teen-ager and his parents depends upon several factors: (1) the personality of the teen-ager; (2) the young person's level of maturity; (3) the parents' attitudes and understanding; (4) the previous relationship between the teen-ager and the parents; and (5) the particular situation.

Although situations vary widely, there are certain characteristic friction spots between teen-agers and their parents. These are directly related to the teen-ager's developmental task of emancipation. People who study what is involved in young people's growing up recognize that often it is not his parents that the teen-ager is rejecting, but rather his own status as a child. The parents are symbols of the young person's outgrown childhood. As a young person matures, he must put aside childish ways and thrust himself far enough from his earlier dependence upon his parents to find his own self-reliance. This takes time and effort. It is a central task of the teen years.

Achieving Adult Economic and Social Status. A great deal is involved in becoming an economically self-sufficient adult. A man must find his place in the world. He must be able to get and hold down a job. He must have what it takes to make good on that job if he expects to earn enough to marry and do his full share in the support of a wife and family.

In the simple world of your great-grandfather's day a young man who was a willing, careful, and industrious worker had little trouble getting launched in his life's work. Education was not as important as it is today. A man did not need highly technical training to get a position. There were relatively few occupations, most of which he could enter with little preparatory training. In 1870, there were only 338 vocations; by the middle of the twentieth century, there were 22,028. Most of these new occupations require technical skills not learned at home or picked up on the job. Today a boy must be trained in advance for almost any job. He needs an education. He must choose his line of work early in order to complete his training early. So vocational guidance is more important now than ever before for teen-age boys.

What about girls? How does a girl establish herself as an adult with full economic and social status? Why is it necessary for her to get an education? Should she train for some useful occupation? Is she expected to work? And is she also expected to find her place in her own home as a wife and mother? These are much disputed questions today, as many people ask, "What is the matter with Modern Woman?" The answer seems to be that most girls expect and are expected to marry. But even with marriage, there are still reasons for developing wage-earning skills.

Three out of every ten married women are now working. In all probability, today's schoolgirls will spend twenty-five years or more in work outside their homes. At the present writing nine out of every ten women are likely

"But where are the extras you advertised? It's only got four exhausts, two spotlights, air-horns and four carburetors!"

Times-Mirror Syndicate, Los Angeles

to work outside the home in the course of their lives.[2] It is no longer a question of whether to marry *or* to work, but rather of how women can prepare adequately for both functions.

Most girls find that training for some remunerative work is imperative for many reasons. First, they may not marry. If they marry young men just getting started, they may need both salaries for a little while. If the husband is incapacitated, the wife's earnings are needed. When the children grow up, there are many years when a useful, creative job makes the difference between a bored middle-aged woman and a happy, growing one. Being able to do something well in addition to being a housewife is important for a woman's self-

[2] National Manpower Council report, *Womanpower* (New York: Columbia University Press, 1957), p. 10.

respect in many cases. Having interests that can be shared with her husband deepens their companionship. Children, too, may profit from the mother's wisely planned outside interests, as these safeguard them against being smothered by "Momism."

Marriage itself has a better chance of success if properly prepared for. Building a happy marriage is fully as complicated as teaching school or running a business. It requires as careful preparation. Both boys and girls should know the principles of child development and care, so that as parents they can raise the wholesome, responsible citizens the world needs. In creating a happy home and a loving family, a man and woman can make good use of any knowledge they have of psychology, health, nutrition, consumer buying, economics, sociology, art, music, religion, and a host of other arts and skills. Girls—and boys, too—need the kind of homemaking courses that will enable them to meet the challenge of twentieth-century homemaking. Study of all such subjects, therefore, is part of education for family life.

Achieving adult status today means the ability to play a number of exacting roles competently. Men and women are expected to succeed as husbands and wives, fathers and mothers, members of a larger family circle, workers, citizens, members of churches, clubs and organizations, neighbors, friends, wage-earners, spenders—all in a given day, week, or year. Such exacting responsibilities cannot be assumed quickly or easily. They require preparation and experience. The ability to become a full-fledged adult is learned in the classroom, the family, and the community through rigorous training and experience over a period of years. It is a big and an important job that many teen-agers are accomplishing exceedingly well.

Developing a Satisfying Sense of Who You Are. You may at times be dissatisfied with yourself. You may wish you were better than you are. Such dissatisfaction is the first step toward new growth. Edward Steichen, the world-famous artist-photographer, tells of the time he tore up every one of the pictures he had spent months making. Then, starting afresh, he launched upon one of the most productive periods of his entire life. The chances are that you will not tear up all you have done, although you may feel like it at times. In a sense, divine discontent is a prerequisite to the search for further development and fulfillment.

You achieve a sense of your real self not only by recognizing what you are not, but also by appreciating what you are. In other words, your growth in realizing who you are consists not only of your discontent, but also of your acceptance of yourself. As you accomplish this developmental task, you are able to accept yourself as you really are, to see your strengths and potentialities as well as your limitations and problems.

By the end of your teens you are expected to have ethical standards and observe the social conventions appropriate for adults in your community.

Your beliefs should be integrated into some consistent system. Your conscience should be developed to the point where you can behave wholesomely on the basis of your own inner controls. The teen years are crucial for you as a developing person. The integration into one well-rounded whole of all you are and want to become is a gigantic task.

Like other big jobs, this one can be seen best through some of its parts. The teen-ager develops a sense of self through many separate activities and experiences, sometimes partly motivated by identification with a particular adult. When an adolescent girl becomes devoted to her dramatics teacher, does odd jobs for her after school, tries out for all the plays, and talks of going into dramatics herself some day, she is exploring one image of her self that she might want to become as a woman.

When a high-school boy shifts from one job to another, to the concern of his employers as well as his parents, he may be trying to find a niche for himself. What he is doing is more important than holding down a job if it helps him round out his sense of who he is and what he wants to become.

When a young person discovers a poem, or a piece of music, or a lovely picture, or a new book that he cannot put down, or an idea that haunts him (and the family perhaps) for days on end, it may be that a new window in himself has been flung open. . . .

A sixteen-year-old girl, at the close of World War II, discovered new meanings in an old, old prayer. She has permitted us to quote her version of it.

THE PRAYER

Our Father who art in heaven
  (and in the hearts of all peace-loving men)

Hallowed be thy name
  (and the names of those who work for righteousness)

Thy kingdom come
  (to aid our bleeding world)

Thy will be done
  (by the will of human understanding)

On earth as it is in heaven
  (where love's warmth reaches all)

Give us this day our daily bread
  (forgetting not Europe's famished children)

And forgive us our trespasses
  (so that *we* may do better)

As we forgive those who trespass against us
  (so that *they* may do better)

And lead us not into temptation
(freeing our minds of selfish greed)

But deliver us from evil
(fascism's poison and atomic destruction)

For Thine is the kingdom, and the power, and the glory forever.
Amen.

Adolescence is a period of exploring, of trying out new roles, of adventuring in self-discovery. The young person who has succeeded in these tasks emerges as an adult filled with enthusiasm and an eagerness to live fully and to do his share of the world's work.

Overcoming Hurdles in the Teen Years

No one slides effortlessly out of childhood into adulthood. The teen years are normally filled with challenges that each individual must meet in order to grow up in mind and spirit. Some of these challenges are found within oneself, some within one's family, some within the confusions of the larger culture, and some within the very nature of life itself.

"My greatest enemy is myself," says one of the world's greatest men. He does not mean that he hates himself, but simply that his own limitations are the greatest hindrance to the fulfillment of his hopes and dreams. You, too, may find that you have certain handicaps as a teen-ager because of problems within yourself. Your present developmental tasks may be difficult because you failed to accomplish earlier ones in your childhood. You may be having trouble in some of your studies because earlier you did not learn to read well. You may have problems with your friends because you have delayed learning how to give and take. You may have trouble keeping a job because it is still hard for you to take responsibility.

There is no such thing as a perfect family. In some ways your family may make it hard for you to accomplish your developmental tasks as a teen-ager. You may have been hindered in your development by being overprotected, overindulged, rejected, intimidated, or neglected. Your family may have been economically deprived, or you may have felt ostracized because of its social, cultural, religious, or racial background. You have either let these handicaps—whatever you have felt them to be—slow down your development as a person, or you have taken them as a challenge to be met and overcome.

Cultural pressures are often hazards in development. The social pressure to conform hinders your fulfillment of yourself as a unique personality. You sense the confusion in the roles of men and women in the world today, and so have difficulty clarifying your own personal goals as a person of either sex. You feel the pressures to be "modern" on the one hand and traditional and conventional on the other, and you become uncertain of just where you stand on all sorts of issues and principles.

Life itself poses problems at every stage of development. You cannot do everything. Most of life's decisions are in terms of alternatives—if you go, you cannot stay; if you do this, you cannot do that; if you choose one way, you thereby forfeit the chance to take another. If you grow up, you cannot remain a child, pleasant as that may have been at one time.

Your character is built on the decisions you make. Dr. Ernest M. Ligon defines character as "the strength with which you throw all of your potential into what seems to you to be the major purpose for which you live." Such a definition sees character being built out of the experiences of life that call for strength. A muscle grows strong with exercise, when it is literally at work. So, too, a person's spirit gains stature and becomes strong in taking on real problems and seeing them through.

You accept life's challanges as you assume responsibility for your own well-being. You accomplish your developmental tasks as a teen-ager in your undertaking of them. The skill with which you tackle and accomplish your job of growing up depends upon three things: (1) your readiness; (2) your previous learnings; and (3) your present opportunities. If you do not want to grow up, if you are afraid of maturity, you may be your own worst saboteur in this job. If you have had a good, varied childhood, full of opportunities to learn, to grow, and to build a sturdy foundation, you enjoy the challenges of the teen years. If you see to it that the opportunities and resources you need for growing up are used to their fullest, you find yourself soon at the threshold of maturity. Your teen years are yours to mold as you can. You are out of the confinement of childhood. You are not yet involved in the press of adulthood. Yours are the years that free men's spirits, years for growth, years for discovering *you*.

Summary

Physical development begins earlier for some teen-agers than for others. It takes longer for some young people to reach maturity than it does others. Progress through the cycle of puberty follows a fairly regular timetable in which all teen-agers follow much the same route, some earlier and faster than others. These differences in the rates of maturing are relatively unimportant except in the way the individual feels about them. All teen-agers face certain developmental tasks that must be accomplished in order to reach full maturity. Five developmental tasks of the teen years are: (1) coming to terms with a changing body; (2) getting along with others one's own age; (3) establishing independence from one's parents; (4) achieving adult economic

and social status; and (5) developing a satisfying conception of self. Everyone has certain hurdles to overcome in the teen years. Accomplishing the
developmental tasks of the teen years brings the individual to maturity eager
and ready for life as an adult.

Suggested Activities

Individual Study

1. Copy the following definitions in your notebook for memorizing and
   review.
   Adolescence—the period between childhood and adulthood, roughly the
   second decade of life. (Sometimes more specifically seen as the period
   following puberty, characterized by social and emotional maturing.)
   Adolescents—people in the process of maturing; teen-age young people.
   Cycle of puberty—the period of increased velocity in growth occurring
   during the early teens.
   Developmental tasks—responsibilities for growing up.
   Growth patterns—processes of growth common to all people.
   Maturation—the process of becoming completely developed; attaining
   full growth.
   Puberty—the cycle of puberty (see above).
   Velocity of growth—the rate of increase in growth, as seen in increases in
   height, weight, size, strength, etc.
2. Plan a school social function that will interest students at the various
   developmental levels in your school. Include some activities that would
   provide experience for developing competence in specific social skills.
   Indicate which of your provisions help meet the needs and interests of both
   the younger and the older, the less and the more experienced, and the relatively immature or mature students. Give your reasons for thinking so.
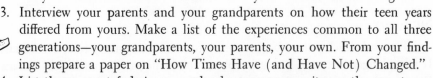
3. Interview your parents and your grandparents on how their teen years
   differed from yours. Make a list of the experiences common to all three
   generations—your grandparents, your parents, your own. From your findings prepare a paper on "How Times Have (and Have Not) Changed."
4. List three recent fads in your school, your community, or the country as
   a whole. These may be fads in speech, dress, or entertainment that have
   been all the rage for a while and then died down completely. Compare
   each one with a custom in the same area that is *always* in style. Can you
   see any characteristics in common among the activities that are always
   popular?
5. Write a paper dealing with your progress in your own developmental tasks
   during the current year. Indicate what tasks you have been working on,

which proves the most difficult and why, in which ones you are achieving well and what is aiding your progress, and what you expect to be at work on in the immediate future.

6. Prepare a confidential memorandum for yourself, entitled, "In Ten Years, I Hope to Be. . . ." Describe all you hope to be doing ten years from now. Include the job you hope to be holding, the kind of family situation you hope to be living in, the place you hope to hold in the community, and so forth. Be sure to include the kind of person you hope to have become by that time. Keep your memorandum for further reference. Talk it over with a trusted friend, your mother, father, or teacher, especially in terms of what you must accomplish to attain your anticipated goals.

Group Activity

1. Organize a panel discussion of boys and girls on "What Makes a Person Appear Attractive?" Encourage members of both sexes to discuss frankly things they find pleasant in each other's appearance as well as constructive suggestions for improvement. Summarize the panel's presentation and discuss in general class session the major points that have been made.

2. Plan a good-grooming program for your school. If feasible, include a series of demonstrations on shampooing and hair-styling, selection and care of clothing, the use of color in make-up and clothes, or any similar topic that seems appropriate and interesting to the students in your school. Talk over your plans step by step with your teacher and carry out those that are of general interest.

3. Give brief demonstrations showing the right and wrong way to handle one phase of each activity listed below.

Making introductions	Gathering in a group on the street
Holding a conversation	Boarding a bus
Telephoning a friend	Ordering food at a restaurant
Making a date	Attending the theater
Calling for a girl (boy)	Mingling with others at a dance
Breaking a date	Attending a program in assembly hall

4. As a class, compile a list of the areas in which parent-youth disputes are most common. Have the list put on the board and take a poll to find out which conflicts occur most often. Into your notebook, copy your class ratings from the most to the least frequent parent-youth problems as a background for the next chapter's study.

5. Plan with your teacher a vocational guidance program in which people engaged in interesting occupations are asked to spend an afternoon at the school talking with small groups of students about their work, their training for it, and employment possibilities available.

6. Arrange a debate on the topic, "Married Women Should Be Encouraged to Work." Have both sides carefully prepare their arguments by becoming familiar with current research and recent statements of American leaders.

Readings

CROW, LESTER D. and ALICE, *Adolescent Development and Adjustment* (New York: McGraw-Hill Book Company, 1956). Part Two, "Adolescent Development," covers such topics as physical growth, maturing mental abilities, changing emotional patterns, and personal and social aspects of personality development through the teen years.

DUVALL, EVELYN MILLIS, *Facts of Life and Love for Teen-Agers* (New York: Association Press, 1956). Part One, "Becoming Men and Women," discusses in detail the questions young people ask about what happens when a girl matures, how boys become men, where babies come from, and the sex problems and promises of the adolescent years.

FAEGRE, MARION L., *The Adolescent in Your Family* (Washington, D. C.: Children's Bureau, U. S. Department of Health, Education, and Welfare, 1955). This well-written booklet about adolescence can be easily read with profit by teen-agers who want to understand better what is happening as they go through the second decade of life.

LERRIGO, MARION O., and SOUTHARD, HELEN, *Finding Yourself* (Chicago: American Medical Association, 1955). An attractively illustrated 50-page pamphlet that reviews for teen-agers the major steps toward adulthood of both boys and girls during their teen years. Prepared jointly by the American Medical Association and the National Education Association.

REMMERS, H. H., and RADLER, D. H., *The American Teenager* (Indianapolis: The Bobbs-Merrill Company, 1957). This book summarizes the Purdue Opinion Polls of representative teen-agers' thinking, attitudes, and concerns about various aspects of their lives in recent years. As such, it interests adolescents as well as the adults who work and live with them.

STRANG, RUTH, *The Adolescent Views Himself* (New York: McGraw-Hill Book Company, 1957). Although every adolescent is different, all teen-agers experience the same difficult growing period between childhood and maturity. This book gives you a realistic look at how adolescents generally see themselves, their world, and the problems of growing up.

Chapter 3
How Mature Are You?

The secret of maturity is the ability to accept yourself, to face your problems honestly, and to handle them intelligently. The test on page 40 is based upon a study by the Research Institute of America. It has been given to managers and personnel directors of several thousand corporations to help them measure their growing maturity. You as a teen-ager can find it quite as provocative as have experienced adults—perhaps more so, for your growth is so much more your central concern.

This is not a test with a "passing" or "failing" grade; rather it is an aid to help you see yourself in the light of the basic principles of maturity. Use the questions below to check your progress in the areas in which you yourself want to improve.

To complete your self-examination, come back to this test at specific times: your birthday, each fall, the beginning of a new year, graduation day, before getting your first real job, and before leaving for college or other special training.

More than anything else you want to be grown-up. You are tired of being treated as a child. You often wish that you might run your own life, choose your own friends, make your own decisions, take responsibility for yourself. You want to go where you want to, when you want to, and stay as late as you want to without the kind of supervision that children get. You want to be allowed to solve your own problems by yourself without the interference of adults.

Becoming mature is a lifelong process. There is no magic minute in any one person's life when he can stop and say with assurance, "Now I am completely mature." Growth and development go on as long as an individual strives to improve and become increasingly mature in the way he faces and reacts to life. Personality is never "done." So, when you think of your maturity, think not only of your abstract ideals or even specific goals, but also of those levels of achievement that indicate whether or not you are ready for adult experiences, privileges, and responsibilities.

CHECK TEST FOR GROWTH [1]

(Do not write in this book.)

In the past year . . .   Yes   No

1. Did you step up your reading?   —   —
2. Did you increase your participation in group activities (clubs, civic associations, church groups, and so forth)?   —   —
3. Did you improve your ability to handle routine and repetitive activities (making beds, completing assignments, preparing dinner, and so on)?   —   —
4. Did you at any time review your past activities to determine which are desirable, which ought to be dropped?   —   —
5. Did you find it easier to deal with people—both family and friends?   —   —
6. Did you have fewer emotional flare-ups?   —   —
7. Did you get greater enjoyment out of your relaxation and recreation this past summer?   —   —
8. Did you devote more time to thinking about the reasons other people behaved the way they did?   —   —
9. Were you able to concentrate on one activity until it was completed?   —   —
10. Did you devote more time to, and get greater satisfaction out of, helping others solve their problems?   —   —
11. Did you improve any of your skills or develop new talents?   —   —
12. Did you come up with some new conclusions about yourself, your personality, your habits?   —   —
13. Did you gain any new insights into your parents and your friends which helped you to understand them better?   —   —
14. Did you go in for new and more varied activities or develop new friends?   —   —
15. Did you find yourself making a larger number of independent decisions?   —   —
16. Did you find it easier to accept the problems for which you had no immediate solutions?   —   —
17. Did you find it a little easier to live in the present?   —   —
18. Did you change some of your opinions and feelings about things?   —   —
19. Did you rediscover an old, simple pleasure?   —   —
20. Did you gain a clearer conviction about and a better understanding of the basic truths, religion, or philosophy in which you believe?   —   —

Birthdays are only one mark of progress toward maturity. Just because you have celebrated a certain birthday does not mean that you are an adult, or that you can expect now to be treated as one. Have you ever known a person sixteen or eighteen or twenty or even forty years old who sometimes acted as though he or she were still a little child? Some grown women cry

[1] Adapted from Dr. Mortimer R. Feinberg, "How Mature Are You?" *McCall's*, Vol. 85 (April, 1958), p. 32. Used by permission.

when they do not get their way. Some middle-aged men get red in the face and rant and rave when other people do not do just what they want them to. There are people of both sexes and of all ages who in some situations act and feel like small children. True maturity is an achievement toward which we all may strive, whatever our actual age.

You do not grow up "all of a piece," evenly and consistently. There are many maturities to consider in any growing individual. The most common types of maturity are:

1. *Chronological* (how many birthdays you have had)
2. *Physical* (how mature your body is)
3. *Intellectual* (how grown-up your thinking is)
4. *Emotional* (how mature your feelings and the ways in which you express your feelings are)
5. *Social* (how mature your relationships with other people are)
6. *Philosophical* (how grown-up your beliefs, ideals, purposes, morals, and values are)

Chronological Maturity

You can tell just exactly how old you are in years, months, weeks, and even days if you care to calculate these figures. Today you are just exactly one year older than you were a year ago today. Next year at this time, regardless of what happens in between, you will be just a year older.

If you are one year older than your brother now, you always will be just one year older. The ratio of your age to that of others changes constantly, but the exact difference remains the same. Suppose your mother was thirty years old when you were born; then she was thirty times older than you. When you were fifteen, she was forty-five and only three times older than you. When you are thirty, she will be sixty, or only twice your age. Yet the difference of thirty years is always just the same. Differences in growth may be great, but birthday differences remain the same.

PHILOSOPHY FOUR [2]

The birthday I was only One
My Teddy came, and he was None.
Now I am Four and he is Three
But he's the size he used to be
While I get bigger every minute
Because my skin has stretches in it.

Beth Duvall Russell

[2] *Book of Uncommon Prayer* (Privately printed, 1944.)

Chronological Growth Is Unalterable. You may catch measles, take a trip around the world, fall in love, lose your best friend, or experience all manner of joys, sorrows, sufferings, or triumphs, but your birthdays march merrily on at the selfsame pace. There is nothing you can do to change your chronological age. As long as you live, your advancing years will tick themselves off regularly, regardless of how you may wish you could hurry them up or slow them down.

Chronological age is important for some things. Getting a driver's license for a car, getting a work permit, obtaining a license to get married, being able to vote, all depend in most states upon your chronological age. There are differences in the ages at which certain privileges are allowed in the various states, but in the main age is recognized as *one* measure of maturity almost everywhere.

The older you grow, the less important age alone becomes. People in their twenties, thirties, forties, and fifties rarely bother very much about the age of their colleagues, or of their own (except for the woman who wants to be coy about her age!). As a measure of how much maturity can be expected of a person, age is of little help.

Physical Maturity

If you want to be technical about how physically mature you are, you consult an expert, who makes detailed X-ray studies of your bones. For all practical purposes, however, there are other more general indications of physical maturation that can be simply summarized.

You have reached physical maturity when you have attained your full height, weight, and strength. As long as you continue to gain in stature year by year, you are still growing and have not reached full maturity. As soon as you stop growing taller and filling out, you are approaching maturity. When you become strong enough to do an adult's work without undue fatigue, your body is at the threshold of maturity. Long before boys and girls are ready for marriage and parenthood, their glands begin to function like those of adult men and women.

Physical maturity is important. To be considered big enough to be allowed to do certain things, you must look big. More is expected of tall, well-developed boys and girls than of their smaller, less well-developed classmates. Sports, dating, jobs, and even relationships at home depend to some extent on how well developed you are physically. Even so, young people themselves tend to feel that this is more important than it really is. Left to herself, nature takes care of physical development rather well. It is just a matter of a few years before your body is mature and ready for adulthood. There are other phases of maturing that are even more important in the long run, and about which you can do something.

Intellectual Maturity

Intellectual maturity is not easy to measure. In fact, there seems to be no common agreement as to just what it involves. Generally speaking, you might think of intellectual maturity along the following lines:

1. A person is intellectually mature to the extent to which he can understand *meanings*. An infant does not understand words or numbers or gestures or signs. As he outgrows his babyhood, he begins to comprehend some of these meanings. The grownup knows what most of the common symbols and signs stand for in his world. He can think abstractly without counting on his toes or fingering objects under discussion. Intellectual maturity involves handling the language of both the words and the signs of one's culture with understanding and comprehension.

2. A person is intellectually mature to the extent to which he can make up his mind. A child waits to see what his parents choose before making a decision. As a person matures, he is increasingly able to make his own decisions without waiting for someone else to tell him what to do.

3. A person is intellectually mature to the extent to which he can look at himself and his problems from outside himself. We call this being objective. It means being able to look at life without being unduly influenced by how one feels. It involves being able to view life without seeing oneself in its very center all the time.

4. A person is intellectually mature to the extent to which he can take responsibility for his own behavior and its consequences. When an accident occurs, some children blame someone or something, rather than admit that they were at fault. As we grow intellectually, we learn that we cannot always be perfect, that all of us make mistakes, and that when a mistake occurs, the grown-up way is to accept the responsibility and work it out as best we can.

5. A person is intellectually mature to the extent to which he is able to postpone judgments. When we are little, we are hasty in judging other people and situations. A little boy or girl says, upon being introduced to a stranger, "I do not like you; go away." A half-grown person may not say it, but will think, "I don't know her and I don't want to. I don't like her, that's all." An adult recognizes intellectually that judgments cannot be made so hastily. Some people call this being open-minded. Most of all it means exercising the mental discipline required to get all the facts before making up your mind about anything. You are an intellectually mature adult when you reserve judgments until you are sure of what is involved.

6. A person is intellectually mature to the extent to which he can take a problem-solving approach to life's questions. When confronted with a new and baffling situation, the child may pretend it isn't there, cry, run away, or close his eyes and dash into the unknown. The more intellectually adult you are, the more able you are to recognize a new problem, accept it as present, have confidence that it can be solved by study and the application of sound principles, and, if it is *your* problem, begin to gather the facts that will eventually help you to work out the solution.

"I've done a lot of thinking in my time . . . and what did it ever get me?"

Times-Mirror Syndicate, Los Angeles

Intellectual Growth Is Up to You. So many things are involved in intellectual growth that its progress varies with the situation and with the person. Recent studies have indicated that the best environment for intellectual growth is one that is stimulating and offers people a chance to tackle real problems that can be solved. When the immediate situation is not stimulating a person seems to mark time. When too much is demanded of him, he tends to become discouraged and stop trying. In between is a happy medium which makes for the best intellectual growth.

As long as you live, you can keep on growing intellectually if you want to. You can begin where you are, at any time, and grow to the next level of mental maturity. You keep from growing intellectually if you become mentally lazy. The alert, alive person who is willing to make the effort can build habits of thinking that will make him increasingly mature. Your most infantile habits of thinking are not fixed forever, unless you like them that way! You can always change for the better.

True intellectual maturity is rich in rewards. It frees the individual for real choices. Anyone who has ever had the thrill of standing on his own feet intellectually, following facts where they lead him, and making decisions on the basis of sound judgment, never wants to return to more infantile ways of thinking. At some times you are more intellectually mature than at others. One reason for this is that your intellectual maturity is so closely related to your emotional maturity.

Emotional Maturity

You learn ways of expressing your feelings from those around you. If you follow the example of mature people, you learn mature patterns of behavior.

The emotional maturity of children often reflects the emotional maturity of their parents. If a mother always cries when little things distress her, or a father habitually loses his temper when things do not go his way, their children may find it hard to learn more mature responses. Parents, like everyone else, have some emotional upsets from time to time. If these are not too frequent, too intense, or too infantile, the children usually grow up to be emotionally healthy and mature.

1. A person is emotionally mature to the extent to which he can restrain himself. When you were very young, you were emotionally explosive. When you felt anything, you expressed it impetuously. As you mature, you become more and more able to restrain these immediate impulses, to wait before expressing yourself.
2. A person is emotionally mature to the extent to which he recognizes and understands his feelings. A little child hardly knows what his

feelings are and cannot tell which are hurtful and which helpful. As you mature emotionally, you learn that some feelings cannot be poured out without making trouble. Hates and jealousies, and even some loves, may do harm if you blurt them out. So you become increasingly skillful at knowing how and when to express yourself, until at last you are capable of recognizing and sorting out your feelings in an adult way. This is a gradual lifelong process.

3. A person is emotionally mature to the extent to which he can express his emotions in wholesome, constructive ways. When Jimmy gets angry and hits his brother with a hammer, he is being harmfully aggressive. When Mary gets so frightened of a neighborhood dog that she cannot eat her supper, that is not good either. When a mother loves her son too suffocatingly, there may be trouble. Learning to express your feelings in ways that leave you and others stronger, happier, better people takes a long while and brings you closer and closer to true maturity.

4. A person is emotionally mature to the extent to which he can carry heavy emotional burdens without cracking up under them. Most people have trouble some time or other. When you were little, minor things could be terribly upsetting. A toy was broken and you thought your heart would break. Later a friend moved out of town, and you felt that the end of everything had come. Your dog got sick, and you cried in anguished grief. As you grow older, you can take such things without becoming that upset. Heavier burdens come along. Your first real friend jilts you. Your mother is rushed to the hospital. Your father loses his job. These crises pass and you right yourself again, only to find other emotional burdens still to come.

An immature individual becomes racked with grief or hot with rage, or cracks up entirely, over situations that more mature persons are able to accept and live with.

You are emotionally mature when, although aware of what is happening, and inwardly sensitive to it, you no longer "go to pieces" in every disturbing situation. You have learned to see situations in perspective and to take them in your stride because you know you can deal with them. This, you may say, is to "act your age" emotionally.

Managing Your Feelings Is Up to You. Feelings are real and cannot be banished. Recognition and acceptance of feelings about yourself and others is the first step in dealing with them. Some feelings you accept but keep to yourself. Some you express and share. Denial of your feelings builds up barriers to friendly relationships. Learning how to enjoy relationships with others and letting them know how you feel about them is part of growing toward emotional maturity.

If you really want to overcome your fears, or get over your temper, or change your emotional habits, you can do so. First you must accept yourself as you are. If you can do this without too much feeling of guilt or shame, that is fine. If you can understand something of why you are as you are, that is so much better. You must realize that changes are not going to take place overnight. If you have spent sixteen years growing a lusty temper, it is not going to disappear by your merely wishing it to. Your progress will be more rapid if you have an understanding friend and counselor to encourage you. Step by step, you learn more and more control, you get more and more satisfaction from your progress and, with practice, find yourself becoming increasingly grown-up emotionally.

Emotional maturity helps you to make and keep friends and to be an attractive, charming personality. It contributes more than anything else to happiness in marriage. It is essential to your social well-being. Most social problems are caused by emotionally ill and infantile people. As more and more people develop emotionally mature personalities, our communities, our country, and our world will benefit greatly.

Social Maturity

Your social age is measured by your ability to get along with people. It involves so many skills and attitudes that it is difficult to measure accurately

You are showing social maturity when you help your family plan a party at which they can meet your friends. Both adults and teen-agers enjoy a buffet supper party at home.

The Gorham Company

for any one person at any one time. As you look back on your growth in relating yourself to others, you are impressed with the changes that have taken place over the years.

When you were a baby, you yelled for what you wanted. You expected other people to answer your demands and meet your needs without question. You were entirely on the receiving end of things for some time. Later on you learned to tease and cajole your parents into giving you what you wanted. This wasn't very grown-up, but such tactics were a step beyond the howling of your baby days. It wasn't long before you began to see that other people liked to have their wishes considered, too. So you developed skills in compromising. Sharing, real sharing, came much later, with the ability to co-operate. It developed slowly, for it is the most difficult, though the most mature, way of getting along with others.

Teen-age boys and girls enjoy doing things together. They need the deepening friendships that develop. Mother-love and family affection are no longer completely satisfying, any more than the milk diet of infancy can satisfy the teen-age hunger for hamburgers. Supervision and guidance are now being supplemented by encouragement in which the teen-ager increasingly assumes responsibility for his own behavior, conduct, and choices. As you grow up, you not only need more and more people of various kinds in your life; you also need different things from them.

The hopeful thing is that social maturity is largely *learned*. You learn how to live in a world of people. From the moment of your birth, you have been learning this through constant experience. How socially mature are you?

Ten Signs of Social Maturity

1. As you become socially mature, it becomes increasingly easy for you to accept others for what they are. You can become more and more interested in the vast variety of human beings, and enjoy exploring each new personality you meet. It is only when you grow really big yourself that you can see the bigness of others, appreciate their potentialities, and respond to the strong common bonds that make all people brothers under the skin.

2. A person is socially mature to the extent to which he can avoid labeling other people. It is childish to respond to the irritating behavior of others with the familiar labels of childhood: liar, piker, cheat, dumbbell, slob, sourpuss, and all the rest. It is only when you do not really understand others that you resort to these easy "false-face labels" which mask the other person and make him appear so unpleasant that you feel justified in behaving toward him as you do.

3. Of course you are not going to like everybody. Few people do. But as you become socially mature, you no longer have to place the blame for your dislike on the other fellow. You can say, "Other people like him (or her or it), and I would like to, but something in me makes it difficult." This approach helps you to avoid the labels that are always so childish, and it leaves the way open for you to meet, to know, and to enjoy a host of people whom you might otherwise miss entirely.

4. A person is socially mature to the extent to which he has emancipated himself from childhood dependencies upon his parents. Expecting your father to come to your rescue every time you get in a jam or looking to your mother to clean up the messes you leave in the kitchen after a snack are marks of dependence whether you admit it or not.

   A socially mature adult can take responsibility for himself. He enjoys making his own decisions and living by them. He consults his parents about his choices and listens to their suggestions. But if he is truly mature socially, the final decision is his own. The task of cutting apron strings from the parents is usually a difficult one for parents and young people alike. But emancipation from one's parents is a step toward social maturity.

5. A person is socially mature to the extent to which he can meet strangers easily. Little boys and girls often cry at the sight of a strange face. Older people do not cry but may be embarrassed when they are introduced to strangers. Blushing, stammering, not knowing what to do with hands or feet, finding nothing interesting to say, and avoiding such meetings are all common reactions among people of even high-school age.

   When you become socially mature, you do not find other people nearly so frightening. You have the skills it takes to put another person at his ease. You openly enjoy making new friends. You feel at ease with people of both sexes and all ages in any number of situations. The nice thing about it is that you yourself can develop this kind of social maturity.

6. A person is socially mature when he can enjoy both being a member of a group, and being alone. As you grow up socially, you discover groups that you genuinely enjoy. You become selective in your activities with friends. You do things with other people that bring you real satisfaction and a sense of well-being. You are increasingly able to refuse invitations to join people or take part in activities that are meaningless, worthless, or harmful.

A socially mature person is not afraid to be alone. Because he has matured socially, he does not have to go on proving his "popularity" to himself or to others through constant participation in groups. He can enjoy being alone with his thoughts, his work, or his interests, without fear of being misunderstood. He is learning to enjoy "the islands of solitude" that every mature person needs in his life.

7. A person is socially mature to the extent to which he can make and keep friends of both sexes. Little children often like people for what they can get from them. At three you liked your favorite aunt because she always brought you toys and candy. At thirteen you liked her because she took you on a trip. Still later you both may be able to enjoy each other as companions, neither of you thinking about what one can do for the other.

Dating in high school can be of two kinds—demanding and possessive, or companionable. The difference lies in the way the friends feel about each other. In both friendship and dating, mature people are not demanding, or possessive, and there is no jealousy involved. They share true affection for each other, take an interest in each other's welfare and development, feel a deep mutual loyalty, and enjoy an easy companionship in which each can be his real self without offending the other.

8. A person is socially mature to the extent to which he can work with others democratically. If he has to be boss all the time, or even some of the time, he still has some growing up to do. If he has to have someone around telling him what to do, he is not mature. The mature person enjoys planning *with* others. He is able to accept others as they are, to approach a problem confidently, knowing that together they can work it out, step by step, to a mutually satisfactory solution.

9. A person is socially mature to the extent to which he can accept and abide by the rules and laws of the group of which he is a part. Children sometimes enjoy seeing how far they can go. Often a teen-ager likes to defy convention just to show how "smart" he is. There may be a thrill in running through a red light, or in seeing what you can get away with on an honor exam, or in stepping over the line in any number of ways, but it is a thrill only the not-quite-grown-up enjoy.

Truly mature people find out what the rules are and adjust to them. If the rules make sense, they obey them. If the rules need changing, they set about changing them; but they do so in orderly ways, according to the rules for changing rules! The socially mature person does not enjoy flaunting convention or sneaking out from under the customs of his group. He takes responsibility not only for himself, but also for the group of which he is a part.

10. A person is socially mature to the extent to which he makes a constructive contribution to the world about him. Children are not expected to contribute to group life. Adults are. Creative, constructive work is an important distinction between children and adults anywhere. As soon as you find something you can do that the world needs done, you begin to feel like an adult. That is one of the reasons why guidance to help you find a satisfying vocation is so important. It is also the reason why our grandfathers thought work was good for the soul.

If you have been mentally scoring yourself as you have read through these ten marks of the socially mature person, you probably have found some areas in which you rated as mature. Possibly in others you did not measure up quite so well. That is to be expected. Social maturity is one of the most difficult areas of growth. Social growth is not at all predictable or regular. The differences among individuals are tremendous. Indeed the different levels of social maturity revealed in the same person are often amazing.

Few other types of maturity are as important as is your social maturity. Whatever you do, wherever you are, you will be dealing with people. The extent to which you can get along with them in socially mature and responsible ways determines the extent to which you will attain success and find real satisfaction.

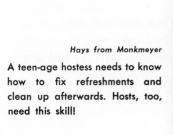

Hays from Monkmeyer

A teen-age hostess needs to know how to fix refreshments and clean up afterwards. Hosts, too, need this skill!

Philosophical Maturity

You can never be quite mature until you have a good workable philosophy of life. Only then will you have the long-term values, the goals worth striving for that will make it possible for you to make choices, keep your balance, expend your energy on worthwhile things, make friends who are true friends, and steer your life in an orderly path of progress. Even falling in love and getting married depend a great deal upon the maturity of your philosophy of life.

When a group of young people were asked to characterize a man who has a good philosophy of life, they mentioned such traits as the eight that follow.[3]

1. *He has few inner conflicts.* He knows who he is. He has come to terms with his role in life. He is not torn apart by every difficult choice he has to make, because he feels sure of the kind of person he is and what that sort of individual does and does not do.

2. *He has a sense of where he is going.* He has conscious goals toward which he is striving. He knows what he wants to become. He sees clearly the vocation he is headed toward and has chosen it carefully in terms of values that are real to him. He sees more to life than his job alone. He is balancing dreams for a home of his own, a "place in the sun," and is working toward the kind of fulfillment that comes to those accustomed to directing their lives rather than drifting along.

3. *He lives for long-term values.* He does not sacrifice the future by impulsively snatching the temptation of the moment regardless of its costs in the long run. He is able to enjoy the present, living fully as he goes along, partly because his values are lasting, permanent ones. He cares more for the on-going joys and satisfactions than for the merely transient, superficial pleasures of life.

4. *He does not worry about non-essentials.* His concern is for things that really matter. He does not need to waste his time in senseless fears, or in anxiety about a multitude of petty annoyances. The things he cares about are bigger than immediate rewards and disappointments. He has enough perspective to remain sensitive yet calm, aware yet poised, "tuned in" to life without living in constant turmoil over its ups and downs.

5. *He regains his equilibrium readily.* When an emergency arises—whether it is a job problem, a death in the family, war, or any other personal or social crisis—he pulls himself together after the first shock.

[3] Adapted and elaborated from William H. and Mildred I. Morgan, *Planning Your Marriage* (New York: Association Press, 1943), pp. 48–49.

He faces the new situation frankly, mobilizes his resources for meeting the emergency, and works it through with poise and hope.

6. *He has a grown-up conscience.* A little child behaves well when someone is watching him, because he knows if he does not, he will be punished. His mother is his conscience at first; when she is absent, he may be swayed by impulse rather than by what he ought to do. With maturity, he is able to exercise his own conscience. The mature person keeps within the bounds of socially approved behavior not because anyone might see him, or find out what he has done, but because he himself has a grown-up, effectively operating conscience.

7. *He has concern for the welfare of others.* An immature person cares primarily for himself and for satisfying his own immediate impulses. With maturity comes an abiding concern for other people, whether close by or not, who might be affected by what he does and says and is. The mature person is interested in the welfare of millions of his fellow men whom he may never meet, but who he feels are his brothers because they share a common humanity.

8. *He is continuing to develop philosophically.* No man or woman can be perfect or complete in any phase of philosophical maturity. The mature individual continues to develop a more adequate philosophy of life as long as he lives. With increasing experience he gains greater perspective and wisdom. With growing maturity, he becomes flexible enough to alter former convictions, opinions, and values, to come to terms with life as it reveals itself to him. The philosophically mature person is flexible and humble.

Where Do You Get Your Philosophy of Life? No one is born with a workable, mature philosophy of life. Just where it comes from, and how, and when, is worthy of your consideration. Where did you get your own values? Who has contributed to your sense of what is really important? What experiences have you had that have helped you develop a sense of who you are and what life means to you?

Your philosophy of life started back in your childhood, in all the things that happened that gave you a sense of direction. Your philosophy has been and continues to be molded by the customs and the values of the people in your home, your church, and your community. The teachings of your religion and your response to them have contributed to the way of life upon which you are already embarked.

You develop your philosophy of life in part through discovery of the great thoughts, the noble ideas, and the views of life that have come down through the ages. In the characters of the Bible and other great books, you are introduced to different designs for living, and often you choose among them. The great writers of all times have left vivid sketches of the life of their day.

Your philosophy of life also comes partly from identification of yourself with people you love and admire. The more mature you are, the bigger the people you try to be like. When you have just started to grow up, your ideal may be a movie star or football hero. Later you are impressed by people who have made some vital contribution to man's welfare. The friends you have, the people you look up to, all help you to build your philosophy of life.

You are as big as the things you care about. Children care tremendously about the pleasures of the moment. Some older people sacrifice all their ideals for comfort, money, or personal power—and often feel, without knowing why, that their lives lack meaning. Most great men have found a sense of purpose through devotion to a great social or intellectual cause. What a man is willing to live for is a measure of his maturity.

When you choose a course of action based on your ambitions and dreams, and are willing to take the responsibility for that action, you are developing a sound philosophy of life. This philosophy is really yours only when it is reflected in your choices and actions. When the poet Browning said that man's reach must exceed his grasp, he meant that men should set high goals for themselves which they must continually strive to reach if they are to grow.

John Dewey once defined a good man as one who, no matter how morally unworthy he *has been*, is trying to become better. It is this unquenchable thirst for improvement that leads to greater philosophical maturity.

Your Growing Personality

Each person must face responsibilities for growing up, at every stage of life. Each act of an individual interacts with those of other people. Each aspect of his behavior relates to and affects all other aspects of his growing personality. A person has a better chance of developing a unified and whole-some personality when he strives to know and understand himself and then works to be his best self rather than to be like someone else. Furthermore, you can only understand and evaluate another's personality fairly if you see it in the framework of his goals and the handicaps he must overcome to achieve these goals.

It is not easy to take inventory and (1) face how you really feel about yourself and others; (2) try to understand what has happened to you in your relations with your parents, brothers, and sisters in your school experiences, and in your adjustment to cultural pressures and economic circumstances; (3) seriously think about what you want life to mean to you; and (4) consider the resources available for improving your life. Yet all of these are important steps if you want to take an active part in your own development.

To look at one's own thoughts, feelings, and behavior honestly and objectively is always to run the risk of discovering something one doesn't want to face. It is important to become aware of assets as well as shortcomings. One must accept oneself as a person of value and worth, trusting one's ability to change gradually for the better. The confidence that one can make reasonably thoughtful decisions and carry them through with reasonable effectiveness is essential to the development of self-reliance.

It is important that you grow in ability to make good decisions about your life in the days, weeks, months, and years ahead, in terms of the values and goals you yourself choose.

Do you want to be distinctive, to have something special that others admire? The better you understand what personal freedom really means, the more often you will choose to be yourself, to follow your own interests, explore your own values and your own unique feelings and ideas. Of course, you know people you admire and want to be like. Today many pressures push you toward following the crowd. You can learn to consider, whenever you are making a choice, to what extent you want to conform and to what extent you can express your independent judgment. Try this when you choose your clothes, plan the use of your time, energy, or money, seek various forms of recreation, select your friends, and think about your career, your hobbies, or your long-range goals.

Have you considered thoughtfully the criteria for maturity presented in this chapter? Do they have meaning for you? Can you use them to help you take increased responsibility for your own development?

The criteria for physical health are probably the most familiar to you. Many of the courses you have taken in school have kept these before you, and your parents, too, have stressed their importance. If you have read thoughtfully the discussion of intellectual maturity, you may have enlarged your concept of the part your intelligence can play in all aspects of maturing, the ways in which you can stand on your own to develop and use intellectual skills in making choices.

Social, emotional, and philosophical maturity are very much involved in personality growth. Study the criteria for each of these again. What questions do they raise in your mind? Many of your questions may be discussed in the chapters ahead, and additional reading will help you clarify your thinking about maturity.

Personal maturity is not easily achieved. Mistakes as well as successes go into the development of a person. Nor is maturity, once achieved, maintained without further effort. Furthermore, the aspects of maturity are interdependent. For instance, good physical health is important for good relations at home, at school, at work, and in community affairs. Good mental health usually makes for a cheerful, enthusiastic approach to people. This in turn brings friendly responses. Seeing yourself as others see you and looking at situations from their viewpoint as well as your own help you develop more mature relationships.

Your ability to continue growing lies in your willingness to improve. You become more mature in proportion to your increased desire to grow and improve. Probably you show a higher degree of maturity in some phases of personality today than you did a few years ago. If you are a rapidly growing person, you will be even more mature by next year or the year after. Your levels of maturity are different from those of other people. You are different in the experiences you have, the way you respond to them, and the growth you make through them. Recognizing how you yourself grow and mature helps you to understand other people. They, too, are striving to mature through their responses to various situations.

Evaluating Progress in Your Personality Development. You are in danger of a retarded personality if you cannot accept yourself as you are, if you dwell on feelings of self-contempt, if you want terribly to be someone other than yourself, or if you are indifferent about your development.

You are making good progress if you can honestly say the following statements are reasonably true of you:

1. You recognize yourself as you are.
2. You are making a conscious effort to improve and grow.
3. You are using your handicaps as challenges rather than as alibis.
4. You recognize the immature methods you sometimes use to get what you want.
5. You realize that wholesome self-expression includes both positive and negative feelings.
6. You try to make your demands on others reasonable.
7. You recognize some of the needs of others and try to meet them whenever possible.
8. You find pleasure in giving as well as in taking.
9. You are assuming some civic responsibility.
10. You feel you "belong" and that other people like you most of the time.
11. You feel increasingly at ease with adults, with children, and with people your own age.
12. You are taking responsibility for setting your own life goals.
13. You are able to seek and take help from competent advisers in attaining your goals.
14. You sense your value as a person and are gaining satisfaction in growth.
15. You are finding life more meaningful and satisfying each year.

Summary

Your chronological age may be important in getting a driver's license, a work permit, or a marriage license, but otherwise it is not an accurate gauge of how mature you are. Your physical maturity may be important in getting a date, or a place on the basketball team, or doing a strenuous man-sized job, but even so there is little you can do to speed it up, except to keep your body in good condition and let nature take its course. Your intellectual, emotional, and social maturities are influenced by others around you, but in the last analysis depend upon you and your efforts to grow up. Your philosophical maturity is reflected in your emerging philosophy of life—a constantly changing set of values which you can continue to broaden and deepen as long as you live. Your growing personality is yours to develop as you assume responsibility for your way of life. You can help yourself to grow up as a person by taking stock of yourself from time to time, facing yourself as you really are, and mobilizing your resources for your future development.

Suggested Activities

Individual Study

1. Take the test in the beginning of the chapter and record your answers in your personal class notebook.
2. Write a confidential paper on what you want to achieve in the years ahead. Include the vocation you want to prepare for and why you are choosing this above all others. Consider the place your own marriage and family life will have in your life as an adult. What firm foundations are you laying down now for your future as you see it? Talk over your dreams with a trusted counselor, and keep your memorandum for future rereading.
3. In your notebook make a table like the one begun below. List six of your own prospective activities in the first column. Fill in the second one as indicated. Answer the question, "Am I Ready?" for each item to the best of your ability. Take your notebook to class for discussion.

(*Do not write in this book.*)

What I Will Be Doing Next Year	Responsibilities Required of Me	Am I Ready? Not Yet	Almost	Yes
1. Driving the car.	a. Obey traffic laws. b. Take care of the car. c. Consult family.		x	
2. Buying clothes.				
3.				

4. Consider the question, "Do privileges always entail responsibilities?" Would you say it is true or not true? Why? Is the answer different for adults than it is for young people?

5. You want to drive a car. Review the various kinds of maturity discussed in this chapter, jotting down all the qualifications necessary for handling a car safely. Draw up a statement entitled, "I am ready to drive a car when . . . " Discuss your paper with your classmates, your teacher, your parents. Check it with the safety rules and local driving ordinances in your community. Have you found that social maturity makes a difference in good driving? Emotional maturity? Intellectual maturity? What about your philosophy of life; does that affect your driving? How?

6. Go over one by one the eight points in the section on philosophical maturity, pages 52–53. Think through what each item means, how the principles involved might look in action, and illustrate out of personal experience, current movies, or fiction an individual who typifies each point. Think of some friends you know who illustrate deficiencies in some of these basic characteristics of maturity in their philosophy of life. Star those items on which you feel a particular need for individual growth. Jot down for yourself some suggestions on how you may develop in the directions you have indicated for yourself.

7. Prepare a book report on one of the books listed in the Readings at the end of the chapter. Be prepared to give it in class. Keep it in your notebook for further reference.

Group Activity

1. Debate the proposition, "It's fun to be mature."
2. Conduct a panel discussion of class members on what seem to be some of the privileges and responsibilities of growing up.
3. Discuss the film, *Farewell to Childhood* (International Film Bureau, 6 North Michigan Avenue, Chicago 2, Illinois, 23 minutes, sound) in terms of growing through the teen years.
4. Invite some respected adult to talk to your class on "What It Means to Become Mature." List the points made for further discussion.
5. Select a situation in which emotional maturity or immaturity is clearly evident in the actions of the people involved. Perhaps the rain has suddenly interrupted a picnic. Perhaps a father has just lost his job. Perhaps the last good tire on the car has just gone flat. Perhaps . . . ?

    Choose roles for an impromptu skit, portraying the way various people on different levels of emotional maturity might act. Change roles and show how these people might learn to act in such a situation.

6. Present for discussion a series of impromptu skits showing socially mature and immature boys and girls at a party, in the schoolroom, on the street, and in a friend's home. Point your discussion toward what each immature person might do to become more socially grown-up. Consider what friends and classmates might do to aid such maturing.
7. Discuss in class the fifteen items for evaluating progress in personality development. Compare the general point of view with the test at the beginning of the chapter. In what basic assumptions are the two similar?

Readings

ABRAHAMSEN, DAVID, M.D., *The Road to Emotional Maturity* (Englewood Cliffs, N. J.: Prentice-Hall, Inc., 1958). An experienced psychiatrist tells you, in language you can understand, the things that could help you become a more mature person. See especially pp. 173–87, where stumbling blocks to emotional maturity are contrasted with the feelings and actions that express emotional maturity.

CRAWFORD, JOHN E., and WOODWARD, LUTHER E., *Better Ways of Growing Up* (Philadelphia: The Muhlenberg Press, 1948). This guide to maturity, written specifically for young people, is particularly helpful in the self-quizzes, checklists, and self-improvement charts that are found throughout the volume.

MOORE, BERNICE MILBURN, and LEAHY, DOROTHY M., *You and Your Family* (Boston: D. C. Heath and Company, 1953). Chapter 8 of this high-school text, "Emotional Climate and Emotional Habits," details the emotional habits that help a young person find a full and satisfying maturity.

PIERCE, WELLINGTON G., *Youth Comes of Age* (New York: McGraw-Hill Book Company, 1948). Chapter 10, "Attaining Maturity," is particularly valuable in the large number of case excerpts that illustrate immature and mature ways of behaving as seen in the lives of young people.

SMART, MOLLIE STEVENS and RUSSELL COOK, *Living in Families* (Boston: Houghton Mifflin Company, 1958). You will find Chapter 8, "The Development of a Way of Life," especially helpful in its discussion of how you prepare for adult responsibilities and go about developing a philosophy of life.

WEITZMAN, ELLIS, *Growing Up Socially* (Chicago: Science Research Associates, 1949). This life-adjustment booklet can help you see how socially mature you are. You can check yourself on the "Test for Social Maturity," pp. 13–16, and see how you measure up as a socially mature person by the listing on pp. 47–48.

Chapter 4

What It Takes to Grow On

If you want to have a well-developed personality, you must satisfy its requirements for growth. For people grow big and beautiful, just the way roses or horses do, by having their needs met. Have you ever had a garden? If so, you have learned that plants need sunshine, moisture, good soil adapted to their requirements, and room to grow in. Without enough sun, plants turn yellow and become weak. Drought dries them up. Poor soil yields poor crops. Plants cannot thrive crowded in upon one another. Favorable physical conditions are necessary for all growing things.

Do you have a pet? Dogs, cats, rabbits, and white mice all have needs that must be satisfied if they are to thrive. Students sometimes use guinea pigs or rats to show how differences in nutrition affect the growth, well-being, and appearance of living things. Well-nourished animals look better, grow bigger, and engage in more activity than animals on an inadequate diet.

Your Needs as a Growing Person

Growing people have ongoing needs. If you want to grow up strong and well, these universal human needs of yours must be satisfied. The needs of a boy or girl are more numerous, and considerably more complex, than those of a puppy or a white rat. Human needs are often neglected because of poor understanding of what they are and how they are best met. The intelligent person who wants to grow up explores his needs and learns how to meet them in wholesome, satisfying ways.

What All People Need. For fifty years or so scientists have been turning their attention to the nature of human needs. C. H. Cooley, Sigmund Freud, W. I. Thomas, John Dewey, George H. Mead, Ellsworth Faris, Henry Murray, James Plant, Daniel Prescott, and many, many others have explored human nature and discussed its basic needs.

Today mankind recognizes certain universal human needs for physical well-being. As we learn more about man's physical make-up, standards for health and hygiene rise. Our physical needs include:

1. *Food* (nutritionally adequate and in sufficient quantity to maintain well-being)
2. *Air* (sufficiently free from harmful chemicals and foreign matter to foster health)
3. *Water* (unpolluted by harmful organic matter, such as bacteria, amoeba, etc., and carrying mineral components helpful rather than harmful to health)
4. *Clothing and shelter* (maintenance of proper temperature and avoidance of harmful constriction or restriction of needed growth and activity)
5. *Exercise and rest* (balanced rhythm promoting vigorous sense of well-being and caution against unduly long periods of enervating lassitude or over-fatiguing activity)
6. *Periodic relief from tensions* (regularity of food intake and elimination, outlets for sexual and emotional energies)
7. *Maintenance of positive health* (preventive services such as vaccination, cleanliness, etc.; adequate medical attention to injured or malfunctioning organs; periodic general check-up)

People Differ in Ways of Meeting Needs. There is tremendous variety in the way in which needs may be met. A hungry man in China picks up his chopsticks and attacks a bowl of rice. The hungry Eskimo takes his knife and hacks off a slab of blubber. A hungry baby tugs at the nipple for his milk. The schoolboy dashes for a hamburger. A housewife out shopping drops in for a cup of tea and a piece of cake. Each satisfies his hunger in his own way.

Hungers are needs that have been modified or conditioned (trained) by particular ways of having been met before. As the need is met, the person feels a pleasurable sense of satisfaction. The Chinese feels good when his stomach is filled with rice, as does the Eskimo with his blubber, the baby with his milk, and the boy with his hamburger. The next time the Chinese feels the need for food, his thoughts turn to the rice which satisfied his need before. The baby cries for milk, the housewife feels "famished" for a cup of tea, all because the memory of the past satisfaction lingers on and carries over to the next situation of need. We tend to repeat, if we can, experiences that bring us satisfaction. So, around our needs we build up habits.

Some habits of satisfying needs are "culturally conditioned"; that is, they grow out of the circumstances of our environment or are copied from others as part of a common way of life. The people of China share their rice as a common, staple food; people of Ireland, the potato; the Italians, spaghetti; Southerners in the United States, sweet potatoes and hot breads; and New Englanders, fish chowders and baked beans.

In governmental distribution of surplus foods, regional tastes are carefully considered. The Chicago family does not eat the hominy grits that the

Memphis family would enjoy. Many Chicagoans realize that the food value of the grits equals that of some of their customary foods, but the culturally conditioned habits of meeting food needs are difficult to change.

Other ways of satisfying needs are more "personally conditioned." John does not eat spinach because his father would never touch it. Jimmy "loves" bread and jam because for years the nicest part of his whole day has been an afternoon snack of bread and jam shared with his mother. Ethel "can't stomach" onions because, at a picnic in her childhood, she was eating an egg and onion sandwich when her father scolded her severely for losing his knife. Only when she was a grown woman, and understood herself and her father better, did she overcome her so-called allergy to onions. So it goes. You pick up your own particular ways of meeting needs not only from the larger group of which you are a part, but also from the intimate day-to-day associations with the people closest to you.

As it is with food, so it is with other needs. Some children cannot go to sleep without a favorite toy beside them. Some people cannot rest well in a

Enjoying and sharing with friends different kinds of foods is one way to broaden your tastes. Our country offers opportunities to sample delicacies of different nations, such as the Italian pizzas these young people are eating.

Sybil Shelton from Monkmeyer

"strange bed." The water in an unfamiliar place may not agree with you, even though it is perfectly healthful. Going to the doctor may be a terrible ordeal to some people, while many little children take their "shots" and accept medical and dental treatment with interest and enthusiasm. The ways in which you satisfy each of your needs depend not only on the need itself, but also upon your past experiences in meeting it.

In so far as you can, you tend to repeat happy, pleasurable experiences and avoid unhappy, painful ones. As you learn to satisfy your needs with particular objects or activities, you form habits by going back again and again to these reliable sources of pleasure. So, in the end, they become so closely associated with the need that they become a part of the hunger itself. Thus a man may be hungry for steak, but he may refuse to touch fish, though it would meet his need for food equally well, because it could not satisfy his hunger for steak.

When your physical needs are not met, you cannot remain healthy. You grow ill when you neglect the vital needs of your growing body. Your personality, too, has needs that must be met if you are to maintain your health.

Learning to Love and to Be Loved

In a crowded swimming pool a mother was teaching a child to swim. Closer and closer paddled a second little fellow. Soon his shrill voice piped up, "Watch me." The woman smiled at the little boy and gave him an encouraging word. All afternoon he hung at her heels like a love-hungry puppy. When it was time for her to go, tears came to his eyes and he asked her if she would not return the next day. A lonely child from a too-busy household can be as starved emotionally as the most pitiful waif on earth. Somewhere, somehow, he must satisfy needs that are as urgent and insistent as any we know of—those for love, affection, and attention.

Everyone needs to feel that he is loved. He needs to feel accepted for what he is, to know he can get a sort of unearned affection just by being himself. He needs to feel others respond to him, look at him as though they really see him, listen to what he has to say, be glad when he arrives, and sorry when he must leave.

These needs are so great that an individual will do almost anything to get attention. Sometimes a child would rather be punished than ignored. He would prefer unfavorable attention to no attention at all. That is why he sometimes acts so silly to make people like him. He just can't stand being neglected emotionally. If you are hungry enough for affection, you may do something, anything, to command the attention of others.

Much as your need for food changes from milk to meat as you mature, so, too, do your love needs change as you grow up. The little child needs to be cuddled, fondled, and held close in order to feel security and a response from others. As he grows older, these physical expressions of affection are to some extent replaced by more intangible ones.

Sympathy, understanding, consideration, and praise assure you that you are loved. Friendships that continue for what you *are* rather than what you *have* or can *do* help to meet your need for love. Having a special place in your family, your clubs, and your classes, where you are respected, appreciated, and encouraged to participate, helps to meet your needs for affection.

But love is a two-way flow. The infant takes love, but gives little in return. As he matures, the other side of love develops—the need to love others. Love, like blood, can nourish only as it circulates. Not to *receive* love is to starve. Not to *give* love is to suffocate. Maturity does not diminish the need for love from others. Rather it increases the need to love others. It is not enough just to be loved. You must love if you are to meet all your love needs.

How You Learn to Love. Your ability to love changes from childhood to adulthood as you go through several developmental phases. Your love first is given to your parents. You loved your mother first of all as she gave you the continuous physical care you needed. Fathers now share in baby care from infancy, so they, too, are included early in the awareness and love of their children. Brothers and sisters come next, then friends of the same sex, and later friends of both sexes. With mature love comes the choice of a marriage partner, toward whom a special quality of devotion is given exclusively and permanently. Love has many elements—companionship, enjoyment of sharing, respect, affection, tenderness, ecstasy, protection, concern for the loved one's welfare and happiness,.and a willingness to give more than you expect to get. These assume different proportions in your feelings for different people and at different times.

Love for others develops slowly. Love brings satisfaction only when it is a two-way process of giving and receiving. In the beginning, infants are almost completely on the receiving end of love. They are completely dependent upon their parents. If they receive "TLC"—tender, loving care—the beginnings of a feeling of security are established. With security, learning to give as well as to receive love begins. Normally each person progresses through the various stages of love from birth to maturity. But development may be stopped at any stage. Often people who are physically adult may be children still in terms of their capacity to love, expecting to receive love without giving it.

The transition from devotion to members of your own sex to love for members of the opposite sex is often difficult. Everyone must achieve such a transition, however, before he can form the kind of relationship essential in a good marriage. It is not that the earlier forms of love are ever abandoned completely, but rather that the quality of love changes as you learn to love.

This need to give of yourself is a basic motivation in such professions as medicine, nursing, the ministry, and teaching. It is the satisfaction of this need that makes many parents look upon the years when their children were small as the happiest of their lives. Your philanthropies, your altruism, your outgoing sympathies to people everywhere—all these help fulfill your need to love maturely.

Jane Addams never married. Yet who can say that she was deprived of two-way affection? She loved widely. People quite unlike herself, people in distant lands, people whom she never met, all were beloved by her. Surely she must have felt, too, the rich currents of affection that welled up around her at Hull House, where she lived close to the heart of her neighbors.

Learning to Become Yourself

You want to *be* someone. You want to be big, to be worthy, to be good, to be growing, to be at home in your world. You want to achieve, to do big things, to be free to be yourself, and to accomplish what you are capable of. Most of all you want to become yourself.

As you grow out of childhood, you want more and more freedom. You need to feel your own independence. You need to feel that you can stand upon your own feet, make your own decisions, and not be too tied to any other person, no matter how close he or she once may have been. You need to feel independent before you can truly experience interdependence with others. It is only when you have found yourself that you can lose yourself again in causes outside yourself.

This need for independence is insistent. It comes out in the negativism of the toddler, the rebellion of the teen-ager, and in frequent clashes in adult circles. It is close to the core of real democracy. It is the threat of every dictator. Man's cry for freedom rings through the ages with the all-or-nothing passion of Patrick Henry's "Give me liberty or give me death."

As a teen-ager, you are learning to be independent without resorting to explosive rebellion. When you insist upon freedom for which you are not yet ready to assume responsibility, you hurt yourself and those who can help you most. At the same time the adults in your life may be underestimating your capacity for independence. As you learn to gauge your development, you find you are more effective in working things out with your parents and teachers in *interdependence*—in which each respects and accepts the other's interest in the situation. Dependence is characteristic of childhood. Independence goes with the early teens' struggle for emancipation. Interdependence is the relationship of maturity.

Finding Out What You Can Do. As a teen-ager, you need opportunities for finding out what you can do. You try out all sorts of things, just to see where your talents and abilities lie. You learn from your successes and you learn from your mistakes as you explore the many possibilities for you in your

world. After a while you become restless just doing any old thing. You want
to do those things that really count.

The time comes in your development when you need to feel that you are
accomplishing something worthwhile. You need to think well of your efforts,
even when you are most realistic about their limitations. You need goals that
are attainable and satisfying opportunities for working toward these goals.
You need to feel that ways are open to allow you to function. You need to
be able to look yourself in the eye with respect and a sense of your own worth
as a person.

The Thrill of Becoming. As long as you live, you need to feel that you
are making progress. This thrill of *becoming* is the exaltation the little child
experiences with his first steps. It is the excitement you feel when you learn
to ride a bicycle, to drive a car, to date more successfully, to write a better
examination paper, to appreciate a passage of music more deeply, or to solve
a family conflict with more harmony. You need to be at home in your world.
You need to feel in tune with reality. You want to understand what life is all
about and where you fit into it. You'd like to know who you are and have
some idea of where you are going. Call it philosophy, call it religion, call it
orientation, call it what you will, you are looking for a serious answer to the
questions, "Who am I?" and "Where am I going?"

How You Take Failure

Cut off a plant's water supply and it dies. Deprive a baby of fondling
and it languishes, as doctors have discovered in their studies of babies seriously
deprived emotionally. Extreme deprivation in any essential human need results
in serious harm. But how about the more common forms of unmet needs?
What do people do when their needs are not fully met? How can you tell
when you yourself have needs that are not being met? What are some of the
ways of reacting to unmet needs? And which ways work out better in the long
run?

You May Withdraw. Withdrawal is one way of responding to unmet
needs. This is what emotionally starved babies do. They just withdraw from
response and become limp and languid. Sometimes people slip back into types
of behavior that they have not used for some time. A child who has been
toilet-trained begins to wet himself when a new baby comes into the home
and deprives him of first place in the attention and affection of his parents.
A lovesick girl refuses to eat when her boy friend does not call. Such back-
sliding is known as *regression*. It is a common type of withdrawal.

Running away from a frustrating situation is an active form of withdrawal. The teacher "does not understand" him, and so the pupil absents
himself from class. Walking out on a problem one cannot fight is sometimes
an intelligent solution, as in getting as far away as possible from a poisonous

snake or a time bomb. The question one must ask is: "Is this a situation to run from?"

Another form of withdrawal is refusal to discuss the unpleasant situation. When the incident is spoken of, you have nothing to say. Daydreaming, with its fantasies and make-believe in which you always come out on top, is another common means of withdrawal from unpleasantness.

One of the most common types of withdrawal is through illness. If you are sick, you cannot be expected to do that which you fear. When you are ill, people are concerned about you; you get attention; you are nursed and coaxed back to health. It is not surprising that many persons have headaches, stomach trouble, allergies, asthma, and all sorts of "attacks" when life gets too rough. Flanders Dunbar and others have even discovered "accident-proneness" in some individuals which gets them into accidents much more frequently than is true of the general public.[1] A current observation about a harassed man "looking like an accident going somewhere to happen" may not be so far-fetched!

Keep in mind that these are mechanisms everyone uses upon occasion. Some withdraw more often than others. People of all ages and walks of life use illness as a way of dropping out of situations with which they cannot quite cope (where basic needs are not being met). A little girl gets an upset stomach every morning, but the illness clears up miraculously as soon as the school bus has gone. The president of the Woman's Club is seized with a violent headache when her rival is elected for an honor she covets. The high-school boy twists his ankle just before the prom he has been dreading. The teacher feels a sore throat coming on when the supervisor is expected. These are not "faked" illnesses. They may be just as real as those without a psychological basis. They are disturbances in the way the person functions, and so they are called *functional illnesses* (brought on primarily by emotional rather than physical disturbances).

You May Defend Yourself. Defending oneself is still another type of response when needs are not met. Defense mechanisms are many. You may resist the active domination of others by negativism, rebellion, or active aggression. When attacked or threatened, you fight back. If you cannot actively fight back at those responsible for your distress, you may take it out on others.

The classic example of this is the man who was reprimanded at the office for something he had not done. He was angry and hurt, but he did not dare talk back to his boss for fear of losing his job. When he got home, his anger spilled over and he spoke sharply to his wife. She, feeling abused at such treatment, slapped her son. He kicked the dog. The dog chased the cat out of the house to the backyard, where the fight continued among the alley cats far into the night! Studies at Yale University have shown the direct connection

[1] Flanders Dunbar, M.D., *Psychosomatic Diagnosis* (New York: Paul B. Hoeber, Inc., 1943).

"You got good grades in history, Dad, because you studied it 30 years ago . . . before anything really interesting had happened!"

Times-Mirror Syndicate, Los Angeles

between frustration of basic needs and aggression.[2] When frustrated, a person may tend to become aggressive. You defend your own interests if you can, when you can, and as best as you can.

Less direct types of defense include the many forms of *rationalization* (the process of finding logical excuses for one's behavior). Thus you defend your position as "wise," "right," and "what I wanted all the time." A Polly-anna, for example, is a girl who thinks everything is just "dandy," whatever happens. In the fable of the fox and the sour grapes, the fox cannot reach the grapes and rationalizes, therefore, that they are sour anyway.

Some people defend themselves by *projection*. Projection is a kind of behavior which includes blaming others for your mistakes and seeing your weaknesses in other people.

[2] John Dollard and others, *Frustration and Aggression* (New Haven: Yale University Press, 1939).

You may defend yourself by *compensation*. If you are not good at one thing, you develop another talent further than you otherwise might. The boy who cannot get into the band may improve his swimming until he leads his team. The girl who does not get good grades may go out for a high dating score, or vice versa. You cannot excel in everything. You are wise when you meet your needs through avenues that are possible for you.

You May Attack the Problem. You sometimes make a frontal approach to a problem. You neither withdraw, nor defend yourself, nor attempt to compensate. You plow right through the obstacle. There was once a boy who was crippled in a school fire. The doctors said that he could never walk again. He was Glenn Cunningham, who later made a new world's record for running a mile. Two important things you have to learn are when and how to tackle the difficulty directly.

Facing Your Mistakes. Facing your mistakes honestly is an important step in learning to live with failure. No one succeeds in everything. Everyone makes mistakes. It is what you do about your errors that determines what kind of person you are becoming. One sort of individual blames others for his mistakes or projects his problems to people or things outside himself. The healthy person learns to face his own shortcomings and to deal with his mistakes wholesomely.

You make mistakes especially when you are in new situations with which you have had little experience. These untried experiences are frequent during your teen years, for it is then that you are stretching away from your old familiar ways, and pushing out into wider, more grown-up life experiences.

When you fall short of your aims for yourself, you can grow from the experience if you can correctly analyze the situation, find out just where you failed, and see what it is that you can try next time to assure a higher level of performance. When you make a mistake that involves others' expectations of you, you can gain their respect by acknowledging your limitations and perhaps asking their indulgence and help so that you can do better next time.

Making Stepping Stones Out of Stumbling Blocks. All of life involves overcoming obstacles of one kind or another. You can approach life's struggles with one of two points of view. You can be sorry for yourself, and feel "put upon" when you meet an obstacle in your path. Or you can approach the barrier between you and your goals as a challenge to be met. Take the first approach and you make life miserable for yourself and others. You waste time feeling sorry for yourself rather than working out any solution to the problem. Take a problem-solving attitude toward the difficulties that confront you and you not only work through the immediate situation, but you learn to make stepping stones of what otherwise might be stumbling blocks. This is the healthy way to live.

Healthy Ways of Meeting Needs

Everyone has needs. Each individual has problems in meeting all of these needs all of the time. Sometimes things outside yourself frustrate you. Someone else dates your girl; the car will not start; or the quota at the college you want to attend is filled. Sometimes two or more of your needs conflict with each other. You need the love of your parents; at the same time you need to grow independent of them. Problems in meeting needs are universal. As long as you live you are faced with both the needs and the problems of getting them met without too much difficulty.

Some ways of meeting needs are poor. When you hurt others in trying to satisfy your needs, you, too, suffer. When you injure yourself in attempting to help yourself, you are like the boy who "cut off his nose to spite his face." Ways such as excessive daydreaming, persistent rationalization, uncontrollable temper, projection, or jealousy are all harmful.

Ten Rules for Mental Health. Good ways of meeting needs are those that help you and others become stronger than you were. These ways are essentially healthful. They come under the heading of what is known as *mental hygiene.* Some of the outstanding principles of good mental health are summarized here:

1. Get acquainted with yourself.
    Know your own strengths and weaknesses.
2. Accept yourself.
    Admit your limitations. Correct your faults as best you can; then forget them.
3. Face the facts of life.
    Truth is often unpleasant, but take it—it can "make you free."
4. Solve your own problems.
    Avoid escapes. Use expert help. Then stand on your own feet.
5. Work hard at what you like.
    Find the things you really enjoy and let them "get you."
6. Earn your successes.
    Stop counting on luck or fate. You can make your own achievements.
7. Try to understand people.
    Don't expect too much of them. Learn to understand how they feel.
8. Develop real friendships.
    Learn to like people. Cultivate companionships. Share yourself.

9. Find yourself in a cause bigger than you are.
   Develop a philosophy in action. Stand for big things.
10. Be alive!
   Exercise your body, mind, and feelings to a tingling aliveness.
   Enjoy new experiences. Don't dry up!

Well-adjusted people maintain their equilibrium even when the going gets rough. They swing neither to one extreme nor to the other, but keep their balance on an even keel. Big men do not try to be perfect. They are satisfied with being themselves, with living and loving, working and playing, and doing the best they can as they go along. They keep their eyes forward, and are pulled ever ahead by the joys and the challenges of living.

Good Families Grow Good People

Human needs are satisfied through human families. Your physical needs, such as food, sleep, clothing, shelter, and medical attention, are met directly through the family most of your life. Personality needs are even more family-based. Love and acceptance, a sense of self, of worth, and of *being* come primarily from your family. That is what families are for today—to help their members grow by meeting their needs.

Good families build good people. Fine, wholesome family life meets the requirements of a growing personality. Families that put their members first recognize the importance of human needs and see that they are satisfied. Such families not only meet the needs of children as they grow up, but they also build in them good habits of living that make wholesome maturity possible.

Some families find it difficult to meet the needs of their members. They may be economically unable to supply the basic requirements for physical well-being. Even though this country is one of the most prosperous in the world, some families are still poorly clothed, poorly fed, poorly housed, and lacking in adequate medical attention.

Families find even more difficult the meeting of personality needs. The love, understanding, and encouragement that all people need from each other do not "just come naturally." It takes a mature, well-adjusted person to give enough of himself to meet the everyday needs of the people he lives with. A nervous mother, a sick father, parents burdened with anxiety and preoccupied with their own affairs, often neglect the emotional needs of their children and of each other. That is one reason why it is so important for each of us to grow as sturdy a personality as we can, so that we can help rather than hinder the growth of others around us.

No one comes from a perfect family. However, most of our homes do remarkably well by us. Most parents are deeply concerned for their children and do everything they can to help them grow up strong, happy, and well. The challenge that each of us faces is to build strongly and well upon the start that our families have given us.

Summary

As long as you live, you may grow. As long as you grow, you have needs to fulfill. Universal human needs include basic requirements for physical health that various people satisfy in various ways. Beyond these basic physical needs is the need to love and to be loved. The ability to love is learned through a lifelong process that starts with self-love and grows out in an ever-expanding circle of warm interaction with others. A healthy personality needs a sense of becoming that involves finding out what can and cannot be done. The way a person meets failure determines his basic personality pattern. Ways of meeting needs either aid devopelment or stunt it. Healthy ways of meeting needs are included in what is meant by *mental hygiene*. People who are mentally well meet their needs in wholesome ways that do not hurt others or themselves. Good families grow good people by meeting their needs and teaching them the habits of life through which needs can be adequately met.

Suggested Activities

Individual Study

1. Keep a weekly record of your own health habits. Do you get enough rest? Do you exercise every day? Is your diet well-balanced, with sufficient quantities of the "basic seven" foods to assure good health? Have you had medical and dental check-ups within the past six months? What are the things you could do to improve your health? Can you start some of these soon?

2. Distinguish between a need and a hunger. Illustrate out of your own experience the difference between needs and hungers for food. List some of the foods you like especially. Which of them are culturally conditioned? Which are more specifically personally conditioned? Are there foods that you would not eat unless you were starving? What are they? Which are the culturally and which the personally conditioned? Is being too fussy sometimes a handicap? Why? What are some of the ways in which we may

keep our habits from becoming too set? How would you recommend that we keep flexible and varied as to the ways in which we meet our many needs?

3. List in your notebook ten names of outstanding persons whom you admire. Beside each name indicate what that person does to gain the respect, attention, and affection of others. How do some of these ways differ from others? Which of them could you not hope to pattern after? Which of these ways might be worth trying? How do they differ from ways which you usually use to get others to notice you? As you get older, are there some ways of relating yourself to others that you hope to cultivate? Can you begin practicing some of these right now?

4. Select some person recently in trouble to whom local newspapers have devoted a great deal of space. From your understanding of basic human needs and the facts you know about the case, try to speculate on what this person lacked to make him a wholesome, happy member of society. Which of his needs were unmet as far as you can see? Discuss this with your class members and compare ideas on what went wrong with this personality. Formulate your hypothesis on the basis that all of us are potentially both good and bad; our behavior hinges on how our needs as growing people are met.

5. Look through the short stories in current magazines for situations that portray functional illnesses. Notice who was ill, what brought on the attack, why it was so threatening to the particular person, what cured it, and how the other people acted toward the person who was ill.

6. In your notebook write a brief theme on the topic, "My Habits Are Homemade." Include the food habits that your family has taught you— the ways of eating, the times, the feelings about foods that you have picked up as a family member. Think about your habits of reacting to people. How are they homemade? Have you taken over some habits of other members of your family: your father, your mother, one of your brothers or sisters? Does a hot temper run in your family? What about religious attitudes? Feelings about other races? See what evidence your class can muster to support the thesis that our ways of meeting various needs usually arise in family situations.

7. List for yourself the ways in which you can help other members of your family meet their needs more easily. What can you do to help meet your mother's needs for affection, encouragement, and sense of growth? Is there anything that you can do to give your father a boost? What needs of your brothers or sisters can you help to meet? How about your grandparents? What do family situations tell you about the needs of the other members?

Do the people in your home occasionally have to fight for what they want? How can you begin to see more clearly what each of you is striving for?

8. Studies show that many teen-agers in our land of plenty do not eat wisely and well. Review Lewis et al, *Family Meals and Hospitality* (New York: The Macmillan Company, 1960), and write a paper on nutrition for American teen-agers.

Group Activity

1. Choose an episode, for dramatization in class, illustrating how a person feigned illness in the face of a difficult situation. Let students choose their roles and play through the episode. They may then exchange roles for the second performance. Now enact the situation again, showing how the various characters could give the chief character enough support and encouragement to permit some solution other than illness. Discuss the points that come out of your role-playing.

2. Discuss in class three defense mechanisms: (a) rationalization; (b) projection; (c) compensation. Give illustrations of each and role-play these in action.

3. Collect mental-hygiene materials from your local and state mental health societies and discuss them in class. Various individuals or groups might be responsible for different emphases made in the materials you are able to gather, with the idea of making a series of class reports.

4. Debate the proposition, "Resolved that great lives are built on failure." Support your argument on either side with illustrations from biographies in which men and women have become great through hardship and failure, or have been broken by defeat.

5. Play the recording, *Sing-Along for Mental Health* (available from your local mental-health society, or from the National Association for Mental Health, 10 Columbus Circle, New York 19, New York). Discuss each of the eight songs in terms of what mental-health principle it emphasizes and what it suggests as good mental-health practices.

6. Review in class Chapter 10, "The Language of Love," in Evelyn Millis Duvall, *Facts of Life and Love for Teen-Agers* (New York: Association Press, 1956), and discuss what it means to learn to love at various stages of human development.

7. Have a class discussion on why it takes good families to grow good people. List on the blackboard the specific contributions families make to personality development. Encourage smaller subgroups of the class to work out

what families contribute: (a) to little children; (b) to teen-agers; (c) to parents; (d) to grandparents; (e) to the children of the neighborhood; and (f) to the community as a whole. Compare the findings of the six committees and conclude with a general discussion of why families are central in society.

Readings

CRAWFORD, JOHN E., and WOODWARD, LUTHER E., *Better Ways of Growing Up* (Philadelphia: The Muhlenberg Press, 1948). Read especially Chapter 1, "About Ourselves," and take the self-quiz around which it is written. This will give you some idea of how well-grounded your beliefs are in actual facts, and how well you understand yourself as a person.

DUVALL, EVELYN MILLIS, *Facts of Life and Love for Teen-Agers* (New York: Association Press, 1956). Chapter 10, "The Language of Love," deals with how your ability to love and be loved develops as you grow, and the progress you make, in your relationships with other people, from dependence to independence and on into interdependence.

ENGLISH, O. SPURGEON, and FOSTER, CONSTANCE J., *Your Behavior Problems* (Chicago: Science Research Associates, 1952). This helpful booklet is written as a guide to understanding why you do what you do, the meaning of misbehavior, moods, and mistakes, with emphasis on how you can choose your behavior and become the kind of person you want to be.

HORNEY, KAREN, M.D., *Self-Analysis* (New York: W. W. Norton & Company, Inc., 1942). This book, written by an eminent psychiatrist, will be of interest to the mature student who wants to try to understand himself, analyze why he does what he does and what his behavior means, and find out what he wants to do about himself.

LANDIS, JUDSON and MARY G., *Personal Adjustment, Marriage, and Family Living* (Englewood Cliffs, N. J.: Prentice-Hall, Inc., 1955). Chapter 2, "What You Are," and Chapter 3, "How We Meet Our Problems," deal with your fundamental needs and the ways in which you try to meet them. A high-school text in wide use.

MENNINGER, WILLIAM C., *Understanding Yourself* (Chicago: Science Research Associates, 1949). This life-adjustment booklet has a particularly good description of the universal mechanisms: compensation, rationalization, idealization, reaction formation, displacement, projection, and conversion in its section on "Your Personality's Bag of Tricks."

SORENSON, HERBERT, and MALM, MARGUERITE, *Psychology for Living* (New York: McGraw-Hill Book Company, 1948). This well-written text for high schools serves well as a basic reference work and is especially relevant to the topics covered in this chapter.

The Flintkote Company

II

How You and Your Parents Feel About Each Other
Getting Through to Each Other
Being a Family Member

Living in Your Family

Chapter 5

How You and Your Parents Feel About Each Other

You and your parents have mixed feelings about each other. Sometimes things go well and there is affection and mutual respect between you. At other times you annoy and worry each other. Just because you care so much, you find that the things your parents say and do (and what they do not say and do) can easily upset you. This makes for difficulties from time to time. It also makes it important to have a mutual understanding of the feelings of each member of the family toward the others. This is especially so during the teen years, when you and your parents are learning new ways of adjusting to one another.

You and your parents may have been getting along quite smoothly throughout your childhood. But now that you are striving to become a full-fledged adult, the ways that once worked out well at home are probably no longer completely satisfactory. Your parents may feel that you need guidance now more than ever as you make the most important decisions of your life—those affecting occupation, education, friendships, love, marriage, and all that you are in the process of becoming.

As a teen-ager, you want freedom to make your own decisions. You may be willing to assume more real responsibility in the major decisions of your life than your parents feel you are ready for. You probably like having your opinions respected and want more than anything else to feel that your parents trust you and admire the kind of person you essentially are.

This is no idle speculation. One need not be a soothsayer to predict such feelings, attitudes, and relationships between teen-agers and their parents. The fact that you are working hard at the developmental task of emancipation from your parental home, as discussed in Chapter 2, accounts for the universality of such differences as those between your parents and you.

79

How Young People Feel About Their Parents

Most young people love their parents most of the time. They usually appreciate all their parents have done for them through the years. There are times when a teen-ager needs parents and likes to come to them for help, guidance, and encouragement. The average teen-ager enjoys doing things with his parents from time to time. He especially enjoys opportunities for co-operative activities around the house. He likes to take responsibility for some of the real work that has to be done.

At the same time, the teen-ager normally wants some privacy. He likes to feel that there are some things that are his alone. It is pleasant to know there are some things he does not have to share with his family. A diary that can be locked away from prying eyes is important for many a young person. A personal chest or bureau or a private drawer that can be one's own exclusive property is more important than ever during the teen years. It is then, too, that teen-agers appreciate the privilege of opening their own mail without having over-inquisitive family members probe into its source and contents. It is not that teen-agers have anything to hide, necessarily, but more often that a feeling of privacy is important to their sense of self, and to the independence of thought and feeling they need.

Young people in the midst of growing up need some time for themselves apart from the rest of the family—time to think, time to talk with friends, time to go out with others of their own age, time to get acquainted with both teen-agers and adults. They expect their parents to allow them such time on their own. Therefore, they are annoyed when their parents upset the plans they make with friends. They may feel misunderstood because their parents make dating and going out difficult. Yet much misunderstanding can be avoided when both young people and their parents know how the others feel and make real plans for a mutually satisfactory working arrangement.

Do Your Parents Understand You?

Frequent polls of high-school students in recent years make clear the way teen-agers feel about all sorts of things and people—including their parents. One of the most reliable of these, the Purdue Opinion Panel, regularly polls thousands of high-school students in a representative countrywide cross section of boys and girls in ninth, tenth, eleventh, and twelfth grades. This means the poll takes account of rural and urban differences, regional views, family income, education, and religion. Findings of these polls tell a great deal about how young people tend to think and feel about their parents.[1]

[1] Data for the following sections are drawn primarily from H. H. Remmers and D. H. Radler, *The American Teenager* (Indianapolis: The Bobbs-Merrill Company, Inc., 1957), a summary of Purdue Opinion Panel reports of recent years. Copyright ©, 1957. Used by special permission of the publishers, The Bobbs-Merrill Company, Inc.

   Two warnings before we go into the findings: (1) These findings are
what young people actually report, not what *ought* to be, or even necessarily
what *truly is*; (2) these findings are what young people think and feel *in
general* and cannot reflect how any one boy or girl would stand on individual
items. In most items, percentages for the various subgroups are different from
those for the total population studied. Individual differences might be expected to be even greater.

   One of the classic complaints young people have against their parents is
that they just "don't understand." Parents frequently are accused of being
old-fashioned, of not realizing that times have changed since they were young.
Teen-agers often feel that their parents are treating them like children, not
letting them grow up as fast as they would like, and not giving them the
respect and appreciation they feel entitled to as maturing personalities.

   Do Your Parents Understand Your Problems? You may be one of the
75 per cent of high-school students who feel that their parents generally tend
to understand the problems of modern youth. Or you may feel, as one out of
four teen-agers does, that parents hardly ever understand their problems. If
your parents never got beyond grade school, you are less likely to feel that
they understand your problems than if they had a high-school or college education, as you see in the chart below.

DOES EDUCATION HELP PARENTS "UNDERSTAND"? [2]

Parents' Education	Teenagers Saying Parents Usually Understand	Teenagers Saying Parents Hardly Ever Understand
Grade school	28%	29%
High school	37	23
College	43	16

   The trend is clear. More teen-agers whose parents have had high-school
and college education feel that their parents usually understand their problems than do those whose parents did not get beyond grade school. The com-
plaint of being misunderstood is nearly twice as frequent (29 per cent) among
students whose parents' education stopped at the grade-school level as among
those whose parents had a college education (16 per cent).

   The reasons for these differences may be in (1) the help education gives
parents for understanding their teen-age children; (2) the respect education

   [2] Percentage of High-School Students Saying Parents "Usually" or "Hardly Ever"
Understand Their Problems, by Level of Parents' Education. Adapted from a portion of a
table. *Ibid.*, p. 109. Copyright ©, 1957. Used by special permission of the publishers, The
Bobbs-Merrill Company, Inc.

wins for parents in the eyes of their teen-age sons and daughters; and (3) the kindred feeling equivalent education of parents and youth offers.

Do Your Parents Treat You Like a Child? Most teen-agers feel that their parents tend to treat them as if they were younger than they really are. When thousands of high-school students were polled, only one out of five (20 per cent) said their parents very seldom treated them as children, while more than half (53 per cent) said "sometimes," and fully a quarter (26 per cent) said "usually." A few did not answer (1 per cent), making a total of practically four out of five (79 per cent) who felt their parents treated them as younger than they actually were.

When these same students were asked to answer the questions the way they felt their mothers and fathers would, an entirely different picture emerged. More than half of the fathers (55 per cent) and the mothers (54 per cent) were thought by their own sons and daughters to be inclined to answer the query with "very seldom." Few of the parents (fathers—7 per cent, mothers—8 per cent) would say that they "usually" treated their teen-agers as younger than they are, according to the students, as is summarized below.

DO PARENTS TREAT TEENAGERS LIKE "BABIES"? [3]

		What Teenagers Think	
	Teenagers' Answer	Mothers Would Say	Fathers Would Say
Usually	26%	8%	7%
Sometimes	53	37	36
Very seldom	20	54	55
Did not answer	1	1	2
Total	100%	100%	100%

From the teen-agers' point of view, it is clear, they are treated like children by their parents far more often than their parents would acknowledge. These trends may be due to several reasons: (1) parents see their high-school-age sons and daughters still as their children, and continue to treat them as they always have; (2) teen-agers may at times act younger than they actually are, and yet resent their parents' treating them accordingly; (3) during the teen years young people grow up so fast that their parents' treatment of them

[3] High-School Students' Answers, and How They Think Their Parents Would Answer the Question, "Do Parents Ever Treat High-School Students As If They Were Much Younger Than They Are?" *Ibid.*, p. 110. Copyright ©, 1957. Used by special permission of the publishers, The Bobbs-Merrill Company, Inc.

cannot keep up with their increasing maturity; and (4) teen-agers are trying so hard to gain full status as mature persons that they are particularly sensitive about being treated as less grown-up than they are.

Should Your Parents Know Where You Are? "When high-school students are out for an evening, should their parents know just where they are?" is a question on which the Purdue Opinion Panel polled American teen-agers. Fifty-three per cent of the students say "often," and 16 per cent say "only sometimes." But 76 per cent of the students feel that their mothers would answer "always," indicating a possible difference of opinion in the matter in a great many homes (as many as 60 per cent is the estimate).

Considerably more teen-age girls (63 per cent) than teen-age boys (42 per cent) think that their parents should always know where their children are in the evening. This probably reflects the greater freedom boys have in these matters.

More students whose parents are still under forty (58 per cent) than those who have older parents (48 per cent) reply "always" to the question of whether parents should know just where they are. This suggests a greater acceptance of parental control among teen-agers whose parents are still relatively young themselves, and more reluctance to talk over their personal affairs with older parents.

Interestingly the age and grade of the students do not greatly affect the way they answer the question of whether parents should know where they are. In this poll 55 per cent of the freshmen and 52 per cent of the seniors say "always"; and exactly the same percentage of seniors as freshmen say "only sometimes" (16 per cent). It may be that as young people mature they realize the importance of the family's knowing where absent members are.

Should Your Parents Choose Your Clothes? There is a wide gap between the way teen-agers think and the way they feel their parents think about this question. Practically half of both high-school girls and boys (47 per cent) agree that parents should "hardly ever" choose their clothing. But only 15 per cent expect their mothers to answer "hardly ever" to the same question. More mothers (26 per cent) than fathers (12 per cent) are seen as wanting usually to choose their teen-agers' clothes. This is what one would expect.

Choosing one's own clothes is a mark of maturity and independence. A young person usually feels strongly about making his own clothing decisions. He wants to dress like his schoolmates rather than the way his parents may feel appropriate.

The mother, on the other hand, has grown accustomed to shopping for clothing for all members of the family and "naturally" continues, on the basis of habit and convenience, to buy things for her teen-agers to wear. She wants her children to look "nice" and to be a credit to her in public. If her standards of dress differ markedly from those of her son or daughter, tension may arise in the family.

Should Your Parents Protect You from Mistakes? The overwhelming majority of teen-agers and their parents agree that parents should try to protect young people from making the mistakes they themselves made when they were young. Many a young person, when he gets in a jam, asks his parents, "Why didn't you stop me?" Many a high-school-age girl, realizing that she should have learned certain important things, accusingly asks her parents, "Why didn't you make me?" Parents frequently preface their admonitions to teen-agers with the phrase, "I wish someone had made me see this when I was your age."

When thousands of high-school students were asked the question, 60 per cent of both boys and girls said their parents should "always" try to protect them from mistakes. The percentage of teen-agers who reply "always" is somewhat greater for freshmen (66 per cent) than for sophomores (61 per cent), juniors (56 per cent), and seniors (59 per cent).

More students whose parents have a grade-school education say "always" (68 per cent) to the question than children of high-school graduates (58 per cent) or those with college-educated parents (47 per cent). This may be due to the tendency of educated people to avoid extremes like "always" or "never." Or the difference may be accounted for by their realizing that young people must learn to live their own lives through mistakes as well as successes.

Are Your Parents Strict Enough? About two-thirds of high-school boys (66 per cent) and over two-thirds of the girls (70 per cent) feel that their parents are handling them "about right." This is a higher rating than these

ARE PARENTS STRICT ENOUGH? [4]			
		What Teenagers Think	
	Teenagers' Answers	*Mothers Would Say*	*Fathers Would Say*
Too strict	18%	2%	3%
About right	68	58	51
Too easy	13	39	44
Did not answer	1	1	2
Total	100%	100%	100%

[4] Teenagers' Answers and How They Think Their Parents Would Answer the Question, "Are Parents Strict Enough in the Way They Handle Their Children of High-School Age?" *Ibid.*, p. 116. Copyright ©, 1957. Used by special permission of the publishers, The Bobbs-Merrill Company, Inc.

teen-agers expect their parents would give themselves. When asked how they thought their parents would answer the question, "Are parents strict enough in the way they handle their children of high-school age?" they replied "about right" for only 58 per cent of the mothers and 51 per cent of the fathers.

There is a fair minority of 18 per cent of the teen-agers who say that their parents are too strict, and another 13 per cent who feel that their parents are too easy with them. These same teen-agers judge that their parents would say they are "too easy" far more often than "too strict" in handling their teen-age sons and daughters, as you see on page 84.

The general picture is clear. Fewer than one in five teen-agers say their parents are too strict, at the same time realizing that their parents do not agree that their management is too strict. Considerably more parents than students are believed to feel that they are too easy with their teen-agers. The great majority of young people agree that their parents are handling them just about right—in fact, most of them feel surer of it than they think their parents are.

Teen-Agers Need Parents

Most teen-agers recognize that they need parents. They agree that they have to have some control and supervision. Most important of all, young people know they need help in growing up and attaining their own maturity.

Families Meet Basic Needs for Growth. People of all ages expect that their needs will be met in the family. That is what families are for in America. Young people are usually dependent upon their parents for fulfillment of their fundamental needs for growth. Food, clothing, shelter, medical attention, all these physical benefits listed in Chapter 4 must come from, or through, the family in our society. Sometimes other agencies supplement what the family can do financially, medically, or otherwise, but even such services are usually obtained through the intercession of the family.

It is the family which first meets personality needs for love, attention, encouragement, security, and a chance to achieve, and which continues longest to meet these needs. Young people expect their basic personality needs to be met within the home. Even when parents fail their children, as parents do upon occasion, the tendency is still to look to one's family for the things one needs most. One man has put it this way: "Youth needs food and love and a place to grow." Parents are expected to supply all three.

You Need Help with Your Developmental Tasks. Like all young people, you are at work on a series of exacting developmental tasks necessary for growing up, as you saw in Chapter 2. These responsibilities for growth take place over a period of years when teen-agers are not entirely ready for complete independence. You presumably still need your parents' help and en-

PARENTS HELP ADOLESCENTS WITH THEIR DEVELOPMENTAL TASKS

Developmental Tasks

Help from Parents

1. Adjustment to a changing body

1. Good example of manhood and womanhood
   Adequate sex education
   Pride and encouragement in growth
   Appropriate clothes

2. New orientation to age-mates

2. Friends welcome at home
   Time for leisure and "fun"
   Encouragement of dating
   Reasonable privileges
   Guidance and understanding

3. Establishing independence from family

3. Easy cutting of apron strings
   Freedom with responsibility
   Guidance instead of "orders"
   Affection without "clinging"

4. Achieving adult status

4. Work opportunities
   Money of one's own
   Suitable education
   Encouragement of social interests

5. Development of the sense of self

5. Good examples to follow
   Religious background
   Introduction to books and ideas
   Encouragement of friendships

couragement in maturing. You probably look to them for guidance through the hazards and difficulties of becoming an adult in today's world.

This is a good time to think through the several kinds of help young people need from their parents in accomplishing the five major developmental tasks of the teen years. Copy the table on page 86 in your notebook adding in the blank spaces two more ways in which parents can help teen-agers accomplish their developmental tasks. Do not write in your book.

How Parents Feel About Their Teen-Agers

It may be a shock to discover that all parents do not love their children all the time. The more we know about family relations, the more we are impressed with the *mixed feelings* normal between people very close to each other. This is particularly true of the way parents feel about their teen-age children. They have many feelings about them. Within the same week, the same day, the same hour, a parent may feel several different ways about the same child.

Pride and Admiration. Most parents are very proud of their growing children. They swell with pride at all the new abilities and accomplishments teen-agers achieve almost every day. They are proud of the increasing size and stature of these children of theirs. The father beams and tells the neighbors that his son is "taller than I am now!" A mother passes the cookies and

Many teen-agers enjoy doing the family's food shopping. In what ways is this activity useful to young people trying to achieve adult status?

Anna Jo Pearce, Alcee Fortier Sr. High School, New Orleans, La.

proudly tells her friends that her daughter baked them. A prize, a good grade, an honor at school, a mention in the paper, will be a subject of family conversation for some time because parents are so pleased with their teen-agers.

Annoyance and Irritation. Have you ever noticed that parents sometimes become annoyed with the behavior of their teen-agers? It is quite common. When young people do not take responsibility for things around the house, most parents feel some annoyance. Pajamas in a heap on the bedroom floor six mornings out of seven make even the most patient mother wish that her young hopeful would take some responsibility for his clothes. A dent in the fender of the car, a chip off the garage door, tools left in the yard, a ring around the bathtub, are frequent annoyances.

The thoughtlessness of youth is another source of parental annoyance. Ann had invited five of her friends over to dinner one night. She had talked it over with her mother ahead of time and had agreed on an evening which, though not particularly convenient for her mother, fitted in best with her friends' plans. Ann offered to come straight home from school and help out with the preparations, so that her mother would not have to cancel her plans for the afternoon. But that day, Ann came home an hour late from school, and then disappeared into her room. Her mother called to her to come down and help. Ann replied that she was sorry, but she was fixing her fingernails and could not help with the dinner. Her mother was very much annoyed. Would you have been?

As young people begin to take more and more responsibility for entertaining, they have to learn *timing*, planning, and working things out with others. While this learning is still going on, it is often their parents who must bear the strain. Like most people forced to do someone else's share of a job in addition to their own, they feel annoyed at the irresponsibility of the other.

An important factor in the annoyance of parents with teen-agers is that often the situation is one in which the boy or girl used to function adequately. Little children sometimes enjoy wiping dishes, helping get the dinner, hanging up pajamas, and putting away their tools and toys. When, instead of doing even better in adolescence, they grow more careless and negligent, parents naturally feel discouraged.

Loss of Authority and Control. When children are young, parents have a great deal of authority. Their word is law. Their suggestions are heeded. Their guidance is taken seriously. A little child is dependent upon his parents' protection and care. But when those same children reach adolescence, parents are no longer so influential.

Parents sometimes feel this lack of control quite strongly. They complain that their teen-agers do not listen to them, do not always take their suggestions, sometimes scoff at them as old-fashioned and out-of-date. As children grow up, parents find they are no longer respected as much as they used to be. Their ideas are more often challenged by teen-agers, who have heard other points of view and have begun to develop ideas of their own.

One father, quite a successful doctor, recently observed, "The hardest pill I have to swallow is having to take second place in my own home." His teen-age son and daughter often contradict him and make him feel that he is no longer the head of the household.

In some families children are encouraged to challenge their parents from childhood on. Parents sometimes enjoy learning with their children and do not have to feel important or right just because they are parents. But even in these homes, parents often feel that they wish they had more influence in the important choices their teen-agers are making.

It is during the teen years that the most important decisions of life are made. What a young person is going to do with his life is decided in his teens. What school he will go to, what he will study, what vocation he will plan for—all these are important decisions that parents like to be a part of, if they can.

The friends you make during the teen years are important for your reputation, your good times now and later, your chances of making a good marriage, and of getting in with the "right set" later on. Parents realize, often more clearly than young people, how important these are. They often try to control their children's choice of friends and face the rebellion that frequently follows. Parents say it is hard to stand by and watch their children choosing friends unwisely, getting in with the wrong crowd, and getting mixed up in dangerous activities. So it is usual for parents to feel both anxiety and concern at their lack of influence just at the time when they feel their children most need help.

Reciprocal Affection. Most parents have loved their children for a long while. They have cared for them since they were babies. They have nursed them through childhood diseases, accidents, failures, and disappointments. They have learned through the years to care very deeply for them.

When children are small, they can love their parents quite openly and freely. A boy can run into the house and give his mother a spontaneous squeeze of affection and appreciation. A girl can curl up on her father's lap and let him know how much she loves him. But when those same children become teen-age, it is much more difficult to express affection for parents quite so freely. Boys often feel embarrassed about letting their mothers or their fathers know how fond they are of them. Girls get too big to be fondled by their folks, and too reticent to express their own feelings openly. Young people often find it much easier to confide in a girl friend or a boy friend than to tell their parents about the things that really matter.

The cooperation shown by this boy and girl, who responded promptly to their mother's call for help, not only pleases her, but also shows active paticipation in family life.

Gratitude thins out as young people grow up, too. When children are small, they can be obviously pleased and grateful for gifts and thoughtfulness of their parents. But these privileges tend to become rights through the years, and in adolescence it seems to become particularly difficult to express appreciation and gratitude to one's parents. One of the reasons for this is that young people do not want to be so obligated to their parents; the more parents do for teen-agers, the harder it is for the youth to emancipate themselves.

Be that as it may, most parents feel unsure of the affection of their teen-age children at the very time when as parents they need it most. When their children reach adolescence, most parents are approaching their own middle years. Being middle-aged is not easy for many people. It means admitting that they are getting older. It means getting a new hold on life, now that the children are no longer the center of their lives. They realize that the rest of their years must be lived on some new basis. It means a change in their stamina and energy, in their feelings, their activities, and the things that mean most to them. It is during these middle years that most parents need the reassurance and encouragement and friendship of their own growing children.

Isabel's mother was unduly strict. She forbade Isabel's going out with any of the boys. She expected her to be home before dark in the evening. She discouraged her from having friends in to see her. Isabel became so upset about her mother's severe regime for her that she consulted her counselor at school. As the counselor talked with her, it came out that Isabel's mother had no other interest in life but Isabel. Through the years when Isabel was growing up, her mother had gradually let go of all of her other interests so that she could devote herself to her child. Now she had nothing else. The counselor pointed this out and encouraged Isabel to try to get her mother out into community affairs again, so she would have something else besides Isabel to give her time to. It took some months, but now her mother is active in church work again. She has joined the YWCA and has helped organize a study club. Already she is beginning to loosen her hold upon Isabel.

This case illustrates the two-way pull of apron strings. Both parents and children must grow up if the children are to mature successfully. Parents can do a great deal to help their teen-agers develop, and young people can help their parents grow, too, by encouraging them to broaden their activities and giving them the assurance and the interest that most parents need from their growing youngsters.

What Do Your Parents Expect of You?

You probably know pretty well what your parents expect of you. They remind you often enough! You have sensed as you grew up what pleased them, what worried them, and what they expected of you, both in general and in specific areas of life.

Some of the things parents expect of their children primarily serve the purpose of peace and pleasantness within the family. When parents want their children to control their tempers, avoid fighting with their brothers and sisters, and assume more responsibility around the house, they are suggesting that young people, too, can share in making the home a pleasant place. The more parents respect their children's ability to co-operate in family living, the more they may expect in some of these areas.

Parents quite generally want their children to be a credit to the family. They prefer to see their children make friends with nice people, go to the better places, and take advantage of opportunities for their growth and development. Parents invest a great deal of time and money in raising their children to the teen years. The Metropolitan Life Insurance Company computed the cost of rearing a child, and found that by the time the child was eighteen, the average parent had already invested more than ten thousand dollars in him. The years of service as a parent, the time required to bring up a child, are even greater contributions. Most parents do not expect to be repaid in any material sense. They had their children because they wanted them. They have given them all the advantages they could afford because they loved them and wanted them to have a good start in life. But most of them expect that by the mid-teens or so their children will begin to show the effects of the parents' devoted efforts. Perhaps certain expectations are not unreasonable.

When the University of Michigan Survey Research Center polled 1,925 girls on the question, "What are the most important things your parents expect of you?" the girls listed eight major areas in the following percentages:

1. Have nice manners and appear well (be a lady, be polite, dress nicely, neatly)   48%
2. Respect others and get along nicely with people (be nice, popular, unselfish)   35
3. Have respect for authority (obey parents, behave, avoid being fresh with elders)   29
4. Be truthful, honest, act decently with boys, not go to bad places, not go with bad kids, not drink, smoke, curse, etc.   26
5. Accept parents' regulations (not stay out late, obey rules, keep parents informed)   15
6. Be independent (stand on own feet, act my age, have high standards, etc.)   13
7. Co-operate with other members of the family (help around the house, etc.)   6
8. Do well in school, finish my education, achieve, etc.   5

This survey finds that the standards parents set are related to the girl's age. With younger girls parents tend to emphasize manners, respect for authority, and getting along with other people; with older teen-agers they stress self-direction and morality. As girls begin going out more and get away from their parents' continuous supervision, they are expected to be increasingly guided by their own consciences and by the moral standards of society.[5]

Parents' Expectations Depend on Who They Are. Parents differ widely. There are millions of parents in America, all as different from one another as people can be. Some are poor; others are well off. Some are farmers; others live in cities and small towns. Some parents have had the privilege of an education; others have had little formal schooling. Some parents have come from old established families; others have had to carve out their own place as newcomers to America. Some parents belong to one race, some to another. Religious beliefs vary even more widely.

Recent studies have shown us the folly of speaking of mothers and fathers as though they were all alike. We know now that every parent reflects in his attitude the influence of the group to which he belongs, the locality in which he grew up, the neighborhood he lives in, his economic and social status, and a host of other cultural determinants.

What parents expect of their children is determined by their economic and social status. The middle-class mother and father expect quite different things from those expected by working-class parents. One study indicates that parents who are more economically and socially secure are apt to be more concerned with the way their children develop intellectually than with whether they keep clean and are obedient. Less secure parents expect much more of their children in terms of what the neighbors will say.

There is some evidence to indicate that older parents are sometimes more rigid than younger ones both in what they expect of their children and in how they train them. Younger parents perhaps have more of the newer ideas about child-rearing; they are less disposed to make children obey, insist upon respect, prove who is boss, or break the child's will than parents who grew up in a generation of stricter discipline. This is not just a matter of age, but depends also on how well informed and up-to-date parents keep. Young people are often a great help to parents who want to be modern.

Calling parents old-fashioned when they disagree with teen-age standards, however, is not particularly helpful. It is much more fruitful to work out together the mutual expectations with which both parents and children can feel comfortable.

Parents Are People. Almost anyone would be annoyed if his belongings were tampered with too frequently. Young people know how they feel when someone gets into their things. Parents are no exception. They, too, feel annoyed when others in the family do not respect their personal property. Mother might be quite willing to lend her nylons; Dad might be agreeable about sharing his new tie. But most parents, like people everywhere, like to be asked. They do not like to have their belongings or their generosity taken for granted.

People generally become upset when their activities are hindered too often or for too long a time. Parents are no exceptions. They may try to understand and accept some interference in long-established habits, but irritation beyond a certain point will try even the most patient person. When a father is locked out of the bathroom for more than an hour just when he must wash and dress, he is apt to feel frustrated and get angry. When a mother cannot place an important telephone call, she becomes annoyed at the teenager who is monopolizing the telephone.

Most people like to feel proud of their relatives. When you are related to someone, you feel that his reputation and his behavior are somehow closely tied in with yours. This is especially true if the relationship is close. Parents feel proud of their children's achievements and feel bad when their children do not live up to their standards. This is one reason parents care so much about how their children behave.

People of every age need to be loved and accepted. Even middle-aged people cannot be happy without affection. Parents are often hurt when their growing children cut the apron strings too roughly. When young people,

"As good as can be expected, I guess, under the laws of heredity."

intent only upon emancipating themselves, shrug off their parents' suggestions and avoid expressions of affection, they forget that parents are people, who need to be understood, accepted, loved, and appreciated as much as does the teen-ager himself. Intellectually parents may understand why their young people do not love them in the same way they used to, but emotionally it may hurt just the same.

Reciprocal Needs of Parents and Youth

Parents, like teen-agers, are growing people, though at a later stage of development. In a quite remarkable way the needs of parents and teen-agers are both parallel and reciprocal. Each needs substantially the same affirmation of life and growth from the other generation within the family, as shown by the following listing:

What Youth Needs from Parents	*What Parents Need from Youth*
1. Encouragement to do and be	1. Encouragement to do and be
2. Appreciation of efforts made	2. Appreciation of efforts made
3. Respect for their belongings	3. Respect for their belongings and
4. Privacy	property
5. Guidance and interpretation	4. Privacy
6. Shared responsibilities	5. Teen-age points of view
7. Support and a sound home base	6. Participation in common interests
8. Affection, trust, and love	7. Shared responsibility for the home
9. Freedom to grow and live their own lives	8. Affection, trust, and love
	9. Chance to plan for the years ahead
10. Respect for themselves as individuals	10. Respect for themselves as individuals

Is it not remarkable how similar these two lists of needs are? Would you have thought that what parents need from youth so closely parallels what youth want from their parents? Had you ever given any real thought before to the possibility of parents' having needs that youth might help to satisfy? Is it a new idea that parents, too, are growing, and that they must broaden their ideas of parenthood, if their children are to be given the chance they need for maturity?

Seeing Both Sides of the Parent-Youth Question. Until their sons and daughters are entirely independent, parents are responsible for their maintenance, their education, and their mistakes. Because of this responsibility, parents have to exercise some control during the teen years. Because they are genuinely interested in their growing young people, they want to know how things are going for them. Parents who do not try to keep in touch with their teen-agers' thoughts and feelings are irresponsible parents. The more interested parents are in their children, the more concern they may be expected to show about their behavior.

During the teen years both parents and young people need to be patient with each other. Parents are not perfect. It is hard for them to realize that their children are growing up so fast. It is easy for them to get "worked up" in their anxiety about a young person's welfare, especially when he has done something foolish, or has not come up to expectations. As parents increasingly realize that teen-agers are learning from their mistakes as well as their successes, patience comes more easily. As young people understand that parents, too, have needs in many ways similar to their own, they may find their interaction more meaningful.

Parents and teen-agers need each other. Members of both generations are growing up in situations that are new and sometimes frightening. The ways are not always clear ahead. There are pitfalls and growing edges in reaching the next stage of one's development that a parent as well as a teen-ager experiences. When both parents and young people meet each other's needs, growth is assured, and their relationship flourishes.

This improved relationship between generations can develop not only in an individual family, but within a school community where parents and teen-agers make an effort to understand each other's point of view and basic rights as human beings. Now, when men and women around the council tables of the world are carving out their declarations of rights, it is fitting that parents and teen-agers are doing so, too.

A Declaration of Rights [6]

In the spring of 1955, 165 senior boys and girls at Hillsborough High School, Tampa, Florida, met with their parents once a week for six weeks. The meetings were conducted by Mr. Dale L. Womble, a family-life teacher in that school. All the students were members of the family-living classes. The objective was to create a better understanding between parents and adolescents. Out of these meetings came the two "declarations of rights" which follow.

A TEEN-AGE DECLARATION OF RIGHTS

(What We Have a Right to Expect from Our Parents)

1. A degree of privacy
2. Honesty
3. Frankness
4. A genuine keen interest in our activities
5. An acceptance of our friends or telling us why not
6. Free choice of religion
7. Keeping family affairs in the family
8. Teaching of responsibility
9. A happy marriage and family relationship
10. A decent example
11. Trust
12. Love and affection beyond doubt (non-partiality)
13. Proper sex education (knowledge and attitudes)
14. Essentials of life (food, clothing, shelter, etc.)
15. Gradual cutting of apron strings
16. Sympathetic understanding of the teen-ager's point of view
17. Democratic practices and procedures (a share in personal and family decisions)
18. Respect for individuality
19. Encouragement for education
20. Family activities
21. A pleasing attitude—(attention to our troubles, keeping communication channels open)
22. Ambition with and for us in achieving goals
23. Training and practice in manners

[6] Dale L. Womble, "A Declaration of Rights," *Marriage and Family Living*, Vol. 17 (November, 1955), p. 358.

24. A feeling of being an asset, not a liability
25. The right to choose own occupation
26. Prompt attention to illness
27. Religious and ethical training and practice
28. A feeling of security
29. Wise counsel and guidance
30. Brothers and/or sisters

A PARENTS' DECLARATION OF RIGHTS

(What We Have a Right to Expect from Our Teen-Agers)

1. Temperance
2. Frugality
3. Honesty
4. Frankness
5. Trust
6. Chastity
7. Humility
8. Industry
9. Sincerity
10. A measure of privacy
11. Keeping family affairs in the family
12. An effort to understand the parents' point of view
13. An understanding of democratic principles and procedures (that there are degrees of freedom, and every government has a provision for a veto)
14. Doing the best possible with the educational opportunity presented
15. Contributing to family activities
16. A pleasing attitude
17. Sharing in family goals
18. Practice of good manners taught
19. Being an asset, not a liability (a fair share of home responsibilities)
20. To understand and continue to practice good religious and ethical training
21. Demonstrations of love and affection (show it)
22. Honor
23. Obedience
24. Appreciation when you have done your best
25. Patience to hear you out before going off on a tangent
26. Respect at least equal to that given those outside the home

Parents who could meet all of youth's hopes and expectations all of the time would be perfect indeed. Most parents try to do what is expected. They want to be good parents. But parents are human beings. They are not perfect. They reflect the homes from which they have come and the neighborhoods of which they are a part. They respond to their children not in a vacuum, but in real-life situations. Parents are influenced by the ways in which their children meet their expectations.

Few teen-agers satisfy all their parents' expectations all of the time. The rebellious youngster who must defy his parents at all costs to prove that he is no longer a child may unnecessarily hurt them and himself until he matures to the place where he recognizes that parents and teen-agers can be interdependent. As young people mature, they are increasingly able to enjoy their parents as people and to measure up to their expectations without violating their own sense of individuality and worth.

You and your parents cannot be expected to see eye to eye on every issue. You inevitably feel different about all sorts of things. You have to be yourself, now that you are growing up and can no longer be satisfied to do everything just the way your parents would. This means that there will be tension and conflict between you and your parents from time to time. If you are ever to become mature, you must pull far enough away from your dependence upon your parents to establish your own identity as a person. At times this will hurt both you and your parents. How painful your differences are depends a great deal on how you learn to live with them, as you will see in Chapter 6.

Summary

The relationship between your parents and yourself is not what it was when you were a child. Now that you are a teen-ager, you and your parents necessarily feel different about each other and the situations in which you find yourself. Teen-agers love and appreciate their parents, but they need some privacy and freedom to grow up without too close dependence upon them. In general, according to polls of thousands of American teen-agers, most high-school students feel that their parents understand their problems, at least sometimes. However, the vast majority of high-school students feel that their parents treat them as younger than they actually are. Parents and teen-agers often disagree about whether parents should know where their sons and daughters are when they go out in the evening and whether parents should choose clothing for teen-agers. Most teen-agers and their parents agree that parents should protect their young people from the mistakes they made when they were young, and that on the whole, parents are handling their teen-agers "about right" rather than being too strict or too easy. Adolescents need parents to meet their growth requirements, as well as for specific help in the tasks of growing up. Parents normally are both proud of and annoyed with their teen-age children. They sense the change in their relationship with them and need more reciprocal affection and co-operation as young people mature. Parents expect their teen-agers to be a credit to them and to conform to the standards of the community. In a real sense parents and teen-agers need each other in remarkably similar ways. Both parents and teen-agers have rights that can be mutually understood and recognized as a basis for harmony between the generations.

Suggested Activities

Individual Study

1. List in your notebook all the ways you can think of in which you and your parents behave differently toward each other now than when you entered first grade. Then write a comment on why you feel your relationship has changed as it has in the past ten years or so. How do you anticipate it may shift in the next ten years?

2. Read and prepare a book review of Ruth Strang, *The Adolescent Views Himself* (New York: McGraw-Hill Book Company, 1958). Conclude your review with your own frank reaction to the questions discussed in the book.

3. Arrange a confidential talk with one of your grandparents in which you can explore some of the problems, and the resources for solving them, that one of your parents faced at your age.

4. If it seems like the sort of thing you can do comfortably, talk over with your parents some of the ways in which life today is different, and has to be different, than it used to be for them when they were your age.

5. Prepare a graphic poster showing some of the youth-poll data in the early part of this chapter, for use as illustrative material in presenting these findings to your class.

6. Prepare a detailed outline of Ernest G. Osborne, *Understanding Your Parents* (New York: Association Press, 1956). Make marginal notes on the outline of your personal reaction to some of the points made. Hand in your outline for your teacher's annotation, and then keep it in your class notebook.

Group Activity

1. Conduct a class poll on the various questions taken up in the youth polls reported in this chapter. This should be carefully prepared as an anonymous questionnaire in which each member of the class is free to check frankly his or her own reactions and opinions without being swayed by the findings of the nationwide polls or by the attitudes of other members of the class. After a committee has tabulated the results of your class poll, they can be summarized on the blackboard as a basis for class discussion. Consider especially how your class differs from, and agrees with, the general findings of the country-wide group of teen-agers, and why you think your poll came out the way it did.

2. Plan a simple get-together in the form of a potluck meal, a tea, or a picnic for members of your class and their parents. After the food has been cleared away, schedule a panel of representative parents and class members to discuss "What Parents and Young People Expect of Each Other."

Choose a panel leader who will encourage each person to speak his or her mind fully and freely and who can keep the discussion rolling comfortably toward the eventual participation of everyone involved. Plan well ahead of time just how this will be done and schedule a class evaluation of the parent-student session at the next meeting of the class.

3. Have a class discussion on "The Kind of Parents We Want to Be Some Day," listing on the blackboard all the things you want to do for your children when they are your age, how you hope to rear them, what hazards you hope to avoid with them when they are teen-agers, as well as the privileges and responsibilities you will want them to assume.

4. Select a committee from your class to prepare your version of "Declaration of Rights for Today's Teen-Agers," following the general pattern used in the one in this chapter, but specifically reflecting what the members of your class feel should be included. Polish the statement in a session of the entire class. Consider submitting it for publication in your local or school paper.

5. Put on the skit, *High-Pressure Area* (available from Mental Health Materials Center, Inc., 1790 Broadway, New York City 19, New York), as a basis for class discussion of parent–teen-ager relations.

Readings

Duvall, Evelyn Millis, and Hill, Reuben, *When You Marry* (Boston: D. C. Heath and Company, 1961). Chapter 14, entitled "What It Means to Be Parents," helps you see how parents' roles change as their children grow up. You will be particularly interested in the section on the interaction between parents and young people.

Jenkins, Gladys Gardner, and Neuman, Joy, *How to Live with Parents* (Chicago: Science Research Associates, 1948). This guidance pamphlet has an especially good section on "Severing Apron Strings" in which becoming independent, meeting conflicting needs, and seeing the other side of issues between adolescents and parents are discussed.

Osborne, Ernest G., *Understanding Your Parents* (New York: Association Press, 1956). A teen-agers' pocket guide written to help young people understand themselves, their parents, and why relationships between the two generations are often strained and difficult. Money, friends, controls, and the little things that irritate are among the topics discussed.

Remmers, H. H., and Radler, D. H., *The American Teenager* (Indianapolis: The Bobbs-Merrill Company, Inc., 1957). The Purdue Opinion Polls regularly find out what representative high-school students feel about all sorts of things— themselves, their plans, and their parents. This book contains the results of such polls in recent years, along with interpretations of what they mean.

Whiteside-Taylor, Katharine, *Getting Along with Parents* (Chicago: Science Research Associates, 1952). The author starts with the recognition that everyone has parent problems, and that these universal conflicts between growing youth and their parents can be understood and worked out—a pamphlet of interest to both generations and to persons of all ages.

Chapter 6

Getting Through to Each Other

Parents say that they want to "get through" to their young people, especially as they go through the teen years. Ninety per cent of the nation's teenagers think that families should discuss things as a group, according to Dr. H. H. Remmers, originator of the Purdue Opinion Panel, whose estimate is based upon recent polls of thousands of high-school students across the country.

Granted that communication between parents and teen-agers is desirable and desired, it still is not always easy. Members of both generations frequently lament that they find it hard to talk things over as children become teen-agers.

With the teen years comes a reluctance to discuss together many things of interest to both parents and young people. Any individual member of either generation can testify to this in general. A recent study of this problem among entering college freshmen indicates specifically just what is most difficult to discuss with parents, and why.

What Teen-Agers Can't Discuss with Their Parents

Dr. Marvin C. Dubbé finds that 99 per cent of the first-year college students he has studied report that they have some difficulty talking over one or more areas of interest with their parents. As would be expected, some topics are easier for teen-agers to discuss than others. Such areas as jobs and summer work, care of property, entertaining friends, and car expenses are mentioned as difficult to discuss with parents by less than 25 per cent of the students. The topics that these older teen-agers find hardest to talk over with their parents are given on page 102 in the order of difficulty.

TALKING WITH PARENTS [1]

Subjects Students Find Difficult to Discuss	With Father	With Mother	With Parents
1. Sex	85%	74%	79%
2. Petting	80	75	77
3. Courtship	60	52	56
4. Late hours	53	55	54
5. Health habits	59	47	53
6. Misbehavior	52	54	53
7. Marriage	56	46	51
8. Engagement	53	45	49

Why It's Hard to Talk with Parents. Why should older teen-agers find it hard to discuss such subjects as sex and petting, misbehavior, and marriage with their parents? Certainly these are topics in which mothers and fathers are interested. Is it perhaps because parents are *too* interested in these areas of life, so that when they get through to their young people with understanding, they press and pry too much? Could it be that members of both generations get too emotional about topics of such intimate and personal importance? What reasons do young people actually give for finding it hard to get through to their parents with comfortable discussion?

In the study described above, young people gave some twenty-two reasons for difficulty in getting through to their parents. One in every five simply said, "I don't know." A very few said it was because they didn't know what words to use. Some said the reason was that they felt superior to their parents, but about the same number blamed the fact that they felt inferior. About one in five said their problem was fear of ridicule, and about the same number feared that they would be condemned.

One in four said the age difference between themselves and their parents blocked their ability to get through to each other. Parents' conservatism and old-fashioned ideas were the reasons given by a full 40 per cent of both boys and girls. Many of the students reported that they had no time to talk with their parents. More than half the girls (52 per cent) said they did not have enough opportunities to talk things over with their fathers.

One of the most prevalent reasons for breakdown in communication between the generations is fear. Forty-five per cent of these older teen-agers said

[1] Rank Order of Subjects Most Difficult to Discuss with Fathers and Mothers by Percentages of College Freshmen Reporting Difficulty in Each. Marvin C. Dubbé, "What Young People Can't Talk Over with Their Parents," *National Parent-Teacher*, October, 1957, pp. 18–20, and personal documents from Dr. Dubbé.

they were afraid to talk with their fathers, and 42 per cent with their mothers, because of the scolding and punishment that might result. More than a third of the students said that their own guilt feelings kept them from talking over some things with their parents. A similar number reported that the signs of embarrassment on their parents' faces when certain subjects were brought up kept them from discussing them freely.

The reasons that topped all others in the eyes of these eighteen- and nineteen-year-old college students were "no need" and "self-reliance." Half of all the freshmen questioned had such a strong need to assert independence

WHY COLLEGE FRESHMEN CAN'T TALK WITH PARENTS [2]

Reasons (in Alphabetical Order)	Percentage of Girls Reporting Difficulty with		Percentage of Boys Reporting Difficulty with		Percentage of Both Sexes Reporting Difficulty with	
	Father	Mother	Father	Mother	Father	Mother
Age difference	24%	24%	30%	26%	27%	25%
Condemned	26	22	18	14	22	18
Confidence violated	12	28	14	30	13	29
Conservatism	44	38	40	36	42	37
Delay	18	16	18	14	18	15
Don't know	26	18	22	22	24	20
Evasion	30	26	26	20	28	23
Fear of power	24	22	24	18	24	20
Fear of punishment	46	42	44	42	45	42
Guilt feelings	38	34	30	32	34	33
Inferiority	4	4	26	16	15	10
Nagging	18	32	38	36	28	34
No need	58	48	54	54	56	51
Position	12	10	14	26	13	18
Pride	38	32	36	26	37	29
Rejected	8	8	0	2	4	5
Ridicule	16	14	30	22	23	18
Self-reliance	40	50	50	42	45	46
Signs of embarrassment	34	34	32	36	33	35
Superiority	16	16	16	16	16	16
Time	52	38	34	28	43	33
Vocabulary	12	2	6	4	9	3

[2] Percentage of Freshmen College Students Giving One or More of Twenty-Two Reasons for Finding Discussion with Parents Difficult. Adapted from tables in Marvin C. Dubbé's personal document reporting doctoral study, Oregon State College, 1956.

that they were reluctant to talk over with their parents topics that they might once have discussed, or might discuss again a little later in their lives. The detailed data are tabulated on page 103 for you to use as a personal check test (see Individual Study, No. 2, page 117).

Parents and young people cannot be expected to see things eye to eye. They have grown up in different generations. Most young people today have grown up in cities, have become accustomed to television, the movies, automobiles, staying out late, and visiting away from home. People of all ages stay up late at night, travel farther away from home, have more money to spend, and are more widely acquainted with people who are not like their own kind than was true a generation or two ago. So there are many areas in which teen-agers and their parents look at life differently.

When Parents and Teen-Agers Disagree

Parents and teen-agers in a given family can disagree about almost anythings. In general, surveys among teen-agers indicate that youth's most frequent disagreements with parents are over: (1) the hours question; (2) use of the family car; (3) money; (4) choosing friends; (5) studying; and (6) dating.

Each of these and many other current parent-youth problems can be seen as reflecting the different points of view characteristic of the two generations. Each problem area can be analyzed for what it means to both teen-agers and their parents. The hours question is here elaborated as an illustration of the kind of interpretation and recommendation that would be relevant for many other conflicts common between the generations.

The Question of Hours. Parents and youth disagree about hours not only because they grew up in different generations (though that, of course, does often play a part in the way they feel about the question), but because parents are concerned about their children getting enough sleep, giving the time they should to their studies, and quite often about what the neighbors will say if their young people come in at all hours.

Teen-agers often want to stay out longer than their parents feel is wise. They hate to break up a party to go home when parents may expect them. They do not want to seem like kill-joys. If they are having a good time, they want to continue. If they have not had a good time, they often want to go some place where they can have fun before they go home. Besides, staying out late makes some young people feel more important than coming home at a more usual hour. Nowadays a date takes longer than it used to. It takes longer to get to the party or the function. Most activities start later than they used to, and they continue longer. It takes a while to get served at even the most modest restaurant, and getting home takes up more time.

The time question can best be decided by both parents and youth together, since both are concerned. Either one can take the lead in opening the

Sybil Shelton from Monkmeyer

Misunderstandings and hard feelings can be avoided if a girl, her date, and her mother discuss hours frankly and easily with one another.

matter for discussion. There are some advantages in the young person's taking the initial responsibility. For instance, Mary is going out to the prom Saturday night. While her mother is helping her fix her dress, she may talk over with her mother the time the dance is to begin, the time it is scheduled to be over, the plans they have for something to eat afterwards, and the time she is likely to get home. In this way her mother has a chance to see what is involved and to express any opinion or feeling she has about it. Then, at the time when the couple is starting out, if Mary turns to her mother, in front of her date, and reassures her mother as to where she is going and when she will be home, all the people involved know what to expect. Mary's date knows when he is expected to have her back. Mary's folks know what time to expect her. She has taken the responsibility and seems to be reliable about it all. If something happens so that Mary cannot get home at the time she has predicted, a telephone call will let her parents know why she is late and what time she will be getting home. This puts the responsibility in the young persons' hands, and at the same time lets the parents in on the plans.

Boys, girls, and parents alike agree that dates or parties in the middle of the week should be over much earlier than during the week-end, when one can sleep later the next morning. Some parents feel that young people in school should not go out at all in the middle of the week. There are schools, however, that do sponsor evening band practice, play practice, informal club affairs, and other activities throughout the week which sometimes make it awkward for young people who are not allowed out in the middle of the week. These things, too, can be discussed with most parents and some comfortable working plan developed, *if* the young people make sure that they are as careful of the way their parents feel about it as they want their parents to be about their interests. Remembering that feelings are a two-sided problem is always helpful in working out disagreements.

Several of the factors involved in working out the hours questions between parents and young people are: (1) where the affair is; (2) who is going; (3) what is going to happen; (4) how soon it is expected to be over; (5) how the return trip home is to be made; and (6) whether or not the parents can be notified if the hour is to be later than expected.

Freedom and Responsibility. Parents and teen-agers often disagree about the amount of freedom and responsibility that the young people are to have. The teen-ager often wants to be free to choose his own friends, select his own courses in school, plan for his own vocational future, earn and spend his own money, and generally run his own life in a more independent fashion than many parents are able to allow.

Parents still feel responsible for their children even when they reach their teens. If anything goes wrong, parents are still considered responsible for their teen-age children by the rest of the community. Parents are rightly interested in the friends, the vocational interests, the recreational pursuits, and the general behavior of their children. And most children want them to be. It is in the way in which freedoms and responsibilities are shared that problems arise in most families.

Problem-Solving Approaches

Most problems between teen-agers and their parents yield best to joint planning and decision-making. Within any given family, disagreements are avoided and problems are solved when all the individuals with an interest in the situation share in working it out. As parents and young people learn how to get through to each other and develop skills in understanding and being understood, even the most difficult problems are relieved.

All of life involves problem-solving. Wherever people come into contact with each other, there are bound to be problems from time to time. Tested experience has shown that some approaches are better than others. On the whole, it does not help to run out on a difficult problem, to bemoan one's fate that it has occurred, or to blame others for the predicament. What does help can be outlined step by step from looking squarely at the problem to following through an effective program for its solution, as shown on pages 110–11.

Getting Through to Each Other. Learning to communicate with others, to solve problems, and to live harmoniously together involves the art of getting through to each other fully, freely, and effectively. It means understanding not only the facts but the feelings, and being able to communicate your own point of view, feelings, and values, so that the other person has a chance of perceiving your situation as you do. It does not help to complain, "You just don't understand." It is your job to see to it that the others "get" your position as clearly as necessary.

Getting through to each other involves not only "sending" but also "receiving." You may have plenty of practice in protesting and in getting your point across. Equally important is your sense of what the other person is thinking and feeling. There are several steps to this process:

1. Ask the questions that will encourage the other person to reveal his thoughts and feelings.
2. Learn to listen to what the other person is saying and how—try to catch the "music" as well as the words, the emotional tone as well as the points being made.
3. Reflect on what is being said in the spirit of, "Is this what you are trying to tell me?" to make sure that you understand what is being said.

4. Make one or more proposals that would satisfy the interests of every-one involved, perhaps starting this way: "Would it help if we . . . ?"

5. Take time to consider any proposals for working out the problem situ-ation amicably.

6. Make an effort to follow any reasonable suggestions, and give others' ideas a fair chance to prove themselves.

7. Realize that good decisions take time, and that the process of working things through together is quite as important as the ultimate answer to whatever question was being considered.

Developing a Parent-Youth Code

We Americans have a heritage of taking the town-meeting approach to our problems. So, today, when pressures and privileges are changing so rapidly, parents and young people gather together in towns across the country to de-velop a code of behavior that makes sense for their particular community. Any questions that either parents or teen-agers have about the many areas of their common life together may become a part of the consideration and ulti-mately of their code. Each of these questions is thrashed out in groups of both young people and parents, separately and together under any suitable auspices. School, church, community association, or parent-teacher association are the most frequent sponsoring groups. When mutually acceptable agree-ments emerge on the major issues involved, statements reflecting the consensus are written out and distributed, either among the families represented or, more widely, through publication in school or local papers. One such code is re-printed here by permission as an example of the kind of thing that is emerging from many such community deliberations of common problems.[3]

Realizing that both adults and young people need to know what is ex-pected of them, and sensing the confusion among members of both genera-tions over acceptable procedures in these changing times, 2,000 high-school students and their parents and teachers, in a series of meetings, came to the following general agreements:

Parent-Youth Relationships. Any matters concerning other members of the family are best discussed within the family. It helps when adults are will-ing to consider new ideas and youth is able to see the wisdom of adult ex-perience.

Members of the family leaving the home are expected to indicate if pos-sible where they will be and when they expect to return. This applies to mem-bers of both generations and is regarded as one of the fundamentals of living together.

[3] Evelyn Millis Duvall, "Toward a Parent-Youth Code for a Midwestern City," *Journal of Home Economics,* Vol. 46 (January, 1954), pp. 36, 37.

"Betty . . . Guess what Daddy gave me for my birthday?"

Parties. It is wise for some responsible adult to be available wherever young people are being entertained. This applies to private homes as well as church, school, and community activities. It should be clear that adult availability does not mean interference or "snoopervision," since youth should be encouraged to be responsible for their own affairs.

Plans for the junior-senior prom are best worked out by the members of those classes in consultation with the teachers and parents most closely involved.

Hours. The hour to be in at night depends upon the age of the young person, the nature of the activity, and the understanding between parents and young people.

In general, it is agreed that hours for school nights and week-end evenings *be no later than:*

	School Nights	*Friday and Saturday Evenings*
7th and 8th Grades	9:30–10:00	10:00–10:30
9th Grade	10:00–10:45	11:00–12:00
10th, 11th, 12th Grades	11:00	12:00–12:30
		(except for special out-of-town affairs that are best left up to the individual families.)

This schedule is seen as most effective when it is interpreted flexibly rather than as a rigid curfew. In the last analysis, these questions belong in families.

A PATTERN FOR PROBLEM SOLVING [4]

Steps	Key Questions	Purpose
1. Face the problem.	What is the matter?	To get problem into words.
	Why do I/we think it is a problem?	To uncover the fear involved.
2. Look at the causes.	What has been happening?	To get the build-up of the problem.
	What has made it a problem now?	To get a clear statement of what is bringing it to a head.
3. Set some goals.	What do I want to accomplish for myself?	To be sure of the desires for self.
	For the other person?	To be sure that decisions will benefit others as well as self.
	What do I/we want the situation to be?	To set a definite change to work toward.
4. Get more knowledge and understanding.	What knowledge is applicable?	To increase understanding.
	Have I studied the question?	To gain insight.
	What has been the experience of other people in similar situations?	
5. Be the other person. (Try to be each of the other persons or groups of persons involved in the problem.)	Just how would I, as this other person, think about it?	To get the other person's point of view and emotional slant.
	And as this other person what does he or she feel?	To allow thinking and feelings of others to be a framework for the next step.

[4] L. A. Lynde, "A Pattern for Counseling," adapted by Girdie Ware, Oklahoma A & M College; and Evelyn Millis Duvall, *Family Development* (Chicago: J. B. Lippincott, 1957), p. 140. Reprinted by permission.

Steps	Key Questions	Purpose
6. Consider what to do.	What could we/I do about it?	To get a list of possible actions.
	Will that bring me to my goals?	To be sure they lead to the goals.
	Will it fit the thoughts and feelings of the other person?	To be sure they will be acceptable to other person.
7. Make a plan of action.	Just how can this be done?	To plan how to do it.
	Who will do each part? How will I do it?	To develop a 1, 2, 3 plan.
	Who will help me?	To select the person to help at each point if needed.
8. Check the plan with the goals.	Will this plan lead you to your goals?	To be sure the plan is really directed at the desired solution.
	Does it provide for each goal?	To be sure it covers all the goals set.
9. Plan the follow-up.	What shall I/we watch for to be sure the plan is working?	To encourage watchfulness in using the plan.
		To encourage abandonment if it seems to be failing.

Automobiles. A young person should be allowed the use of the family car as soon as he or she has a driver's license, has demonstrated the ability to be responsible for the use of the car, and has legitimate use for it in getting to and from recognized activities. These are matters for family consultation, the parents understanding what the use of the car means to young people, and youth recognizing the basis for their parents' concern. In general it helps to plan ahead for the use of the car.

Going out in the car, attending drive-in theaters, etc., depends upon the responsibility of the boy and girl to protect their reputations and the good names of the family. Sitting in the car after a date does not look well to some people, it is agreed.

Allowances. The amount of allowance given a young person depends upon the family income, what the allowance is supposed to cover, the willingness of young people to be responsible for their expenditures, as well as their ability to earn some or all of their own money. Such questions need to be reviewed from time to time and adjustments made to fit new developments.

Responsibility for Mistakes. A young person making a mistake should be allowed to redeem himself and should be expected to make amends for harm caused others. Malicious gossip among adults is considered irresponsible and destructive to the best interests of both adults and youth in the community. The branding of all youth as undependable because of the irresponsible behavior of a few is to be discouraged.

Opportunities for Learning. Adults are expected to provide youth with wholesome opportunities to gain the knowledges, skills, spiritual attitudes, and moral values involved in learning what it means to grow up and become a responsible, successful adult. At best, these educational opportunities through helpful books, classes, and counseling are provided by the homes, schools, and churches within the community.

Mutual Trust. As adults and youth work together for common interests in the home as well as in the larger community, they often learn to appreciate and to trust each other.

Recommendation. It is recommended that this statement be distributed as revised to those families in the community with young people of high-school age.

In conclusion: These agreements and understandings have come out of a process of mutual consultation that is to be continued between the adults and youth of the city. It is expected that as situations change and new developments occur, new agreements must be reached.

This is the democratic way of solving problems. Within this process lie the strengths of the family, the integrity of the community, the stability of the nation, and the hope of the free world.

Practicing Democracy in the Family Brings Happiness

A very wise person defines a good family as one in which "everyone spoils everyone else." By this he means that a family is a place where each person—parent or child—has a right to be heard, to have his values respected and his feelings accepted with loving tenderness.

This climate of mutual acceptance and support is best developed in an atmosphere of democratic interaction, where each family member feels free to raise his voice and to be heard on any matter that concerns him.

One recent study found that democracy in the family is closely related to the happiness of that family. Professor Slocum studied 2,000 seniors from thirty-five high schools across the state of Washington. He found that family happiness and democratic controls go hand in hand in the ratings of these high-school seniors, as we see below.

The data are clear. In homes where democratic controls are "nearly always" practiced, the great majority of the high-school seniors rate their families as "very happy," and only a very small percentage say their families are "unhappy." In families where controls are undemocratic not one of the boys and only 7 per cent of the girls rated the home as "very happy," and nearly half of the boys and two-thirds of the girls rated their families as "unhappy."

DEMOCRACY AND THE HAPPY HOME [5]

Rating of Home Life

Democratic Control	Sex	Very Happy Per Cent	Fairly Happy Per Cent	Unhappy Per Cent	Total Per Cent	Number of Seniors
Nearly always	B	59	37	4	100	318
	G	67	30	3	100	369
Usually	B	42	50	8	100	279
	G	38	54	8	100	245
Half and half	B	27	54	19	100	127
	G	29	56	15	100	113
Undemocratic	B	0	55	45	100	11
	G	7	29	64	100	14

Reading down the "Very Happy" column, you find a gradual decline in percentages of students rating their homes as "very happy" as practices in democratic controls diminish. Reading down the "Unhappy" column, you find a gradual increase of percentages of students rating their homes as "unhappy" as undemocratic controls increase. Reading across the top line, you see by far the largest percentage of homes practicing democratic controls are rated as "happy," with only a small percentage considered "unhappy." Reading by contrast, across the last line, representing homes characterized by undemocratic controls, you note that very few students are "very happy," and a relatively large percentage of those questioned are "unhappy."

Families in which parents and teen-agers discuss their problems are rated conspicuously happier than those in which discussion is not common. This

---

[5] Happiness and Democratic Practices in the Family as Rated by High-School Seniors. Walter L. Slocum, "Some Factors Associated with Happiness in Unbroken Homes," *The Coordinator*, Vol. 6 (March, 1958), p. 37.

is not just a happy guess. One of the statements these senior boys and girls were asked to check was, "With regard to family problems, my parents discuss them with me: (1) always; (2) usually; (3) about half the time; (4) seldom; and (5) never." At the time of the study, the students were asked to rate their homes as "very happy," "fairly happy," or "unhappy." When the results of the two items were tabulated and compared, a close relationship between family happiness and discussion was clear, as we see below.

DISCUSSION AND THE HAPPY HOME [6]

| | | Students' Rating of Family Happiness | | |
Discuss Problems in the Family	Number of Students	Very Happy	Fairly Happy	Unhappy
Always	96 girls	70%	22%	8%
	69 boys	56	32	12
Usually	364 girls	58	37	5
	307 boys	58	37	5
Half the time	190 girls	39	53	8
	205 boys	42	54	4
Never	15 girls	13	60	27
	22 boys	9	59	32

Reading the top line of this table, you see that in families that always discuss their problems, 70 per cent of the girls rate their homes as happy in contrast to 8 per cent who rate them as unhappy. Reading down the column of students rating their homes as very happy, you see a steady decline in the percentages as the amount of family discussion decreases from always to never. In these several ratings girls' responses are not unlike those of the boys. In fact, reading across the "usually" line (second from the top) we see that the responses of the two sexes are identical.

It is clear that family happiness and discussion are related—a reflection perhaps of the need family members have to get through to each other, to feel that the others in the family understand how they feel, care about their opinions, and appreciate their participation.

[6] Relationship of Family Happiness to Discussion of Family Problems as Rated by 2,000 Senior-High-School Students. *Ibid.*, p. 38.

Companionship Through Family Recreation

Companionship is built by doing things together. Family recreation enjoyed by the family as a whole or by various members playing together in mutually satisfying activities brings a pleasant sense of mutuality and belonging. Tensions can be released by many forms of recreation—through games, sports, gardening, "do-it-yourself" projects, music, dramatics, or any other pastime that a particular family finds is fun.

The 22nd National Recreation Congress defines recreation as "any form of activity in which the individual feels a sense of freedom and of self-forgetfulness, and to which he gives himself wholeheartedly because of the satisfaction he gains by participating." Recreation so defined puts the emphasis on the *how* rather than on the *what*. It actually makes little difference what the family does in having fun together, as long as there is real satisfaction for the individual members and for the family as a whole. This is the point of the saying, "The family that plays together, stays together."

Values in Family Fun. In the teen years boys and girls naturally pull away from some family activities in favor of doing more with their own age group. Yet to drop all family fun is to miss out on important values in personal and family living. Some of the types of family fun worth cherishing can be simply stated for further elaboration in your thinking and discussion.

1. Increasing sense of companionship through family participation in various forms of music, art, nature study, crafts, sports, and other activities.
2. Improving communication skills through family discussion of books, plays, movies, television programs, news events, political issues, people enjoyed, and personal observations about life.
3. Developing skills in entertaining friends and relatives as a family, with planning and responsibilities jointly shared by the various family members.
4. Broadening horizons through family trips and vacations to visit distant family members, explore new terrain, or make new family friends.
5. Developing in the family social skills for use in wider social situations, such as winning and losing graciously, observing expected courtesies, and learning specific skills such as sports, dancing, and public speaking.
6. Participating in civic, social, and church responsibilities as a member of the family identified with certain groups, causes, projects, and affiliations as the proving ground for one's future associations.

7. Enjoying the satisfactions of giving and receiving surprises at birthdays and anniversaries, Sunday and holiday meals, picnics, and various special celebrations, unexpected as well as expected.

Family Rituals Enhance Communication. Most family rituals have pleasant associations. Often they center about holidays, birthdays, anniversaries, and other happy occasions. Family rituals are a particular family's ways of doing things that tend to be repeated time after time, until a sense of rightness accompanies them. Because these recurring occasions are so meaningful and so pleasant to the family as a whole as well as to the individuals in the family, they tend to continue.[7]

Whenever you find yourself saying to your family, "Let's do it just the way we always used to," you are requesting the continuation of a family ritual that has become meaningful to you. The particular activity itself is not important. It may be something very simple like Father's cooking hamburgers for the family at a favorite picnic spot, or your surprising your parents with breakfast in bed some Sunday morning. It may be a real celebration like a family trip to Big Town, or a bang-up birthday party or a big Thanksgiving dinner with all the family pitching in to make it a grand affair.

It is the family ritual, large or small, that gives meaning, warmth, and color to family living. The older you grow, the more fondly you think back on the good times you had with your parents as you were growing up. Your reunions will be dotted with reminiscences that begin, "Do you remember the way we used to . . . ?"

Such a precious heritage is built by the years of interaction between you and your parents. It does not just happen. What you do together now is what you will look back upon later with either pleasure or regret. What you enjoy together now is worth doing again and again for all it contributes to the quality of your family life.

Summary

Communication between parents and youth is important to members of both generations. But for various reasons young people find it hard to talk many things over with their parents. Seeing both sides of the parent-youth question in terms of the need each generation has for the other aids communication. Disagreements occur in the best of families. Differences can be worked through in harmony as family members discover what a problem situation means to the others and seek a solution that protects the values of

---

[7] James H. S. Bossard and Eleanor S. Boll, *Rituals in Family Living* (Philadelphia: University of Pennsylvania Press, 1950), p. 89.

each person involved. This means shared responsibility, joint planning, and mutual confidence in the individual family and in the community through such communication-in-action as that found in developing parent-youth codes. Values in family fun and recreation enrich companionship and build meaningful family rituals through the years. Efforts at free full communication are central in democratic living within the family.

Suggested Activities

Individual Study

1. Write a paper based on your own experience, as well as your readings in this chapter, on "Why Family Discussion and Happiness Go Together." Illustrate your material with examples and episodes of how you felt when questions (a) were discussed; (b) were not discussed with you in your own family. Conclude with your own plan for talking things through with your children when they are your age.

2. Copy the list of twenty-two reasons for the difficulty of discussion with parents, page 103, in a column down the left-hand page of your class notebook. Then make two headings for columns to the right—"My Difficulty with Father" and "My Difficulty with Mother." Check those reasons that apply to your problem in discussion with both of your parents. Then compare your checks with the percentages of those for college freshmen of your sex. Discuss with a trusted counselor the similarities or differences between the table in the text and your own in your notebook. If feasible, make a plan for facilitating your future discussion with one or both of your parents.

3. Try out step by step the "Pattern for Problem Solving," pages 110–11 of your text, in working through some everyday difference of opinion or disagreement with one of your parents. Write up what you did at each step in the process, according to the outline. Tell what the reaction was in terms of the way your parents acted and the way you felt as a result of the effort to solve the problem. Describe what eventually emerged as a solution to the problem and the extent to which you felt it was a good one or not. Did the recommended procedure work or not? Why? Why not? What will you try in a similar situation that may arise in the future?

4. Plan a surprise for a member of your family. Carry it through and be prepared to report how it worked out. How did the family member feel about your effort to please? How did you feel about it? Did you feel closer than you had before? Were you able to communicate more easily with each other before or after your surprise?

5. Make a list of the rituals in your family that you have most enjoyed through the years. Check each one that you hope you will be able to continue when you have a home of your own.

6. Describe the birthday you remember most vividly. How was it celebrated? What makes it stand out in your memory?

Group Activity

1. Have a class discussion concerning the most frequent situations in which young people feel that they are not understood by their parents. Just when do these misunderstandings most often arise? Over what kinds of issues? Make a list of the most common areas of disagreement.

2. Divide your class into four groups and plan a series of psychodramas on "Was He (or She) 'Burned Up!'" Let each spontaneous skit portray some episode from a family in which a teen-ager has done something that greatly annoyed one of his or her parents. Keep the situations as normal and usual as you can. Such things are common. Many young people feel self-conscious about them. So bringing them out into the open in spontaneous skits may make them seem amusing. At the same time, the point at which parents are often annoyed with typical adolescent behavior can be put across as parents see it.

3. Invite in two older couples to tell about dating in their own youth, and to discuss with you how many things have changed in just the last generation or two. Ask the visiting adults to tell you how they used to arrange dates, where they went, what they did, how much it cost, and when they were expected home at night. Ask the visitors questions about points that are not quite clear. Compare their memories with stories or movies like *Margie, The Late George Apley, Life with Father, Meet Me in St. Louis,* and other stories of life at the turn of the century. Try to keep from too quickly labeling past customs as old-fashioned. Rather try to get the feel of what it must have been like to be young at that time. See if you can sense how you would have felt then as a young person in love, let us say. Can you imagine how you would feel about your own children if you had had that kind of youth yourself?

4. Consider, in a class discussion, the following specific cases in terms of the questions, "Whose responsibility is it?" "Is the teen-ager responsible?" "The parents?" "Both?" "Who takes the next step?"

   a. John had an accident with the family car last night. The repair bill came to nearly fifty dollars. Whose responsibility is it?

b. Mary ran down an old man at a crossing as she was bicycling home from school last week. The man's family is suing for damages. Whose responsibility is it?

c. Harry and Ken became boisterous at the corner clubroom last Saturday and some furnishings were broken. Whose responsibility is it?

d. Edith expects two of her friends to spend the night with her next Friday. Her room has not been picked up all week. Whose responsibility is it?

e. Emil lives with his widowed mother, who needs an operation. It will take all of her savings and more. Emil has some money he has earned summers and after school. His mother will not be able to work for some weeks. The bills will have to be met. Whose responsibility is it?

f. John's steady girl has broken up with him because he continues to drink occasionally on dates. Whose responsibility is it?

g. Ellen lost her favorite friend when he heard her use profanity. Whose responsibility is it?

h. Herman wants to drop out of school and get a job. He has the aptitude for going on into engineering, for which he has been planning for years. Whose responsibility is it?

5. Arrange to show the film, *You and Your Family* (Association Films, 291 Broadway, New York City 17, New York), as a basis for discussion of right and wrong ways for both parents and young people to handle the late-hours question. Discuss ways of working out the problem that will safeguard the interests of both the parents and the young people.

6. Produce *Which Way Out*, a 23-minute play written about teen-agers who are having difficulty understanding their emotionally disturbed father. The cast includes two teen-age boys and three teen-age girls. Producing packets containing seven scripts and a discussion guide are available through the Mental Health Materials Center, Inc., 1790 Broadway, New York City 19, New York. Plan the discussion following the play very carefully, inviting in as consultant, if possible, a person trained in guidance or mental health.

7. Consider ways of developing a parent-youth code for your community. How could you go about getting parents to discuss such questions? Talk with some of the leaders in the Parent-Teacher Association, the mothers' clubs, or with some of the parents of students in your own home room. Would they be interested in working out such a code with your class? Outline the steps necessary to launch such a community activity.

8. Discuss in a class session some of the listings individual students have made of their most meaningful family rituals (Item 5 in Individual Study above).

Readings

ECKERT, RALPH G., *What You Should Know About Parenthood* (Chicago: Science Research Associates, 1953). This life-adjustment booklet written for young people about what it will be like to become parents provides an excellent two-way look at their relationships with their own parents that could facilitate communication between the generations.

ENGLISH, O. SPURGEON, M.D., and FOSTER, CONSTANCE J., *Fathers Are Parents, Too* (New York: G. P. Putnam's Sons, 1951). A book on the role of the father in the family that has much to tell young people about their relationships with their own fathers in Chapter 10, "Father and Adolescence."

FAEGRE, MARION L., *The Adolescent in Your Family* (Washington, D. C.: Children's Bureau Publication 347, 1955). One of the clearest descriptions of the relationships between adolescents and the rest of the family, with many valid recommendations for better ways of getting through to each other with more effective communication.

LANDIS, JUDSON T. and MARY G., *Building Your Life* (Englewood Cliffs, N. J.: Prentice-Hall, Inc., 1954). Chapter 19, "Your Parents," and Chapter 20, "Your Family and Your Decisions," include sections on getting through to each other about the choice of a young person's friends, his right to privacy, and such decisions as whether or not to smoke.

PIERCE, WELLINGTON G., *Youth Comes of Age* (New York: McGraw-Hill Book Company, 1948). Chapter 2, on "Getting Along with Your Family," starts with the inevitable rumblings and grumblings of normal disagreements within the family and goes on to the ways in which the two generations can get through to each other to enjoy family good times.

Chapter 7

Being a Family Member

Being a family member has definite privileges and rights. It also entails certain responsibilities for each member. If you are to enjoy the privileges, you are expected to assume the responsibilities. Only by accepting both can you become a participating part of the family.

Privileges of Family Membership

Because you are a member of your family, you bear its name and are accepted without question as a member of the group. You do not need to be voted in, nor can you be voted out. You *belong* to your family regardless of what you do or what happens. There may be times when you wish that you could leave your family far behind. There may be occasions when you feel that certain family members would rather not have you around. But feel as you will, you still remain your parents' child and a member of the family.

Your rights and privileges as a family member are legally protected. If anything should happen to your parents, your rights to a share of their property would be safeguarded by law in most states. If anything happens to you before you reach legal adulthood, your parents are responsible. As long as you live, your place as a member of the family is secured for you.

Your Share of the Family Money. As a member of your family you are entitled to a just share of the family income for the meeting of your real needs. Basic rights commonly include food, shelter, essential clothing, necessary medical and dental costs, and the education provided by your community. In addition there are certain expected privileges that vary greatly from community to community and from family to family. Some families pay for music lessons, bicycles, vacation trips, desired items of clothing, parties, special educational opportunities, and many other advantages that the family willingly provides for its children. These are not *rights* which the family must provide. They are *privileges* that the family wants its children to enjoy.

121

Most families try to be fair in distributing the family money. No one child gets all the advantages while others, like Cinderella, are neglected. There may be times in any family when certain family members have needs greater than others. Then it is considered appropriate for the family to meet those costs even if it means letting some desires of others in the family wait for a while. A sister may have to wait for a new dress while her brother gets his tonsils out. A father may postpone the purchase of a new coat in favor of a new washing machine. The mother may make over her old hat so that her daughter may have a new suit. And so it goes in millions of families.

Your Allowance. Practically half of the 1,925 teen-age girls (49 per cent) studied by the Survey Research Center of the University of Michigan receive an allowance. Most of these girls have been getting an allowance since before they were ten years of age. This is in accord with the general recognition that each child in the family should have a regular allowance as soon as he or she has use for money. Whether you get an allowance or not depends upon your family's stand on the question, and perhaps on what other sources of income you have as a teen-ager.

ADOLESCENT SPENDING [1]

Percentages of Girls by Age Groups

Items	Under 14	14–16	Over 16	Total
Clothes	40%	57%	61%	50%
Entertainment—cokes, movies	35	37	23	34
School expenses—bus, lunch, books	18	19	29	20
Personal expenses	10	11	13	11
Gifts	11	6	7	9
Church, charity	5	2	3	4
Hobby equipment	5	3	2	4
Supports self, or helps with family finances	1	2	3	2
Saves money	20	14	12	16
Other	7	8	8	7
Has no money	2	2	2	2
Not ascertained	9	8	8	8
Number	844	822	259	1,925

Note: Totals are more than 100 per cent in each column because girls gave more than one response.

[1] How 1,925 Adolescent Girls Spend Their Money. Survey Research Center, *Adolescent Girls: A Nation-Wide Study of Girls Between Eleven and Eighteen Years of Age* (Ann Arbor, Michigan: Institute for Social Research, University of Michigan, 1957), p. 87.

How much a teen-ager's allowance should be depends upon many factors: the family income, the parents' confidence in their teen-ager's ability to use his money wisely, the amount one's friends receive, and the various items one's allowance is expected to cover. The largest number of girls studied by the University of Michigan report receiving between $1.00 and $5.00 a week, which they spend variously for clothes, entertainment, school and personal expenses, as itemized on page 123.

Allowances often cover at least some of the teen-ager's clothing needs. By the time they graduate from high school, some young people are buying most of their clothes. Others are capably handling almost all of the family's finances. Some few have practically no money of their own, and little opportunity to learn how to spend money. The great value of an allowance for a young person through the years is the experience it gives in handling money. Another way of learning to use money wisely is through participating in family spending plans.

Family Decisions on Spending. Increasingly, families decide how the money shall be spent by planning sessions in which each family member takes part. No one member decides all by himself what the others shall or shall not have. Meeting as a unit, the family members explore their needs and wishes, count up their assets, and decide which are most important and which shall come first. This has great advantages, not only in making every member feel a real part of the family, but also in giving the younger members of the family training in planning and decision making. Since this is a new approach, it is often up to young people to introduce it into their families as a working plan.

14- TO 16-YEAR-OLD WORKING BOYS [2]

Number of Hours Worked Last Week	Percentage of Those Who Work	Percentage of Total 1,045
Under 6	14%	6%
6 to 12	33	15
13 to 20	23	11
21 to 30	18	9
31 or more	8	4
Not ascertained	4	2
Hasn't got a job		53
	100%	100%
Number	491	1,045

[2] Number of Hours 14- to 16-Year-Old Boys Say They Work a Week. Survey Research Center, *A Study of Adolescent Boys* (Ann Arbor, Michigan: Institute for Social Research, University of Michigan, 1955), p. 41.

Your Earnings as a Teen-Ager. Almost half the 1,045 teen-age boys studied by the University of Michigan Survey Research Center have some kind of job. Three out of four have jobs with strangers, somewhat less than one in five works for his family, 2 per cent work for friends, and another 2 per cent are self-employed. Most of the teen-age boys who work spend more than six hours a week at their jobs, as is seen on page 124.

In most communities young people of high-school age can earn money in many ways. Boys deliver papers, work for stores as clerks, packers, and delivery men, and get part-time jobs in local plants when business is good. Girls serve as baby sitters, saleswomen, and do various other types of work.

By law the money earned by minors belongs to their parents. Actually most parents do not expect their children's earnings to be turned over for family use except in dire need. Many parents, however, like to know that their teen-age earners are using their money wisely. They often expect them to save at least some of their earnings for future needs. They quite often object to unreasonable extravagances and wastefulness. It is not just the money they are concerned about. Parents usually want their children to develop good money habits and to learn to spend what they have intelligently. Wise young people budget their money and so learn to handle their finances.

Learning to Handle Money Wisely. You learn to manage your money wisely in actual situations where handling money is involved. You learn a great deal about money by participating in family decisions about it. Your chief sources of personal income as a teen-ager are (1) your earnings; (2) your allowance; and (3) special gifts you get from your parents, other relatives, and friends.

Learning to manage your finances involves dividing your available money between amounts you want to spend, give, and save. Your savings may be for a short-term special thing like a new article of clothing or for long-term goals such as summer camp, travel plans, an automobile, or your college education.

Even though the amounts are small, you learn good or bad management in the way you use your money. The money you have goes further if you practice good buying habits. Getting the most for your money is something you learn with experience. You will find that your money buys more of what you want as you develop skill in wise spending.

TEN GUIDES TO GOOD MONEY MANAGEMENT [3]

1. Buy only what you really want and need.
2. Guard against squandering money in many little extravagances.
3. Use scientific tests instead of sales or advertising claims.

[3] Adapted from Evelyn Millis Duvall and Reuben Hill, *When You Marry* (Boston: D. C. Heath, 1953), pp. 218–24.

4. Avoid fads that are here today and gone tomorrow.
5. Buy where you can get good quality at low prices.
6. Take advantage of bona fide sales at reputable stores.
7. Consider second-hand items where feasible.
8. Keep what you have in good repair.
9. Plan immediate and long-term spending within your income.
10. Build up a "cushion fund" to use in emergencies.

Enjoying and Changing Your Home

Enjoying the use of the home is one of the privileges of family members. Changing things at home is a very special privilege, too. Let us look at both of these.

Making Use of Home Facilities. Have you ever realized how much you take for granted in your use of family equipment? You raid the icebox, bring your friends in to hear a record, use the telephone, all as a matter of course. When you were still quite young and immature, you may have abused these privileges and taken advantage of others' good nature. Then you were more apt to leave the bathroom in disorder, forget to close the icebox door, or hang onto the telephone when someone else in the family wanted to use it. As you mature, you learn to become responsible for these privileges and to keep from being a burden on the others in the family.

If you had to pay for the facilities you use in entertaining your friends, you would find that the costs would run startlingly high. You would discover, too, that you would have to make arrangements well in advance. It would not be likely that you could bring the crowd in to eat on the spur of the moment. Only the most expensive clubs can afford to cater to the spontaneous whims and wishes of their members. Yet many of you make use of these services quite readily in your homes. It is only fair to make sure you do not inconvenience other family members. It is usually expected that you will plan with the family before inviting others in except for the most informal gatherings. Conscientious young people assume some responsibility for providing simple refreshments and for cleaning up afterward. Even in a public park you are expected to leave the picnic grounds as clean as you found them. You should observe the same courtesy in your home.

Making Changes at Home. One of the real advantages of belonging to a family is that you can make changes with relative ease. It takes a long while to bring about changes at school or in the community. You have to get a great many people to see things your way and to back the change you are proposing. Then you have to convince the administration of the school or town that the change you are proposing is a good one that they can afford and which should not be delayed. By the time the proposal has gone through all the necessary channels, considerable time has elapsed and a great deal of energy has been expended. At home the process can be simple.

Sybil Shelton from Monkmeyer

Gardening is a chore that brings immediate rewards in the improved appearance of the yard. Most other household jobs can be fun, too, when family members pitch in together, as this brother and sister are doing.

Some changes at home take place so easily you hardly realize it. You have your evening meal at five-thirty instead of at six so that you can get to the band concert. You have your breakfast early because of a special examination. You hang some pictures on your wall. You install new shelves for your books. You paint the kitchen chairs. Such things take place as a matter of course in the family. They would not be simple in an institution. There you must conform to set rules. At home the routines can be changed to fit your needs and interests.

Even more drastic changes are possible at home. Ellen did not like the way the living room looked. She talked it over with her parents and got them to agree to let her change it around and fix it up with an agreed-upon amount of money. She drew a floor plan of the room. Then she took the project to school and, with her teacher's help, made a plan for redesigning the whole room. She and her mother selected material for slip covers and curtains, which they made themselves. Before long her mother and father were proudly telling their friends how Ellen had redone the room. Ellen learned a lot from the experience, the most important part of which was that if you do not like something, you can change it!

Similarly Joey repainted the family car. And Alec planted a garden at the back of the house in the spot that had been an unsightly dump. And Jessie got her family to eat more vegetables. The illustrations are limitless. All over America young people are making improvements at home. When these changes are entered into thoughtfully and carried out successfully, the whole family gets satisfaction from them.

Respecting the Persons the Changes Affect. If you were a Robinson Crusoe, you could make all the changes you desired without affecting anyone, except perhaps your man Friday. Around home other people have to be considered. Some things are easier to change than others, depending upon how strongly people feel about them. Sometimes people get attached to things the way they are and do not like to see them changed. Then innovations can be introduced only slowly and with consideration for the feelings of the persons involved.

On the whole, things are easier to change than people. You can paint the porch furniture, make new curtains, or even change the pantry around without causing much of a stir. But when you begin to try to remodel some other member of the family, you find that you need a great deal of skill and diplomacy. Once you can convince the other person that you are sincerely interested in him or her, half your battle is won.

Lucy wanted to help her mother comb her hair more stylishly. She began by calling her mother's attention to hair styles in magazine advertisements. One night while she and her mother were alone, she tried fixing her mother's hair a new way. They both agreed that it was becoming, and after another experimental session, her mother adopted the new hair style. Notice that Lucy did not begin by scolding her mother for being old-fashioned. She considered her mother's feelings and when they were alone she gave her a positive demonstration that was helpful. Just criticizing rarely does much good. Criticism must be positive, with some specific suggestion for change, before it can persuade anyone to change.

Father may have some habits you find annoying, or you may think his whole attitude toward you needs some readjusting. You may have some wonderful ideas for reforming the personalities of your brothers and sisters. But before you tell them your ideas on the subject, or even begin nagging, stop to think how you would like it if someone started to make you over without your consent.

You have a right to change some things around the home. But respect for another's personality should keep you from trying to reform him too drastically. This phase of individual development is most successful when it is launched with the full knowledge and co-operation of the person being changed. And that goes for everyone.

Assuming Responsibility in Your Family

Most teen-agers have some responsibilities at home. When 1,925 girls of junior- and senior-high-school age were asked, "Do you have any regular work at home?" and "Are there some jobs around the house that are your special responsibilities?" nine out of ten of the girls (92 per cent) replied in the affirmative. In general, the older the girl, the more major responsibility she carries, as you see below.

GIRLS' DUTIES IN THE HOME [4]				
	Under 14	14–16	Over 16	Total 1,925
Has *light* responsibility at home	54%	36%	29%	44%
Has *moderate* responsibility at home	28	36	38	32
Has *major* responsibility at home	5	13	15	10
Has some responsibility, degree unknown	6	6	6	6
No responsibilities at home	7	9	12	8
Total	100%	100%	100%	100%
Number	844	822	259	1,925

[4] Home Responsibilities Reported by 1,925 Girls Eleven to Eighteen Years Old. Survey Research Center, *Adolescent Girls* (Ann Arbor, Michigan: Institute for Social Research, University of Michigan, 1957), p. 61.

The great majority of all teen-age girls carry some responsibility at home. Even those under fourteen years of age are generally assigned at least light or moderate responsibilities. The number of girls reporting no home responsibilities increased slightly with the age of the girls, from 7 per cent of those under fourteen to 12 per cent of those over sixteen. This may be due to the increased work load of older teen-age girls outside the home.

Factors influencing the responsibility of teen-agers in the home are: (1) mother's health; (2) mother's employment; (3) number of younger children in the family; (4) number of adults in the family; (5) amount of hired help, if any; (6) teen-ager's willingness and ability to carry responsibilities; (7) teen-ager's outside responsibilities; and (8) family pattern of mutual activity.

Teen-age boys are as affected by these eight factors in distribution of responsibility as are the girls of the family. A boy whose mother is ill or working outside probably has more to do at home than one whose mother is well and a full-time homemaker. The young person with several younger brothers or sisters is used to carrying more responsibility than an only child. Adult relatives, older brothers and sisters, or household help may reduce the demands on the teen-ager. Most families expect less from the boy or girl with an exacting program of school work, employment, and community activities. Some families, however, expect a degree of active participation from children as well as adult members. There are very real values, beyond those of getting the work done, in sharing family duties.

Sharing Home Duties. Girls and young women can profit from first-hand experience in homemaking to prepare them for marriage. More and more, as the roles of men and women are changing, boys, too, need to know how to help run a home, perform housekeeping operations, and appreciate the challenge of homemaking.

Every educated person should know how to select food for optimum nutrition and how to prepare it attractively. Malnutrition in our country is a problem not of supply, but of education. A neat, clean, attractive home ranks high in the expectations of both men and women for themselves and their families. Skills in selecting furnishings and keeping them in order are learned —in action. Every girl or boy profits from knowing how to (1) clean a room and put it to rights; (2) wash, iron, and care for clothing; (3) plan and cook a meal; (4) choose new items that go well with what is already at hand; (5) plan a tasteful, wardrobe or a room; (6) put on a simple or fancy party for family and guests; and (7) work co-operatively with others in a variety of homemaking activities.

Both boys and girls profit from activities that teach lifelong skills in making the home a pleasant place. Home projects that encourage the development of such skills are:

1. Planning meals and preparing them attractively within the limits of time, money, and facilities available.
2. Choosing equipment and utensils wisely, and sometimes repairing or improving those at hand.
3. Arranging work and storage space efficiently and conveniently.
4. Making the home safe, comfortable, and attractive.
5. Keeping the home safe, comfortable, and attractive.
6. Making, renovating, and altering clothing and furnishings as needed.
7. Taking responsibility for the care of the children.
8. Making day-to-day, as well as special, family purchases on the basis of sound money-management principles.
9. Assisting with budget planning and the keeping of household records.
10. Participating as a family member in community, church, and wider areas of social responsibility.

FAMILY ECONOMIC ACTIVITIES [5]

			Family Member		
Activity	A Shared Activity *	Father	Mother	Teen-Age Son	Teen-Age Daughter
1. Selects large household equipment	61.9%	68.7%	90.2%	5.0%	6.8%
2. Shops for furniture and furnishings	61.3	62.3	93.5	4.6	13.7
3. Shops for groceries	55.1	42.5	84.1	32.0	37.4
4. Plans family's savings	47.2	68.8	73.2	3.0	2.1
5. Shops for family's clothes	46.4	29.3	95.6	30.1	44.3
6. Shops for family's new car	46.4	91.3	46.5	10.8	15.0
7. Provides children's spending money	45.7	77.3	56.1	21.4	4.6
8. Pays bills	39.7	76.8	58.2	7.4	7.6
9. Earns money for family	38.3	97.9	32.8	15.7	2.2

* A shared activity is one that is usually participated in by two or more members of the family.

[5] Percentages of Fathers, Mothers, and Teen-Age Sons and Daughters Participating in Selected Family Economic Activities in 1,027 Families. Theodore B. Johannis, Jr., "Participation by Fathers, Mothers and Teen-Age Sons and Daughters in Selected Family Economic Activities," *The Coordinator,* Vol. 6 (September, 1957), p. 15.

Working together in sharing family responsibilities can be fun—for every member of the family. Planning a party or special event can be particularly pleasant when everyone is in on the planning. Getting the house ready for a special holiday like Thanksgiving or Christmas is something that every family member can share. Even weekly chores like cleaning the yard, washing the car, and doing the shopping, are lightened when the whole family pitches in on them. Many families find the same principle holds for getting a meal on the table, cleaning up afterwards, or straightening things up before everyone leaves in the morning.

Shopping for household furnishings and equipment is a shared activity in six out of ten families. Mothers are often the major purchasing agents of almost all household possessions except the family car, which fathers have the main vote in choosing. In 1,027 families studied, teen-agers tended to be most active in family economic activities in buying their own clothes and family groceries as seen on page 131.

In some families there is much wider participation than in others. The traditional patterns of husband being the breadwinner and wife the home-maker, with the children playing minor, secondary roles, are being modified today. An increasing number of wives are earning money, and more and more husbands and children are taking part in household activities. This is a promising trend in family relationships that augurs well for the development of individual members of the family as well as for their democratic interaction.

Brothers and Sisters in Your Life

Are you annoyed when your brother reads your diary? Does your sister irritate you when she rummages in your dresser drawer without your permission? Do you wish that your little brother and sister would keep out of the living room when your friends call upon you? Would you prefer that your older brother not try to run your life for you? Would you like it better if your older sister were not quite so critical? These feelings are common among brothers and sisters from time to time.

Nice, happy feelings among brothers and sisters are common, too. Talking things over with an understanding sister is very satisfying. Going on a trip with a brother can be exciting. Doing things together—gardening, playing games, even the chores around the house—can be fun with brothers and sisters if we know how to make them so. Part of this know-how starts with understanding that some feelings of rivalry and jealousy are common among brothers and sisters and that there are deep-seated bases for such feelings.

Rivalries and Jealousies Among You. The oldest child in the family had his parents all to himself before his brothers and sisters arrived. He was the center of things, with his parents always near to meet his needs. Then along came a little newcomer to share this paradise of his. The new baby took up a great deal of *his* mother's time. There were exclamations of pleasure over the new baby. It is understandable that the older child felt left out and saw his baby brother or sister as the cause of his demotion. Way back there began a series of hostile feelings and jealousies—of little acts of aggression such as taking the baby's bottle away, hiding his rattle, pushing, patting too hard, and all the other ingenious ways little children have of venting their negative feelings about someone they are supposed to love.

Younger brothers and sisters soon learn to react to these petty hostilities and to defend themselves in one way or another. They cry and the mother comes running. They hit back, pull hair, poke fingers in eyes, tear up precious papers, push over toys, and have a gay time making life annoying for the bigger, stronger children who have the upper hand.

In many families these early hostilities among the children dwindle down to occasional bickering and teasing episodes interspersed with long, happy periods of companionship. In families where these early hostile feelings have not been understood and wisely channeled, the brothers and sisters may continue a sort of open warefare through the years. Quarrels may be intense and frequent. Feelings may mount, and each one may get on the other's nerves. Then it is not easy to get along lovingly together. The unpleasant habits of the past continue as too strong an influence. Even then, understanding and insight help greatly.

Coping with Competition in the Family. Brothers and sisters have to be different from one another, as you saw in Chapter 1. Each child in the family struggles to carve out for himself a niche that will be all his or her own. Each person strives to establish a uniquely meaningful place in the family. This means that inevitably there is competition among the various children in any one family. No one can be the handsomest, the brightest, the most able, the most responsible, and the most fun, all rolled into one. But each child in the family can be first in something. One can usually be the first to get the point of a joke, another to volunteer his help in some chore, another to finish his homework; another can excel in sports or in music. There are dozens of ways in which individual people may distinguish themselves.

A certain amount of competition in the family is good training for the competition we must all meet in our culture, competition in business, in social life, in education, in sports, in politics, in community affairs. Competition is unhealthy when it is unfair, unsportsmanlike, or weighted by favoritism. Even then you must be able to deal with it without letting it throw you. You learn your first lessons in coping with competition through your dealings with your brothers and sisters.

To cope with competition effectively, you need the ability to improve your relationship with another person in a given situation. Improving a relationship involves, basically, a sequence of four steps:

1. Analyzing the situation (What happened? Who is involved? How do you feel about it? How does he/she feel? In what situations have you been involved with this particular person before? How have you usually reacted in previous encounters with this person? What are the customary reactions of the other to you? What makes this situation a problem? Why does it matter—to you, to the other person?)

2. Clarifying the incident (Describe clearly just what happened, in what sequence, who did what and how, what was said and in what order, what gestures and postures were used, and all other relevant facts, much as you would be expected to testify before a judge if he were to question you about details.)

3. Understanding the relationship (What early experiences color your reaction to this person? What feelings and behavior repeatedly appear in your relationship with this individual? What are the central feelings you have toward each other and why?)

4. Improving the relationship (What can you do to more fully understand the feelings and respect the values of the other person? How can you communicate more fully what it is that bothers you in the relationship? What positive factors can you build on? What specific steps can you take to improve this relationship? What is the next thing that seems feasible to do? When can you attempt it?)

Enjoying and Learning with Each Other. Only children are often wistful that they have no brothers and sisters to grow up with, share with, and enjoy the companionship of, through the years. There are real values in having brothers and sisters. Growing up with other children in the family, you learn to share, to give and take. You learn to take a stand and to make yourself understood in order to get your share of attention. You develop standards of fair play and know what you can get away with and what is just not allowed by the other children in the family. You learn to love and be loved, and to accept one another so completely that nothing, not even your occasional skirmishes, can dim your loyalty to each other. If you are fortunate enough to grow up in a family where there are both brothers and sisters, you have the chance to learn what boys and girls are really like in daily living.

As brothers and sisters learn to enjoy each other for the real people they are, their relationships become increasingly harmonious. It is always pleasant to see brothers and sisters really enjoying one another. There is something fine and sturdy in the loyalty between two brothers or the special warmth between two sisters. There is something unique in a close brother-sister relationship. But such things do not just happen. They are built up through the years by the children of the family.

Lois Ann was annoyed that her young brother, Tim, always hung around when her boy-friends came to call. He seemed to enjoy showing off and being a nuisance on these occasions, much to her distress. Lois Ann talked it over with her mother, who suggested that Tim seemed to be looking for more attention from his sister than he received. Lois Ann thought it over and realized that on the days when she had a date coming she was particularly aloof and uninterested in Tim. The next Friday afternoon, when she came home, instead of going at once to her room to fix her nails, she played catch with Tim for half an hour. Then she admired his rabbit and helped him fix a broken catch on the hutch door. That evening Tim volunteered to dry the dishes in Lois Ann's place, and when her date came, he was the model of discretion. Not a bad return for one hour's time, Lois Ann realized. She realized, too, something even more important—that when things go wrong between people, the trouble is very rarely in only one of them. Either of them, by changing his attitude and deepening his understanding, can make a difference in the whole relationship.

Grandparents and Other Relatives

Is your grandmother old-fashioned? Does she expect you to do things the way she did when she was young? Is your grandfather shocked by some of the things your crowd think of as correct? Are any of your relatives surprised about the amount of money you spend in a week? Has one of them ever

Ewing Galloway

Young people who learn to accept their grandparents as human beings find many satisfactions in the relationship. A new point of view, sidelights on old events, and even an interesting new hobby are among the rewards of this kind of companionship.

reminded you that that much money would have been enough to feed a whole family on a couple of generations ago? If not, you have most unusually up-to-date grandparents and other relatives!

Problems in Perspective. Times have changed so rapidly in the last two generations that very few people have been able to keep up with the changing scene. Never in our history has life changed as much or as fast as it has since your grandmother was a girl. In her lifetime she has seen the coming of the automobile and the disappearance of the "surrey-with-the-fringe-on-top." She has witnessed the coming of the telephone, the radio, and television. She has lived through radically changing styles in clothing, music, literature, drama, recreation and work. She has had to unlearn most of the things she was taught in her girlhood in order to keep in step with the changing ways of the world. It is not surprising if she represents in her behavior some of the experiences and attitudes of an earlier day.

The wonder is that as many of our older adults are as modern and youthful as they are. Those who have kept young in spirit usually have been blessed with children and grandchildren who have not left them behind, but have shared with them the ideas and experiences and affection that has kept them growing, interesting people.

Young people do not have all the answers. There are many insights and understandings that come with the years. That is one of the things you learn as you mature. Do you remember what Mark Twain said about his father? He said that when he was sixteen he was ashamed of how ignorant his father was; but when he reached twenty-one, he was surprised at all his father had learned in the last five years! This is a common experience.

Enjoying Older Relatives. Some young people have learned the secret of enjoying their older relatives. They start by accepting their grandmother and their Uncle Jim as real people, and not just as peculiar characters playing parts as relatives. They realize that older people as well as younger ones have sensitivities, pride, and individuality that deserve recognition and understanding. Finally they try to profit from the rich background of these older relatives.

Ezra was named for his grandfather. They were very fond of each other and had grand times together. On their frequent fishing trips together, Ezra particularly enjoyed hearing his grandfather talk about the good old days when he was young and the country was just opening up. One day Ezra asked about the days when his father was courting his mother. Some of the things Ezra learned about his mother and his father as young people helped him to understand their attitude toward his dating adventures. Strangely enough, as Ezra and his grandfather became closer, the years between them seemed less important and the young lad, his parents, and his grandfather, could enjoy each other's company without thinking much about the large difference in their ages. This experience is a rewarding one for anyone willing to work for it.

Building Family Loyalties

When families become closely knit, it is largely because their members are so genuinely loyal to each other. Their deep sense of belonging grows out of family loyalty. Such strong cohesiveness is developed through years of happy living together. Family loyalty requires continuing mutual thoughtfulness in many ways, such as these:

1. Realizing that relationships in the family change and that what once might have pleased either you or another member of the family may be inappropriate later.
2. Recognizing that all family relationships are normally made up of both positive and negative emotions. Rivalry and jealousy are practically universal feelings; love and hate go hand in hand. The feelings that predominate in your family relationships are partly your responsibility.
3. Gradually cultivating less savage and destructive feelings as you grow up, by striving to understand yourself and the others in your family.

4. Honestly acknowledging your real feelings in any relationship or family situation. This is usually more helpful than refusing to admit unpleasant emotions or running away from the situation that brought them forth.

5. Becoming genuinely interested in your parents, brothers, sisters, and other relatives as persons, an important step in learning to enjoy your relationship with them.

6. Practicing the art of really listening to others with increasing sensitivity to the feeling as well as the meaning behind their words.

7. Participating with other family members in activities you mutually enjoy. Sharing common interests builds a strong sense of unity. Learning new skills and activities together is one effective way of getting to know each other better.

8. Recognizing that every member of the family needs privacy at times, and that each person has the right to withdraw and be alone without being misunderstood by the family as a whole.

9. Realizing that differences are inevitable in any family and that each person can be enjoyed, respected, and encouraged for the contribution he makes to the group.

10. Using family discussion to make plans, to make a place for differences, to resolve conflicts, and to evaluate situations as they come along within the family.

11. Taking time to express genuine appreciation, affection, and love in daily interaction with other members of the family.

12. Taking pride in your family and its members, for past history, present accomplishments, and future promise, because they are not like any other family you will ever know, and because they are your family.

Summary

Being a family member gives you certain rights, privileges, and responsibilities. Your share of the family money is determined in action within the family. Half of the teen-age girls studied receive a regular allowance from their families. The amount of the allowance depends on many things, including what it is expected to cover. Practically half of the teen-age boys studied earn at least some of their own money at jobs taking up to thirty hours or more a week. Learning to handle money wisely involves an understanding of economic values and the principles of good management. Using and enjoying the privileges of your home involves assuming accompanying responsibilities. Most teen-agers have some regular duties in their families, depending upon such things as mother's health and outside employment, the number of younger and older people in the household, the amount of hired help, and the young person's outside responsibilities. Sharing home duties has values beyond the work done, such as homemaking skills learned as a participating member of the family. Rivalry and jealousy are often part of brother-sister relationships. They are outgrown as the children mature and learn to cope with competition in the family. Brothers, sisters, grandparents, and other relatives can be enjoyed as problems are seen in perspective. Family loyalties are built through the repeated application of mutual thoughtfulness and a growing sense of unity.

Suggested Activities

Individual Study

1. Make plans for a simple party that you can afford and can arrange yourself. Estimate the cost of the refreshments. Make a list of things you will do to help your guests have a good time and to keep the party moving. Write out specifically what you want your mother and father to do and *not to do* while your guests are there. Talk over your plans with your family either as a definite project or as something you would like to do some time. Keep your plans in your class notebook.

2. Keep an accurate record of all the money you earn and spend in a week. Make a budget for yourself, allocating sufficient amounts for the various needs in terms of your expected income. Talk over your budget with your parents. Revise it as may be necessary and then copy it into your notebook as a guide for the next week.

3. Write to *Consumer's Research*, Washington, New Jersey, and to *Consumers Union*, Mount Vernon, New York, for descriptions of their buying guides and services. Prepare a display of the materials you receive for presentation to your class.

4. Compare prices on identical items of food and clothing in several stores in your neighborhood. Note the differences and write up your comparative findings in your notebook.

5. Write a paper on the usual home responsibilities you assume each week. Which of these do you do alone, and in what activities do you work with other members of your family? Which do you most enjoy? Most dislike? Why? How do you feel about teen-agers assuming responsibilities at home?

6. Prepare a detailed description of some particular situation in your family that recently made you angry. Tell who was involved and just what happened. Try to analyze why you felt and acted as you did. Suggest insights that might result in your more mature handling of a similar family situa-

tion in the future. Give your paper to your teacher for her annotations. Talk it over with her or, if you feel it would help, with the member of the family involved.

7. Come to class prepared to report (a) the things you enjoy about your brothers and sisters; and (b) those that are most annoying. Copy these two lists into your notebook. Check each list for those things which you might be able to do to improve the relationship.

Group Activities

1. Discuss the question of how friends can have fun together when some individuals have much more money to spend than others.
2. Debate the proposition, "Resolved that an allowance for a teen-ager helps build good money habits."
3. Act out a family situation that often leads to quarreling between brothers and sisters. Play it as it usually happens. Then replay the same episode to show how the problem situation might be handled constructively.
4. Invite a number of articulate grandparents to participate with members of your class in a panel on "What Grandparents and Grandchildren Enjoy Most about Each Other." Prime your panel leader to draw out the points that members of both generations have to make about what the other does that is annoying or unsatisfactory, as well as the pleasurable items. Conclude the panel with a class discussion on what makes for mutually harmonious relationships between grandparents and teen-agers.
5. Plan a visit to the old people's home in your area. Think of what you could do while there, questions you would ask, etc. Talk your trip over with your parents and grandparents.
6. View and discuss the film strip, *Future in Hand* (McGraw-Hill, sound) in terms of what it means to be a family member.
7. Put on the skit, *The Room Upstairs*, about old and young people living together (30 minutes playing time). Available as a producing packet of six scripts (one for each actor, the director, and the discussion leader) from The National Association for Mental Health, 10 Columbus Circle, New York 19, New York.

Readings

ELLENWOOD, JAMES LEE, *There's No Place Like Home: A Family Lives Together* (New York: Charles Scribner's Sons, 1939). An easy-to-read account of the way one family worked out the relationships between three generations under the same roof—entertaining and highly discussable material on what it means to be a family member.

FORCE, ELIZABETH S., *Your Family Today and Tomorrow* (New York: Harcourt, Brace and Company, Inc., 1955). Chapter 3, "Understanding Yourself and Your Parents," and Chapter 4, "Reducing Family Friction," review the areas of friction most common between teen-agers and other family members and offer suggestions for working them through.

LEVY, JOHN, M.D., and MUNROE, RUTH, *The Happy Family* (New York: Alfred A. Knopf, 1938). A modern classic that continues to be a leader in its field because it offers so much insight and understanding on personal and family problems. You will find Chapter 1, "How Families Begin," particularly interesting and helpful.

MONEY MANAGEMENT INSTITUTE, *Money Management for Young Moderns* (Chicago: Household Finance Corporation, 1954). A booklet written especially for teen-agers to help them see where their money comes from, where it goes, and how to make a practical spending plan that will help them get more of what they want for the money they have.

MOORE, BERNICE MILBURN, and LEAHY, DOROTHY M., *You and Your Family* (Boston: D. C. Heath and Company, 1953). Chapter 9, "Family Living Poses Problems," takes up some of the reasons why being a family member is not always easy, why family members annoy and worry each other, and how they can live more harmoniously together.

TROELSTRUP, ARCH W., *Consumer Problems and Personal Finance* (New York: McGraw-Hill Book Company, 1957). This book written by the Head of the Department of Consumer Education of Stephens College contains a wealth of money-management information and advice that the mature high-school student will find quite as readable as the student in college.

ULLMAN, FRANCES, *Life with Brothers and Sisters* (Chicago: Science Research Associates, 1952). This attractive booklet written in co-operation with the Child Study Association of America can be read equally well by both younger and older brothers and sisters, as well as by the senior-high-school student, to the benefit of their relationships in the family.

Lew Merrim from Monkmeyer

Finding and

III

Becoming Popular and Having Friends
Getting and Enjoying Dates
Going Steady

Keeping Friends

Chapter 8
Becoming Popular and Having Friends

You want to be popular. You like to be liked. It is only human to want to feel that others find you nice to be near. Especially as a teen-ager you want to feel that you belong.

Just what it is that makes one person popular and another lonely is a good question. Why is it that Sue—good-looking, intelligent Sue—walks home alone from school, while Alice, who is neither as pretty nor as smart, always has a cluster of boys and girls around her?

What Makes a Person Popular?

Popularity is achieved by a combination of qualities that make a person generally liked by other people. The popular boy or girl has many friends, is invited out to parties and to social activities, and is the kind of person that others like to have around.

You Cannot Buy Friendship. Others may flock for a while around the boy who has lots of money to spend, but this is not real friendship, any more than is the temporary popularity that stems from getting a new car, or the transitory interest that comes with a new style or piece of clothing. Such things are for the moment—here today and gone tomorrow. True friendships are based on more solid, lasting qualities that persist over time.

Clothes Aren't Everything. Clothes do not make the man or the woman. It takes more than a fancy wardrobe to make people like you. In fact, many people are not much aware of what you have on, as long as you are appropriately dressed. In several high schools a number of boys were interviewed on the morning immediately following the big party of the year. It may be surprising to you to learn that *most* of the boys had no clear recollection of what their dates had worn to that party just the night before! Their replies to the question were vague, even when they were appreciative, as note the following typical statements: "She was a dream in soft blue"; "She looked O.K. to me, I guess"; "She wore my flowers in her hair"; "She looked sweet—she always does."

Looks Aren't Enough. There is general agreement that you do not have to be beautiful to be popular. Most popular people are *attractive*, but that is a long way from being truly handsome or beautiful. The perfect features, ideal figure, and silken hair that make a cover girl are not enough to make a girl popular with the hometown teen-agers. The qualities that make a person attractive to them often have little relationship to strictly physical beauty.

If you believe everything you see in the advertisements and accept all you hear in the commercials, you may come to believe that all you need to get friends is to wash your hair with a particular brand of shampoo, apply the right deodorant, or brush your teeth with a certain toothpaste. To listen to some advertising claims, you would almost think that if you applied the right potions in all the right places, friends would be drawn to you as to a magnet. This appeal is as old and as potent as the magic love potion of the fairly tale.

There is just enough truth in the underlying idea to make it seem valid. Dirty, oily hair is unpleasant; clean, sweet-smelling hair is attractive. Bad breath and unpleasant body odors are generally avoided, while the person who regularly keeps his mouth and body fresh and clean makes a more welcome neighbor. Rough, red hands are unsightly; smooth, soft skin feels pleasant to the touch and looks nice, too. So it goes. Good grooming is important. But the particular brand of toilet preparation you use is relatively unimportant.

Much more serious is the wishful dream that when you happen to get the right combination of applications, or find the brand that suits you, the doorway to popularity will open up as by magic. There are no such short cuts to friendship, no magic formula that guarantees personal appeal. You must learn how to get and keep friends the hard way, as everyone does.

Personality—What Is It? Ask any group of teen-agers what makes for popularity and the chances are you will hear "personality" mentioned more frequently than any other quality. When the University of Michigan Survey Research Center asked nearly two thousand girls (1,925) what makes a girl popular, they found more than one out of every three (37 per cent) of the girls over fourteen saying "good personality"—a considerably higher percentage than mentioned any other characteristic. Just what is this mysteriously potent combination—personality?

For the social scientist, personality is the sum total of all that a person is. Your personality is all that you are—up to now. It is a combination of all your traits, habits, attitudes, values, and characteristic ways of behaving that make you uniquely yourself. Your personality is YOU in action. As such, it is the reflection of what you have been, what you are now, and what you are in the process of becoming.

In its general sense, as the factor essential to popularity, personality seems to mean all that goes toward making a person attractive to others. It may include the individual's vicacity and alertness. It may cover winsomeness, sweetness, and modesty. The popular definition of personality may include such qualities as "fun-loving," "good sport," "one of the gang," "someone you can count on," and a dozen other characteristics. It almost always includes the quality of *friendliness*.

Persons who are known as having "personality" are usually friendly people. They like others and let them know it. They enjoy being with others. They go out of their way to be nice to others. They find many little ways of letting others know they are liked and respected.

When a television panel of teen-agers recently discussed the question of popularity, they agreed that it is achieved by the person who knows how to get along with people. These articulate young people agreed that it is foolish to try to follow any "personality formula," but rather that being truly popular involves learning how to make friends and keep them.

The Girl Everyone Likes

The University of Michigan asked over a thousand girls between the ages of eleven and eighteen the question, "Think of a girl that everyone likes. Why do they like her?" These teen-agers mentioned many qualities that make a girl likable to others. On some characteristics there was general agreement. The majority mentioned such tendencies as being aware of others in terms of

THE GIRL EVERYONE LIKES [1]	
Why Everyone Likes Her	Per Cent of Girls Responding *
1. Awareness of others (nice, friendly, kind, understanding, etc.)	84%
2. Social skills (equalitarian, good personality, fun to be with, etc.)	63
3. Character traits (honest, dependable, good sport, optimistic, etc.)	43
4. Appearance (good-looking, pretty, well-dressed, neat, clean, etc.)	17
5. Morality (good reputation, decent acting, goes to church, etc.)	5
6. Other (from a good family, is polite, has nice manners, etc.)	6

* Totals more than 100 per cent because some girls gave more than one response.

[1] The Girl Everyone Likes—Descriptive Summary from 1,273 Girls. Survey Research Center, *Adolescent Girls: A Nation-Wide Study of Girls Between Eleven and Eighteen Years of Age* (Ann Arbor, Michigan: Institute for Social Research, University of Michigan, 1957), p. 99.

being friendly, interested in people, kind, understanding, and having the ability to keep confidences. Nearly two-thirds of all the girls mentioned social skills such as having a good personality, being fun to be with, and contributing to good school spirit. More than four out of every ten mentioned character traits such as honesty and dependability, good sportsmanship, optimism, and modesty. If a girl is talented or a good leader, many people will like her. The summary of qualities appealing in girls is seen on page 147.

The older the girl, the more often she mentions such factors as being aware of others and having social skills as what makes a girl likable. Ninety per cent of the girls between fourteen and sixteen mention being aware of others as important. Being kind and keeping confidences are both mentioned more often by the older than the younger girls. Four times as many of the older girls as the younger mention having a good school spirit as important. The older girls seem to be aware of the social skills that matter most in becoming an attractive, popular person.

To Have Friends You Must Be Friendly. In order to have friends, you have to become a friendly person. You need to learn how to get through to the people who can become your friends. You must learn how to get acquainted with people easily. You must learn how to project your personality well enough so that they feel that they are getting acquainted with you. At the same time you become expert in sharing yourself with your friends in a two-way flow of mutual friendship.

Some are more expert than others in making friends. It almost seems at times that some people must be born popular, they do it so easily. Yet, we know that each individual really learns how to become friendly. Even though some find it easy, and others much harder, each individual starts at one point or another to learn what friendliness involves.

You Learn to Be Friendly—First in Your Family

You were born with the potentialities of becoming friendly. But these potentialities do not develop by themselves. No one bursts full-bloom into a happy, lovable person with the fully developed capacity for making and keeping friends. It takes many years of learning to become that kind of person.

This process of becoming a friendly person does not start in your teens. It begins way back in a person's baby days and continues throughout childhood, the teen years, and adult life. What happens when you are growing up makes a big difference in the kind of skills you develop, and the sort of things you do and do not learn. What you do about learning to be friendly from now on determines to a great extent your progress in social development.

Because you grew up in a family, as most people do, your family started you off in the kind of friendship skills you have acquired so far. Because you spent most of your early years at home, these early family relationships are very important in your social growth.

A Friendly Family Helps. If you grew up in a friendly, socially active family, you were fortunate. In that kind of setting you had a chance to learn both by example and by practice how to become a friendly person.

If your mother and father were active in social affairs while you were growing up, you probably were taken along with them to meetings and social affairs. You met people and they met and knew you. You learned how to be introduced and how to acknowledge an introduction. You learned the essentials of fitting easily into a new group of people, as well as making your way among people you knew well. If you grew up surrounded by people who knew and liked you because they knew and liked your parents, you started with a

To have friends, a person must be a good listener as well as a good speaker. He must be warm and outgoing and able to bring as much interest and vitality to a gathering over a soda-fountain table as to a more formal date.

Dorothy Reed from Monkmeyer

healthy feeling that people are friendly. You learned not only how to *be* friendly, but also to *expect* friendliness wherever you go. When you anticipate being liked, you are ready to be friendly, because your experience has taught you that friendships are both easy and pleasant to cultivate.

On the other hand, if your family had very little to do with other people while you were growing up, you very possibly have a great deal to learn about making and keeping friends. If your mother disliked people, or your father was extremely reserved and aloof, so that very few people ever came to your house when you were young, and you were seldom taken to social gatherings, then your friendliness learnings have been delayed.

Eloise, for instance, grew up on a farm a long way from other families. Her father was an unhappy, blustery man who always felt that other people were going to get the best of him if he did not watch out. Eloise was never taken to church or community affairs. She very rarely left the farm until she started school. Even then she saw very little of the other children. Her father discouraged her bringing other childen home from school with her. When she became old enough to be interested in boys, her father was so suspicious of them that she dared not mention a boy or let one come to see her for fear of her father's anger. By the time she was fourteen, she had many imaginary friends and dream lovers, but very few flesh-and-blood relationships either with boys or girls. Eloise was held back in her social development by the isolation of her family and her father's unfriendly attitudes.

Ralph grew up in quite a different family. He was one of six children in a family that lived in a rambling house, loved to entertain people, and enjoyed all of the various activities of the whole town. He learned while he was still a little boy to mind his table manners, so that when he grew up, he was never uneasy in a strange household. Before he was old enough to go to high school, he had played host to his older sister's high-school-age friends, passing refreshments or sitting happily on a stool listening to their chatter. He grew up in such a friendly family that he felt easy and comfortable with people. He knew how to act, having practiced many social skills all his life. Becoming a friendly person was as easy and natural for Ralph as eating his meals or keeping himself clean, and for the same reason—he had learned how from the example of his family.

Few families make it as easy to become friendly as did Ralph's. Many have some handicaps in the social scheme of things. Eloise's home was an extreme of social isolation; Ralph's was at the other end of the scale. Most individuals come from families that fall somewhere in between these two extremes. You are probably neither as deprived of social opportunities as Eloise nor as advantageously situated as Ralph. You can understand both your assets and your liabilities by reviewing how families help and hamper the development of friendliness.

BECOMING POPULAR AND HAVING FRIENDS

Families Help Develop Friendliness by:	*Families Hinder Friendliness by:*
Encouraging children to bring friends home to play, for meals, etc.	Not allowing children to invite friends into the home.
Being active in community affairs.	Being socially aloof or isolated.
Encouraging children to join clubs and participate in social activities.	Keeping children away from groups and activities.
Letting the children feel more important than the material things of the home (furniture, clean floors, etc.)	Keeping such an immaculate house that the children are not allowed to have fun in it.
Helping a child learn good manners by practicing them at home.	Setting such a poor example of how to behave socially that children have to learn a whole new set of manners when they go out.
Sharing responsibilities with the children.	Letting children grow up without the ability to take care of themselves.
Emphasizing interdependence and the importance of belonging.	Accentuating differences and being too proud or ashamed of being different.
Enjoying all kinds of people.	Being snobbish.

Stretching Beyond Your Family. Your family was the beginning but not the end of your friendship learnings. It started your social education, but it is up to you to continue the job of becoming a friendly person. Especially now, as a teen-ager, you must stretch away from your family and find other friends who mean a great deal to you. These are the days when you are neither what you always have been, nor yet what you will become.

You have a two-way outlook as a teen-ager. You look back toward the family from which you have come and see much you want to perpetuate. The warm, friendly customs that made life such fun you want to continue now that you are a person in the position to live your own life. You look ahead and plan what life will be like when you have a home of your own. Perhaps you say to yourself, "Believe me, when I get married, I'm going to have things the way I like them." Right now you are tied completely neither to past nor future. You are free to choose the kind of friends who mean most to you.

During your teen years other adults besides your parents may become especially meaningful to you. A particular teacher, the coach, your minister, one of your youth leaders, or an especially understanding neighbor may already have become the sort of sympathetic older friend to whom you can take your troubles and with whom you can share your dreams without fear of ridicule. He or she may be the kind of person you want to become when you get to be that age. You may have learned a great deal about the deeper meanings of friendship from this special friend.

In all probability you have been in and out of others' homes all your life. But now, when you visit another family, you see things that you never noticed before. You observe the way the members of some families respect and appreciate one another. You notice how they welcome one another's friends into their home and create a warm, friendly atmosphere in which everyone feels at home. You can choose models for your own future family as you see various kinds of families in action. You find new dimensions of hospitality and friendliness sprouting within yourself.

So it is with your relationships with all kinds of people as you stretch beyond your roots. You find friends among people your family never knew. You learn to care about people who grew up halfway across the world. You find yourself becoming aware of millions of people you will never meet and feeling a spirit of kinship with all men everywhere. There is no end to the growth that is possible if you keep striving toward greater understanding and fellowship.

Finding and Keeping Friends

Very young people sometimes dream of becoming the kind of persons whom *everyone* will like. This is an almost impossible dream. You have probably found that there are some people whom, try as you will, you cannot like. So, too, there are some persons who do not like you. You may not know the reason, and they may not understand it themselves, but they just do not feel warm toward you. Rather than believe you can appeal to everyone, you might try to understand why some people do not like you while others do.

The individuals who do not like you may associate you with some previously unhappy experience. They may avoid you because you resemble some person they used to dislike. They may feel that you do not like them, or they may feel they are unworthy of your friendship. They may be looking for more popular people as friends, though this is an unsound basis for real friendship. They may find their needs satisfied better by others than by you. They may not like the things you seem to them to like.

There are many reasons why your friends are your friends. Your friends like you because you are associated with pleasant experiences. They like you because you make them feel worthy and because you include them in your activities. They like you because you satisfy some of their real needs as persons. They like you because they enjoy the things you enjoy—because you share common interests, tastes, and ideas.

There are general characteristics that thousands of teen-agers say they do and do not like in each other.[2] These teen-agers say they like a person who

[2] Harold T. Christensen, "Dating Behavior as Evaluated by High-School Students," *The American Journal of Sociology*, Vol. 57 (May, 1952), pp. 580–86.

By learning new sports, skills, and hobbies, you become a more interesting person. At the same time, you are making friends by participating in new activities.

1. Is physically and mentally fit.
2. Is dependable and can be trusted.
3. Takes pride in personal appearance and manners.
4. Is clean in speech and action.
5. Has a pleasant disposition and sense of humor.
6. Is considerate of others.
7. Acts his own age and is not childish.

When 8,000 teen-agers in this survey listed what they do *not* like in members of the same and the opposite sex, some interesting distinctions were made. Boys tend to be criticized more often than girls for being vulgar in speech and action, for wanting too much necking and petting on dates, for withholding compliments, for being careless in dress and manners, and for being disrespectful to girls. It is interesting that both boys and girls tend to agree that boys offend more often in such traits than do girls.

Girls in the same national survey are criticized for being too easily hurt, being shy and self-conscious, being emotionally cold, being too possessive, and acting childish and silly. Girls agree with boys that these faults are more frequently found among girls than among boys.

Courtesy Makes Friends. The courteous person finds doors opening that are closed to others. The boy who behaves courteously when he calls for a girl impresses her parents and wins their confidence. The girl who is gracious in a gathering of strangers may find future friends among them.

There are certain social forms expected of people generally. It is expected that you will not speak while others in your immediate circle are talking, that you will not interrupt or contradict unpleasantly, that you will not use a voice that is stridently unpleasant. It is expected that you will say "Please" when requesting something of another person, and "Thank you" when receiving anything. It is assumed that you will say "Excuse me" when interrupting anyone, stepping in front of him, or in any way interfering with him. These are essential minimums of good social usage for any fairly well-brought-up person.

There are special forms that are appropriate for particular occasions— good eating habits and courtesies at the table, good manners in public places, on public transportation, in an automobile, in the schoolroom, and at church. You are expected to conduct yourself with consideration for the other people in the situation.

Boy-Girl Manners. Certain courtesies are expected in the relationship between a girl and a boy. The boy is expected to rise when a girl or a woman comes into a room. He is expected to open the door for her and to stand aside and let her precede him through a doorway. In conducting a girl to his automobile, he is expected to open the car door for her, wait until she is seated before closing the door, then go around and get in at his side. In acknowledgment, the girl gives the boy her nod and smile of thanks. Between good friends, and in casual situations, such formalities may sometimes be dispensed with. But in general it is a good idea to know what is the courteous thing to do, and to do it whenever possible.

Boys often complain that the girls they know do not give them a chance to be courteous. The girl dashes through the door before the boy gets a chance to open it for her. She jumps into the car before he has an opportunity to escort her, and she hops out before he ever gets around to open her door for her. The boys have a point. The courteous thing to do is to expect and make way for good manners. As a girl matures, she learns that when she expects a boy's respect and attention, she gets it.

The older you grow, the more people you meet and the larger your circle of acquaintances grows. The foundation of courtesy you build now, through daily practice, will show in your good manners as an adult. Gracious, poised behavior helps you find and keep friends.

What Should a Friend Be? What kind of person is appreciated as a friend? When such questions were asked of several hundred girls in a national study, some interesting findings emerged. The ten top-ranking characteristics of a friend as given by adolescent girls appear in the table on page 155 with the percentage of girls mentioning each quality.

Girls under fourteen years of age mention some qualities far more often than do girls over sixteen; twice as many of the younger girls mention the importance of a girl's being "nice, friendly, or amiable" (32 per cent and 16 per cent respectively). More than three times as many younger as older girls say it is important for a girl to be "co-operative, unselfish, or fair" (20 per

WHAT A FRIEND SHOULD BE [3]

| | *Per Cent of Girls Responding* * | | |
Rank Order of Qualities Mentioned	Under 14	Over 16	Total
1. Loyal, dependable	24%	32%	30%
2. Nice, amiable, friendly	32	16	25
3. Not a gossip	18	23	21
4. Likes the same things, enjoys things together	19	22	19
5. Supports you in trouble	13	17	16
6. Co-operative, unselfish, fair	20	6	14
7. Trustworthy	7	14	12
8. Has moral courage, honest, independent	9	16	12
9. Likes and understands you, considerate	10	12	12
10. Can talk to and confide in her	6	21	11

* Percentages total more than 100 per cent because some of the girls gave more than one response.

cent and 6 per cent respectively). The older girls are more inclined to list such qualities as loyalty and dependability, trustworthiness, moral courage, and the ability to confide.

It is abundantly clear that the best way to find and keep friends is to become a good friend yourself. You hinder your own growth as you continue poor social habits. The time you spend in self-pity is wasted, for the more you mope and moan about how lonely you are, the less likable you become. Belittling those who are popular only serves to make you less attractive. Avoiding social situations in which you might appear shy and awkward or pretending absorption in other interests, fools no one but yourself and delays your development as a friendly person. Only as you make progress in becoming a good friend will you find your friendships increasing in number and improving in quality.

Ten Steps to Becoming a Good Friend

There are some established principles for becoming socially adequate that yield rich returns in friendship. These approaches are not necessarily easy, but they are effective. Few of these methods produce results overnight. But given a real chance, they work, because they are based upon the sound, irrefutable fact that you must do the learning and the growing for yourself.

[3] What 1,273 Girls Say a Friend Should Be. Survey Research Center, *Adolescent Girls* (Ann Arbor, Michigan: Institute for Social Research, University of Michigan, 1957), p. 92.

1. *Accepting and liking yourself as you are.* No one is perfect in anything. Each individual has certain strengths and also certain weaknesses that can be accepted and understood. Expecting yourself to be infallible is self-defeating. Trying to hide your faults is useless, though understandable. Blaming your problems on others only delays your efforts to solve them. Only when you can accept yourself with neither shame nor false pride can you become wholesomely outgoing.

2. *Accepting and enjoying others as they are.* You will never find another person who is just like you. You can expect that every person you meet and come to know is uniquely himself or herself. You can learn to live with the infinite differences among people as you learn to enjoy each for what he is. You like some people "naturally," because they are "your kind of folks." You enjoy them for certain qualities they have in common with you, for the likes and dislikes you share. When you learn to enjoy people who look at things differently than you do, you can deepen your understanding of others and widen your circle of friends.

3. *Speaking kindly and generously of others.* As you go out of your way to be kind in your judgment of others, you find that they begin to appear more worthy in your eyes. When you speak well of another

"Oh, I haven't been waiting long—I went home and ate."

person, you feel more friendly toward him or her. The more generous you are to others, the more kindly you feel toward them. You become friendly by acting like a friend toward people. In time, as you learn to be positive and supportive in your attitude toward others, you become a friend worth having, whom others can truly enjoy.

4. *Being loyal to your friends and justifying their confidence in you.* One of the characteristics of a good friend about which young people feel strongly is that of being the kind of person who is loyal, trustworthy, in whom one can confide without fear. The gossip is rightly avoided. The tale-bearer makes a poor friend. The ability to be loyal, supportive, and trustworthy not only makes you a good friend to others; it also makes you feel more satisfaction in yourself. You know that you are the kind of person whom your friends can count on in a crisis.

5. *Joining with others in doing the things you like to do.* The chances are that you meet your friends doing the things you mutually enjoy. Research studies at Cornell University [4] find that you tend to make friends among people congenial to you. As you follow your interests out into the group life of the community, you find others with whom participating is mutually enjoyable. You join a group interested in things in which you are interested—music, drama, speech, sports, or whatever they are—and you find friends among those looking for the same activities. One of the first steps in making more friends is to become an active member of groups that represent your central interests.

6. *Participating co-operatively in school, church, and neighborhood affairs.* There are all sorts of jobs to be done in the setting in which you find yourself. There are projects to plan and carry through at school. There are programs and activities to carry out in your church groups. There are community jobs that can be undertaken. In joining others to get these tasks done, you become a participating member of a team. You find friends among those with whom you work. You may get an unexpected chance to be a "big wheel" in serving with a clean-up committee, or working behind the scenes in a play.

7. *Focusing your interest and attention outside yourself.* As you mature in your ability to be a good friend, you find that you are less self-centered and more interested in other people and new activities. You can find your own greatest rewards in friendship by losing yourself in worthy causes and thoughtfulness of others. When you get absorbed in something beyond the present moment, you forget your own petty

[4] Carlfred B. Broderick, *Predicting Friendship Behavior: A Study of the Determinants of Friendship Selection and Maintenance in a College Population* (Ph.D. Thesis, Ithaca, N. Y.: Cornell University, June, 1956), p. 231.

annoyances. Through your devotion to a real purpose, you may find your little frustrations ironing themselves out.

8. *Enjoying the give and take of interdependence.* When you were small, you leaned on your parents and other members of your family as a dependent child. Then, as you became an adolescent, you asserted your independence and insisted upon standing on your own feet and living your own life. As you mature in your relationships with others, you find fulfillment in being interdependent. You enjoy doing kindnesses for others. You get pleasure from their doing favors for you. You no longer worry about keeping things "even" or reciprocating tit-for-tat.

9. *Practicing the pleasant, socially approved ways of behaving with others.* No matter where you grew up, or how, there are some rough places in your make-up that can be polished. To win friends, you must become as attractive, graceful, and socially poised as possible. You learn what is the socially accepted thing to do in different situations. Then you practice doing the correct thing until it becomes second nature to you. Becoming a gracious person who makes others feel good is based on a combination of social arts that are learned in conscientious practice in real life situations.

10. *Relaxing and enjoying your life for all that it offers.* The individual who tries too hard to make a success of himself is not a pleasant person to be around. The pushy person who pretends to be something he is not is rarely happy. To keep on growing in a healthy way, you must find satisfaction in each new day and in simple things. Try to relax and feel the fullness of life all about you, the beauty of nature. You can revel in the daily joys and satisfactions of living. You can relish being alive. Then you can personify some of the charm that draws friends to those who know how to live with a deep sense of fulfillment.

Popularity Changes in Time

The person who was most popular in junior high may not be the senior-high favorite. The person who is popular in high school may or may not be later on. Qualities that are generally admired by one group are not those that are most desired in another. This is encouraging. The person who does not rate at the moment may have his turn later, especially if he continues to make the most of his potentialities.

These trends are clearly indicated in the University of Michigan study of 1,273 adolescent girls. A significantly greater proportion of girls under 14 than over think that appearance is what makes a girl popular with boys (56 and 38 per cent respectively). On the other hand, only about half as many younger girls as older ones recognize the importance of social skills in popularity, as is clear in the table below.

WHAT MAKES A GIRL POPULAR? [5]				
	Opinions of Girls			
	Under 14	14–16	Over 16	Total
Appearance (pretty, neat, clean, good figure, etc.)	56%	39%	38%	47%
Way she relates to boys (friendly, sensitive, etc.)	39	44	53	42
Social skills (good personality, nice manners, etc.)	25	47	48	37
Personal resources (not affected, stuck-up, etc.)	31	32	31	30
Morality (good reputation, not sexy, fast, etc.)	7	9	10	9

The change in emphasis as girls mature through the teen years is clear in these findings. The younger girls, who have little experience with boys as yet, put their emphasis on appearance. The older girls, who have begun to date, see what is important for popularity and what is not. So they put their emphasis more on the way a girl relates to boys and her behavior in social situations than on her appearance alone.

A goodly number of both boys and girls who are not particularly popular in high school come into their own later on. They are usually the individuals who are not discouraged by not rating in a crowd, but find and keep friends as they go along. As their friendship circles increase and their social skills improve, they find themselves more and more at home with other people. They do not seek popularity as an end in itself, but rather find it as a by-product of the satisfactions of friendship.

Summary

You want to be popular and have friends. As you analyze what makes a person popular, you realize that you cannot buy friendship. You see that clothes aren't everything, that looks aren't enough. Developing a friendly personality is what counts most. Research studies show that the girl everyone likes is aware of others and has well-developed social skills first of all. In order

[5] Girls' Responses by Age Groups to the Question, "What Makes a Girl Popular with Boys?" Survey Research Center, *Adolescent Girls* (Ann Arbor, Michigan: Institute for Social Research, University of Michigan, 1957), pp. 110–11.

to have friends, you must be a friendly person. You learn to be friendly first in your family. There are ways in which families both help and hinder their children in becoming friendly people. Your families were your beginning, and now you grow on from there as you stretch beyond your roots. With experience, you find that you make friends more readily with some persons than with others—for reasons that can be understood. There are certain qualities that are generally admired. There are basic courtesies and manners that any well-brought-up person must acquire. Studies show that teen-agers think a good friend should be loyal, amiable, compatible, faithful in trouble, trustworthy, honest, considerate, and the kind of person who can share confidences without gossiping. The evidence is that the way to find and keep friends is to become a good friend yourself. There are ten established steps to becoming a good friend that you can use as a guide. If you are not a popular person now, you may have your turn later. For popularity changes in time—as you do.

Suggested Activities

Individual Study

1. Send for the series of nine letters called *Milestones to Marriage* (Mental Health Materials Center, 1790 Broadway, New York 19, New York). Reserve the set for use at appropriate times in your coúrse. Review Letter #2, "Personality and You," in oral or written form, or both.
2. Review Chapter 6, "What Boys and Girls Expect of Each Other," in Evelyn Millis Duvall, *Facts of Life and Love for Teen-Agers* (New York: Association Press, 1956), and compare the research findings summarized in it with those in this chapter. Which ones point in the same general direction? What conclusions do you draw from these surveys of youth?
3. Make a chart similar to the one below in your class notebook. Fill it out as completely as you can by yourself. Then discuss your findings with some of your close friends. If this seems appropriate, consider with your teacher the possibility of having a class discussion on the pros and cons of falling in love at first sight.

MY FRIENDS AND HOW I FOUND THEM

(Do not write in this book.)

My Best Friends	Where We Met	When We Met	How Long It Took to Become Best Friends

4. In your class notebook add to the following two columns the ideas raised in the class discussion supplemented by your own experiences and knowledge.

People feel included when I	People feel left out when I
Smile at them.	Do not look at them.
Ask their advice.	Seem to know all the answers.
Speak to them.	Ignore them.
Use their names when addressing them.	Fail to remember them.
Consider their opinions.	Belittle their ideas.

5. Make a list of clubs and groups in your school that are organized around particular interests and skills. Mark "x" those to which you belong now. Put "xx" next to those you would like to join if you could. After each of these latter, suggest in a word or two what you would have to do to get into the group. Your notebook entry may look like this:

INTEREST GROUPS I WOULD ENJOY

x Those I already belong to
xx Those I would like to join

(Do not write in this book.)

Groups	Skills I Would Have to Develop
x Glee Club	
xx Orchestra	Ability to play a musical instrument
x Swimming Team	
xx Wranglers Forum	Ability to speak out in a group
Basketball Team	
Stamp Club	
Outing Club	
x Y-Teens or Hi-Y	
xx Social Action Club	Keeping up with current issues
Camera Club	
Dramatic Club	
Debating Team	

6. Outline plans for a school fashion show that might be given by your class or club. Include plans for inviting one of the boys' clubs or classes in for criticism or judging. Plan score pads for the boys to mark on the various types of styles if you believe a scoring plan will be valuable in getting the boys' honest opinions.

Consider what might be done to have the girls evaluate boys' school clothing, too. Are there some things that girls would like to change in boys' fashions? Devise in your planning ways for these suggestions to come out.

When each member of the class has made these plans, they can be discussed in class so that a class plan can be made for putting them into effect. Perhaps your teacher and the girls' adviser would be willing to help you sponsor such an event during a club hour or assembly meeting. You may want to recruit the interest of some of your mothers, of one of your town's dress-shop buyers, and perhaps of the boys' department head of your men's clothing store.

Group Activity

1. Produce the skit, *The Ins and Outs* (20 minutes, available from your state Mental Health Association, or from the National Association for Mental Health, 10 Columbus Circle, New York 19, New York). Cast three boys and two girls, including as leading characters the school idol, the most popular girl in the school, and a boy who wants to get "in." Allow ample time after the presentation for discussion of the material.

2. Have a class discussion of the booklet, *Understanding Yourself*, by William C. Menninger, M.D., available from Science Research Associates, 57 West Grand Avenue, Chicago 10, Illinois. Bring out in your class discussion the reasons why people act the way they do toward others.

3. Arrange a showing of the film, *Races of Mankind*, distributed by the Public Affairs Committee, 22 East 38 Street, New York 16, New York. Immediately following the showing of the film, discuss together "Where We Get Our Prejudices."

4. Hold a class debate on the question, "Should Fraternities and Sororities Be Abolished?" In getting ready for it, try to bring together for consideration the many social and psychological factors that are important in the social experiences of people.

5. Put on a series of reality practice scenes in which groups of students act out the behavior that will be expected of them as they (a) ride on the bus to a nearby community; (b) attend a formal banquet; (c) take the train to the state-college campus; and (d) serve as hosts and hostesses at the next school open house or other activities coming up in the near future that will involve the participation of the members of the class.

6. Arrange a panel discussion of boys and girls who are known leaders in your school on the topic, "What Boys and Girls Expect of Each Other." Request your panel leader to turn the discussion over to the entire class for

general participation as soon as the panel has had its first round of shared observations.

7. Interview your school psychologist or guidance director before your class on what personality is and how it is cultivated during the teen years. Ask him or her particularly what is most important for the development of an attractive personality.

Readings

BAILARD, VIRGINIA, and STRANG, RUTH, *Ways to Improve Your Personality* (New York: Whittlesey House, 1951). Two outstanding youth authorities have written this book explicitly to help today's young people grow into friendly, likable, effective people. If you are ready for this kind of guidance, you will want to read the entire book.

BURKHART, ROY A., *The Freedom to Become Yourself* (Englewood Cliffs, N. J.: Prentice-Hall, Inc., 1956). An experienced youth counselor and wise pastor outlines what it takes to become the kind of friendly, effective person who has the capacity of "becoming." See especially in Chapter 12 the section on "Growing Toward Awareness."

CRAWFORD, JOHN E., and WOODWARD, LUTHER E., *Better Ways of Growing Up* (Philadelphia: The Muhlenberg Press, 1948). You may want to take the self-quiz, "How Do I Feel About My Friends?" on pages 97 and 98; and if you are puzzled by friendship problems, ask yourself the five questions on page 99 as a guide to diagnosing the trouble.

DUVALL, EVELYN MILLIS, and HILL, REUBEN, *Being Married* (Boston: D. C. Heath and Company, 1960). Chapter 1, "Dating and Friendship-Making," reviews recent research on who makes friends with whom, when and how, and what it takes to become a friendly person who is ready to enjoy others and to begin satisfactory dating.

PIERCE, WELLINGTON G., *Youth Comes of Age* (New York: McGraw-Hill Book Company, 1948). Chapter 5, "Learning to Be Likable" goes into detail about the habits that make a person friendly, the traits that make you likable, with forty-five questions to ask yourself about your progress in becoming a friendly person.

STRATTON, DOROTHY C., and SCHLEMAN, HELEN B., *Your Best Foot Forward— Social Usage for Young Moderns* (New York: McGraw-Hill Book Company, 1955). This revised edition of a popular book contains up-to-date information on the latest social practices among teen-agers based upon over 9,000 questionnaires sent to young people across the country.

Chapter 9

Getting and Enjoying Dates

Being a teen-ager means having dates—in the minds of most high-school students. In actual practice, dating is not always a part of high-school experience. There are some boys and girls that date. There are others who do not. Who dates? How often? By what age? What do you have to do to get a date? And what do you do with a date when you get one? These are all frequent questions in the minds of today's teen-agers.

When Dating Begins

There are great differences in the ages at which young people begin to have dates. Some girls start having dates while they are still in grade school, and are experienced daters before they reach high school. Other girls and most boys start dating much later and do not actually date much until late in their teens.

When more than a thousand (1,045) boys between fourteen and sixteen years of age were asked whether they were dating or not, more than half of them reported that they were.[1] By the age of sixteen almost six out of ten boys (59 per cent) are dating. Many of the remaining 41 per cent would like to take girls on dates. In another phase of the same study, the 430 boys who were not dating were asked if they would like to date. In reply, the non-dating boys divided about equally, 42 per cent saying "Yes," 43 per cent saying, "No." and the remaining 15 per cent undecided.

A companion study of adolescent girls finds that between the ages of fourteen and sixteen, 73 per cent are dating, in contrast to 59 per cent of the boys. These findings confirm the general observation that girls start to date earlier than boys. Beyond the age of sixteen practically all girls say that they are dating, most of them quite frequently, as we see in the table on page 165.

[1] Survey Research Center, *A Study of Adolescent Boys* (Ann Arbor, Michigan: Institute for Social Research, University of Michigan, 1955), p. 42.

164

Present Dating Experience	GIRLS' DATING EXPERIENCE [2]	Age		
	Under 14	14–16	Over 16	Total
More than on weekends	1%	9%	22%	7%
Weekly, every weekend	4	36	44	24
Fairly frequently, few times a month	3	10	7	6
Occasionally, once a month	4	8	7	6
Rarely, a few times a year	3	5	5	4
Yes, dates, unknown how much	2	4	6	4
Depends on meaning of date, mixes with boys	2	1	1	2
No, don't date	81	27	5	47
No, is engaged or married	–	–	3	–
Total	100%	100%	100%	100%
Number	844	822	259	1,925

Eight out of ten girls under fourteen are not yet dating. In the fourteen-to-sixteen age group there is a sharp increase in dating with only a little over a quarter of the girls not dating at all. Beyond sixteen, more than seven out of ten girls date regularly, and a handful are already engaged or married (3 per cent). Just a few report they do not date at all (5 per cent).

There are many factors determining when a young person begins to date. Encouragement from family, friends, and community are important inter-related factors that make for differences in the age at which dating begins. Even more important is the teen-ager's personal readiness for dating—the level of his or her own maturity and the extent to which the skills of dating are being developed.

Developing Dating Skills

Dating success depends upon ability to develop a set of highly compli-cated skills. Two young people out on a date and obviously enjoying it hugely often make the dating know-how seem very simple. Actually getting and keeping dates is difficult, just about the most complex skill you ever learn!

Learning how to get and keep a date interested is fully as complicated a process as learning how to execute a perfect swan dive. Poised on the end of the diving board, the expert swings out in a long, lovely curve and cuts the water in perfect harmony of motion. The beginner goes through many waste motions, hovers perilously near the edge of the board, makes two or three

[2] Percentage of Teen-Age Girls Dating at Reported Frequencies. Survey Research Center, *Adolescent Girls: A Nation-Wide Study of Girls Between Eleven and Eighteen Years of Age* (Ann Arbor, Michigan: Institute for Social Research, University of Michigan, 1957), p. 107.

false starts, tenses all over, and then, in one final effort, throws himself into the air and hits the water with a resounding thud. It hurts. But it's all part of learning how, in diving or dating. The first efforts are clumsy, but after a great deal of practice, the feeling of ease comes and the person is "smooth."

The skills required for a "smooth" dating technique are perfected, as are all learnings, by understanding what is expected, by practice, and then by more practice. Consider briefly some of the fundamentally essential dating skills that all boys and girls must develop in order to become successful in dating.

Conversational Ability. You learned how to talk many years ago, but you still have to polish up your conversational ability when it comes to chatting with a member of the other sex. Teen-age boys and girls have a way of talking with each other that differs considerably from children's chatter. There are some things that are considered good topics of conversation, and others that are just as definitely taboo. There are rules and unwritten laws about breaking into each other's sentences, about holding the floor too long, about holding up one's own end of the conversation, that every young person has to learn for himself by experience.

There are short-cut words and symbols that may express a whole idea for a crowd. There are witticisms and touches of humor that keep conversation alive and bubbling. There are moments for serious deliberation and other times when being solemnly intelligent is inappropriate. What these various procedures are, how to use them, when, and with whom, often makes the difference between the person rated as a good date and the one passed by as dull.

How to carry on a conversation that suits the time, the place, and the person is an elaborate skill. It means being sensitive to the mood of the other people present. It means being really aware of what is going on under the surface as well as on top. Above all, it means being able to listen, and to hear what others are saying.

A good conversationalist is not the one who is always talking. On the contrary, the highly skilled in conversational ability often speaks very little. He is skilled in his ability to keep up with what is being said, and to contribute particularly appropriate and effective comments that are rightly timed. This does not mean that a good conversationalist waits patiently for others to cease talking so that he can chime in with his story, but rather that he listens to what others are saying and reacts appreciatively to the others' moods and ideas. This *response* to others is important, especially in dating and in mixed-group activities.

Most boys and girls want to feel that they are appreciated and enjoyed for themselves. They like to have reassurance that others are really listening to them when they speak. They look for and enjoy indications that others are responding to them in the social situation. When one can give that reassurance and response, he is considered a good conversationalist, even if he has actually said very little.

Topics to talk about are a puzzle to some young people. The answer in general is really quite simple. You talk about the things in which you both are interested. You talk about the things and the people you both know. You explore each other's experiences and preferences and interests in an effort to get better acquainted with each other. You do not have to memorize jokes or cute sayings or pretend to be informed on subjects about which you know nothing. You are on safer ground when you are yourself and encourage your companion to be himself, too.

Facial Expressions and Gestures. There are gestures that speak volumes between two people, and non-verbal language that is more effective than some of us realize. The boy who has learned to look at girls as though he likes them and is neither afraid of them nor too familiar attracts a girls' friendship without having to say a great deal. The girl who appears to be friendly has already taken the first big step toward getting dates.

Shy, uneasy people, who keep their eyes on their toes or look absently over another's shoulders when they are talking with them, often want to be just as friendly as the person who looks friendly. The difference is that the one has not learned the gestures and the facial expressions that tell other people how he feels. Often it is the shy, embarrassed girl and boy who get the reputation for being "stuck-up," when actually they merely lack some of these little gestures and ways of expressing their interest in others.

When in doubt, *smile*. If someone smiles at you, you feel recognized, accepted, and encouraged. You feel *in*. A smile between two people makes them feel a special mutual acceptance that is warmly pleasant to both of them. A smile is the self-starter to many a conversation. The boy or girl who has learned how to smile, and smiles as though he or she means and feels it, is the person who is off to a good start in dating.

To look directly at the person with whom you are talking is another good general principle to follow. If you do find it hard to look into another person's eyes, it may be because you have been too self-conscious to try really to see the other one. Practice looking directly at others in your relationships with some of your close acquaintances. See how this effort to watch another person's expression heightens your interest in him, and makes you feel like responding to his mood.

Your face should reflect the mood of the situation. If the conversation is light and gay, your face should be relaxed and bright. When the atmosphere is sad, when another person is relating something that hurt him deeply, your face should reflect your feeling of sympathy and understanding. You will find that you understand people better and enjoy them more when you become skilled in sympathizing with them through the situations that you share together.

Some people become artful in special little gestures and expressions that are peculiarly their own. Hank has a winsome little one-sided smile that looks tender and defenseless. It expresses his spirit of genuine friendliness almost better than anything else he says or does. Girls like him when he smiles, and they stay around long enough to like him better, too.

There are some gestures and postures that are so obviously designed to be seductive that they look crude. The boy who winks at all the girls gets the reputation of being unselective. The girl who tries a "come hither" expression too freely runs the danger of being considered common or too "easy." There are many crude gestures, ways of walking and of looking at others that people often resent. These are expressions it is best to avoid.

If handshaking is customary in your community, you should be aware of the fact that your handclasp speaks for you more eloquently than you may realize. The girl with a limp, cool handshake is apt to leave her new acquaintance feeling that she is not very much interested in him. The girl who grabs a boy's hand and pumps it too vigorously may very likely scare him off with her aggressiveness. Somewhere in between is the warm, firm, friendly grip that invites further acquaintance and confidence.

In general you are on safe ground in developing gestures and facial expressions that convey your sympathetic understanding and interest in others. Your manner should be one of easy, comfortable warmth and comradeliness, if you hope to be attractive as a date.

Introducing Yourself into a Group. One of the hardest things that some boys and girls ever have to learn is how to join a group without being either too forward or too retiring about it. If you are too aggressive in attempting to get into a group, the group is apt to close tightly against you and resist your getting in. If you sit back and wait for others to notice you, you may have a long, cold wait.

This skill is especially important for the young person who is new in the community, as is frequently the case these days when families move about so much. It takes some young people a long while to become accepted in the already organized groups in the new school. Those who get into the group easily are those who have perfected the skills of introducing themselves in ways that are pleasant and that make them seem like worthy group members.

Selecting the right group or groups for you is a part of the problem. As you probably recognize, there are some groups that rate in a given school, others that are less well thought of, and still others that have a definitely negative reputation. To associate with the group that has a bad reputation is to take on part of that reputation for yourself. Making sure that the group that you are about to join enjoys a favorable rating is especially important for a newcomer who is apt to be labeled by the company he keeps.

Joining groups should be based on similar interests and tastes as much as possible. In most schools there is a variety of clubs and organizations to appeal to many different interests. Not all boys and girls are happy in the same groups. It is up to you to choose the people who seem most like your kind, who like to do the things that interest you. It is in such associations that dating flourishes, because the boys and girls have interests in common.

Becoming accepted in the group of one's choice may be accomplished in many ways. Cultivating the acquaintance of one of the group members and letting that person sponsor you into the group is generally one of the most effective methods. Another way is to attend an open meeting and assume some helpful responsibility that indicates both your interest and your willingness to be helpful. Sometimes letting an adult sponsor know of your interest in joining a club is sufficient to get you started. In some very close-knit groups it may take some maneuvering from the outside to get you favorable consideration for membership.

Most dating starts from mixed-group associations. So skills in becoming socially active are important requisites for getting into the dating crowd. The boy and girl who are able to introduce themselves easily into group life greatly increase their dating possibilities and choices.

Social Arts in Dating. By the time you are old enough to date, you should have acquired most of the basic social arts that make relationships with people "smooth." There are certain fundamental courtesies that cannot be overlooked if one expects to succeed in dating. Acknowledging introductions pleasantly, expressing gratitude for kindnesses, greeting people pleasantly, saying good-by easily, introducing people gracefully, are all skills basic to feeling comfortable in a social situation.

Even if you have learned most of these things as you were growing up, going out on dates brings many new situations that call for a review of these old learnings and the cultivation of new social skills. Going to a theater involves certain forms of social behavior that both the boy and the girl should recognize if they are to make each other feel comfortable.

Ordering food in a restaurant, etiquette in eating out, and paying the check all require certain specific sets of know-how for both the boy and the girl, if their date is to be really "smooth." Riding a bus or streetcar, taking a cab, traveling on a train or plane requires still another combination of do's and don't's best learned by finding out what to expect and putting this knowledge into practice.

There are many books on manners and the social arts that are generally helpful. Some of them are listed at the end of this chapter. However, it is well to remember that there are differences in what is considered good taste in different groups and communities. It is therefore very important to discover what is expected by your community and the region in which you live. That is the reason why talking over what is expected of each other on a date is so helpful both to boys and girls in any school.

Activity Skills. It is the individual who can do things who has the most opportunities to know people. That is one way of saying that as you cultivate activity skills you enlarge your field of acquaintance and increase your dating possibilities. The girl who plays a musical instrument not only may have access to all the other activities and groups, but also may join the band or orchestra, if she is interested. The boy who can engage in sports and photography moves in a wider circle than does the one who is just interested in photography.

Learning to play tennis, to swim, to skate, to dance, and to do some of the other things that the young people your age are doing pays off in more invitations to join others of both sexes, to go places, and do things.

Cinderella got by on her fairy godmother's skills. Susan and Mary and Alfred today know that no fairy godmother is going to rescue them from their corner. They themselves must get out and associate with others, learn what it takes to do what others are doing, and become socially active, if they are to have the friends and enjoy the dates that most young people of both sexes want.

Your Parents and Your Dates

Your parents have an interest in your dating. They have ideas as to how old you should be before you start to date, whom you should and should not date, how often you should go out, where, and for how long. Parents are rightly concerned with how long you stay out at night, since, after all, they are responsible not only for your safety but also for your reputation. If the neighbors begin to talk about your behavior, they quite often lay the blame for your conduct at your parents' door with this kind of comment: "If I were her mother, I'd see to it that she . . ." Mothers and fathers feel these community pressures; they are actually the go-betweens for both the neighborhood and their children.

Parents and young people often do not see eye to eye on many dating questions. How old should you be before you start to date? How often may you have dates? How about dating on school nights? How well should you know each other before dating? How late is too late to be out? What places are all right and which are questionable places for dating? All these and many others are often questions on which parents and young people disagree.

The methods suggested in Chapter 6 for parents' and young people's discussions of some of these controversial questions are pertinent here, and might well be reviewed at this point. Beyond this is the recognition that parents are people interested in your welfare and, even when they seem to make things difficult, they actually have your interests at heart.

Young people must learn to understand their parents as they are and to take some responsibility for helping their parents understand what things mean to them as children. We find, for instance, that parents often are stricter with their older children than they are with the younger. It is not that they want to make things hard for the first-born child, but rather that they need to become accustomed to their children's growing up and going out and having dates and all the rest that is involved in a child's becoming more mature. If the older children realize this, they can recognize that theirs is the challenge of parent education—of getting their parents acquainted with the activities of the teen-agers and establishing the mutual confidence that helps both parents and young people through the strains of getting started in dating.

Why Some Do Not Date

With so much emphasis on dating among teen-agers, questions about why some persons do not date are inevitable. The answers are many and

"I have the feeling your father doesn't trust me."

complex. Actually, to find out why any particular individual does not date, one would have to know and understand him, or her. There are some reasons for not dating, however, that are common enough to bear summarizing.

1. Some girls, and even more boys, of high-school age are not personally ready for dating. Some individuals mature later than others, and are not physically, emotionally, or socially ready for dating when others of their age are. The answer for them is to seek as many maturing experiences as they can—in mixed-group activities that do not involve dates, until they do build up dating readiness.

2. Some parents are so opposed to their sons' and daughters' dating that they make it difficult for their teen-agers to start having dates. There are some fathers and mothers who openly say that there is plenty of time ahead for going out with members of the other sex and that during high school, time should be applied to school work. A young person in these circumstances who wants a date risks his or her parents' displeasure or the difficulties of having dates without the family's encouragement, in which case knowledge of the date may get back to the parents anyway.

3. Older sons and daughters in large families often carry so much responsibility at home that they have very little time for the socializing that leads to dating. They are the teen-agers who usually have to hurry home from school to care for younger brothers or sisters, help care for the family business, prepare the evening meal, and otherwise carry heavy family responsibilities not shared by other young people. There are satisfactions in feeling that one is carrying real responsibility at home, but these usually do not substitute for those that come with dating experience. In fact, such responsible young people sometimes have to be openly encouraged to mix with other young people and get into situations where dating becomes a possibility.

4. Some boys and girls are so preoccupied with all-absorbing interests and preparations for the future that there is little time or interest for the dating activities. The girl who is preoccupied with her plan for becoming a physician or a musician may forego the pleasures of dating in order to keep her grades up or do the practicing that will assure her of the further technical training that she needs to realize her dreams for future achievement. The boy who has his eye on becoming a research physicist or an electronics engineer may literally have no time for girls.

5. There are some persons of both sexes who never relate personally to members of the other sex. There are not as many unmarried men and women as there once were, but there are many persons of both sexes

who find their satisfactions in areas other than romance and marriage. Many of these individuals live rich, full, interesting lives with quite as much satisfaction as those who rush pell-mell into early commitments in love, marriage, and family life. It is important to recognize that there are all kinds of people in the world, and that just because most people do certain things—like dating, falling in love, and getting married, for instance, is no reason why all others should—unless they want to.

Feelings Affect Dating

The way you feel about yourself and members of the other sex affects you in the way you date and in whether or not you date at all. If you like yourself and are fond of members of the opposite sex, the chances are you enjoy being with them and find fun in dating. If you have feelings of inadequacy about yourself, you may be hampered in getting into the dating scheme. If you are afraid of members of the opposite sex, the chances are your feelings affect your friendships with them, the dates you get and do not get, and your success in dating.

A girl or boy growing up with a feeling of being unattractive and unworthy for any of a number of reasons may not be able to develop easily the skills of getting through to others that come so naturally to many teen-agers.

The girl who grows up with a fear of men is likely to avoid the boys who might be her friends. She may have come by her fear in perfectly understandable ways. Her mother may have confided the painful experiences she had with a brutal husband. The girl herself may have had a frightening experience with a boy or boys early in her life that has made her wary of any further relationship with boys. She may have such a distorted understanding of the nature of sex that she is revolted by any kind of contact with boys.

The boy who grows up under the domination of an overpowering woman may have it in for women, or he may avoid any future relationship with any female who again might dominate him. A boy who early gets the idea that girls are females to be exploited whenever possible shows such a distorted attitude that girls are apt to avoid him as the potential wolf he is. He finds it hard to make a real friend of a girl who might be a pleasant date.

Attitudes Toward Sex Are Central. In any dating situation it is the attitude that each sex has toward the other that determines the nature of the relationship. A boy who accepts girls as persons is able to think of them as dates. A girl who is not afraid of boys is able to enjoy her dates with them.

Sex is a normal part of living. Sex can add deep satisfactions to all phases of life, or it can torment and destroy everything that a person holds dear. The difference lies in the way the person feels about being a member of his sex and in his attitudes toward the opposite sex.

Unwholesome attitudes toward sex are easy to distinguish. One is the tendency to deny or to overemphasize the importance of sex in life. A second is to limit one's sex interest to sheer physical satisfaction, with none of the rich overtones that make sex more completely a human experience. A third is thinking of sex as evil or unworthy or unclean. Such negative feelings about sex emerge out of unfortunate or inadequate sex education.

Limitations in Sex Education. Today's teen-agers are limited in their sex education. Although everyone agrees that a growing young person has a right to know the facts of life, only a relatively small portion get their sex information from what are usually considered reliable sources, as you see in this table.

HOW TEEN-AGERS LEARN ABOUT SEX [3]						
"Where Did You Get Most of Your Information About Sex?"			Mother's Education			
	Boys	Girls	Grade	High	College	Total
From people my own age	53%	42%	49%	47%	45%	48%
From parents	15	32	20	27	26	24
From other older people	7	7	8	6	7	7
From a course in school	5	6	8	4	3	6
From other than above sources	19	10	15	13	17	15

Practically half of all teen-agers get their sex education from friends and others of their own age—usually considered an unreliable source for information of this kind. Only one out of four high-school students whose mothers have a high-school or college education say they got their sex information from their parents. Only one out of five teen-agers whose mothers have a grade-school education got their sex education at home. A very small proportion of all high-school students report getting their sex information from a course in school, and only slightly higher percentages give credit to adults other than parents—perhaps physicians, coaches, physical-training instructors, youth leaders and the like.

Although authorities agree that sex education should begin as soon as a child asks questions about the differences between boys and girls and where

[3] Sources of Sex Information Reported by 8,500 High-School Students. Purdue Opinion Panel, *Report of Poll Number 50, High-School Students Look at Science* (Lafayette, Indiana: Purdue University Division of Educational Reference, November, 1957), pp. 9a–10a.

babies come from, only 1 per cent of the teen-agers polled say they got their information about sex before they started school. The great majority (91 per cent) get their sex education after they had reached the sixth grade.

With such limitations in sex education, some distortions in sex attitudes are to be expected. There are many young people growing up today who will be hampered in their dating because of the limitations in their sex education. There are many other teen-agers who openly seek the guidance that was lacking earlier so that they may find fulfillment in dating, falling in love, and eventually getting married.

Gaining the Values of Dating

Successful dating during the teens has values for the developing personality that cannot be ignored. Get into the swing of things in dating, and you feel "in"—you feel you belong, that all is well with you. Fail to make the grade as a good date and somehow you feel that you are not progressing as you should. Some of the explicit values of dating can be summarized as follows:

1. *Growth in personal attractiveness is rewarded.* Good grooming, appropriate clothing, pleasant manners, and attractive ways with others are often motivated by dating and the desire for dates. Becoming attractive is part of the experience of dating. When a girl feels she rates with the boys as well as with other girls, she reflects her success in a glow that lights her face and wins more admirers. When a boy feels that "his girl" is fond of him, he develops a thoughtfulness and manliness that an unloved boy lacks. Dating success comes with being attractive, and attractiveness comes with dating success.

2. *Poise in social situations develops.* With the new social and cultural interests that dating brings comes a greater feeling of ease in new situations. As a boy and girl learn to enjoy each other's interests, both of them grow in their social skills and their range of activities.

3. *Development of social skills is encouraged.* With dating comes an insistent need to learn the things that are done on dates. A girl and boy have to learn to dance to be part of the dating crowd. They learn to skate because that is fun to do together. They probably learn a number of new sports that they had not mastered before their dating days. Interest in music, art, literature, and other cultural pursuits often encourages new skills and interests with the shared participation of dating.

4. *Understanding members of the other sex is facilitated.* The girl who grows up in a houseful of brothers may know all about boys from them. The boy with several sisters has probably learned a great deal

Since the person at the other end of the telephone cannot see your smile, you must let him "hear" it. This requires not only clear speech and a pleasant voice, but also a warm response to what he is saying.

Bell System Photos

about girls. The teen-ager who has no brothers and sisters close enough in age may have missed out on first-hand contacts with members of the other sex until he or she begins to date. Getting to know individuals of the other sex as people is important in becoming a man or woman. Members of the opposite sex make up roughly half of the total population. Not to know any of them fairly well in a personal way is to miss out on a lot of living.

5. *Forming new friendships is encouraged.* Start to date and you get into situations where you meet many people you would not otherwise know. You get acquainted not only with more members of the other sex, but also with more of your own. As you move freely among other young people, you become part of the paired-off kind of crowd that makes up most of young adult and adult society. Two by two, men and women move together through most social affairs. As you learn to be a member of such a twosome you become the kind of socially accepted person who knows and enjoys all kinds of people.

6. *Learning to live with differences is required.* You grew up in the tight little island that was your home and your neighborhood. As you became a teen-ager, you moved further out into the community, where you met all kinds of people. Dating gets you into first-hand give-and-take experiences with people who are new to you and who have different ideas, different backgrounds, different life styles. You become able to understand, appreciate, respect, and live with these differences as you meet them in the security of the dating situation. Through dating you learn to deal with your differences as they come along.

7. *Learning to plan and to share becomes imperative.* You cannot date for long without having to learn to plan with another person for what you are to do together. You may have been spoiled before you started to date. Perhaps other people always gave in to you. Your date may not be quite as docile, and soon you find that you have to learn to share, to give and take, if your dating is to continue. The time comes in your dating when sharing with another is so much more fun than doing things alone that you find little satisfaction any more in being selfish or bossy. You have learned to work as part of a team.

8. *Developing a sense of humor is encouraged.* You cannot move among others in the dating crowd without learning that a sense of humor saves the day in many an awkward situation. You learn to use humor in your social relations, to kid your way out of embarrassing episodes, and to see the funny side of otherwise tense situations. With experience in dating, you gain perspective on yourself and your immediate problems so that you can relax and get the fun out of everyday situations. In dating you learn the kind of humor that helps rather than hurts. You develop a sense of humor that serves as a lubricant in your human relations.

9. *Establishing ethical standards is a requisite for dating.* You and your date find yourselves in all sorts of situations, facing many kinds of temptations, with many new possibilities from which to choose what you will do, and when, and how. Dating poses such problems as when, whether, and how much to drink or not to drink, to pet or not to pet; when to follow the crowd and when to do what you think best. As you date, you have to come to terms with the kind of person you are, what you are going to stand for, and what you will and will not do. Your standards develop as guides to follow in the normal process of dating.

10. *Standing up for what you believe is right is required.* You have to learn to stand on your own feet and express yourself when you begin to date. Your standards and beliefs are challenged by those with whom you go out. You find yourself put on the spot where you have to stand up and be counted for what you are and what you believe in as a person. This gives you important practice in developing your moral sense and becoming capable of running your own life with poise and responsibility.

You become a good date by learning to respect another's individuality, to conform to your parents' and community's expectations of you, to uphold your own standards without imposing them on others, to accept responsibility for your conduct as a maturing young person free to move among others and find life opening up all about, and to find the fulfillment that comes through wholesome relationships between the sexes.

Summary

Dating begins in the high-school years for most teen-agers. Approximately three-fourths of the girls and six out of ten of the boys are dating by the time they reach their sixteenth birthday. Dating involves the learning of many complex skills including (1) conversational ability; (2) learning attractive facial expressions and gestures; (3) knowing how to introduce yourself into a group; (4) developing social arts in dating; and (5) learning the necessary activity skills. Your parents are necessarily interested in your dates and have a significant place in your dating from the beginning. There are many reasons why some persons do not date, including (1) immaturity; (2) parents' objections; (3) heavy responsibilities at home; (4) preoccupation with other interests; (5) lack of interest in intimate interaction with members of the other sex. Your attitudes toward yourself, toward members of the other sex, and toward sex itself affect your dating. Your attitudes toward sex reflect the adequacy or limitations of your sex education. Most young people get their sex education from persons of their own age after they have reached the sixth grade in school—falling far short of the sex education recommended for wholesome development. There are values to be gained in dating that cannot be overestimated. These include growth in personal attractiveness, learning poise in social situations, achieving skill in social graces, understanding members of the other sex, forming new friendships, learning to live with differences and to plan and share with others, developing a sense of humor, establishing ethical standards and standing up for what you believe is right.

Suggested Activities

Individual Study

1. In your notebook list the most frequent dating activities in your community, and opposite each the approximate cost for a couple participating in that kind of date. Which dates are the least expensive? Which are the most costly? Which are the most fun in your experience? Are the most expensive dates always the most enjoyable? Why, or why not?
2. Prepare an autobiographical sketch outlining the history of your own sex education. When did it begin? How? From what sources did you find out about the facts of life? Which episodes in your sex education remain most vividly in your memory? Why? What books have you found most helpful

in answering your questions? To whom do you take your questions about sex, love, and marriage now?

3. Review Evelyn Millis Duvall, *Facts of Life and Love for Teen-Agers* (New York: Association Press, 1956). Would you recommend such a book as this for your younger sister or brother? Do you wish you had had this book when you were entering your teens? Are most of your questions about life discussed? As fully as you want? What other questions might be taken up in such discussions for teen-agers?

4. Talk over your present dating worries with a trusted counselor, teacher, or youth leader. Prepare yourself for your conference by jotting down the questions you want to ask and outlining in your mind the problems you find baffling in the dating situations you face from time to time.

5. Copy the following list in your notebook. Then put an "x" next to those skills that you have already developed. Put "xx" after those that you would like to develop. Make a definite plan for learning one of these desired skills within the next few months. Write yourself a letter in your notebook outlining what steps you will take to cultivate the desired activity.

ACTIVITY SKILLS

(*Do not write in this book.*)

(x means "I know how"; xx means "I want to learn how")

Bicycling	Baseball	Backgammon
Swimming	Basketball	Chess
Skating	Other sports (specify)	Picnicking
Folk Dancing	Bridge	Hiking
Social Dancing	Other card games (specify)	Photography
Tennis	Checkers	Other hobbies

Group Activity

1. Arrange a symposium of active daters in the senior class on "What You Have a Right to Expect of Your Date." Allow time for the class to query the members of the symposium at the close of the formal presentation.

2. Discuss as a class the characteristics of those who are most successful in dating in your school. Consider how these qualities are developed. What helps? How do dating skills grow?

3. Invite your mothers to a class tea. Serve simple refreshments and then open a general forum session on one of the pertinent questions about dating in which the parents are interested. Summarize the discussion on the board. If there are many helpful points brought out, mimeograph a page of suggestions offered by the mothers and the young people. Send a copy to each home with your class's compliments.

4. Enlist your teacher's help in developing a series of skits portraying "Not that way—but this" in dating etiquette in the following situations:

    a. A school party.
    b. A movie date.
    c. A snack at a restaurant.
    d. A trip to a ball game.
    e. Entertaining at home.
    f. A formal party.
    g. Any other situation of particular interest to you.

5. Arrange to show the film, *You and Your Friends* (available through Association Films, 291 Broadway, New York 17, New York) to the members of your class. Discuss the questions suggested as to good points on manners essential for dating.
6. Role-play the right and the wrong way of acknowledging an introduction to the new girl on a double date—for a boy, and for the other girl. Discuss.
7. Divide the first ten chapters of *The Art of Dating* (New York: Association Press, 1958) among members of your class for a group book review. After each brief report, encourage class discussion of the main points chapter by chapter.

Readings

DUVALL, EVELYN MILLIS, *The Art of Dating* (New York: Association Press, 1958). You will find this entire book given over to how to get started in dating, what is expected of you when you date, how you can have a good time and be a good date. The first ten chapters are especially concerned with getting and enjoying dates.

DUVALL, EVELYN MILLIS, *Facts of Life and Love for Teen-Agers* (New York: Association Press, 1956). The two most frequent questions of 25,000 young people were (1) How do I get a date? and (2) What do I do with a date when I get it? Part 2, "Getting and Keeping Dates," takes these questions up in detail in Chapters 5, 6, 7, 8, and 9.

DUVALL, EVELYN MILLIS, and HILL, REUBEN, *When You Marry* (Boston: D. C. Heath and Company, 1961). Chapter 2, on dating, reviews what you want to know about the kinds of dates there are, how and when you get started in the dating crowd, where to go and what to do on a date when you get it.

KIRKENDALL, LESTER A., and OSBORNE, RUTH FARNHAM, *Dating Days* (Chicago: Science Research Associates, 1949). This life-adjustment booklet is written by two youth experts who offer you sound guidance on what to do if you don't date, how to get off on the right foot in dating, and what problems you can expect to meet in your dating.

LANDIS, PAUL H., *Coming of Age: Problems of Teen-Agers* (New York: Public Affairs Pamphlets, 1956). Aspects of the dating problem discussed in this helpful booklet are: What if you don't have a date? How do you behave on a date? What about a kiss on the first date? What about dating and sex?

Chapter 10

Going Steady

What about going steady? Is it all right to go steady while in high school? Why do parents object to your going steady? How far should you go with a "steady?" How can you say "No" to a steady friend without losing his friendship? Can you expect high-school friendships to last? These are typical of the questions that both boys and girls ask. They are good questions, deserving the best insight you can bring to bear upon them.

Going steady is an understanding between a boy and a girl to date only each other. The understanding may or may not be arrived at by discussion and agreement, but it is none the less real to the boy, the girl, and their friends. When a boy knows he can count on a girl to save all her dates for him while he asks her and only her to go out with him, they are going steady. To go steady with a person is to have an option on the other's dating time. As long as two people remain available only to each other for social engagements, they are going steady.

What About Going Steady in High School?

Teen-agers are not in complete agreement about the question of going steady. Some believe that it is a good thing to do, others strongly disapprove it, and still others say, "It depends."

When thousands of tenth-, eleventh-, and twelfth-grade students were polled in 1957, half of them approved of going steady, one out of four was undecided, and almost one out of five said high-school students should not go steady.[1] More boys (53 per cent) than girls (46 per cent) approve of going steady while in high school. Only 16 per cent of the boys and 20 per cent of the girls say high-school students should not go steady.

There are more juniors and seniors (25 per cent) than sophomores (20 per cent) undecided about the question. Slightly higher percentages of tenth-

[1] Purdue Opinion Panel, Poll No. 49, *Youth's Attitudes Toward Various Aspects of Their Lives* (Lafayette, Indiana: Purdue University, April, 1957), p. 9a.

182

graders (52 per cent) than of eleventh-graders (47 per cent) and twelfth-graders (49 per cent) approve of going steady.

Going steady is more generally accepted among certain groups than among others. A significantly greater proportion of urban than of rural teenagers think they should go steady while in high school (53 per cent and 41 per cent respectively). More young people from high-income (52 per cent) and medium-income (57 per cent) families than those from families with low incomes (43 per cent) approve of going steady. Fewer students in the South (44 per cent) approve of going steady while in high school than in other regions of the country (West—56 per cent, East—51 per cent, Midwest—50 per cent).

When several hundred dating high-school boys between the ages of fourteen and sixteen were asked, "How often do you date?" only 7 per cent said they were going steady, as is clear from the table below.

BOYS' DATING PATTERNS: AGE 14–16 [2]	
"How often do you date?"	Per Cent
Going steady, as often as there is time for it	7%
Weekly, every weekend, twice a week	30
Fairly frequently, a few times a month	22
Occasionally, once a month	21
Rarely, a few times a year	17
Not ascertained	3
Total (617 dating boys)	100%

In a parallel study of adolescent girls, less than a fifth of the girls between eleven and eighteen years of age had a clearly positive feeling about going steady. Almost half of nearly two thousand girls expressed negative feelings about the whole idea, as you see on page 185, in the rank order of attitudes toward going steady.

With so many negative and conditional attitudes about going steady, the next question is, why is going steady so common? Why do teen-agers go steady?

Why Couples Go Steady

Sometimes couples start going steady almost by accident. At other times, going steady is the result of slow, considered deliberation. Here are some of the more frequently mentioned reasons couples give for going steady.

[2] Frequency with Which 14- to 16-Year-Old Boys Date. Survey Research Center, A Study of Adolescent Boys (Ann Arbor, Michigan: Institute for Social Research, University of Michigan, 1955), p. 44.

Mutual Preference. When a boy discovers a girl whom he likes better than any of the others, he may ask her to go steady with him. If she would rather go with him than with any other boy who might ask her, she may consent to be his steady girl. From then on they save their dates for each other and do not go out with others as long as they are going steady.

Sometimes even young boys and girls love each other so much that they prefer each other's companionship to that of all others who might be available. When you are in love, you want to be near the one you love. You try to get the entire attention of the loved one, and like to know that your affection is returned. Going steady with the one you love assures both of you time together and protects each of you from the intrusion of outsiders. This brings a sense of belonging that is important and a kind of security with each other that means a great deal. But mutual affection is only one of the reasons why couples go steady.

Social Security. When a girl has a steady boy friend, she is sure of having a date when she wants one. She need not fear missing parties and social affairs when she has a boy she can count on as an escort. Boys, too, report that even though they may take the initiative in asking a girl for a date, there is much more security in knowing that they will not be turned down when they are going steady than when they are making a new choice each time they date.

Conformity to Local Customs. There are some communities where so many of the young people are already paired off in steady couples that young people are almost required to go steady. Schools differ widely in their social make-up. In some schools most of the social affairs are planned on a stag or group basis where a regular date is not necessary. In others, most of the fun is on a couple basis requiring a date for participation. Where couples are already paired off as steadies, you almost have to have a steady in order to go out at all.

Social Pressure. Sometimes getting started as a steady couple occurs almost by accident. John takes Mary to a game Friday night. They are seen out together the next week, and before they realize it everybody is expecting them to go only with each other. The other boys consider Mary John's girl, and so do not ask her to go with them. The other girls begin to assume that Mary is going with John. They are invited to affairs as a couple. Mary begins to expect that John will call, and she waits for his invitations. John knows that he is expected to pair off with Mary, and that she is anticipating her dates with him. They have not discussed whether they should go steady. They may never have agreed that they wanted to go steady. They simply *are*.

Practical Considerations. Girls are surprised sometimes to discover that boys have some very practical matters to consider in their dating. When a boy takes a new girl out, she expects him to "show her the town." Buying her

GIRLS' VIEWS ON GOING STEADY [3]

"What do you think about the idea of going steady?"	Under 14	14–16	Over 16	Total *
		Age		
Negative Responses: (Total)	25%	55%	66%	44%
Not good, prevents knowing other boys	9	22	22	16
Not a good idea—general	4	3	5	4
Not good while in high school	3	5	9	4
Too serious, implies intention to marry	2	5	4	4
Not good, I don't like it, miss too much fun	2	5	5	3
No training for picking a marriage partner	–	3	2	2
Just done to be sure of a date	–	2	6	2
May get too involved sexually	–	1	1	1
Other	5	9	12	8
Conditional Responses: (Total)	28%	38%	49%	34%
All right if you really like the boy, know him well	11	16	20	14
If involves serious relationships, if plan to marry	4	4	11	5
If girl has first known a lot of boys	2	3	5	3
If it's not too demanding, if they don't get too serious	2	5	4	3
If the girl's parents approve	3	2	1	2
Other	6	8	8	7
Maturity as a Condition: (Total)	34%	27%	17%	29%
If the girl is old enough—general	12	10	5	10
The girl should be 17 or 18	9	7	4	7
The girl should be in high school	4	2	–	3
The girl should be mature enough	2	4	5	4
Other	7	4	3	5
Reaction Is Generally Positive: (Total)	14%	19%	23%	19%
I like it, good idea—general	8	7	6	8
Learn to get along with boys	2	6	7	5
You get to know a boy well	1	2	4	2
Other	3	4	6	4
Don't know	11%	3%	–	6%
Not ascertained	3	6	3	4
Total numbers	844	822	259	1,925

* Percentages total over 100% because some girls gave more than one response.

[3] Teen-Age Girls' Attitudes Toward Going Steady in Rank Order. Survey Research Center, *Adolescent Girls: A Nation-Wide Study of Girls Between Eleven and Eighteen Years of Age* (Ann Arbor, Michigan: Institute for Social Research, University of Michigan, 1957), pp. 108–9.

flowers, taking her to a play, buying refreshments, paying taxi fare, and all the other expenses involved, oftentimes make this kind of dating rather expensive. A steady girl, on the other hand, is apt to be more thoughtful of her escort's finances. She may propose less expensive dates from time to time. She may reciprocate by inviting the boy over to her house, or out on a picnic which she supplies. They may find a great many things to do together that cost very little: taking walks, studying together, coke-dates, visiting museums, the zoo, city parks, trips with each other's family, and many, many other pastimes available to couples who know each other well enough to relax from the more expensive forms of formal dating.

Probably most couples have never analyzed just why they are going steady. If they did, they would quite possibly find that there was not only one reason, but many factors involved in their going with each other.

Advantages of Going Steady

Many of the advantages of going steady have already been mentioned or implied, as summarized here. When you go steady, you

1. "Belong" to someone who "belongs" to you.
2. Go with someone whom you prefer to others.
3. Are sure of a date when you want one.
4. Are in the social set made up of steadies.
5. Can have informal, inexpensive fun with a person with whom you can relax.

Steady couples often find a tender thoughtfulness growing into their dates that is warmly satisfying. Each waits until the other has expressed his wishes before a decision is made. Each considers the other before committing himself to social engagements. Each becomes interested in the other as a person as well as a date. It is not infrequent for a girl to encourage and stimulate her friend to do better in his school work. He may listen to her troubles and help her make important decisions. They find that as they stand together in various issues, each feels more secure. They discover the satisfaction of having someone to confide in who understands, and so increasingly they share with each other things that mean most to them.

This quality of thinking and feeling and acting as a couple is a sort of dress rehearsal for the companionship of marriage. As such, it may contribute a great deal to the emotional development of a boy or a girl. In their concern for other factors, adults may not appreciate these real advantages that mean a great deal to the young people involved.

Disadvantages of Going Steady

Parents often regret the tendency of young people to start going steady so early because they see its many disadvantages. Since an intelligent understanding depends upon seeing both sides of a question—its advantages and its limitations, let us look at the hazards involved in going steady too soon.

Friendships Are Limited. When a boy and girl start going steady too soon, they cut off the many possibilities both might have for dating and knowing other people whom they might enjoy if they gave themselves a chance. When you consider that the teen years are the only ones in which people are generally free to go around with many others of the opposite sex, you see that going steady limits these opportunities for becoming acquainted with the kinds of boys and the kinds of girls that there are. As parents often point out, once you settle down, you have to go together for a long while. Therefore, there is a point in taking advantage of the freedom for variety that "open-field" dating offers before you settle down into going steady.

Choices Are Narrowed. You marry someone you know. When you know only the one with whom you have been going steady, you have a very narrow choice indeed. Only by dating many people can you exercise any real choice in deciding on a lifetime companion.

One of the hazards of very early marriages is that the partners have not given themselves a chance to discover the kind of person who will be a permanently satisfying companion. When you start going steady too soon, you deprive yourself of the opportunity of finding out what it feels like to go with someone else. Later you may look rather wistfully at other kinds of companions whom you might have tried out in dating if you had not been in such a hurry to go steady.

Someone has suggested that going steady is something like going down the cafeteria line and getting ice cream for dessert every time. We have nothing against ice cream; it is a good food. You might decide you wanted to have nothing else but ice cream. But if ice cream becomes a habit too soon, you may never learn how good pie or cake or strawberry shortcake tastes, and so you miss out altogether on any real choice.

Choosing a mate wisely is an important step toward a permanently satisfying marriage. To limit your choice by not having a variety of possibilities is, on the whole, a short-sighted and ill-advised policy.

Personality Development May Be One-Sided. It is commonly recognized that we develop and grow out of our responses to the people with whom we are associated. Look at this from the viewpoint of your own experience. Have you ever noticed that you feel different with each of your various friends? Did it ever occur to you that you are a slightly different *you* with different people? With one person you may be self-sufficient, with another dependent, with still another you may take the responsibility for both of you. With one friend you may feel "good," with another just slightly naughty, while still another makes you feel relaxed and normal. With one friend you may be able to talk very easily, with another you find it hard to express yourself, with still another you may find yourself in sparkling repartee that amazes you. This comparison has countless possibilities. The more friends you have, the greater the variety of your own reactions. The more different responses you experience, the fuller the development of your personality.

To be truly mature involves in part the exploration and development of the various facets of our own personality. When you limit the scope of your friendships, you close off whole areas of your potential development as a person. In these days when you live in such a complex and demanding world, it becomes increasingly important for you to round out your growth in many directions before you become too set in one way or another. To go steady too soon handicaps your fullest development of the variety of responses of which you are capable.

Getting Involved. Some couples become so involved with each other that all else takes second place. Close friends of the other sex are of course exciting, and they may be highly stimulating and satisfying. But when they take up so much time and attention that there is little place for anything else, then they may rightly become a cause for concern.

Jill and Andy have been going steady for some time now. They see no one else. Andy calls for Jill in the morning so that they can walk to school together. They sit beside each other at school. They eat lunch together. He walks home from school with her. He calls her up every evening. Three evenings a week they have a date together. Jill's life is so full of Andy that she finds it hard to study. When he isn't sitting by her side, she finds herself daydreaming about him. When she sits down to study at night, ideas of what she can tell Andy when he calls come chasing through her mind. He, too, finds it hard to keep his mind on his studies. Other friends, their families, their work, their other interests all are neglected. This one relationship becomes so absorbing that nothing else seems important. Is it any wonder that their parents, their teachers, and their friends feel that they are taking each other too seriously?

Responsibility for Standards

There used to be a time when the responsibility for the conduct of a couple rested almost entirely with the girl. She was supposed to know how intimate she should let the boy be and see to it that he met her standards. The boy, on the other hand, felt justified in going as far as the girl permitted. If anything happened, she was to blame. Standards were her responsibility.

Sybil Shelton from Monkmeyer

People going steady share many informal, inexpensive activities. This is one of the ways by which they can find out how much they really have in common.

This situation still prevails in some communities, but it is not as common as it once was.

Intelligent people today realize that the boy has some responsibility for his conduct, too. Girls are no longer looked upon as mere playthings, but are increasingly regarded as companions who are appreciated, respected, and recognized as persons.

Now that many girls and boys share responsibility for the extent of their intimacies, it becomes increasingly important for them to know how far they may safely go in expressing their affection, and when it is wise to stop.

Becoming Too Intimate. When a normal girl and boy see a great deal of each other to the exclusion of everyone else, the usual expressions of affection soon seems inadequate to express the depth of their feeling for each other. There comes a time in the experience of many couples when friendly hand-holding, a good-night kiss, or a tender pat may not meet the deep-felt need to communicate in some especially close way the peculiar attraction that pulls them together. Then it is that parents, who are often cannily wise in these things, begin to worry if the couple is alone too much. Then it is that the young people themselves face a critical point in their relationship.

Maintaining Standards. How can a couple know when they are going too far in their love-making? What signs and signals should they be on the look-out for? These are good questions, worthy of your most careful thought.

When either or both members of the couple feel urgently impelled to continue the love-making, it is time to stop before it gets out of bounds. Nature causes lovers to respond in a spiraling crescendo of feeling that is easier to halt in its early stages than when it is near the peak of excitability. Two people who really love each other enough to protect themselves from ill-advised behavior guard against becoming so intimate that they are compelled to continue.

When a boy and girl go so far that they are left tense and over-stimulated, they have gone too far. If either of them has difficulty in getting to sleep after they have had a date, they probably have gone farther than they can take comfortably. If they find themselves spending their time together anticipating the hour when they will be alone for their love-making, it probably has begun to assume compulsive proportions.

When either or both members of the couple feel embarrassed the next morning, when they cannot meet each other's eyes in the same old friendly way, when she wonders how he feels about her now, and he feels guilty about having gone so far, they have gone too far.

Refusing to Be Exploited

There are some people of both sexes who enjoy seeing how far they can go in exploiting their dating partners. Occasionally a girl exploits the boy she is out with by getting him excited and tempting him into actions that get them both into trouble. Such a girl may be trying cold-bloodedly to "get her man" by making him responsible for their continuing relationship. She may be impulsively "playing with fire" not because she loves the boy, but because she wants to see how far she can get him to go with her. There are some female teasers who delight in getting the boy so excited he can hardly contain himself and then shrugging him off. Such ways of tempting a man are as old as Eve, and may end in both partners' banishment from the garden of bliss.

Even more common are the exploitive tactics of the male who aggressively tries to take his date farther than their relationship calls for. Recent studies show clearly that most girls have to "fight off" aggressive boy friends several times in their senior year at high school. Many of these exploitive attempts take place on first dates. Others occur between couples who are going steady. Before they have gone steady very long, most girls find it necessary first to define their relationship in terms of just how much intimacy is appropriate, and then to refuse to become involved beyond that point.

Wanting to Do the Right Thing. Most teen-agers want to be accepted and respected. They want to do the right thing in so far as they are able. And from time to time they need to be reminded of their goals and given a chance to see the sense in doing the right thing.

The greatest satisfactions in life come in your associations with other people. The warm glow of friendship, the gentle tenderness of true affection, the rich depths of marriage and parenthood, all are built on foundations of mutual respect and consideration. As you learn to care for others, you want their happiness as well as your own. You leave behind you many tendencies to exploit others for your own immediate satisfaction as you grow out of childhood and into more mature love relationships.

Moral codes are built upon the experience of the centuries in protecting the rights and values of people in their relationships with each other. These rules for living with one another are so bred into you that you cannot comfortably depart very far from them. As you yourself grow up to the place where love and marriage and children of your own become goals worth striving for, you find yourself increasingly willing to make the investments of patience and worthy living that they require.

There are always some young people in every school who disregard the rules and try out dead-end routes to happiness. We all know them. Agnes and Anthony were up before the principal for indiscreet behavior at the last school party, while Zelma and Mitzi were sent for treatment of their love-sick crush on each other. Such things are common enough to make us wonder what the trouble is in such a case.

The evidence is that most people who seriously deviate from the moral standards have something the matter with them. Sometimes they are unhappily disturbed personalities who will become happy and well-adjusted only under helpful treatment. More often they are inexpert learners who need to develop the skills for behaving more adequately. A considerable number of young people get involved in relationships beyond their depth just because they have not yet learned how to say "No."

Saying "No." Saying "no" does not need to be difficult. It is better to stop at a middle ground that you can live with comfortably than to go on to a point that is wrong for you. One of the most important things any boy or girl has to learn is how to avoid temptation, keep out of danger, and say "No" effectively. Here are five steps in refusing an unwelcome invitation to more intimacy than seems right to you:

1. *Who You Think You Are.* As soon as you know who you are, what kind of person you are and want to become, it becomes relatively easy for you to decide what you will and will not do. If you are always upset with a fear that you will miss something if you refuse an invitation or resist a temptation, your life will be in turmoil. You start your learning of how to say "no" with a base line of understanding of who you are.

2. *Be Kind, Be Firm.* You do not need to make a scene when you say "no." You do not need to slap a boy's face or run or make a crisis out of the situation. Suppose that someone is suggesting something (by word or gesture) that you do not want to do. Very firmly you let the other person know that, although you like him (or her), you do not like the proposed behavior. You are gracious about it when you keep the atmosphere casual and comfortable.

3. *Help Save Face.* Our Oriental neighbors follow a very important principle. Whenever another person might be hurt or put in an embarrassing position, they are careful to see that he "saves face." They recognize that his feelings are important. If he feels less worthy, or bad, or insulted, he has lost face, and the friendship suffers.

   Girls must learn that they can resist a boy's advances without losing his friendship. When a girl must refuse a boy the intimacy he seeks, she must be particularly careful to protect his opinion of himself, to save face for him. As she learns to handle such situations, she discovers a wide variety of easy, comfortable devices to help both him and her stay on an even keel.

4. *Discussion Helps.* Boys and girls are beginning to discover that they can understand each other much better when they discuss frankly the things that bother them as they come along. There is no reason why the discussion of feelings and behavior between a boy and girl cannot be both wholesome and helpful.

Group discussion is often especially helpful under good leadership. When boys talk over what they expect of a girl on a date, it helps them clarify their thinking and gives the girls some knowledge of how most boys feel about it. Conversely, it helps boys to hear girls discuss what they expect of a boy on a date. It is for these reasons that young people's groups in churches, YMCA's and YWCA's, and similar agencies so often schedule panel discussions of boys and girls on such questions of dating behavior as have been discussed here. Many schools, too, offer opportunities for young people to think through together the kinds of conduct and codes of behavior that are appropriate for their times.

Breaking Up

Many "steady" attachments don't last very long. The American girl typically goes steady with from five to seven different boys before she eventually finds the man with whom she wants to spend the rest of her life. Some relationships break up in an angry flare-up of contention. Others just fade away, leaving neither of the pair very sorry that they are "washed up."

Most high-school romances do not last long enough to lead into marriage. This is nothing to worry about. To grow up means to develop interests, to clarify values, and to mature beyond childish attachments. Friendships at every age are important in themselves. They are satisfying and meaningful to the people at the time. Each leaves its contribution in the lives of those who share them. Even if a steady couple breaks up never to meet again, each will continue to influence the other in the many shared experiences and feelings they developed together. One of the finest arts in growing up is being able to move on and not cling to the old milestones. Knowing when to break off and when to make up and start over again is one of the learnings to be developed in any relationship.

Parting may be "such sweet sorrow," as Shakespeare expressed it, when you are leaving the relationship where it can easily be picked up again. Breaking off a relationship that has meant a great deal can be, and often is, a bitter, painful experience. Yet relationships do break. Friends part. Couples who have been going steady frequently get to the place where breaking up seems to be the only possibility.

Why Steadies Break Off. There are many reasons why couples who have been going steady break off. One of the most frequent reasons is that they have outgrown each other. This is especially true in the teen years, when development is so rapid. Then interests, needs, skills, and habits shift and change as growth takes place, so that a quite congenial companion at one stage of development becomes boring and uninteresting at the next.

Elise was appealing to Jonathan when he was first beginning to notice girls. She had a cute little-girl way about her that made him feel grown-up and important. But as he became more at home with other girls and boys of his age, he was no longer satisfied with Elise as a companion. He broke off with Elise when he was ready for more variety in experience. It was not Elise's fault. They had just outgrown each other.

As your interests change, your companions shift, too. Gloria had been going steady with Tim for many months. They were good pals and had great fun with the crowd of other couples at the teen canteen in their neighborhood. Then Gloria won a scholarship and began thinking seriously about going on to college. Larry was studying for his entrance examinations at the same time, and before either of them really knew the extent of what was happening, Gloria was too busy to spend much time with Tim and was seeing a great deal of Larry. Perhaps it is in this area of common interests that the old saying, "Birds of a feather flock together," is most often true.

"Please return all my childish, mushy letters, Laurie. I want to use them again."

Times-Mirror Syndicate, Los Angeles

Steadies sometimes break off when their relationship has gained a momentum that one or both of them finds uncomfortable. When they have become deeply involved with each other to the exclusion of all else, the relationship may break of its own weight. Carey broke off with Mae quite suddenly after a heavy date when he had gone further in his love-making than he could face up to the next day. He had literally scared himself with the feelings that were aroused as he caressed her, to the point where he just could not continue to see her. This is a more common reason than many young people realize for sudden, unexpected, and unexplained breaks in boy-girl relationships.

What It Means to Break Off. Breaking off with a steady is often painful. Sometimes, of course, both tire of the relationship at about the same time and mutually agree to see less of each other. Or there may be an emotional scene over some issue which leaves each partner hurt, angry, and perhaps a little resentful of the other. This is the "I never want to see him again" kind of break that comes like the eruption of a volcano, sudden, dramatic, unplanned, and unexpected.

When one person cares more than the other, there is apt to be real hurt at the time of the break. Such uneven involvements are common. Take Janice, for instance. She simply adored Stanley through the months that they were going steady. She glowed in his presence. She talked unceasingly of him both at home and at school. He filled her life completely. Stanley, however, was not nearly so interested in her. He enjoyed the boys on the team, and the other young people of both sexes at church. If he had been really honest about it, he would have preferred not going steady at all, but he didn't want to hurt Janice, so he never mentioned it until her clinging adoration simply became intolerable. When he finally broke off with Janice, she was terribly hurt, while he felt both relieved and guilty about it.

Or take Becky, for example. Roger has been a faithful friend for a long while. He assumes that she will always be waiting for him. But she does not feel the same way about him. Now that Josh has begun to show an interest in her, she would like to discourage Roger's constant attention. But she does not want to hurt his feelings. What shall she do?

How to Break Up. There are two extreme ways to break up. The one extreme is just to walk out. One day you may be going steady and the next there may be nothing there. Boys often break up this way. They simply do not come around any more. No telephone calls. No notes. No significant glances. No anything to mark what was once a steady boy friend. This method works, but it hurts. The girl left without any explanation whatsoever is bewildered, confused, lonely, defenseless in front of her friends. She has no answer to the question, "What happened?"

The other extreme, more frequently used by girls, is the long, drawn-out harangue of slights and hurts. "What have I done to lose your love?" the girl persistently asks. "What can I do to make you love me again?" All in vain, too often. Because he doesn't know either! Few can understand enough about why and how they love each other, especially when they are in the midst of such an involvement, to be able to analyze it very well. These prolonged probings into why things can't "be like they used to be" are apt to keep the wound open without helping much.

In between these two extremes is the happy medium in which both try honestly to recognize and accept the cooling-off of their relationship and gradually see less of each other. This method requires a real sensitivity to needs of both partners. It requires a considerable degree of maturity, too. Only a relatively mature boy or girl can admit to himself or herself that he or she is less lovable to the other one than before. The ability to accept the waning as well as the waxing of friendship comes with experience. Only after it has happened a few times do most people learn to relax and go on without being too deeply crushed. Everyone must learn how to be wiser about these things, and somehow each must learn for himself.

Drifting Apart. Many couples drift apart after a while. Being away on a vacation over the summer is enough to put an end to many steady relationships. When one or both members of the couple get off to another spot, meet new people, and develop new interests, they often find that when they meet again in the fall, they do not "click" as they once did. This is especially true if they have not kept up their correspondence during their separation. Letter writing is an art that comes with experience. Communicating meaningfully with another person whom you do not see over a period of time requires a maturity of devotion that is often lacking during the teen years. And so the partners drift apart.

Taking a Breather. Breaking off with a steady is often somewhat of a relief. It gives you a chance to clean up your room, catch up on your reading, and even see something of the family for a change. There are some real students who knock off going steady for several weeks around examination time so that they can get some serious studying done! Others enjoy the shift in tempo and the breather that comes with the release from heavy concentration on the "one and only."

Katie seemed to come alive again when she and Don broke up. First she cleaned out her dresser drawers, and that led to rearranging her whole room. She felt so pleased about how things looked, that she had some of her old girl friends over for lunch, something she had not had time to do for months. The following weekend she visited her cousin, who lived a three-hour bus ride away, and had great fun visiting relatives she had not seen in ages. She

"You worry unnecessarily, Laurie. If I were in love with Natalie Wood, wouldn't SHE be here on Lookout Mountain with me?"

Times-Mirror Syndicate, Los Angeles

so enjoyed being free again that she took her time about getting back into circulation. She found it a relief to be on her own without a devoted friend hanging around all the time. Boys say that when they break off going steady they, too, sometimes experience a sense of relief that has its own satisfactions.

Getting Back into Circulation. If you find that life goes on, and is even fun without dates for a while, you will not have trouble getting back into circulation again. If not, you may waste hours of anguish trying to blow warmth into the cold ashes of your last love. Or you may get so into a panic about not having a dating partner that you overplay your hand and find more difficulty in getting started once more than if you relax and gradually ease back in. When you are ready to have dates again you can go to mixed affairs either alone or with a friend of your own sex. If you are friendly to everyone, and if the situation seems right, you may see a likely girl home (or may be seen home by a boy). A movie comes along that you may see together. You may both work on the same committee at the church. And before you know it, you have a date whenever you want one.

Dividing your time among several people who interest you is a good plan. Then you give yourself a chance to date without being tied down to any one person. You are wise to cultivate a variety of interests and to associate with several different groups. Friends and interesting companions appear in many of these varied groupings. You can string along with several of them without having to battle the green-eyed monster, jealousy. At this stage, it is not fair to lead one date on which the false expectation that he (or she) is the only one. Nor is it sensible to talk extensively about your other dates when you are paired off with still another. Being a pleasant companion and neither giving nor expecting too much exclusiveness is the secret to success in getting back into circulation again.

Marriage May Be the Next Step

There are high-school couples who fall in love while they are very young, go steady all through school, and then get married soon afterwards. There are many other things to consider before marrying and settling down besides the feelings two people have for each other.

There comes a time in the life of the typical young adult when the person with whom he or she has been going steady begins to appear as a potential marriage partner. Although most marriages take place between men and women who first knew each other as steadies, going steady is no insurance that two people will find each other suitable as mates. In fact, most people marry only after making and breaking several steady attachments, as you saw earlier in this chapter. When two people going steady get well enough acquainted to know each other's hopes and dreams, feelings and values, a sense of mutual understanding develops. When both members of the pair sense they are right for each other, and feel mature enough to make a permanent decision, marriage, for them, is the next step.

Summary

Going steady is not universally approved by either boys or girls, for many reasons. But many teen-agers report that they go steady for such reasons as (1) mutual preference; (2) social security; (3) conformity to local customs; (4) social pressure; and (5) practical considerations. There are real advantages in going steady, one of the greatest of which is the "we-feeling" that grows through the companionship. The disadvantages of going steady mentioned most frequently are: (1) friendships are limited; (2) choices are narrowed; (3) personality development may be one-sided; (4) getting involved may be over-absorbing; and (5) the temptations to intimacy may become a problem. Both boys and girls are responsible for standards of conduct. Both must learn how far to go and how to stop their expressions of affection in time to keep their relationship on a wholesome basis. Both sexes have to learn how to refuse to be exploited. This means wanting to do the right thing and learning how to refuse invitations to inappropriate intimacy. Some romances don't last. Breaking up often indicates changes in goals and expectations of one another. Breaking up may be a part of growing up. As values and interests change, your needs in friends do, too. You must learn when to break up and when to make up in order to make the most of going steady. After going steady the next step is marriage—for some couples.

Suggested Activities

Individual Study

1. Write a paper on "What I Think of Going Steady." Include your readings, your personal experiences, your ideas, your parents' attitudes, and your personal plans for your own future. Keep your paper in your notebook to refer to later.
2. Write a letter to the person with whom you would like to go steady, telling him or her why you would like to go steady. Be as specific as you can. When you have finished your letter, read it over to yourself in an attempt to discover whether you want to go steady enough to make a real effort in that direction. You might find it helpful to discuss it with a friendly adult adviser in whom you have confidence.
3. Describe a situation in which you found it hard to say "no" to an invitation to greater intimacy than you thought right. Go into detail on just what happened, what you did, and what you wish you had done. What would you do another time in a similar situation? Talk over your plans with someone you trust.
4. Write a letter to a cousin of yours in a distant city who has just written that she has broken up with a fellow she had been going steady with for some time. Give her what comfort you can from what you know about going steady. Suggest a book that she might read that might be helpful to her now.
5. Review Chapters 12, 13, 14, and 15 in The Art of Dating (New York: Association Press, 1958) and be prepared to give your report orally in class as well as in written form for your teacher's comments.
6. Talk over with your parents, your religious adviser, or some other trusted adult why grown-ups so often frown on the practice of going steady among

teen-agers. Find out whether going steady was a common practice when these adults were your age. How many people did they go steady with before getting married? How do present ideas of going steady look to adults now? Write up your interview and keep it in your notebook.

Group Activity

1. Arrange a panel discussion of several popular boys and girls in your school who are currently going steady, on the topic, "Why We Are Going Steady." After each has had a chance to give his or her first thoughts, turn the panel over to the class for their further questions and comments.
2. Role-play a number of ways in which a couple who have been going steady can break up without hurting each other too greatly. After a given episode has been presented once, stop the action and encourage discussion of what was just shown. Follow up suggestions in further role-playing presentations. Change roles and let girls play the boys' parts and the boys take the girls' roles to see how each feels in the other's situation. Discuss the various methods in terms of which is kindest, quickest, most effective.
3. Discuss what the school social committee can do to plan the kind of social event in which couples who are not going steady or dating regularly can have a good time and feel quite as much a part of the party as those who are going steady. Put on the board your ideas for activities that would encourage all to participate. Send your suggestions on to the social committee's next meeting for their consideration.
4. Invite into a special meeting of your class: (a) a mother who encourages her daughter to go steady; (b) a parent who feels strongly that teen-agers should not go steady; and (c) an outside youth leader from a local church or YMCA, YWCA, or 4-H Club to present a program on "The Value and Limitations of Going Steady While in High School." Ask each person to speak for five or ten minutes; then encourage them to discuss their points among themselves and with the members of your class.
5. View the film, *How to Say No* (Coronet Instructional Films, 65 East South Water Street, Chicago 1, Illinois, sound, black and white, 14 minutes), and discuss the ways of refusing an invitation to intimacy without losing your friends.

Readings

COTHERN, FAYLY H., *I've Been Wondering: Questions and Answers for Teen-Agers* (Nashville, Tennessee: Broadman Press, 1956). The first chapter has such pertinent sections as "Why go steady?" "How old should you be before you date steadily?" "Should you go steady if you are separated?" and "How do you break off?"

Duvall, Evelyn Millis, *The Art of Dating* (New York: Association Press, 1958). Chapter 15, "Going Steady," discusses such questions as how adults see steady dating, why young people go steady, why not go steady, how to break off the relationship, and how to get back into circulation again.

Duvall, Evelyn Millis, *Facts of Life and Love for Teen-Agers* (New York: Association Press, 1956). Chapter 15 sees going steady as giving a feeling of belonging and security, then goes into detail about how to get over a broken heart when you have stopped going steady, what it means to be pinned and to have an understanding before marriage.

Duvall, Evelyn Millis, and Hill, Reuben, *Being Married* (Boston: D. C. Heath and Company, 1960). Chapter 2, "Becoming Involved," discusses the process of getting in deeper than ever in going steady, getting pinned, and becoming mutually committed in anticipation of marriage.

Eckert, Ralph G., *Sex Attitudes in the Home* (New York: Association Press, 1956). Chapters 8 and 9 discuss frankly how to understand and deal with the sex feelings that are aroused when a boy and girl see a great deal of each other before marriage.

Lemasters, E. E., *Modern Courtship and Marriage* (New York: The Macmillan Company, 1957). This college text is so clearly written that the mature high-school student will find much of interest in it. Read especially Chapter 6, "Going Steady," for a review of studies about steady dating and case histories illustrating some problems involved.

Joy Time, Inc.

Anticipating

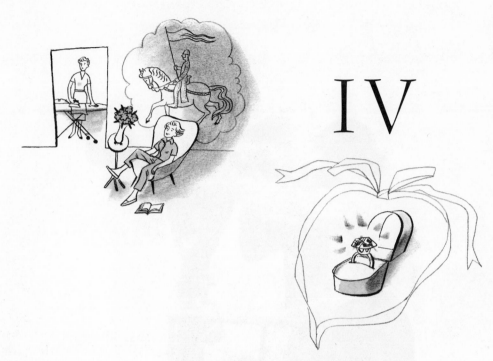

IV

Will You Make a Success of Marriage?
When Are You Ready for Marriage?
Your Engagement Plans
Early Marriage Adjustments

Your Marriage

Chapter 11

Will You Make a Success of Marriage?

You expect some day to get married and live happily ever after. But realistically you know that many couples who want to succeed in marriage fail to find happiness with each other. Will your marriage succeed or fail? What does it take to find happiness in marriage? What kind of people are happily married? There was a time when such questions would be a matter for speculation. Today, thanks to years of social science research, you have some basis for knowing what is important for the success of your marriage.

What Science Says about Success in Marriage

In recent decades there has been a great deal of scientific study about many things. Hundreds of millions of dollars are poured into industrial research every year, bringing us new products, new equipment, new resources—in fact, a whole new way of life. Billions of dollars are spent in the development of military defenses. Men and women have been at work, too, in the physical sciences, learning about atoms and ions and the penetration of the stratosphere and outer space. Others have been studying the frontiers of the human mind and spirit in the social sciences. One of the relevant aspects of social science investigation is that of the prediction of success or failure in marriage.

There has been enough study of what makes a successful marriage so that we can predict *in general* which marriages will succeed and which will fail. The emphasis in this last statement is on the two words *in general*. In other words, we take the same kind of risk that insurance companies do. We know enough about how long the average man in a given group will live to enable an insurance company to make a good business predicting longevity. The future of any one particular person cannot be foreseen accurately in a crystal

205

ball. The approximate future of the average person in any group can be predicted quite reliably, however, for length of life, and marital success even before the marriage takes place.

Statistically, your chances of a happy marriage are not as great now as they would have been fifty years ago. One reason why more marriages fail today than a few generations ago is that so much more is expected of marriage than ever before.

You Expect More of Marriage Today

There was a time when a man and woman simply had to stay married whether their marriage was happy or not. Your great-grandmother had no other place to go if she did not want to live with her husband any longer. Before women could get jobs outside the home, they were entirely dependent upon men to support them. Men, too, were dependent upon women for the basic essentials of living then. Before the days of canned foods, chain groceries, delicatessens, bakeries, and restaurants, a man needed a woman to cook for him. When there were very few laundries, apartment hotels with maid service, nurses, or ready-made clothing, a man had to have a woman who could wash and iron his clothes, keep his house, nurse him through illnesses, and do his sewing and mending. If your grandparents were not happy in their marriage, there was very little either of them could do about it except stick it out.

You Want to Be Understood. Men and women today expect to be understood deeply and intimately, often better than they have ever understood themselves. They look forward to a deep sense of mutual sympathy in which each appreciates and feels with the other as a person. They want to be fully and permanently loved, more completely than either of them has ever been loved before. This is a lot to expect of marriage and of each other.

You Want to Be Loved. Americans marry for love. People of other cultures have their marriages arranged for them by their families for economic profit or social advantage. But we want more than anything else to find love in our marriages. This is especially true today.

As millions of us move so often, we have many acquaintances but few intimates. Therefore we need more all-pervading, deeply fulfilling affection from our mates than was necessary in simpler days when emotionally satisfying relationships were also possible with other relatives, neighbors, or friends.

You Want Companionship. It is companionship that makes a marriage satisfying. Two people who can "talk each other's language" and communicate all the little overtones of feeling and response that remain unexpressed in casual contacts are usually the one who find rich satisfaction in their relationship. If they are able to know what and how the other is feeling, to read between the lines, to understand almost without being told, they feel a oneness that is unique. If they have a sense of common purpose, of joint endeavor, of real partnership, their marriage is likely to last.

People who make the kind of marriages that succeed in being more richly satisfying with each passing year are those who are willing and able to learn, to share, and, in the fullest sense, to live together.

You Want to Be Yourself. When you marry you still want to be yourself. You want to be free to make some choices, and to live your own life without too great curtailment. A man wants to continue to be himself and not just his wife's appendage. Most women today want some independence and the feeling of being themselves as well as wives and mothers.

One way of judging a good marriage is to see the extent to which the two individuals continue to grow as persons after their marriage. When each is free to be himself and to develop his own talents as best he can, he finds fulfillment as an individual as well as in a mate.

Ten Requisites for a Happy Marriage

Twentieth-century social scientists have been studying what is important for a happy marriage. Several of these investigations have continued over the past thirty years, testing, retesting, and appraising the marriages made by engaged, married, and divorced couples.

From their long study of the marriages of one thousand engaged couples, Professors Burgess and Wallin [1] find ten factors especially important for success in marriage. These are:

1. *Loving and Being Loved.* When love fails, the marriage is a failure, and the two people can become indifferent or actually hostile to each other. When love grows in marriage, there is a greater satisfaction with the marriage and with each other through the years. Some men and women have grown up in demonstrative families and have learned to love openly and without embarrassment. Love is expressed not only in hugs and kisses, but in a thousand little thoughtful ways in any happily married couple's life. Devotion in marriage finds concrete expression in the home the two persons build together, in the children they bear and rear, and in all they both hold dear.

2. *Sex Satisfaction.* There is a great deal of evidence to indicate that most couples have to learn to respond fully in their most intimate moments together. Newly married couples may be clumsy and awkward, even embarrassed, with each other. With tenderness and

---

[1] This section is drawn from Ernest W. Burgess, Paul Wallin, and Gladys Denny Shultz, *Courtship, Engagement and Marriage* (Philadelphia: J. B. Lippincott Company, 1954), p. 267.

patience and the recognition that it takes time to learn the language of love-making, as it does to become fluent in any other language, the two become more relaxed with each other and more competent in helping each other to full sex satisfaction.

Successful marriage and good sex adjustment go together, but which is cause and which is effect is not so clearly understood. There are some happily married couples who report that their sex life has not been particularly satisfying. There are others who are most compatible sex partners, but miserable in their marriage. About the only conclusions that can be drawn are that (1) while sex satisfaction is important, it is by no means the only factor in marital happiness; and (2) a couple's sex life is usually closely related to many other facets of their total relationship.

3. *Emotional Interdependence.* When two people come to depend upon one another emotionally, they are bound together by their increasing reliance upon one another. Otherwise they may go about their independent ways with little regard for each other. The studies indicate that when husband and wife depend upon each other mutually, their marriage is greatly unified.

Two people who marry set themselves the task of developing together the emotional climate that will be good to grow in. When such an emotional atmosphere is established in the home, the marriage tends to be mutually satisfying to all members of the family.

4. *Compatibility.* Few couples are compatible in every respect. There are enormous differences in personality make-up between any two individuals. Naturally the differences are even greater when one of the individuals is a man and one is a woman. Some differences between people are good for a relationship. Others irritate and annoy both members of the pair.

Most couples grow in their ability to accept and live with their differences. The rigid person who sees another's behavior as different from his own, and says with indignation, "I would never do that," has more problems of incompatibility than the person who can be flexible and not expect his mate to be just like himself.

5. *Similar Backgrounds.* The general tendency is for a person to marry someone with a similar background. Marriage within one's faith is more common than interfaith marriage. Marrying someone from the same general social and economic level is more common than "marrying across the tracks." Getting married to someone from the same general kind of family is more frequent than marrying into an entirely different kind of family.

Mixed marriages do, however, take place. Some of these marriages work out well, but more such couples break up than is true among those more alike in background. Although differences in background are not necessarily disastrous, they are almost always a challenge to the members of the pair whose job it is to merge not only their own different personalities, but also the different ways of life they represent.

6. *Common Interests*. Successful marriages are built upon common interests. Some interests tend to be more binding than others. Burgess and Wallin find that interests in sports have little binding effect; that friends, reading, and dancing have some binding effect; and that the greatest binding effect of all comes when the husband and wife both work together in the same profession, community service, or other cause.

Common interests and the way the two persons feel about them become evident in courtship and engagement. Some dating couples find that there is little they enjoy doing together except going to ball games and drive-in theatres—hardly adequate for a lifetime of marriage. Others have many meaningful interests in common, work on projects together, devote themselves to similar causes and by the time they marry have built a wealth of common interests as a foundation for their life together as a couple.

7. *Domesticity*. Domesticity is defined as the desire for the comforts and pleasures of home life. Persons of both sexes vary greatly in domesticity. Some men and women care for nothing but their homes, spending every waking hour with the family in home-centered activities. Others blend their domestic interests with outside activities of various sorts. Some individuals escape as much as possible from the responsibilities of home life.

Studies indicate that the extremes of domesticity and non-domesticity are not as successful as is the happy medium of combining home interests with interests outside the family. The Burgess-Wallin research on this point concludes, "The golden mean which blends domestic and vital outside interests appears most favorable to success."

8. *Expectation of Success*. When a man and wife expect that their marriage will continue through the years, they make long term plans for their life together. They want children, often recognizing that bearing and rearing children will be a major responsibility for twenty years or more. They plan ahead for their children's education, often before the first baby is out of his cradle. They make sacrifices to get

a home of their own and equip it for the years ahead, all because they expect their marriage to go on and on. They increasingly recognize that building a good marriage that will last through the years is their joint responsibility. Such an attitude of expectation of success contributes to the permanence of marriage.

9. *Co-operativeness.* When a man and woman marry, they become a team. Together they face the tasks of earning money, setting up and maintaining a home, and having a family. These things always have been shared. Once upon a time it was the man's job to work to support his family, and the woman's job to keep house and care for the children. Today the roles of husbands and wives are not as rigidly defined as they once were. Many married women work outside their homes to help support the family and establish the kind of home that would be impossible on the husband's earnings alone. Many husbands find pleasure in being at home with their families, helping with the housekeeping and the homemaking, in ways unknown to their fathers and grandfathers. Family co-operation in today's changing times requires true adaptability, as we see in the next section.

10. *Adaptability.* Burgess and Wallin define adaptability as "the capacity of the person to change his roles, his attitudes, and his behavior to adjust to those of other persons or to a new and modified situation." In marriage adaptability enables a couple to cope with new situations that affect their marriage through the months and years.

To be adaptable a person has to (1) want to adapt; (2) see the situation from the other person's viewpoint; (3) be flexible; and (4) be competent in taking on the new attitudes and skills that the new situation requires. These often necessitate real working out by both members of the couple.

Now that you have reviewed the ten factors most important for success in marriage, you can use them as a guide in choosing your marriage partner.

Choosing the One for You

The person you choose as your marriage partner is by your side a long while. You will share together life's hurts and happiness through the years. Together you expect to find meaning in your work, joy in your home, and satisfaction in everyday living. Your mate is not just a date for a while, but a partner for a lifetime. Therefore, who makes a good marriage partner is of prime importance to you.

Your choice involves more than the selection of an individual. It includes, whether you realize it or not, the simultaneous selection of (1) the mood and atmosphere of your future home; (2) its level of intellectual, aesthetic, and recreational life; and (3) the other line of your children's ancestry. The disposition of your marriage partner and the way you affect each other will largely determine the emotional climate of your home life. The kind and quality and breadth and depth of your mate's cultural interests and potential tastes will greatly influence not only his or her individual recreational pursuits but also such joint concerns as which television shows will be turned on, what outside activities you share, and the kind of music and reading matter and people brought into your home. Finally your husband or wife becomes irrevocably the father or mother of your children. Such sobering realizations show how important it is to choose someone suitable.

The courtship period is filled with planning and dreaming, exchanging gifts and shopping together. In marriage the couple will also have to share more humdrum tasks.

Sybil Shelton from Monkmeyer

Someone to Live With. If your marriage is to work out happily, you must pick someone that you can live with. You must therefore find someone you can *like* as well as love. And the two feelings are not the same, you know. It is quite possible to be madly in love with someone with whom it would be impossible to live. You could be violently attracted to a person with whom you have almost nothing in common. Yet to be happily married, you must enjoy being together. Sharing all the homey little everyday things in marriage—getting the car washed, shopping for groceries, drying the dishes, entertaining each other's families, deciding what to do on a Saturday afternoon—all these and thousands of other little things are the real proving-ground of marriage. Unless you enjoy being together, doing things together, sharing a great deal of life in common, your marriage will not be built soundly on foundations of real companionship.

Having Enough in Common to Marry On

The ten requisites for a happy marriage drawn from research studies underscore again and again the importance of having enough in common to marry on. This means similarity in backgrounds, interests, tastes, ideals, and values, as we now see in greater detail.

Opposites Attract—Sometimes. There have been more than one hundred different studies to date that show clearly that the old saying, "Opposites attract," is true of only a minority of all marriage choices. Research into the question as to who gets married to whom reveals some interesting findings. For instance, there is a tendency for tall people to marry tall people, dark-eyed people to marry dark-eyed people, the blind to marry the blind, the deaf to marry the deaf, and so on down an amazing list of physical similarities. Even more striking than the data concerning outward characteristics is the fact that there is a tendency to be attracted to, fall in love with, and to marry people from the same general social background. These social characteristics are much more significant for the success of a marriage than such factors as eye-color or tendency of the hair to curl. So let us see what is involved.

Similar Backgrounds. Statistically speaking, your marriage has a greater chance for success if you and your partner share a common background—if, for instance,

1. You grew up in the same kind of family.
2. You came from the same nationality background.
3. You are from the same racial stock.
4. You share a common religious faith.
5. You grew up in the same type of community.
6. You both came from the country or a small town or a city.
7. You were brought up similarly.

8. You agree on what is important.
9. You do things the same way, like the same things, share many habits in common.

This does not mean that differences in background cannot be worked out in marriage. What it does mean is that more people find success in marriage who have a great deal in common than who come from widely different backgrounds.

There will always be individual cases that are exceptions to the rule. You can build a strong, durable marriage quite counter to the statistical probabilities. But, other things being equal, the right one for you is someone like yourself, from the same general kind of background. When you share a common beginning, you are more likely to have common habits, interests, values, and ways of looking at life, that give you a common base for life together.

Similar Interests and Tastes. When you like the same things, enjoy the same activities, like (or dislike) the same people, you tend to like each other and get along well together.

Actually you have more chance of meeting and knowing people with your own tastes and interests than with dissimilar ones. For you tend to be near those who are interested in doing the same sort of things. The boy who enjoys sports meets other boys and girls on the playing field. The girl who likes dramatics meets other dramatics-minded people at rehearsals and plays. Your interests bring you together, and they keep you together.

Taste is limitless. Some people like a great deal of activity. They are the action type of persons. Others are more quiet, contemplative, not needing many activities. Since marriage is a partnership involving at least some shared pursuits, it stands to reason (as well as being proved data) that two people who share some common tastes and interests have a sound basis for a good marriage.

Similar Ideals and Values. You have to feel that the same things are important to be happily married. In America today all kinds of values are held by all kinds of people. There are those who act as though having a good time is the most important value in life. These people seek pleasure in many ways and do not allow much to interfere with their good times. Then there are those who act as though making money were the most important thing in life. They sacrifice everything for the "almighty dollar." Many people are deeply religious, believing in a higher power and devoting their lives to serving their God as they understand Him. Others fight for human rights and for the recognition and appreciation of the individual in the social scene. So on and on, through a scale of values from the most self-centered and calculating to the socially sensitive and spiritually motivated. Any great difference in the basic values represented in a couple is apt to lead to trouble.

Martha May was a pious girl who had been brought up in a religious home to believe that God watched over every step, and to put herself second always to others. While on a vacation one summer, she fell head over heels in love with Lester, who believed that the world owed him a living. Lester was a big, handsome fellow, easy-going and full of fun. He was attracted to Martha May's quiet thoughtfulness, and possessively drove off the other boys who might have dated her. After a whirlwind courtship that summer they were married, and then the trouble began. Lester started out that fall by quitting his job and announcing that "only suckers work." He took up betting on professional football games and became quite enthusiastic about a nice little racket he and one of his pals had worked out for increasing his winnings. Martha May was shocked at her husband's philosophy of life and tried in every way she knew to reform him. Her tears and nagging cooled his ardor, and he left home. Martha May returned to her family, her marriage broken and her faith in men shattered.

A marriage counselor could have predicted the outcome of this marriage fairly accurately. Anyone with real experience with people and a knowledge of the combinations that are successful could have foretold the tragic ending of this match. When two people are headed in opposite directions and have contrary philosophies of life and entirely different value systems, something has to give. In these days that something is usually the marriage.

One Test—"Going My Way?" If your partner is going in the same direction in which you are developing, you will be good for each other. If, on the other hand, you are headed in opposite directions, you will pull apart. In a real sense, you can become a team only when you are going in the same direction. You must pull together to make the marriage work. You must care about the same things, think the same values are important, and share a common sense of direction and of destiny to join hands in the kind of marriage that will last.

One young man applied this test very simply. He says, "I was going along enjoying life, feeling the tug of the future and the joy of the present, and there beside me was a girl who thought as I thought, dreamed as I dreamed, and cared as I cared; so I took her by the hand and married her."

Mixed Marriages Are Apt to Be Difficult

Mixed marriages are usually harder to work out than are marriages of people who have more in common. Marriages across racial and nationality lines are more generally opposed than are marriages between people from the same general backgrounds. The same thing is true of marriages across wide social and economic chasms. The Cinderella marriage may sound romantic, but it rarely works out as well as do marriages of two people from the same economic walk of life.

The problems common to interfaith, interracial, international, and other mixed marriages are several. There is first of all the tendency of the families of the couple to regret the marriage of their child outside the group in which he has been brought up. Parents and other relatives usually feel that the young person is marrying well when he or she selects a mate from within the family's culture. When a choice is made from another quite different group, there is a tendency to feel that it cannot work out well, and to expect that difficulties will result. This tendency to expect trouble makes it hard for the young couple to weather the normal strains of early marriage adjustment. If any little problem comes along, the families tend to take sides and to feel that if their children had married their own kind, they would not be having such troubles.

Young people selecting partners outside their own group are often called upon to explain or to defend their choice in ways not required of others who married as they were expected to, within their own group.

Janice was about to marry a fine young man with whom she had been in love for some time. They were well suited to each other except that Janice was a minister's daughter and Sol was a liberal Jew. Somehow, wherever they went as a couple, they had to *explain* their relationship. Janice's friends and family thought that it was peculiar that Janice could not find some nice young man in her own father's church. They could not see what Janice saw in Sol because they looked at him with a far more critical attitude than they would have looked over a young man from her own faith. So it was too with Sol's folks. They thought Janice was a lovely girl, but they could not see what made her so much more desirable than a half dozen fine Jewish girls Sol might have chosen. When Janice and Sol married, there was still a question about the marriage in the attitudes of both families and sets of friends. For years, every little adjustment that the young people made to each other was exaggerated and magnified by expectation of failure on the part of both families.

Most difficult of all is the misunderstanding that arises from time to time between the couple themselves. Different groups see things in different ways and bring up their children to share these views. When marriages occur between members of two quite different groups, there are bound to be areas in which there will be clashes of opinion, values, and habits. Angela, brought up in an Italian home, thinks nothing of drinking wine on social occasions. Ned, from a Scotch Presbyterian family, feels that any alcoholic drinking is bad, and gets quite upset with Angela and her family at what he calls their irresponsible tippling. What to serve his friends and her friends when they entertain as a couple has become a major problem for Angela and Ned to work out.

Bridging Your Differences. When you marry, you make a contract to build a bridge between yourselves. This bridge of communication must be strong enough to bear the weight of both of you at your points of greatest difference. It must be solid enough so that you can get through to each other with sympathy and understanding in the tender, intimate kind of companionship you want in marriage today, as you saw in Chapter 6, "Getting Through to Each Other."

When you and your partner come from similar backgrounds, the gulf between you is a narrow one, and the bridge you must build is therefore short and erected without too much difficulty. When you come from widely separated social, religious, national, economic, or cultural groups, the chasm between you is a wide one that will involve the building of a longer and more complicated bridge of communication before you can get through to each other with the shared feelings and purposes that make for real unity.

Your marriage will work to the extent to which you can bridge your differences satisfactorily. If your bridge needs to be a long and complex one, it will take longer and be more difficult than if you need only a short runway between you. But however long and complicated the task, it is up to *you* to build your own marriage.

How Much Difference Can You Live With? How you feel about your differences is quite as important as the actual distance between you as a couple. Take Gretchen and Gordon, for instance. After four months of marriage, Gretchen came in tears to consult a marriage counselor. With a sob she told how miserable they both were, and then said, "But of course, ours is a mixed marriage." The counselor said, "Yes? In what way is yours a mixed marriage?" To which Gretchen replied, "Well, you see, I'm a Baptist, I'm a *good* Baptist, and Gordon is *just* a Methodist." Gretchen went on to say that theirs had been a whirlwind courtship, filled with moonlit nights and many tender words of love between them. One evening before they married Gordon had told her that he loved her so much that he would gladly do anything she ever wanted him to. She believed him then, and was crushed to find after their marriage that he was not willing to join her church. Gordon thought that Gretchen was being somewhat childish in her demands, especially since his own church meant so much to him. He had been president of his Methodist young people's society, had recently represented his church at a summer conference and enjoyed the crowd at his church too much to give them up as completely as his new wife expected.

The difference between a Baptist and a Methodist is not great unless you *feel* that it is. If Gretchen felt that being a Baptist was *that* important, she would have been wise to have picked a boy from her own church. Some people from far more different churches marry and work out remarkably strong marriages. Usually such persons do not feel so strongly about their particular religion, and they are more apt to have a broader view of the spiritual life and to be able to live with a wider range of difference.

The test for any given person is, "How much difference can I take in my marriage?" No one whom you marry will be your exact twin. Inevitably there will be differences between you. Your task is to determine which kinds of differences you can live with most comfortably and to select the kind of person who comes within these limits of your acceptance.

Differences Can Be Advantages. Certain differences of temperament seem to be an advantage in marriage. An effervescent type of girl married to a stable, quiet young man often finds rich satisfaction in his poise and calmness at the same time that he finds her vivacity stimulating. A dominant, masculine man often prefers a quiet, submissive woman to the more high-powered type, who would not be as comfortable with his dominance as would her quieter sister. And so it goes through a wide range of temperamental differences between mates.

Meeting Each Other's Needs. Most of all it is important to marry the kind of person who can meet your needs and whose needs you can meet. The girl needing a strong, reassuring man who will encourage her to do things and to grow as a person will do well to marry that kind of man, if she can find him. The boy wanting a companion who will share his interests, go with him on hunting trips, work beside him in his business, and meet his needs for an

"I think she's going to regret marrying a doctor."

ever-present comrade should seek out this kind of girl in making his final choice of a life-partner.

The right one for you is the person who is good for you, who will encourage you to be yourself, to grow, to develop, and to realize your potentialities as a person.

Choosing a Personality That Meshes with Yours

Your choice of a marriage partner involves finding the kind of personality that goes well with yours. You will have to interact as a team in many ways. As much as you can, you are wise to choose as a mate

1. Someone whom you feel you understand, and who seems to understand what you really are.
2. Someone whose faults you can see and accept, and who can take your limitations in stride.
3. Someone who comes vitally alive in your company, and who stimulates your interests, concerns, and creativeness.
4. Someone who is maturing socially, emotionally, and spiritually, and who encourages your continued growth as a person.
5. Someone who glows with love for you, and whom you love, admire, and enjoy being near.

Of all these, the one about which there is most general confusion is that of love. We Americans are a romantic people and sometimes our ideas about love and romance get all mixed up. So let us look at what being in love is like.

Being in Love

Of course you will marry someone you love. But how are you going to know for sure whether your love will last? You very likely have been in love, or thought you were, several times before. Now as you look back on some of these past infatuations, you probably are glad that nothing came of them. How are you going to be sure when the time comes for your final choice? The first thing to recognize is the hold that romantic illusions have on your thinking about love. There is so much you hear that is just not so!

Fallacies About Love and Romance. By now you know you do not "fall in love" as romantic fiction has it, but rather you tend to *grow into love* over time and mutual acquaintance. Sometimes of course, you feel instantly attracted to a person of the other sex. But such spontaneous "love at first sight" attractions sometimes do not last for more than a few dates. So there is little likelihood that you will know for sure the instant your "one and only" comes along. Since there is no one Ideal Girl for each boy, no Mr. Right for each girl, it is rarely true that "when they meet they know it." Rather, in thoughtful people there will be inevitably some questions about your suitability for each other all along. The fairy-tale idea that "if you are in love, nothing else matters" is a poor philosophy. A great deal matters besides being in love, especially when you have still to decide whether or not you are so deeply and permanently in love as to make plans for the future.

Infatuations Come and Go. Studies have shown some distinctions between infatuation and love that are pertinent here. In general, infatuations tend to be prevalent in the lives of young teen-agers, while love more often characterizes relationships between more mature persons. The tendency is for infatuations to be brief and transitory. Most boys and girls can recall any number of sudden infatuations that were exciting at the time but that lasted but a short while. Infatuations tend more often to occur between two persons who do not know each other well, while love grows with longer acquaintance.

Love Enough for Marriage. If some strong feelings of attraction are not love at all, but only short-term infatuations, how is a person to know when he or she is really in love? The following tests of love may be helpful to you:

1. Love is outgoing, not centered in oneself alone, but spilling over into concern for the other person, the relationship, and causes and concerns beyond the pair of lovers.
2. Love releases energy, is vitalizing, creative, motivating each of the lovers to his own best effort, his finest achievements and productivity.
3. Love wants to share and to be shared, in all the many ways that two persons can share each other's interests, feelings, activities, thoughts, and dreams.
4. Love gives a sense of togetherness, of unity, of a we-feeling in which plans and hopes and daily life are experienced as happening to two-in-one.
5. Love grows with further acquaintance and becomes richer, deeper, more varied, more satisfying over time.[2]

Getting to Know Each Other

The surest way to find out whether you have the kind of love that will grow rather than fade away when another attractive person comes along, is to get to know one another. As you get better and better acquainted, you discover a great deal about each other, and you find out how you feel in each other's company in a wide variety of circumstances.

Seeing Each Other in Many Situations. If you do the same thing date after date, you have little opportunity for getting acquainted with each other

[2] Excerpted from a fuller discussion in Evelyn Millis Duvall, *Facts of Life and Love for Teen-Agers* (New York: Association Press, 1956), pp. 253–72.

in different settings. But when you find opportunities for seeing each other in all sorts of situations, you become familiar with what you are both like in daily life. By working together, you can discover a great deal about each other's work habits. By sharing the care of children or pets or some other dependents, you can learn how each of you responds to the needs of others. By participating not only in active sports but also in quiet pursuits, by seeing each other in the company of other people as well as in more solitary situations, you can gain a great deal of understanding about each other and about how well your personalities mesh.

Most of all, it is important to find out how each of you feels in various emotional situations. How do you feel, for instance, when your loved one gets mad? sad? disappointed? cocky? nervous? worried? enthusiastic? Does the other's emotional state set off reciprocal feelings in you, or are they antagonistic? Are you good for each other emotionally? Or do you tend to set each other on edge when one or the other of you is upset? These things are very important to learn, as much before marriage as is possible.

Accepting Each Other As Is. As you get better acquainted with each other, you find out a great deal about yourselves that may have to be accepted if you are to be happy with each other. Each of you has certain limitations, faults, and difficulties that may become a burden to the relationship if the other cannot face and accept them fairly well. Just closing your eyes to the other's faults or to your own does not wipe them out of the picture. In fact, refusing to admit and face your problems may make them worse for you both. Getting to know each other involves first of all finding out what you both are really like, how you got that way, and what it means to you.

Getting Acquainted with Both Families. If you like a person, you want to get acquainted with his family. You want to know the persons who are important to him or her. You want them to like you. And you want to know them well enough to become genuinely fond of them for the people they are as well as for the place they hold in the life of this person you love. But more than that, you see in your lover's family the background that is uniquely his. You see in the way he acts with his father and mother and brothers and sisters and other relatives something of the way he has been brought up. You sense what things are important to his family, as well as to him, and what ways he has been taught to follow all through childhood.

You cannot completely sever any person from his or her own roots. You have to marry all that a person's family means in terms of special loves and fears and dreams and values. Soon after marriage, if not before, you discover that your mate's relatives are your family, too. Those other parents are to become your children's grandparents. That other home will be where at least some holidays are spent and where a sense of being a family originates.

Taking Time to Decide

Finding out whether you are really suitable for each other takes time. It means a considerable amount of mutual exploration and discovery. It involves seeing each other in many different situations and emotional climates. It depends upon a depth of mutual acquaintance that cannot take place all at once.

Impulsiveness and Whirlwind Courtships. You occasionally find a girl who boasts that her man "swept me off my feet, and before I knew it I was married." Such impulsive behavior is characteristic of emotionally immature, childlike people who are swept along on a tide of emotion from one situation to the next. Whirlwind courtships occur in great numbers in times of stress and insecurity. In wartime it is not unusual for a couple to meet and marry during a two-week furlough. When the world seems full of uncertainties, many people seek something definite to cling to through marriage. Unfortunately such hasty ill-considered marriages are the least secure of all.

Doubts and Uncertainties. Most sweethearts have some questions about whether they are right for each other, as well as when and how they should progress from one step to the next in their relationship. They quite rightly wonder just how involved it is wise to get at various stages of their affair. They may have doubts about whether their love will last long enough to dare make plans for the future.

Such questions are not an indication that the relationship is a poor one. Rather some doubts can be an indication that the two people care enough for each other and for their love to want to lay a firm foundation for the future before rushing too hastily into marriage.

Being Increasingly Sure. As a couple becomes better and better acquainted and sees more and more of each other in all sorts of circumstances they either grate upon each other or grow more in love. They tend either to find that they are not suitable, and break off their affair, or they become more and more sure that they are right for each other. Only time and further acquaintance can reliably bring a sense of more and more certainty that this is the right choice. Then the time comes when commitment and marriage are the inevitable next steps.

Becoming Good Marriage Material

The happiness of your marriage depends not only on the kind of person your mate is, but especially upon the kind of person you yourself are. There are some persons who could be happy with almost anyone else, and there are others who would find little happiness regardless of who their partner was. The secret of success in marriage as in life lies within the individual.

After you marry, you will still be you. Your marriage may help you grow up in many ways. You may find that you are a better person for having married. But basically you will still be yourself after marriage as before. If you are the kind of person who strives to become worthy of another's affections, you will find in marriage a continuing adventure in becoming, in a satisfying sense of self-realization.

Getting Along with Yourself. Your ability to get along with another person in the closest of all associations—marriage—depends primarily on how

"But I don't want to learn anything about housekeeping, Mother—I want to be a sweet, innocent bride."

well you have learned and are learning how to live with yourself. If you expect too much of yourself, and are always punishing yourself for what you have done or have not done, you will continue to have problems with yourself, whether you marry or not. If, on the other hand, you are making real progress in learning to know yourself, and to know what you can expect of yourself, and how you most readily improve and grow, you will probably be the kind of person who can marry and find happiness in your marriage. As you get along with yourself, you can face your faults without blaming the other for all the problems you are having with yourself. This takes some doing, but nothing is more important for your happiness as a person or your success as a marriage partner.

Becoming Good to Live With. You become good marriage material by cultivating the qualities that are good to be near. You may need to become more lovable and less irritable, more understanding and less impatient, more mature and less demanding, more faithful and less fickle, more honest and less insincere. The kind of person you really are becomes strikingly evident in marriage. You may live behind a façade of pretense in other relationships, but you have to be yourself in marriage. The fulfillment you find in becoming a finer person is a precious dowry to take into marriage.

Good Marriages Are Made by Good People

There is overwhelming evidence that successful marriages are made by good people. One study [3] compares happily married with divorced couples in an effort to find out why some marriages succeed and others fail. The 929 men and women who contributed their experiences as happily and unhappily married persons were representative of the general population. This study finds, as do others, that certain characteristics are associated with success in marriage. In general, the findings are that the person who succeeds in his or her marriage is responsible, sociable, and religious.

Being a Responsible Person. When happily and unhappily married men and women rated their mates on the degree to which the spouse assumed responsibility readily, there were marked differences between the two groups. Happily married men and women far more often describe their mates as being responsible than do those who have been divorced. Those whose marriages have failed, on the other hand, describe their divorced former partners as irresponsible far more often than do happily married husbands and wives.

The differences in the way these husbands and wives rate their mates on the degree to which they assume responsibility readily are so significant that they could not have occurred by chance. For instance, not one happily married

[3] Harvey Locke, *Predicting Adjustment in Marriage* (New York: Henry Holt and Company, 1951).

man or woman described the married partner as "not at all" responsible, while one out of four of the divorced men (23.4 per cent) and women (29.2 per cent) rated their mates as "not at all" responsible.[4]

Sociability and Friendliness. There have been many studies that conclude that the ability to make friends and to get along happily with people generally is a quality associated with happiness in marriage.

The sociable person, who has had many friends before marriage, is a better marriage risk than the lonely soul who reports having had almost no friends before marriage. Locke's study further indicates that couples who enjoy mutual friends after their marriage are more likely to be happily married than those with few or no mutual friends.

Such findings as these are not hard to interpret. The individual who has learned how to enjoy friends is the kind of person who can give of himself or herself and knows how to maintain a pleasant friendly relationship. The socially less competent person may be basically as fine a person, but not as experienced in making and keeping friends as the sociable one. Fortunately these social skills can be learned. There are persons of both sexes who "find themselves" as young people and continue to grow in their ability to be friendly.

Religious People and Practices. People who have never studied the question may mistakenly believe that they can leave religion out of their choice and build a sound marriage and family life without regard for religious values. The evidence is all to the contrary.

Research studies all agree that there is a close relationship between religious activity and happiness in marriage. Couples who get married in a church and by a minister, priest, or rabbi have a better chance of a permanently happy home than do those who marry without the blessing of their church. Unfavorable atttiudes toward religion and unconventional behavior are associated with unhappiness and with marital failure according to a number of studies. Investigations of some 25,000 marriages show three times as many marriage failures among non-religious as among religious people.

The reasons for a close relationship between religious living and happiness are not hard to see. We Americans believe in churches and in what they stand for in our lives. We know that man does not live by bread alone at any time. We feel deeply the need of a spiritual orientation. Many of us seek direction through religion, which has been a symbol of the good life through the ages. This is simply putting our heritage into practice.

Good people make good marriages. When you marry, you share all you have and are with the mate you choose. If that mate is a person who tries to live a good life, you have a sound basis for your trust.

[4] *Ibid.*, p. 177.

Summary

The success of your marriage depends upon the kind of persons you and your mate are. You expect more of marriage today than men and women used to. You expect to be understood, to be loved, to find companionship, and yet to be yourself even after marriage. This is a lot to expect of marriage, and some fail to find happiness. Scientific studies tell you what makes marriage successful. Ten requisites for a happy marriage are: (1) loving and being loved; (2) sex satisfaction; (3) emotional interdependence; (4) compatibility; (5) similar cultural backgrounds; (6) common interests; (7) domesticity; (8) expectation of success; (9) co-operativeness; and (10) adaptability. In choosing a mate, you also choose the mood of your future home, the nature of your life together, and your children's ancestors. The chances are that your marriage will be built upon common interests, tastes, ideals, and values between you and a mate who is going the same way in life. You are wise if you choose someone whose personality meshes well with yours, so that both of you may feel alive and grow in each other's company. Being enough in love to marry on involves more than the many romantic illusions clouding your vision. But you can guide yourself by some of the tests of love, and take time to be sure. Getting to know each other well before you finally commit yourselves involves seeing each other in many different situations, accepting each other as you really are, and getting acquainted with each other's families. It is important for you to become good marriage material yourself by learning to be the kind of person who will be good to live with, who can live with himself and find happiness in marriage as in life. Being religious is good for marriage and family life, for in the last analysis, it takes good people to make good marriages.

Suggested Activities

Individual Study

1. Into the three columns below put the qualities you will look for in a marriage partner. Think through carefully in which column to place the various characteristics.

THE ONE I MARRY WILL HAVE TO BE

(*Do not write in this book.*)

Essential Qualities	*Important Qualities*	*Desirable Qualities*

2. Write a paper on "The Marriage I Look Forward To."
3. Prepare a book report on James H. S. Bossard and Eleanor Boll, *One Marriage: Two Faiths* (New York: The Ronald Press Company, 1957).
4. Prepare a chart of "Who Is a Good Marriage Risk?" using data gleaned from your review of the various studies listed and quoted in your Readings. Summarize your findings in a paper on the topic. If it seems advisable, copy your chart on the blackboard to serve as a basis for class discussion.
5. Write a letter to yourself to be opened on your wedding day telling the kind of person you hope to have become by then.

Group Activity

1. Conduct a symposium on the ten requisites for a happy marriage as outlined in your text and elaborated in the Burgess-Wallin study. Search out detailed data from the research study to document the points of the presentations. Illustrate from your own observations and experience.
2. Invite a panel of women married twenty-five and fifty years ago to discuss with each other and with your class what was expected of a wife at the time of their marriages. Save time for members of the class to question the women in further detail.
3. Show and discuss in class the film, *Choosing Your Marriage Partner* (Coronet, sound, 13½ minutes).
4. Invite a Protestant minister, a Jewish rabbi, and a Catholic priest to tell your class their policies about performing a mixed marriage.
5. Have the members of your class collect materials from their own churches dealing with official church policies about marrying outside the religion. Use these materials as the basis for a class discussion on the subject.
6. Study together the film strip, *Is This the One for Me?* (Radio and Film Commission, 1001 Nineteenth Avenue, Nashville 2, Tennessee).

Readings

BLACK, ALGERNON D., *If I Marry Outside My Religion* (New York: Public Affairs Pamphlets, 1954). This wise booklet takes a long look at interfaith marriages, explains why they have increased, what the position of the various churches is on marrying outside their faith, and what problems and challenges face a couple taking this step.

BURGESS, ERNEST W., WALLIN, PAUL, and SHULTZ, GLADYS DENNY, *Courtship, Engagement and Marriage* (Philadelphia: J. B. Lippincott Company, 1954). This is a popular edition of the much-quoted Burgess-Wallin study of 1,000 engaged couples. You will find Part Three, "What Makes a Marriage Succeed," an invaluable background for this chapter.

DUVALL, EVELYN MILLIS, and HILL, REUBEN, *When You Marry* (Boston; D.C. Heath and Company, 1961). Chapter 6, "Will Yours Be a Happy Marriage?" reviews the findings of various studies on predicting success or failure in marriage, discusses mixed marriages of various types, and considers the kind of persons who get married and live happily ever after.

DUVALL, SYLVANUS M., *Before You Marry* (New York: Association Press, 1959). Chapter 8, "Who Is Right for You?" and Chapter 9, "What About Mixed Marriage?" take up one by one the most frequent questions young couples have about their chances for success in marriage and answer each one clearly and explicitly out of the best that is known from research findings and clinical evidence.

ECKERT, RALPH G., *So You Think It's Love!* (New York: Public Affairs Pamphlets, 1950). You will find this entire booklet of interest, but read especially the sections on "Love at First Sight," "Do We Fall in Love?" "How Can I Know It's Really Love?" and "Finding the Right Person."

LANDIS, JUDSON T. and MARY G., *Personal Adjustment, Marriage, and Family Living* (Englewood Cliffs, N. J.: Prentice-Hall, Inc., 1955). Chapter 10, "Likes or Opposites in Marriage," includes discussion of such differences as age, education, economic status, racial and international aspects of mixed marriages and the challenges they present.

LOCKE, HARVEY J., *Predicting Adjustment in Marriage: A Comparison of a Divorced and a Happily Married Group* (New York: Henry Holt and Company, 1951). This basic research report will interest the mature student, who will find Chapters 9, 10, and 11 particularly pertinent in their review of the personality traits associated with happy marriage.

Chapter 12

When Are You Ready for Marriage?

You will probably marry some day; the big question now may be, "When?" The possibility of marrying very soon may have already presented itself to you. Or you may be one of those people who feel strongly that it is better to wait until you have finished your education before you marry and settle down. In either case, you undoubtedly have wondered whether the young people who are rushing off into early marriage are smart, or whether it is better to wait until one is more truly ready for marriage.

Young Marriages Are on the Increase

There is a common assumption that Americans used to get married at much younger ages in Grandmother's and Grandfather's day two or three generations ago. According to the official records of the United States Bureau of the Census, however, the age at which men and women marry for the first time *is younger now* than ever before in this century. Table, page 230, shows the median age (the *middle* age in the sequence from youngest to oldest persons) for the first marriages of men and women in given years between 1890 and 1955.

Two trends are clear in the figures given. First, there has been a general tendency ever since 1890, decade by decade, for both men and women to marry at younger ages, until now they are marrying, on the average, when the boy is in his twenty-third year and the girl is barely twenty. Second, there is a general tendency for men to marry women two or three years younger than themselves, a trend that has been going on for some time.

Differences in Age. The census figures support the popular notion that the man should be a few years older than his wife. Research studies indicate that difference in age is not a particularly important item in successful marriage. Strangely, these studies show that some of the happiest marriages are those in which the woman is a little the older—just why, we do not know as yet.

228

Clinical experience with individual couples seems to show that the actual difference in age is second in importance to the way the two people feel about it. If the woman, being older, is jealous of younger women more nearly her husband's age, there will be trouble. If she feels insecure, she may exaggerate the importance of her age, or try to simulate a youthfulness that is not comfortable to either of them.

When the difference in age is twenty years or more, the older is apt to feel somewhat like a parent. It is not uncommon for such an older husband to think of his wife as a child, and even to call her "Baby," as he plays a protective, paternal role with her. She in turn frequently reflects this role by calling him "Daddy" and acting more like a daughter with him than an equally mature companion. Similarly the very much older wife may baby her younger husband, who responds to her mothering like a son. Such marriages sometimes work out satisfactorily to both. There are problems, however, when and if the younger one grows up to the place where he or she is no longer satisfied with a parent-person for a mate, but wants a partner more nearly his own age.

In general, differences of a few years one way or the other between the couple are not important. Far more significant for the success of the marriage is the level of maturity achieved by the two people.

Young Marriages Often Fail

Generally speaking, marriages of very young people are less stable than those of more mature persons.[1] There have been many studies of the relationship between age at marriage and the happiness of the marriage. These studies agree on the whole that while age at marriage is not the most important factor, it is significantly related to marital happiness. Terman and his associates found that the best age for marriage for the man was twenty-two and over, and for the woman twenty and over. Burgess and Cottrell in their research found that the period from nineteen to twenty-one was the most hazardous, and that the best age for marriage for husband and wife was between twenty-two and thirty.

Marriage as an Escape. One of the reasons why so many young marriages fail is that they are founded to escape from an unhappy situation. Marriage as an escape rarely works. Many young people struggling for independence, for a life of their own away from their folks, feel that marriage is the way out. If things are not right at home, it is easy to dream about getting married and getting away from it all. The trouble is that such marriages are often complete and utter failures. Before you marry, you should have had some success in working out your own problems. You should marry for marriage

[1] Paul C. Glick, *American Families.* (New York: John Wiley & Sons, Inc., 1957), pp. 56–57.

MEDIAN AGE AT FIRST MARRIAGE [2]		
(United States Bureau of the Census)		
Year	Men	Women
1890	26.1	22.0
1900	25.9	21.9
1910	25.1	21.6
1920	24.6	21.2
1930	24.3	21.3
1940	24.3	21.5
1950	22.8	20.1
1955	22.7	20.2

itself and not just to get out from under some difficult situation that is too much for you—that is, if you want your marriage really to succeed.

Take Amy, for instance. When she was seventeen, her mother left home, leaving the furniture to Amy. Her father, crushed by his wife's leaving, gave Amy some money and sent her to her grandmother's to live. The grandmother was old-fashioned and strict and made life miserable for Amy. About that time, Jim came to town. He had left school and was living with his father, who drank. He met Amy at the drugstore where he worked. He was earning money of his own for the first time in his life. He resented his father's alcoholic dependence upon him. He and Amy consoled each other, and within a very short time decided to marry. Amy had the furniture, Jim had a job . . . and so they married! It is not surprising that their marriage did not last through the first year. Teen-age marriages often break up. They are too often as precariously based as this one, founded only on a mutual feeling of misery.

Forced Marriages. A considerable number of young marriages take place because they "have to." The girl becomes pregnant, and marriage seems to be the inevitable next step. Comparisons of the dates of marriages with the dates of the first child's birth registration made by Dr. Christensen and others found that a considerable number of brides in one county were already pregnant at the time of their marriage. This is a situation known to many communities. High-school students generally are aware of the many questions that must be faced by both the boy and the girl in such a situation.

The pregnant unmarried girl is immediately faced with such questions as "Shall I go ahead and have my baby?" "How shall I care for it?" "Do I really want to marry the baby's father?" "Will I have to drop out of school?" "What will my parents and my friends say when they find out?" "Is it better to marry now, or to brave my condition through somehow?"

[2] *Ibid.*, p. 54.

The boy in the situation has his questions, too, of which the following are typical: "Am I the only fellow involved?" "Do I have to marry the girl because I may have got her pregnant?" "What will happen if I refuse to marry her?" "If I do marry her, will I have to drop out of school and get a job?" "How much help can I expect from my family?" "What happens to my plans and hopes for the future if I marry now?"

Young people of both sexes agree that such difficult questions as these are a poor start for any marriage. They sense that what may have started as genuine fondness for one another may turn to bitterness and resentment under the pressure of a premature marriage. Wise are the members of both sexes who do not risk the forced marriage. They prefer to wait until they are ready to marry and settle down rather than get trapped into what is called a "shotgun wedding."

Marry While in School?

When 10,000 students from high schools all over the nation were polled on the age at which they would most like to marry, only 5 per cent said under age 18. Three out of four (73 per cent) said they preferred getting married between 19 and 24 years of age.[3] Actually the figures show that only a small minority of young people do marry while they are in high school. The February, 1956, Purdue Opinion Panel Poll No. 43 found that of the thousands of high-school students of both sexes polled, only 2 per cent of the boys, and 1 per cent of the girls were already married. The reason why more boys than girls in high school were already married is quite possibly because more boys stay on in school after they marry than do girls.

Should the Boy Stay in School? In the case of a high-school marriage, should the boy leave school and go to work, or should he stay on and finish his education? Years ago there would have been little question about it. When a man married, he was expected to support his wife and family. In recent years there have been a number of other factors generally recognized as important. When a boy has already married, he faces real responsibilities not only now but for the years ahead. If he has the ability and the interest, he will realize more of his potentialities, and can support his family better, with an adequate education than otherwise. Realistically his answer will depend upon what resources he and his wife can count on. If she can support him while he completes his schooling, that may work. If his family or hers is willing and able to lend a hand and help the little new family get on its feet while he stays on in school, that may be a real solution. If there are no such resources, or if his pride makes it impossible for him to take such help, then he may have no alternative but to quit school and go to work at anything he can get.

[3] Purdue Opinion Panel, Poll No. 27 (Lafayette, Indiana: Purdue University, December, 1950), p. 34.

"Did you ever stop to consider that perhaps I'm the best she can do?"

What About the Girl's Education? It has been only in recent years that a girl had a choice of whether she might continue her education after she married. Always before when a girl married, she was expected to become a full-time homemaker. Now a girl who marries while she is still in school may elect to continue and graduate as she would have had she not married. Her reasoning in this decision is often sound. She realizes that now that she is married, education is more important than ever. With graduation behind her, she quite possibly can get a better job if and when she does go to work than if she does not finish. She senses the truth of the saying, "Educate a woman and you educate a family," in that her intellectual and cultural level will influence her family-in-the-making. She may quite possibly have special talents and abilities that call for specialized training to develop fully. She may have aspirations beyond being a humdrum housekeeper, which act as a challenge to her to make something of herself.

Whether a girl can continue with her education after she marries depends greatly on her total situation. If her husband wants her to finish, her race is half won. If his family or hers backs them with financial help and sincere encouragement, that may be all that is necessary. But if her husband resists the idea, and if there is no one else to lend a hand, she may have no choice but to drop out and do what she can to help support herself and her family.

Attitudes Toward High-School Marriages. The public generally takes a dim view of marrying while in high school. Recent studies in New Mexico and California indicate that there are many high schools that force married students to withdraw from school. Even more high schools discriminate against married students by barring them from sports and social activities, from holding office, and from representing the school in public appearances. Some communities are more liberal than others on the matter of student marriages. Some families are more lenient than others on the question. Circumstances alter cases, in the minds of members of both generations. In general, however, both adults and young people agree that it is best to wait until after graduation before getting married.

Marriage and Military Service

With military service looming as a real possibility for the rank and file of young men, the question as to whether it is better to marry before going into service or to wait until one's stint for Uncle Sam is completed is almost universal.

Marrying Before Going into Service. If the marriage takes place before the boy goes into service, the young couple have the sense of having things settled between them even while they are separated. But they face a number of urgent questions about how they will manage their marriage. Their first big decision is what the wife will do while her man is in service. Will she plan to follow him for as long as and as far as she can? Or will she stay home and wait for his return? If she remains at home, will it be with her parents, with his family, or by herself? Will she get a job? Stay in school? Have a baby? Or some combination of all three?

How will the boy make out so far away from his wife and home? Will he be lonelier than if he were not married? How can he tell? What recreation will be out of bounds for him as a married serviceman? How often can he get home to be with his wife? How good will they be at keeping in touch with each other between their actual meetings?

In actual life situations such questions as these tend to be secondary to the more immediate one of "Do we feel sure enough about ourselves to get married before military service separates us?" The couple who have been going together for some time may quite wisely choose to marry before the boy goes into the service for the simple reason that they feel ready for marriage, while the couple that knows each other only slightly may wisely postpone their final decision to marry until they see how they feel afterward.

Getting Married After He Is Out of Service. There are many couples who choose to wait until the boy is out of service before getting married. They put it this way: "When we marry, we want to live together, and not be torn apart by his service duties." If they both agree that they want to wait until after he is out to get married, they mutually reinforce their decision. Then they both plan on how they will keep their love alive and what the girl will do in the meanwhile. Even so, they will be wise not to rush into marriage as soon as he is released from duty. He may need a time to readjust to civilian life before becoming a husband. They both may need a chance to get reacquainted with each other before getting married. They both may want to plan together the many details that go into marriage in a way that would be difficult if they were separated until the eve of the wedding.

Parents and In-Laws of the Serviceman. Recent years have shown how important parents are in the lives of young people who are separated by the boy's military service. If the couple has not married before he went into service, the girl may stay on with her parents until he is out and ready to marry. If they have married before he went off, he leaves his wife, and often a child or two, to fend for themselves while he is away. Most of the time, the girl either goes back to her parents or lives with his family until he is out of the service. His parents or in-laws take his place in the everyday details of life, are at her side when the baby comes, help out financially, and keep the little family intact until they can be reunited. The vast majority of young couples are appreciative of their parents' co-operation in such situations. There are some who resent having to take help and make it hard for themselves as well as for their families by attempting a complete independence that is not appropriate.

WHEN ARE YOU READY FOR MARRIAGE?

Where Will the Money Come From?

Two cannot live as cheaply as one. In fact, it is doubtful if two can live as cheaply as two, when the two are married! For marriage brings new needs and desires: for equipment, furniture, supplies for entertaining, setting up a new home, and getting ready for children. All these are expensive, and at the same time the previous needs for food, clothing, recreation, and all, keep right on for both the man and the woman.

In the first years of marriage when the needs for money are so great, the income of the young couple is usually small. The man is just getting started and ordinarily is earning much less than he will in a few years, when he will be established in his job. So the newly married couple faces the peculiar problem of having its greatest financial needs at the time when its income as a couple is lowest. This calls for one or more supplementary sources of money, none of which is a completely satisfactory solution for today's young people.

Many proposals are being made for getting young marriages launched with some financial security. There are several ways of underwriting the young marriage that newlyweds themselves are working out. Let us look at them one by one.

Parents' Help. Some parents are willing to help finance their children's marriages. They have already made a heavy investment in them, many thousands of dollars by the time they reach maturity. They want their children to be happy and to do what seems best for them. They, the parents, would be giving their children allowances if they were not married and not working, so they continue giving them an allowance after marriage until they get on their feet. This argument is found especially among those parents whose incomes are sufficient to cover their own needs and leave a comfortable margin besides. It makes sense in that the father's income is often at its peak at the time of the marriage of his children, although his costs, as head of his own household, are relatively low after the children leave.

Only a small proportion of America's families are in a position to finance the newly formed households their children establish, so parental subsidy is a possibility for only a few. A further obstacle is the general feeling that young people should be able to take care of themselves when they marry. Even if the parents are able and willing to help out, the young man often resents their aid and is reluctant to be dependent either upon his folks or his in-laws for the establishment of his own home. He frequently reflects the common feeling that a man ought not to marry until he is ready to support his wife. The girl in the case may not feel quite so strongly about it, but she, too, looks for independence in marriage and prefers their being "on their own."

G. I. *Allowances and Allotments.* For men and women who have had military service there are the G. I. allowances and allotments which finance, partially at least, the completion of schooling and getting started in a vocation. These benefits are slightly larger for the married than for the single man, and so help out if and when he marries. It is most unusual for a couple to be able to live entirely on these G. I. funds, and almost all such married couples must find some other source of income to supplement the help they get from Uncle Sam.

Special Funds and Resources. There are some fortunate young people who have accumulated some money through savings, insurance, or inheritance that can be used to help set up housekeeping when they are otherwise ready for marriage. These couples are few, however, and even they are reluctant to spend the nest-egg that spells security for day-to-day living expenses.

The Man Works—Full- or Part-Time. There is nothing new in the man's working to support his wife and family. That is traditionally expected. The thing that is new is that now when so many very young marriages take place, the man is not always ready to assume the full burden of *financial* support at first.

There are some men who get and hold a full-time job even when they are carrying a full program in school or college. This is pretty strenuous and requires more stamina and ability than many men have. It means, too, that the young husband will have little time for his wife and family at the very time in their early relationships as a family when doing things together is most important.

A part-time job is an answer for the husband who still has general or specialized training to complete before he is ready to become fully established vocationally. He carries on his vocational preparation as his main endeavor, and holds the part-time job as long as he can to help make ends meet until he can take over the full support of his family.

The Wife May Work—for a While. The most frequent way of subsidizing the young marriage today is through the wife's working. Her income added to her husband's often makes the difference between having enough money to marry on and having to postpone the marriage indefinitely. In many ways the ability and willingness of the modern woman to earn money after marriage is her dowry. Today her parents do not settle money upon her as often as they see that she gets an education and is able to earn a living either before or after her marriage.

There are many problems involved in a wife's working outside the home which must be faced by the individual couple. In general there are two big problems to consider. One is the prejudice against working wives that the wife, her husband, their family, and friends may have. The second is the problem of being able to adjust to being "just a homemaker," as so many women put it, when the time has come for her to stop working and start having a family.

Lever Brothers

Running a home involves many management chores, such as caring for and keeping track of linens and other household supplies and furnishings.

Each couple must face such questions squarely and plan wisely in the light of the situation as it exists for them.

Ready for Marriage Financially. The great majority of young people agree that it is best to postpone marriage until they have saved enough to get married on without too much of a struggle. When the Purdue Opinion Panel polled thousands of high-school students (January, 1957) on the question, "How much money should one have saved before getting married?" 72 per cent of all students gave the figure as more than $500. Only 6 per cent of all students said they felt one should marry with less than $100. This seems to indicate that high-school students generally are sensible about the responsibilities they are to assume as soon as they marry, and on the whole realize that marriage is not something to be taken lightly or rushed into prematurely.

Maturity Is Most Important

Marriage is not child's play. It is a serious undertaking, demanding a great deal of responsibility and maturity for success. Although maturity consists of much more than chronological age, as we saw in Unit I, still age is one tangible factor worthy of our consideration.

Two people are ready for marriage when they are mature enough to enjoy its privileges and responsibilities. They must be grown up enough to be both ready to cast off their childish ways and establish themselves as adults both in their home and in their community. They must be ready to find satisfaction in real responsibilities, hearty co-operation, vigorous interdependence. They must be ready to settle down.

Being Ready to Settle Down. There are many years of general exploration between childhood and maturity. Teen-age young people enjoy going places, doing things, being with different people, loving and being loved. Attachments during the teen years are often very deeply felt and moving experiences, but they tend to be short-lived.

Ruth was very deeply in love with a boy she met at camp one summer. By the time they left for home in September, they both believed their feelings would never change. But as autumn passed, their letters became more and more infrequent until by Christmas Ruth was just a girl to send a card to, and she was already dating another fine chap at school. Make no mistake, they had been truly fond of one another. But being young, they were not yet ready for lasting, permanent love.

When you marry, you must be sure that your love is mature enough to last. What feels like love one month may not be there a year later. So, how can you be sure? That is a good question.

If you give yourselves time before marriage to be sure that yours is the kind of love that will last, you do not run the risk of marrying as a result of one of the exciting but short-lived varieties of attachment that cannot weather the adjustments and intimacies of marriage. We are very sure that in order to be happily married, the two people must enjoy the day-by-day living together. It takes time to learn to enjoy the same things, to learn how the other feels, to find yourself in the intricacies of such a truly personal relationship.

Summary

Young marriages are on the increase, but generally they are more difficult to establish successfully than marriages of more mature persons. There are many questions that a boy and girl face as they contemplate marrying before he goes into military service or waiting until after he has finished his service requirements. Whatever their situation, the couple face the question of where the money will come from when they marry. They may get help from their families, from Uncle Sam if the boy is a serviceman or veteran, from special funds and savings, or more usually from his work and/or hers. In general young people themselves believe that one should have at least a modest nest-egg in terms of savings before getting married. However they settle these practical details, they are wise to give their relationship the test of time before assuming the responsibilities of marriage and family life.

Suggested Activities

Individual Study

1. Draw up a budget for a young couple getting married in your town. Use actual figures of what it will cost them each week for food, clothing, health, recreation, etc., on (a) a modest budget; (b) a comfortable budget. Consult advertisements, catalogues, and merchants for prevailing prices.
2. Find out how your local businessmen feel about employing married women (consult your Chamber of Commerce, and interview merchants and employment officers in your neighborhood). Report your findings in class.
3. Send to the Household Finance Corporation, 919 North Michigan Avenue, Chicago, Illinois, for materials on costs of getting married. Review these in class.
4. Study *Housing and Home Management*, by Lewis et al. (New York: The Macmillan Company, 1961) and write a paper on "The Home I Want to Have Some Day."
5. Write a letter to your younger sister telling her why she should stay in school even though she is very much in love with the boy she has been going with for six months.
6. Checking back on Chapter 3, compile a list for yourself of tests of personal maturity for marriage under the heading, "I will be ready for marriage when. . . ."

Group Activities

1. Conduct a class poll on the question, "Should a couple count on parental subsidy for their marriage?"
2. Arrange to see and discuss the film, "Are You Ready for Marriage?" (Coronet, sound, 16 minutes).
3. Hold a symposium of the advantages and disadvantages of marrying (a) before the man goes into service; (b) while he is in service; and (c) immediately after he returns from service.

4. Arrange a debate on the topic, "Resolved that Teen-Agers Are Too Young for Marriage."

5. Role-play a situation in which an ardent young high-school boy is urging his sweetheart to marry him at once, while the girl protests with various reasons why it would not be wise to do so just yet. Reverse the situation and have the girl pressure the boy to drop out of school and get married, while he tries to point out the wisdom of postponing their marriage until he has finished his education. Discuss the roles played and replay them with the suggestions offered by the members of the class.

6. Invite in one or more couples who have been married five to ten years to tell how they managed when they married. What did they live on at first? Where did the money come from? Were they glad they married when they did? Did either of them feel it might have been better to have waited a while? Allow time for questions and discussion both while the guests are present and after they leave the class.

Readings

DUVALL, EVELYN MILLIS, *The Art of Dating* (New York: Association Press, 1958). Chapter 16 of this book, written especially for young people, deals with such questions as: What is the right age for marriage? Should you get married while still in school? What about marriage while he is in service? and How do you go about preparing for marriage?

ELLZEY, W. CLARK, How to Keep Romance in Your Marriage (New York: Association Press, 1954). Chapter 7, "Immaturity—A Killer of Romance," discusses in ways that are easy to understand how immaturity spoils a relationship under such guises as illness, drinking, and snobbery.

FORCE, ELIZABETH S. *Your Family Today and Tomorrow* (New York: Harcourt, Brace and Company, 1955). Chapter 9, "How Ready Are You?" distinguishes between age and maturity as a basis for marriage, discusses what's wrong with teen-age marriages, and then looks at the practical side of getting married.

KIRKENDALL, LESTER A., *Too Young To Marry?* (New York: Public Affairs Pamphlets, 1956). Here are 28 pages of sound consideration of the pros and cons of early marriages and how a young person can go about observing caution before rushing into a too-early marriage.

LANDIS, JUDSON T. and MARY G., *Personal Adjustment, Marriage, and Family Living* (Englewood Cliffs, N. J.: Prentice-Hall, 1955). Chapter 11, "Age for Marriage," has a particularly challenging section on school attitudes toward marrying while in high school.

LANDIS, PAUL H., *Your Marriage and Family Living* (New York: McGraw-Hill Book Company, 1954). Chapter 7, "Deciding at What Age to Marry," has a clear chart depicting the increase in young marriages in this century and a two-page spread graphically relating the age at marriage to marital happiness.

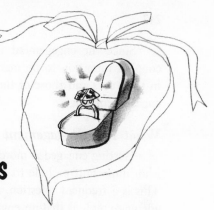

Chapter 13

Your Engagement Plans

There comes a time when you are sure enough of your relationship to begin to plan definitely for the future. You may have been going steady for some time. You may have been wearing each other's rings to show you felt "that way." You may have been "pinned." You probably have had an understanding between the two of you that some day you would belong finally and definitely to each other. He may have just asked and she accepted the proposal with but little preparation for the engagement. However it came about in your case, the engagement is marked by a public announcement to family, friends, and all who know you that you are planning to marry each other.

Is a Diamond Necessary?

It is usual for the man to give his fiancée a ring as a symbol of their betrothal. This she wears on her third finger, left hand, where later her wedding ring also will be worn, so that all may know the status of their relationship. Traditionally the engagement ring is a diamond solitaire, chosen either by the man, his family, or by the couple.

Some couples who are struggling to save enough money for wedding costs, for the backlog they will need to furnish their home, for the purchase of their first car, and for the financing of their first baby, ask quite sensibly, "Is a diamond ring actually necessary?" As a matter of fact, modern couples have already devised numerous variations on the custom that make sense to them.

On some campuses, the man's fraternity pin worn by his fiancée is taken to mean engagement (although on other campuses it simply means "pinning," with less specific commitment to marriage). An occasional couple may exchange class rings. These, worn on the third finger, left hand, together with the explicit announcement that they are engaged, serve the purpose for them. One student nurse, working in a hospital with a ruling against the wearing of rings on duty, wore a gold cross on a neck chain in place of a ring when she was engaged. There are as many other possibilities as there are couples with ingenuity.

241

Since the engagement is marked by the public announcement of the couple's intention to be married, anything that symbolizes their new status in their eyes and those of their friends and families serves the purpose of an engagement ring.

What Your Engagement Is For

Getting engaged is more than buying and wearing a ring. Being engaged is an important prelude to marriage. How long should your engagement be? This is a frequent question, for which a definite answer is sought. The only adequate reply is that an engagement should be "long enough"—long enough to accomplish the jobs that must be done during engagement to ready the two people for their life together in marriage.

Studies show that, in general, the couples who have had relatively long engagements have a greater chance of happy marriage than those whose engagements are very short. Such findings seem to suggest that it takes a while for most couples to complete their preparation for marriage through the engagement period.

Your Trousseau Is Just a Beginning. For many girls the engagement period is the time when they get their clothes ready for the wedding. To read the engagement and wedding notices in a daily paper, one would think that clothes were the most important item in a marriage, at least from the woman's point of view! These accounts give detailed descriptions of what the bride wore, but not a single mention of how she feels inside or of how really ready for marriage she is. Indeed, such news stories give almost as little attention to the groom. An oversight if there ever was one!

What the bride wears is important only in how she feels about it. Many modern girls are beginning to question the expenditure of large amounts of money for wedding finery and are saying to their dads, "Let me have a very simple wedding and use the money for some of the many things we will want for our home when we marry."

Getting to Know Each Other Well. It is during the engagement period that the two young people have a chance to learn to know each other well. Their friends and family realize that they prefer being alone and give them more privacy than they may have had before their engagement. Now, too, that they are safe in each other's affection, they can drop the many little ways of getting and holding each other's attention which may have been necessary when other competitors were around. They may at last focus their whole attention on getting fully to know each other.

It is the sharing of intimate thoughts, feelings, dreams, disappointments, hopes, and aspirations that brings a couple close together and gives each member a sense of understanding and of being understood that is important for marriage. As the engaged couple does all sorts of things together, such as the things the man has enjoyed and the things his fiancée wants to share with him, each partner learns to know the other as a whole personality.

Many, many experiences help this mutual exploration. She visits his home and sees his baby pictures, hears his mother tell personal family anecdotes of his childhood, sees the look in his father's eyes when they talk with one another, and gets the feeling of what it has been like to grow up in his family and be the kind of person he is. He becomes an accepted member of her family during the engagement period, sees how her brothers and sisters feel about her, sees her in action with them all, perhaps has a part in some of the family fussing and teasing. So he, too, becomes more personally acquainted with this girl of his and begins to see her as a real person with all the many characteristic ways of thinking, feeling, behaving, and responding to others that she will carry over into their marriage.

Getting to know each other well before marriage is an important function of the engagement period. Nothing else can take its place. If, during their engagement, the two have learned to know each other deeply and well, they are ready for the many adjustments and adaptations ahead of them in marriage.

Getting Your Families to Know You as a Couple. Up until the actual engagement, both families may or may not have been acquainted with you both. They may have taken a "let's wait and see" attitude while you were going together. But when the time comes that you are actually engaged, they have to take the relationship more seriously. Now they face the responsibility of getting well acquainted with this person who soon is to come into the family. Even more important, both families have to get accustomed to thinking of you as a pair. They may need time to get used to considering you both in all their thinking and plans.

You can help your families become well acquainted with you both in many ways. You can include members of both families in special little festivals and celebrations. You can include more and more members of your families in your own plans and pleasures. The girl can make a special effort to get to know her future mother-in-law as a person, knowing that her acceptance will mean much to the future happiness of the union. As soon as you both realize how much you can do in getting your families used to thinking of the two of you as a new branch of the family tree, you will find many ways of making yourselves felt on both sides of the house.

Learning to Respond as a Couple. One of the important functions of the engagement is to become truly accustomed to being a couple, to thinking, feeling, and acting as a couple instead of as two separate individuals. We knew a man once who, in arranging transportation for his honeymoon, bought only one ticket! That seems ridiculous, and yet it is the kind of thing that is all too common. After having been single for so many years, it takes time to learn to think and feel as two.

Before marriage both persons need to become comfortably accustomed to being accepted as a couple among their friends and acquaintances. They need the experience of being invited everywhere as a pair rather than as two individuals. Their families and close friends need to get used to thinking of them as a unit instead of as two separate entities. This takes time, not only for the couple but also for all the people who know and love them. One of the things to be done in the engagement period is to let the relationship between them become settled, accepted, taken as a fact in a comfortable fashion by all the people involved.

Discussing Future Plans

Planning and preparing ahead for the marriage adjustments to come is one major function of the engagement period. In much the same way that two people would plan ahead for a journey, looking up alternative routes, talking with those who have been on such a trip before, deciding what they will do and how, estimating their probable costs, and finding out how they both feel about the various details of their planning—so, before marriage, a couple devotes time and attention to serious planning for what lies ahead.

What Kind of Home Will Be Yours? Never before have young couples had such complete freedom to decide the kind of home they want to have. The modern young couple can choose almost any type of living accommodations that they wish, and few will either praise or blame them for their choice. They may marry on a shoestring and set up housekeeping in a trailer or a temporary furnished apartment; or they may wait until they have enough money for a down-payment on a house of their own. They may settle down near where they always have lived or pick up and move halfway around the world. Almost any conceivable way of life is a possibility.

For the couple that has waited until the man is vocationally settled and ready to support his wife and family, the problem of housing is: Which possibility available in the community where he works will be best for them? They may decide to rent some inexpensive place until they can build up a backlog between them. Or they may decide that their wisest move is to buy a place of their own, making monthly payments on their own place instead of in rentals. In this case, they must have enough ready cash to make some kind of down payment, and carry the rest as a loan or mortgage.

During engagement it is wise to see rather specifically not only the kind of place that you will call home the first few months, but also to get some perspective for the years ahead. After you have been married for a while

"On the other hand, the drainage is wonderful."

and have children, you will need a large and permanent type of residence more urgently than you did as newlyweds. When your children reach school age, your housing problem will reach its peak. By the time they are adolescents, some refurnishing will be needed to fit your home for teen-age entertaining. Then, as your children leave home, your needs as a couple will be for a smaller, more easily cared-for home. Such a long view helps in many of the decisions that must be made on the kind of home to look for, the type of furnishings to get, and the way of life that allows for the expansion and contraction of your family in the years ahead.

Who Will Do What? Will yours be the kind of family where the man of the house is its sole support and breadwinner? Or is your home to be one where the "little woman" helps out financially? Is your preference more for "woman's place is in the home" or for jointly shared responsibilities around the house as well as in the large community? Do you believe, specifically, that a man should help wash the dishes? Prepare the meals? Do the laundry? Do the heavy cleaning? Care for children? Do you see yourselves doing things together, or dividing the jobs to be done between you? The engagement period is not too soon to begin to think through your own feelings and preferences among the bewildering possibilities open to young couples today. Your decisions, to be good enough to live with, must be made upon the basis of mutual discussion, planning, and decisions now as well as later.

How Will Decisions Be Made? It's all very well to laugh at the married man who reports that he never had any question about who would make decisions in his house, because he made all the big ones, and his wife made all the little ones. Their only trouble was they never agreed on which were the big decisions and which were the little ones! When you come down to actual cases, the question of who makes the various decisions that go into married living is a complicated one. Some couples prefer the man to be the boss, in others "the woman wears the pants," and still others operate democratically with both husband and wife taking part, each contributing his or her own special abilities and interests in behalf of the common welfare. Such questions are not just a matter of philosophy, but actually expressions of the kinds of people both partners are. That is why it is important to find out early in your relationship how each of you feels about who should make decisions. During the engagement many decisions have to be made in which the two people can see how they function as a team and begin to iron out the problems that arise as they come up rather than saving until marriage the problem of who makes the decisions and how.

Your Expression of Love, Sex, and Affection. Love-making may be more difficult to discuss than any other phase of your relationship, though it may be the most important matter to talk over. Each of you probably has different kinds of needs for emotional support and tenderness as well as for physical love. One of you may need continued reassurances of being loved, while the other may just as naturally prefer to take things for granted and be unaware of the need for saying, "I love you," in many little ways every day. These differences can become serious friction points unless they are faced and worked out fairly early in the relationship.

Few persons grow up in identical families. In one home the expression of affection is full and free, with everyone kissing everyone else in the morning, at bedtime, at homecoming, at departures, and at any little incident in between. In other homes overt expression of affection is more rare, not because the persons necessarily love each other less, but simply because they express their affection differently. As two people near marriage, they come face to face with the problem of what forms of affection and love-making are most mutually satisfying, and what irritates or disappoints one or the other. Such aspects of lovers' lives are all too often kept hidden at the very time that it is most important that they be faced fully and frankly. This is one of the tasks of the engagement period that two people must work out with each other to find happiness.

What Place Will In-Laws Have? If you are planning to move in with one set of parents or the other, you may realize the importance of this discussion. If one of you has a dependent parent whose home is to be with you, you probably have faced the part that such a relative will play in your marriage. But it is not just in such extremes that in-laws are to be considered. Ordinary questions such as where you will spend your holidays, whose home you will visit for the big family festivals, which set of grandparents will be closest to your children, and how you will feel about accepting sizable gifts and aid from both sets of relatives are quite possibly as important as the major issues.

When you marry you find yourself with three families—HIS, HERS, and YOURS. How you are to divide yourselves between the three is already being determined in your engagement relationships, whether you realize it or not. The smartest thing is to see where you stand with both sets of in-laws and come to some mutually comfortable arrangement that fits your situation and the needs of everyone else involved.

How Will You Bring Up Your Children? It is possible that you have already discussed how you both feel about children, and in general how you are going to bring them up. You may have come to some agreement about whether you want to raise them strictly, so that they will be quiet and well-mannered, or permissively, so that they may have the chance to develop their own full capacities. One or both of you may feel strongly that when you have children of your own, you don't want to repeat the mistakes you feel

In planning a home, it is wise to try to anticipate future needs, which may shift as your family grows and changes.

your parents made with you. Maybe you already have said with determination, "Believe me, when I have children, I'm going to bring them up to mind." Now is the time to sort out these feelings that you both have and come to some consensus about the children you hope to have. Such discussions are so much easier and more rational before the children arrive than afterward.

Whose Friends Will Be Yours? After you marry, whose friends will you associate with as a couple? Will HER friends be yours, or HIS, or neither? Of course, some of these things cannot be fully foreseen. It will depend a great deal on where you live and whom you live near. But already you have begun to find that some friends are not enjoyed by both of you, and that one of you likes some people more than the other does. How will marriage change all that? Will you each be free to see the persons you like, or will you be discouraged by your partner's lack of enthusiasm? When you don't see eye to eye about a particular friend, how will you work it out between you? During your courtship and engagement days, you begin to face such questions. By forming the habit of working them through as they arise, you can prepare yourself for some of the further questions of whose friends will be yours as a married couple.

Recreation—as a Couple, as Individuals. The popular stereotype is that after marriage a man must have "one night a week out with the boys," as well as having recreation in mixed company with his wife. Some women very much enjoy their associations with other women and after marriage want to continue these "women only" activities. There are other couples to neither of whom such recreational pursuits within their own sex mean very much, so that few problems ever arise. The big issue is more often over the jealousy or possessiveness of one member of the pair, so that the other feels fenced in or restricted from various enjoyable activities. You cannot foresee all the problems, but some are already evident in your engagement. These may be the testing grounds for working through patterns of joint and individual recreation in your marriage.

Religious Affiliation and Participation. Whether yours is an interfaith marriage or not, you may find it helpful to discuss your church affiliation with each other and with your religious leaders during the engagement period. You may need to decide which church will be yours after you marry, where and how you will give your children their religious education, and just how religious your home is to be. You may find that the big question lies in the different ideas you both have about the importance of certain observations and practices. How you both feel about regular church attendance, blessing at meals, individual and family prayers, contributions to church and charitable organizations, and participation in religious activities generally can be matters on which you completely agree, or on which you are so far apart that you are almost afraid to discuss your differences. During the engagement period it is wise to discover as much as you can about your similar and different views and to plan realistically how you are going to develop the religious side of your marriage.

Community Activities. There are some people who look forward to marriage as a chance to set up a kind of open house where all friends, acquaintances, and neighbors are welcome any hour of the day or night. There are others whose concept of a home of their own is a place with few intrusions, a quiet place to which they can retreat at the end of a day. There is nothing basically wrong with either of these extremes or with the many variations that lie between. Problems arise when one mate holds one point of view and the other a contradictory one.

Participation in the larger community can require a great deal of time and expense. It is a great deal to ask of a person who is reluctant to spread himself too thin. The checks and balances between running oneself ragged at one extreme and becoming a recluse at the other must be worked out between two people who are to share a way of life that makes sense to them. This takes time and patience and work, both during the engagement and the marriage.

Are You Right for Each Other?

One important function of the engagement period is to test the relationship for its marriage possibilities. When the two do not see things eye to eye in enough of the important areas of life, they may be wise to recognize it soon enough to spare each other the misery of an unhappy marriage. Many a young person has felt trapped into marriage simply because he or she did not know how to break off effectively a relationship with an unpromising partner in time.

The reasons for feeling that you are not right for each other vary. There may be the discovery that each of you fades as a personality in the other's presence. Sometimes there is the growing recognition of incompatibility of background. There may be the realization on the part of one that the other is not the individual he or she seemed to be in the early dating stage and that the personality as now revealed is not acceptable. Often there is the realization that one partner is not ready for marriage and its responsibility. Frequently there is an accumulation of guilt and shame over sex activity that does not seem "right" before marriage. There are numerous other personal reasons for breaking the engagement which may or may not be recognized fully by the members of the couple.

Discussing one's feelings as frankly and freely as possible with one's betrothed is recommended as the first step in breaking off. Telling family and friends, overcoming the emotional turmoil involved, and getting back into circulation again are further steps in the process. Often consultation with a particularly helpful adviser is invaluable when doubts and uncertainties arise.

Premarital Consultation

With so many questions to be discussed during the engagement, how are two people to know when they are far enough along in their preparations to be ready for marriage as the next step? One way that helps is through consultation with those who are in a position to give expert guidance.

Medical Examination. There are many couples today who get a complete medical examination to be sure that everything is all right before they get married. Even before they go for their blood tests, now required by most states as proof that neither of the pair has a communicable venereal disease, the two people visit their doctors for a premarital examination. They want to make sure that they are all set to marry and have a family. They face with their doctors any possible physical difficulties. And they ask any questions either of them may have about what it means to become a wife and mother, a husband and father.

Personality Exploration. In some cases there is a rather special need to appraise the personality of one or both of the pair before they marry. A girl who has had a traumatic experience during her childhood may need individualized help in overcoming her fears. A young man who has had a nervous breakdown during early adolescence may need to be sure that he can go into marriage without anxiety. Previously unhappy persons who are in danger of carrying into marriage the personality problems that have already proved a burden may require professional help. Quite normal persons of both sexes find that personality tests and appraisals are helpful in getting insight into their prevailing tendencies and inclinations, their strengths and their weaknesses, especially as these personality factors affect their relationships with others in intimate situations.

Religious Conference. In all the three major religious faiths in our country, there are pastors, priests, and rabbis who insist that the couples they marry should first talk with them not only about plans for the wedding, but in preparation for the marriage. Most couples find such conferences helpful in guiding their thinking through many of the decisions that they are making as they prepare for their life together. In some places classes for engaged couples, like the Pre-Cana Conferences of the Roman Catholic Church, and the series offered regularly by local churches, YMCA's, YWCA's and Jewish temples, serve a real purpose in opening for discussion some of the questions that all couples face before marriage.

Talks with Both Families. One general tendency that has unfortunate repercussions is for young couples to take the attitude, "What we do is nobody's business but ours." Of course in a sense that is true. But in another sense, what they do as individuals and as a pair does affect many others, especially those who are related to them in both families. Studies show, for instance, that many young married couples need and take help from their families to get established, to buy a car, to get a down-payment for a home, to pay for the first baby, and to weather the many crises that are a part of marriage and family life. If the families have been consulted as plans for the marriage were made, they are far more likely to go along with what it is eventually going to cost them than if they suddenly are expected to foot bills for which they have been unprepared. Even if money is not the issue, other things inevitably are between the generations in almost any family. Talking out problems and plans as decisions are being made helps make everyone feel IN, and goes a long way toward getting a good start in marriage.

Preparing for the Wedding

You will have some preparations to make for even the simplest wedding. There are many types of weddings from which you may choose the one that best fits your situation, at a cost you can afford.

What Kind of Wedding for Yours? Yours can be a simple home wedding with just the immediate families present. It can take place after a regular service in your home church at a time when many of your friends and your pastor are already there. It can be a garden wedding, a country-club wedding, or an orchard wedding at blossom time. It can be a grand pageant with all the trimmings. It can be whatever you and your families prefer. But the choice must be made in time to prepare for it.

Deciding the Size of the Wedding. How many persons will you have at your wedding? If neither of you has a host of friends you want near you on your day of days, you may prefer a simple wedding to which just your closest relatives come. If one or both of you have many social obligations, or come from a family where such things are expected, you may feel you just have to have a big church wedding to satisfy everyone. Your first job as a couple in preparing for your wedding is to decide how big and elaborate yours is to be. This will depend somewhat on how much you want to pay for the wedding.

How Much Will It Cost? You can have a simple home or church wedding for practically nothing besides the clothes you wear and perhaps simple refreshments afterwards. Or you may spend many thousands of dollars for a great big affair. Young married couples discussing this choice usually agree on two things. One, that they were glad that they had something nice to remember as their wedding day, and two, that they often wish that they had spent less on their wedding and saved more of the money that was available for establishing their home after they were married. These two values can conflict, especially if the girl is not satisfied with something fairly simple as "nice to remember as her wedding day." Some girls have been so full of dreams of wearing long white satin wedding dresses, and trailing down the aisle behind a parade of ushers and bridesmaids, that more modest weddings leave them with a feeling of being cheated.

The most important thing to decide is just how much the wedding trimmings mean to the two of you and to plan for the kind of wedding that will keep within what you feel you want to spend on it.

Bringing Both Families into Your Plans. If one or both families are prominent in the community, the young couple may find that their wedding is a community affair from the first, with their families taking over many of the plans and arrangements. Most couples may make many of their wedding decisions themselves and yet agree that consulting their families about the various details provides a nice sense of participation to everyone concerned. All too often the bride and her mother take over and leave the groom's family so much out of the preparations that even he feels himself an outsider. Modern couples sense that their marriage does not have to be taken over by the women, and that joint consultation with interested members of both families is well worth the effort.

Your Honeymoon Plans

Your honeymoon plans are yours to make. It is possible that one father or the other will stake you to an exciting trip for a few days or a few weeks. More likely you will be dividing your own money between some of the wedding costs, your early marriage expenses, and your honeymoon.

What Will Your Honeymoon Mean to You? It is generally recognized that most young couples want to be alone right after the wedding so they have a chance to find out what it means to be married. They want and need privacy to establish the more intimate aspects of their life together. They usually need rest after the strenuous excitement of preparing for the wedding. They may want some new experience or trip that they can enjoy together. They need a chance to feel really married at last.

Where Will You Go? During the engagement it is necessary to decide just where you will go on your honeymoon, how you will travel, and how long you will stay. Many factors come into these decisions—how much money you have to spend, how much time you can take, what each of you prefers as a honeymoon, and what each of you thinks appropriate. Usually you will keep your honeymoon plans a secret from everyone except possibly some trusted friend like the best man, who may help you make travel arrangements.

If You Can't Afford a Honeymoon. You need not feel cheated if you cannot afford the time or the money for a honeymoon away from home. There are many couples who simply slip away after the wedding and go to their new home for what time they have before duty calls them back to work. All around the world one finds older married couples happy as can be at taking their long postponed honeymoon. They are often quite eager to tell how when they married there was no time or money for a real honeymoon, so they went right into their first little home and "played house" from the very beginning. Then after some years they found the time and had the money to take a real honeymoon. This makes sense to a good many couples—more sense sometimes than the opposite extreme of spending so much and having such a strenuous honeymoon that there is little time for the rest and just being together that a honeymoon is for.

Making Your Decisions Democratically. By the time you are engaged, you have probably already discovered whether one of you tends to boss the other and run off with the authority that rightfully belongs to you both. By the time you reach marriage, you should be aware of the tendencies of each toward independence or dependence, an autocratic or democratic attitude, strength or weakness in upholding a point. Each of you has his or her own tendencies that show up quickly and frequently whenever decisions must be made.

As you learn how to be more and more democratic in the way you make your decisions, you build a broad mutual basis for future decision-making. These things are important in any relationship, and most of us need to work on them to be competent.

How Long Should Your Engagement Be?

At the beginning of this chapter we suggested that the only good answer to the question of how long an engagement should be is "long enough." Now we can see something of what this means in detail. An engagement should be long enough to accomplish its purposes and to bring the couple to their wedding day ready for their marriage. For some couples who take the time and have the opportunity to work effectively on these many tasks, the actual time may not need to be long. For other couples, who are widely separated, or who for one reason or another cannot work full-time at the jobs to be accomplished during the engagement period, the time required will be longer, or they will have to carry over into marriage the unfinished business of the engagement.

In general engagements of six months or more work out better than those of shorter duration. The Burgess-Wallin studies found that engagements that lasted two years or more worked out better than those that were just too short.

Engagements that go on and on without getting anywhere may indicate that one or both members of the pair do not really want to get married. There may be some reason or other that can be diagnosed by counseling or psychotherapy. Engagements are too long, also, when the couple grow restless, frustrated, and overstimulated at being too ready for marriage over too long a time.

Your engagement should be long enough to bring you to the altar ready for each other and for marriage. How long that takes will depend upon you and your use of the time you have together.

Your Engagement Foretells Your Marriage

Studies of one thousand couples through their engagements and on into their marriages have been made by Professors Burgess and Wallin over many years. The overall conclusion of these research investigations is that the couple's engagement adjustment tends to foretell the way they will adjust to each other in marriage. When you stop to think of it, this is understandable. After all, you will still be you after you marry, as before. Your mate will not greatly change after marriage. Your relationship with each other now is basically what it will be after you are married. Through the engagement period the groundwork is being laid for the years of marriage ahead. This is so important that it cannot be slighted without some risk of handicapping the future.

Summary

There are functions of the engagement period that must be accomplished to prepare yourselves for marriage. These are generally: to get to know each other; to get acquainted with both families; and to place yourselves as a pair in the eyes of those who know you. Discussing future plans is an important part of the engagement. It involves deciding the kind of home you will have, who will assume responsibility, how you will make your decisions, how you will express your affection and love for each other, what place your in-laws will have in your marriage, how you will bring up your children, whose friends will be yours after your marriage, where and how you will find your recreation as a couple, what religious affiliations and participation will be yours after marriage, and how active you will be in community life. Premarital consultation includes a premarital medical examination, religious conference, personality exploration, and talks with both families. During your engagement you will plan the details of your wedding, including its size, type, costs, and family participation. Your honeymoon plans may be your secret and can take whatever form best fits your needs and meets your dreams at the price you want to pay. The way you plan together lays the foundation for your life together. Your engagement should be long enough to bring you to marriage ready to assume its responsibilities and enjoy its privileges. Studies show that engagements foretell marriage adjustments—which we study in detail in the next chapter.

Suggested Activities

Individual Study

1. Study Part I, "Growing Families in Changing Times," in *Family Development*, by Evelyn Millis Duvall (Philadelphia: J. B. Lippincott Company, 1957). Summarize the way in which family developmental tasks parallel the major factors to be considered in "Discussing Future Plans," in this chapter. Write a paper on "How Engagement Plans Prepare for Family Living."
2. Read and summarize the findings of the research study by Ernest W. Burgess, Paul Wallin, and Gladys Denny Shultz, *Courtship, Engagement and Marriage* (Philadelphia: J. B. Lippincott Company, 1954). Prepare a report on your findings.
3. Investigate the question of broken engagements by surveying the literature available in your library and classroom. Explore especially the works suggested in the Readings that follow.
4. Write a letter to a girl who is about to elope after a very short courtship telling her why you feel she would be wise to postpone her marriage until a more adequate engagement period is possible.

Group Activity

1. Review the book by Edward Streeter, *Father of the Bride* (New York: Simon and Schuster, Inc., 1948) as a basis for class discussion on the dangers of letting wedding plans become too elaborate.
2. Have a debate on the proposition: "Resolved that a girl has to have a diamond in order to feel engaged."
3. Role-play a series of situations suggested by the ten areas under the section. "Discussing Future Plans," in this chapter. Portray various ways in which these situations might be handled.
4. Invite a panel of married couples to discuss with your class the kinds of honeymoons they had and how they feel about the relative merits of various honeymoon arrangements. Leave time for the class members to question the participants and express their own views.
5. Ask a local pastor, priest, or rabbi to tell your class something about what is being done in your community to prepare engaged couples for marriage, either in groups or in private conferences. If possible, send a delegation to a class in preparation for marriage held under responsible auspices, reporting back on who came, who led the session, and what was discussed.

Readings

BURGESS, ERNEST W., WALLIN, PAUL, and SHULTZ, GLADYS DENNY, *Courtship, Engagement and Marriage* (Philadelphia: J. B. Lippincott Company, 1954). An easy-to-read edition of the basic research study taking 1,000 couples from engagement on into marriage. Part Two, "The Engaged Couple," is especially relevant background reading for this chapter.

CAVAN, RUTH S., *American Marriage, a Way of Life* (New York: Thomas Y. Crowell, 1959). Chapter 9, "Engagement, the Anticipation of Marriage," in this college text will challenge the mature student and serve as excellent background for both teacher and pupil in the study of the uses of the engagement period.

DUVALL, EVELYN MILLIS, and HILL, REUBEN, *When You Marry* (Boston: D. C. Heath and Company, 1961). Chapter 5, "Getting Engaged," covers most of the questions that concern high-school students studying the meaning of the engagement period and how it best serves to prepare a couple for their marriage.

DUVALL, SYLVANUS M., *Before You Marry* (New York: Association Press, 1959). Chapter 3, "Fact and Fiction About Sex," discusses frankly how far an engaged couple should go before marriage and how to understand sex standards before and after marriage as a basis for a good life together.

FORCE, ELIZABETH S., *Your Family Today and Tomorrow* (New York: Harcourt, Brace and Company, 1955). Chapter 11, "Making Good Use of the Engagement Period," has excellent sections on the possibilities of reforming each other, on meeting each other's families, and on the practical considerations that confront the engaged couple.

LEMASTERS, E. E., *Modern Courtship and Marriage* (New York: The Macmillan Company, 1957). Chapter 8, "Engagement," contains an intriguing chart on page 160 of the areas of one's personality that are exposed to the other in random dating, going steady, being pinned, engaged, and married, as well as a clear discussion of the engagement period that will interest the advanced student.

MORGAN, WILLIAM H., and MORGAN, MILDRED I., *Thinking Together About Marriage and Family* (New York: Association Press, 1955). A wealth of material in the form of discussion outlines, resources, and activity suggestions. See especially those in Chapter 9, "Engagement to Marriage."

Chapter 14

Early Marriage Adjustments

The old-fashioned fairy tale usually ends, "Then they were married and lived happily ever after." There is no suggestion that the married couple have to work out ways of living together happily. The fact is that living together as man and wife has to be learned. The two people inevitably face many areas of life where adjustments have to be made if the marriage is to succeed. Many of these adjustments can be foreseen and prepared for long before the marriage itself takes place.

Before you apply for a job in your chosen vocation, you plan ahead and prepare for it. You find out what that kind of position demands of you, what your responsibilities will be, and what satisfactions it will offer. You study for it and train for it by getting some supervised experience in situations like it, so that, when you eventually find yourself with such a job, you will be ready to succeed in it.

So it is with marriage. If you want your marriage to succeed, you plan for it and prepare for it long before you actually marry.

Adjustments Are to Be Expected

Some very young, romantically inclined young people believe that a good marriage is one in which there are no problems, no adjustments, and no conflicts. Actually such a marriage is a myth. All marriages are built on adjustments. All married people have problems to solve in their marriages. These adjustments and problems can be anticipated, just as vocational problems may be foreseen and prepared for.

Four hundred couples happily married for more than twenty years once were asked how soon their marriage adjustments were made. They reported adjustments in six important areas of married life. The indications were that

258

some couples worked out these adjustments much more quickly than others, and that those who were successful in their adjustments were significantly happier than others. We have every reason to suppose that people who prepare for marriage succeed better than those who marry blindly and in ignorance of what to expect.

Making Decisions Together. Decision-making involves a number of steps in a process that leads to a completed action. First of all comes the recognition that a decision is needed in a situation. Husband or wife faces some alternative that calls for a choice and senses that a decision must be made.

The next step is that of stating the problem so that the other person in the relationship can see it clearly. One element of this is clearing the issue of extraneous elements. Fritz Redl reminds us that one difficulty we have in our relationships in our families is that of "kitchen-sinkism," the tendency to drag into any discussion everything but the kitchen sink. Clear-cut decisions, on the other hand, start from clear, clean statements of the problem at hand.

After the situation is clearly defined, the next step is communicating to the partner how one feels about it. This involves making one's values as explicit as possible, and conveying to the other the implications and meanings of the situation as best one can. This step is familiar, since each of us has had some considerable experience in "selling our point" or "campaigning" for what we want all through childhood and youth.

The next step requires more maturity because it involves listening to the other's viewpoint and really hearing what the other person's values and feelings are. The petulant, demanding person who has been "spoiled" by always having his or her own way finds it especially hard to wait until the partner's wishes are made known before insisting upon the decision. Nevertheless, this two-way aspect of decision-making is important in a good marriage, and its difficulties must be worked out by husband and wife in many situations before they feel that they can make decisions easily as a team.

The next step calls for the weighing of the various values and seeing the possible outcomes of alternate proposals. The two people look at what would happen if they made the decision one way, and how they would like that outcome, both as a pair and as individuals. One by one they take up other possibilities, looking at the pros and cons, the advantages and disadvantages of each alternative to each of them and to both of them. Sometimes they need further facts at this point. It helps to get all the relevant data available to make the alternatives objectively clear.

The final step is that of deciding from among the various possibilities which one best seems to meet the situation at hand, preserving as many values and preferences as possible at a cost that both are willing to pay. This is hard for many individuals, and even more so for couples. There are few decisions where the pluses and minuses are pure black and white. Usually there is no one line that is so far superior to all others that it is by far the best. So the decision must be made in terms of selecting the least of the evils and taking responsibility for its outcome.

Such a complicated process requires considerable maturity and self-discipline on the part of both partners. So it is not surprising that in many marriages the adjustments to be made in decision-making require considerable time, effort, and mutual responsibility.

Ability to Make Decisions Is Learned. Growing up in a family where decisions are made openly and democratically helps in learning how to make decisions in action. We saw in Chapter 7, "Being a Family Member," that as children learn to assume responsibility for their role as family members, they learn how to participate in family discussions and live with family decisions. Then, when they marry, they put into practice what they learned in their childhood homes.

Tom and Mary get along wonderfully well in their marriage. Whenever any matter comes up that concerns them both, they talk it over together and make a joint decision about it. Mary never commits Tom to social functions without consulting him first. Tom does not buy equipment which Mary will have to use without making sure that it is just what she wants. They recognize that each is interested in certain common areas and make sure that choices and decisions are made by both of them together. It has been fairly easy for Tom and Mary to work things out this way because that is the way they were both brought up. Tom's father always deferred to his wife in those things that affected her, while she recognized his rights and interests in most things too. Mary's family had been even more freely democratic, discussing and planning together all of the big and little things that a family shares. So when Tom and Mary married, they brought their training and skill in joint decision-making to their new marriage adjustments.

But what of those who have had little if any experience in making decisions together? Some people grow up having all their plans made for them by a strong-minded mother, father, older brother, or sister. There are persons, too, so independent that when issues and choices come along, they think only of themselves. Such persons have trouble making the many adjustments to be expected in marriage, unless they begin to learn how to work and live with other people co-operatively. Marriage demands a great deal of hearty co-operation. This must be learned through actual experience. One of the best ways to prepare for marriage is to begin beforehand to adjust co-operatively to others.

Settling Your Differences

Every couple must work out its own ways of coping with the differences that arise in a marriage. As decision after decision has to be made, some adjustment must be made by each member of the pair if the total relationship is to grow smoothly and well. One big reason is that men and women, being human beings, are often irrational and unreasonable, especially when they are upset or disturbed.

Differences Are Inevitable. No two people can share the long-term intimacy of marriage without discovering many areas in which they do not see eye to eye. Sometimes couples take out on each other negative feelings that have arisen outside the marriage relationship itself. Just because a husband and wife feel safe with each other, they may use their marriage as a sort of emotional safety valve when things go wrong outside.

Enid was very much worried about her mother, who had had several heart attacks. After the last one, the doctor had warned the family that she could not pull through many more like that. Enid not only felt bad because she did not want to lose her mother, but she was especially upset because she felt guilty about all the things she might have done (and had not) to make her mother happy through the years. When she returned from her mother's bedside, she was anxious and upset. Without realizing what she was doing, she became irritable and over-critical of her husband. She would not let him sympathize with her. She accused him of not caring what happened to her mother. She did not really believe that he did not care. She was simply venting on him all her own guilty, unhappy feelings about her mother. While she was so upset, all sorts of differences arose in her marriage. Little, insignificant things that her husband did irritated her, and she nagged and fussed for no outward reason.

What happened to Enid might happen to anyone. When a man is concerned about the security of his job, when a woman is working out a personal problem, when either is anxious about the children, or household cares, or money, their differences will loom large not only in the big things, but in all the little areas of life together, too.

When people live together, difficulties may arise over the equipment that is to be shared. Such differences are so common that most of us know about them from first-hand experience.

Since all marriages and all families have differences from time to time, the question is, "How can we handle our differences comfortably for all of us?" The family that fights and fusses all the time creates a stormy place in which to live. The marriage where one partner always gives in to the other is not a full, mutual relationship. In between constant bickering and chronic

Courtesy B. F. Goodrich & Company

By making joint decisions not only about major problems but also about such minor ones as placement of a chair or who is to do a certain chore, conflicts can sometimes be avoided.

giving-in is the more wholesome alternative of settling your differences constructively. You can begin learning this right now.

Keeping Lines of Communication Open. Getting through to each other so that each understands how the other feels about situations is one of the most important foundations of a happy marriage. If you feel that you are understood, and that your partner is concerned about how you feel, you can live with a good many other little frustrations. If you feel that you know "what is eating" your partner even during the most unpleasant episodes, you can work them through together. It is when communication bogs down and you can't get through to each other that the relationship is threatened.

Some persons are fortunate in having grown up in families where members openly and clearly communicated with each other, as we saw in Chapter 6, "Getting Through to Each Other." Others experienced the frigid silences, the inarticulate helplessness that taught them only the dangers of poor communication. Whichever kind of family background was yours, you must go on from there. Every person can improve his ability to communicate with others, especially in emotionally loaded situations and in intimate interaction. But you improve only through the willingness to learn what is required.

One fairly simple approach is that of hesitating before emotions become too explosive and asking the other person, "What does this mean to you, dear?" When each is encouraged to get his or her own feelings expressed and shared, both can better understand the total problem from both points of view, and each feels that he is better understood. Sometimes just putting one's feelings into words drains off the emotion to the place where one can relax and work through the problem constructively.

WORKING CONFLICTS THROUGH [1]

If you must quarrel, there is a knack to it that every married person should learn. Certain techniques are absolutely harmful. Others are rather risky. Some are almost universally constructive. You quarrel constructively when you finish with your marriage stronger than it was when you began. Here are some of the ways in which it is done:

1. Accept the fact of the conflict without being ashamed or pretending it isn't there. Remember that conflict is normal. Face the fact that you and your spouse are human beings. Don't be alarmed when differences arise from time to time.
2. Try to find out what the whole thing means to your mate. What's "eating" him? or her? How does he feel about it and why? Keep as calm as you can yourself while you encourage him to talk it all out.
3. What does it matter to you? Why are you annoyed or irritated by it? Ask yourself honestly why it is that you are so excited about it. (For instance, Andrew discovered that he got "riled" whenever his wife set her mouth in a thin little line because that habit was associated in his experience with an extremely dominating aunt who made his life miserable when he was a little boy.)
4. Adopt a problem-solving approach to the situation, but keep remembering that many situations need not really become problems. On the basis of your mutual acceptance and understanding, try to see what can be done to work things out comfortably. Don't let tensions pile up day after day. Work them out as they come along.
5. Try to agree on some next step for taking care of the situation. Get busy on it together as soon as possible.
6. Do what you can to help the other to save face, to feel stronger, and to feel your love no matter what. Avoid sniping at each other. Keep your energy focused on the *problem* as much as you can, rather than on the *other's faults*.
7. Be patient. Be willing to take a little time for the solving of your difficulties. Don't expect miracles. Count on spending some time on the problem.
8. Before the whole situation gets beyond you, get some competent counseling help.

Difficulties Can Strengthen Your Marriage. Coping with conflict constructively leaves your marriage stronger than it was before. After you have worked through a difficult situation together and have a solution that you both feel comfortable with, you are apt to feel deep-down satisfaction in

[1] From Evelyn Millis Duvall, *Building Your Marriage* (New York: Public Affairs Committee, 1946), pp. 23–24. Used by permission

the new dimension of your togetherness. "We worked that one through; now we can take on almost anything," you say to yourselves, realizing that what once threatened your relationship and made you flare up at each other has become a further bond in your mutual understanding and partnership.

A new marriage is essentially an untried union. After two people have been married awhile, they have lived through enough different situations so that they know where their strengths and vulnerabilities, are. They are stronger as individuals and as a team for having coped co-operatively with real problems as they have appeared and worked them through together.

When Wives Work

When wives work, adjustments have to be made in the relationships between husband and wife, and later between parents and children. There was a time when such questions did not arise. Traditionally, when a woman married, she expected to find her place entirely in the home. Now more and more women are employed outside the home after they marry.

More Wives Work Now Than Ever. The National Manpower Council's official statements published in 1957, *Womanpower,* Columbia University Press, tell us that now nine out of ten women are likely to work outside the home in the course of their lives. At the close of the century fully half of the adult women never entered paid employment, and most of those who did were unmarried. Now only one-fourth of the twenty-eight million women who work during the course of a year are single, and three out of every ten married women are working. Under these circumstances, early marriage adjustments are different than many men and women have been led to expect.

Why Women Work After Marriage. A woman's work used to be home-centered. Only in recent generations, as more and more outside employment has become available, have we raised the question as to whether women should work or not. Your grandmother would have considered such a question ridiculous, because she worked and had no choice about it. Most of the things that your grandmother made in the home are now bought. Today's wives have time for outside employment, especially before children come. They are trained for it. Their earnings are needed in the great majority of new marriages, for the husband's income is low and needs are great. Most girls prefer working for a year or two instead of postponing the marriage until the man is earning enough to support them both and establish a home. Furthermore, many girls enjoy the work experience itself. Especially if they have been educated for a certain vocation, they want at least a little experience in it before settling down to motherhood. The social contribution of woman's work is significant. Then, too, some women say that they are better people to live with if their outside interests are rich and challenging.

Budgeting Time and Energy. When wives work, both husband and wife face the challenge of budgeting their time and energy so that things at home go smoothly even though both of them are employed outside for much of the working day. These are adjustments that vary with each couple and shift with each new situation. They call for elaborate patterns of planning and co-operating to get things done without undue strain on any one person at any one time. If the wife carries a full-time job, she often finds herself overworked with the responsibilities that are hers at home, too. A man may come home from work and rest. A wife hurries into the house only to find the housework to be done, dinner to get, and a hundred other things awaiting her attention. Most co-operative modern husbands realize the fairness of dividing the home tasks when both partners are working outside. Even with such adaptability, couples must work out the routines and methods of getting things done with a minimum of strain. To accomplish that is bound to take time and effort.

When babies come, most wives feel that they should discontinue their outside work while the children are small. Yet many wives find that the twenty-four-hour-a-day duty with little children requires a big adjustment after the stimulus of outside work with other adults. Trying to carry an outside job and a home and small children is an almost superhuman task which few women do well and easily. Postponing children indefinitely is no answer, either. Too many couples postpone their babies until it is too late and they lose forever the privileges of parenthood.

Choosing What Is Important. Every family unit has the challenge of planning so that what is most important to them as people can be protected. This is especially true when a wife faces the possibility of working outside the home. Many values are at stake that only wise planning can safeguard. How is the wife's strength to be conserved, with the responsibilities of both home and job facing her each day? What place will children have in the couple's life? What operations in the home can be simplified or eliminated entirely when other things loom larger in importance? How will the food be prepared? Homemaking and housekeeping done? Friends entertained? Clothing cared for? Family obligations met? Relaxation and recreation as a couple protected?

Husband and wife together determine what is essential for their marriage. They decide what can be taken on only as an occasional luxury. In such decisions they are actually determining a hierarchy of values in which some things are given top priority and others are relegated to the "when we have time" category. Answers to such basic questions of relative values cannot be found in any book. They must be worked out by the people who are to live with them—the individual husband and wife.

Sharing jobs in the kitchen can bring couples closer together and give the husband as well as the wife a sense of creative participation in family living.

Getting the Work Done at Home

Studies at Michigan State University find that many more young husbands are participating in housekeeping and homemaking activities than are those married twenty years or more. Now that many more young wives are working outside the home, more men are finding themselves at home in their families. These changing roles of men and women mean that more activities are shared by husband and wife than once was the case. But it means, too, that husbands and wives today have more joint decisions to make, more adjustments to accomplish and more problems to solve in more areas of life than in former days. Then there were definite divisions between men's work and women's work that individuals understood and followed as their parents had before them.

Professor Theodore Johannis at the University of Oregon recently studied the participation by fathers, mothers, and teen-age sons and daughters in selected family activities and found that many modern families co-operate in getting things done at home. In the 1,027 families investigated more than one-half of them shared in shopping for groceries, and fully one-third of the teen-age sons and daughters participated with other family members in this activity. Even more girls (44.3 per cent) helped in shopping for family clothing, an activity in which 30.1 per cent of the teen-age boys participated also.

In 38 to 62 per cent of the families studied, the economic activities of the household were usually participated in by two or more family members.

Sharing Family Tasks. There is plenty of work to be done in even a very simple home. There is no longer a definite division of woman's work and man's work, so most couples have to decide for themselves who shall do what and which necessary skills are involved. These decisions are usually made on the basis of their previous experience and their ability to plan constructively and fairly for the just division of labor.

Because certain jobs always used to be woman's work, or man's work, many of us tend to feel they somehow should continue to be. The big division of labor in many homes is between the work inside and the work outside the house. Men and boys do the outside jobs, mow the lawn, carry out the ashes, sweep the walk, paint the garage, put on screens. The women and girls do the inside work, the cooking, mending, cleaning, washing and wiping dishes, and taking care of little children. Such rules often work hardships. Some girls really enjoy mowing a lawn or painting a fence. Many men like to take care of the baby and enjoy helping with the dishes. Choices no longer can be left to older ways, which make little sense for us. The work at home should be divided on the basis of more important factors.

Time, Interest, and Flexibility. One fair basis for division of labor is *time*. Who has time for the given job to be done? Can he do it? Can they do it together? Many tasks that might be unpleasant are fun when shared. Doing the dishes or the washing, fixing the yard, cleaning the porch, are jobs which lend themselves to joint efforts. A second factor is *interest*. If she enjoys mowing the lawn, why not? If he likes to bake the waffles, is there any reason why he should not? Modern couples are flexible about such things and work out their work program around their individual preferences. A third factor is *fairness*. No one likes to be imposed upon; we all like to be considered. If the day has been an unusually heavy one for the wife, an understanding husband will volunteer with the dishes. If he has been through a crisis at the office, his wife will not insist that he put on the screens right now. If she is very understanding, she will suggest something that he will greatly enjoy doing and let the screens go for a while.

Such flexibility offers many advantages over the older rigid system of man's work and woman's work, but it also needs to be worked out wisely to succeed. Begin thinking and talking about possibilities long before you marry. Your ideas about who should do what will carry over into your marriage.

Money Management in Marriage

There is never enough money for everything. No matter how much or how little money you have when you marry, you will face the challenge of managing your finances. If you marry on a shoestring, as many young couples do, your problems of having enough money to cover all you want and need may be very real.

Making a Money Plan. The first task in money management is making a financial plan that will work for you. This means specifically finding out how much money will be coming in each week or month and then allocating it among the various items of expense you will have.

There are certain predictable expenditures that can be provided for regularly in your budget. Such items as food, clothing, housing (rent or monthly payments, taxes, and heat), utilities such as gas, water, electricity, telephone; medical expense, recreation, donations, and savings can be plotted month by month with reliable predictability for most items. At times there will be sudden unexpected expenses because of an accident, an illness, or the unexpected need to take a trip. But even these can be absorbed if there is a contingency fund for emergencies. If the regular month-to-month costs are covered adequately by each month's income, with some savings left over for a rainy day, the money plan usually works out comfortably.

Living Within Your Income. As long as your costs are less than your income, you can get along. But as soon as your regular expenditures get dangerously close to your total income, then you have no margin for error or emergency. It is not hard then to get so far behind that it will take a minor miracle to catch up on your payments.

Buying on the installment plan has special hazards in trying to live within your income. It sounds so simple to pay a little bit down and a little bit more each month. But when you are paying on a washer and a refrigerator, and perhaps a television set, all at once, your payments can take a sizable bite out of each pay check so that the "little bit" becomes an almost impossible burden. Living within your income means calculating all possible drains on your income and providing for the contingencies that may throw your whole financial plan out of kilter.

Being Smart Buyers. Whole books are written on better buymanship and wise consumer policies. These are full of suggestions for getting more for your money. There are many ways by which you can stretch your money for more of what you want, such as (1) making weekly menus and shopping lists from among the specials that are advertised regularly by most food stores; (2) planning ahead on what is needed so that you can take advantage of sales and discounts on all sorts of items; (3) buying clothing after the peak season has passed, and household goods at annual clearance sales; (4) patronizing the less expensive rather than the high-status stores where costs are higher; (5) having more do-it-yourself items in which you can save the costs of labor by finishing the product yourselves; (6) learning to read labels and buy the more economical product in terms of quantity, quality, and price;

"Look, darling, our first bills!"

and (7) following the recommendations of consumer-service publications such as *Consumers' Research*, Washington, N. J., and *Consumers Union*, 256 Washington Street, Mount Vernon, N. Y.

Husband and Wife Are Partners. The evidence shows that more young couples today are sharing in earning the money that keeps their marriage afloat financially. Many studies show, too, that they enjoy being partners in planning where their money is to go and in carrying out their money plans together. It is not at all unusual these days to see husband and wife together shopping for groceries or furniture or clothing and seeming to enjoy their joint responsibility as a basic part of their marriage. This sense of being partners in a going enterprise can bring real satisfaction to both members of the pair. Being true partners in homemaking certainly is a sound foundation for a marriage.

Recreation for Each and for Both

Good times in marriage do not just happen. Leisure-time fun comes out of learned enjoyment and the ability to plan for it.

Doing Things Together. Married couples find great pleasure in doing things together. If both of them are musical, they will enjoy their music and each other the more for sharing their pleasure in it. When couples pursue their mutually enjoyed activities together, whatever they do takes on a special pleasure. Perhaps that is one of the reasons why marriages of those who have common interests work out so exceptionally well.

Pursuing Personal Interests. In looking forward to marriage, you may realize that you will want to continue some personal pleasures which you cannot easily share with your mate after marriage. Stella enjoys knitting. Harry likes an occasional game of pool with the boys. Yet these separate interests need not handicap their fun in marriage. Of course they will be free to enjoy their personal pleasures as long as they are not so absorbing that the mate is continually left out.

Carry-Over Interests. Before marriage it is a good idea to sort out each other's interests in terms of which will well carry over into marriage. The boy may find that football, once so absorbing, has little place in marriage. The girl may realize that "hen" sessions with the girls will give way to discussions with her husband. So it is with many, many forms of recreation. Some activities, such as bicycle riding, swimming, music, and reading, are as much fun or more after marriage as before. Others do not transplant into marriage as well. Before you think seriously of marriage you may want to consider what interests you have in common, what things you will enjoy together, which activities you will enjoy apart, and then develop some common plans for good times after marriage.

Enjoying Mutual Friends. Whose friends will be your friends after you marry? Will the people you enjoy now be those that you both enjoy as a married pair? These are questions a couple should already have raised during their engagement, as shown in Chapter 13. If each partner recognizes that certain people have been very meaningful friends to the other through the years, and that very possibly these friendships will continue, husband and wife can develop a mutual acceptance of loyalty to old friendships while at the same time they begin making new ones as a couple.

Parents, In-Laws, and the Couple

You have probably heard about the young man who said, "I am marrying the girl, not her family." That young man needs to learn about marriage. He needs to know that families and friends are a real part of every marriage. What the family thinks is important. They cannot be entirely disregarded.

How friends feel, and how the couple feels about their friends is a vital part of their marriage. All married couples have to work out adjustments to their families and their friends.

In-Law Problems. Mother-in-law jokes sound as though in-laws were a definite peril to a marriage. This is true only if one or both members of the couple are still emotionally tied to their parents. If the young wife is really grown up, she will not have to run home to Mother every time her husband does not agree with her. If she is mature enough for marriage, she will settle her differences with her husband and leave her mother and other childish securities out of it. The same is true of the man. If he is emotionally ready for marriage, he will not compare his wife's cake with his mother's, nor long for the safe harbor of his parental home during the marital storms that come and go.

Some middle-aged mothers and fathers have to be encouraged to let their children go. The mother who has not kept up interests and activities of her own may cling to her married children and interfere more than is good for any of them. Such an attitude is understandable. Often she feels that she is left high and dry as her children grow up and leave home. For years she has devoted her entire life to them. Now life looks bleak and lonely without any reason for being. But it does not help her to let her meddle in the newlyweds' marriage. She should be encouraged to take up interests of her own that will satisfy her needs.

Finding Harmony Among In-Laws. In a study [2] of more than five thousand in-law situations, it was found that harmony among in-laws depends on two central factors: acceptance and mutual respect. If the members of the larger family feel that they are accepted and loved as persons, they are apt to get along well with one another. But when a young bride comes into the family expecting that she will not get along with her mother-in-law just because she is a mother-in-law, there may very possibly be difficulties between the two women. When the bride feels that her mother-in-law accepts her and takes her into the family as a real daughter and daughter-in-law, the feeling of being "in" helps in the total family relationship.

Mutual respect for each other as people is evident in many ways. It includes respecting each other's wishes and values and interests. It means treating each other as real human beings with tastes and special qualities. It means expressing appreciation for one another from time to time, so that each can feel respected and admired and loved for what he is, as well as for what he does.

Harmony among in-laws does not just happen when the marriage is consummated. It grows and develops from mutual concern, appreciation, acceptance, and respect. It thrives on the satisfaction found in being members

[2] Evelyn Millis Duvall, *In-Laws: Pro and Con* (New York: Association Press, 1954).

"I want my mother!"

of the larger family and in finding positive advantages in being and having in-laws.

Grandparents Can Be Assets. Grandparents can be a joy in a family. The sense of continuity as a family, the tie with the past, the on-going affection, the personal interest, the help in a crisis, all make parents of married children invaluable. As little children come, grandparents come into their own, and can greatly enrich the lives of the children as well as the parents. We are not always smart about these widening relationships. All of us, grandparents, parents, and children, have much to learn in deriving the full value of these potentially fruitful relationships.

The Children You Will Have Some Day

A marriage is not a family until children come. Most couples want children of their own. Few realize how many plans and preparations can precede the coming of the first baby. Here, for instance, are some of the questions that young people may realistically consider long before they marry.

About Your Children

1. How many children do you want? (Are you realistic about this in terms of the number you can afford, take care of, and rightly expect?)

2. Do you very much prefer boys? girls? (Be careful about this; strong preferences for one sex or the other make for trouble when a member of the other sex comes along.)
3. Are you sentimental about such things as curly hair, twins, or dimples? (Such things cannot be "ordered" and are not very important anyway, you know.)
4. Have you thought about how you want to bring your children up? (It would be a very good idea to give considerable attention to this. It is very important.)
5. How well do you agree with your friends on how children should be raised? When you discuss such things, are you able to stand some opinions that differ from yours? (You had better, for the person you marry may have quite different ideas about one phase or another in child-rearing.)
6. Do you like the idea of prenatal classes for mothers and fathers before their children come? (We hope so, for they are a great help.)
7. Will you be willing to study about children after yours arrive? (Parent education has proved itself, and you will gain much from such opportunities for study.)

The point here is that thinking about children is a part of your preparing ahead for marriage. Do not let yourself feel embarrassed about it. It is one of the most exciting and rewarding things you can do.

Bringing Your Dreams into Reality

Long before you actually get married, you dream about how it will be. You say to yourself, or to some trusted confidant, "When I get married, I know just how I'll want things to be." As soon as you approach marriage with your partner at your side, you are at the point of bringing your dream into reality. As you plan ahead for the kind of home that you will have, you are making your dreams come true.

How Will Your Home Be Different? As you sift out your hopes and plans, you will be deciding how your home will be different from any either of you has ever known. In some ways your home-to-be will resemble your family. You will want to share the pleasant rewarding ways of doing things that meant a great deal to you as you grew up in your family. Likewise your partner will want to continue some of the family ways of life he has known. This is what makes your marriage uniquely your own, expressing your values, embodying your dreams, channeling your own special way of life in common.

Your Kind of Family. As you face your wedding and work through your early marriage adjustments, you are determining the kind of family you are building together. You are in the process of deciding many things—where you will live and on what, how you will work out your relationships with each other and with the other special people in your lives.

Beyond these specifics, you are determining, too, the foundations of your home in the choices you make for it. You are establishing a pattern of behavior which generally favors spiritual goals or which stresses material objectives. You are facing choices in which you must often weigh your interest in people against your interest in things. You are setting precedents in homemaking that may lean to the rigid and unchanging or the flexible and resilient, or perhaps fall somewhere in between. You are setting the stage from the start for the type of family rule you want, whether dictatorial or democratic.

Your home expresses you. What you put into it is what comes out of it. If you want the marriage and family that you are to build to express the part of your life that you most want to preserve and develop, now is not a minute too soon to start thinking about it.

Summary

Adjustments must be expected in marriage and can be planned ahead. Experience in making joint decisions with others is good preparation for marriage. You will need to know how to settle your differences in marriage in ways that are constructive. One question you will need to settle is whether the wife is to work. Dividing the work to be done and developing the needed skills can be on the basis of time, interest, and fairness. Families and friends can be an asset to a marriage. Good times must be planned. Thinking about the children you will have some day is part of preparing ahead for marriage.

Suggested Activities

Individual Study

1. In the section, "Why Women Work After Marriage," are seven arguments for wives working a while after marriage. Number them and copy them into your notebook. Add to them other points which you think of, or which you discuss in class. Talk with women you know who combine marriage and work. Get their points of view on how it can be done successfully.

2. Check the following list for frequency of "fussing" in your family over the objects listed:

CONFLICTS OVER COMMON FACILITIES

(Do not write in this book.)

Facility Which Several Family Members Want to Use at the Same Time	Very Frequently	Often	Hardly Ever
Bathroom			
Living Room			
Kitchen			
Radio			
Automobile			
Clothing			
Others (name)			

3. Copy the following table into your notebook. Then check the column which seems right to you for the following tasks.[3]

WHO SHOULD DO WHAT AROUND THE HOUSE

(Do not write in this book.)

	The Husband	The Wife	Either	Both
Washing dishes				
Wiping dishes				
Firing the furnace				
Washing windows				
Mending socks				
Washing clothes				
Doing the ironing				
Keeping the budget				
Putting things in their place				
Baking				
Cooking				
Canning				
Gardening				
Washing the car				

[3] You are thinking in terms of a modern co-operative marriage if most of your checks appear in the *either* or *both* column. You are still a little old-fashioned if many of your checks appear in the first two columns.

4. Gather data on how much it actually costs to buy and keep a car in your community. Consult the chapter on "Money Matters" in Duvall and Hill, *When You Marry* (see Readings), and other references that will help you see the various items that must be included in a realistic appraisal of the cost of an automobile for a young married couple.
5. Review and write a report on Arch W. Troelstrup, *Consumer Problems and Personal Finance* (2nd ed., New York: McGraw-Hill Book Company, 1957).
6. Write a paper on the religious participation and practices you want to continue when you have a home of your own.

Group Activity

1. Invite into your class for a panel discussion young wives who have found different answers to the question, "Should women work after marriage?" Choose one whose sole attention is given over to her marriage and home, one who carries a part-time job as well, one who carries a full-time job and her home responsibilities with the help of a co-operative husband. Ask one who has managed the threefold job of home, employment, and children. Encourage members of the class to ask questions and to discuss the various points raised.
2. Debate the proposition, "Resolved that husbands and wives should have separate vacations." See that the main points made by both sides are written on the blackboard and copied in your class notebook. Write your own personal opinion about the question at the close of the class listing.
3. Discuss the film strip, "Parents Preparing Youth for Marriage" (The Radio and Film Commission, 1001 Nineteenth Avenue South, Nashville 2, Tennessee).
4. Have class committees find out what it actually costs young couples to live in your community on a low, medium, and generous income. Have the housing committee find out what local rentals are for various types of accommodations, clip advertisements of apartments and houses for rent, and gather data on what it costs to buy a home in your community. Have a food committee collect food sales announcements from your daily papers and plan the menus and food costs for one week for a newly married couple. Have the clothing committee plan a budget for the married couple's clothing. The recreation, health, and other committees similarly share responsibility for computing actual allotments from a couple's budget on a low, medium, and a generous income. Plot these three budgets on the board and discuss.
5. Role play a series of decision-making episodes between a husband and wife during the first months of marriage. Have the class participate in

choosing the problems and discussing the various situations as each is
acted out.

6. Assign a committee to give a group report of the exploratory study of in-
law relationships, Evelyn Millis Duvall, *In-Laws: Pro and Con* (New
York: Association Press, 1954). Discuss freely, encouraging the frank
airing of feelings.

Readings

CAVAN, RUTH S., *American Marriage: A Way of Life* (New York: Thomas Y.
Crowell, 1960). This is primarily a college text that is clearly enough written to
be of value to the advanced senior-high-school student. Chapter 12, "Learning
to Live Together," is particularly relevant to early marriage adjustments.

DUVALL, EVELYN MILLIS, and HILL, REUBEN, *When You Marry* (Boston: D. C.
Heath and Company, 1961). You will find much that is pertinent in all of Part
II, "What Being Married Means." We suggest that you read especially Chapter
8, "Newly-Weds" with its detailed coverage of the adjustments the newly married pair have to make to each other and to marriage.

LANDIS, JUDSON T. and MARY G., *Personal Adjustment, Marriage, and Family Living* (Englewood Cliffs, N. J.: Prentice-Hall, Inc., 1955). In Chapter 16, "What
It Means to Be Married," is a clear report of the authors' research findings on
the length of time it takes to make various adjustments in marriage and the
marital happiness of the couple.

LEVINE, LENA, M.D., *The Modern Book of Marriage* (New York: Bartholomew
House, 1957). An understanding woman physician has written this practical
guide to marital happiness, discussing wisely some of the many questions young
married couples have brought to her about their own marriages. The answers
are short and to the point, as well as reassuring and helpful.

LEVY, JOHN, and MUNROE, RUTH, *The Happy Family* (New York: Alfred A.
Knopf, 1938). This modern classic has two chapters that are directly pertinent
to the discussion in this chapter. Chapter 4, "Sexual Satisfaction," and Chapter
5, "Living Together." In both of these chapters you get the individual persons
in perspective through the marriage relationship.

MACE, DAVID R., *Marriage: The Art of Lasting Love* (Garden City, New York:
Doubleday and Company, Inc., 1952). If you have ever read the *Woman's
Home Companion* articles by Dr. Mace, you may recognize the materials in this
book. We suggest that you read his Chapter 3, "The Early Weeks of Marriage,"
in connection with your study of early marriage adjustment.

Courtesy B. F. Goodrich & Company

V

Getting Along with Children
How Children Grow
Caring for Children

Children in Your Life

Chapter 15
Getting Along with Children

Do children like you? Do you enjoy them? When you are with children, do you know what to do? Are you able to be an interesting companion with most children you know? Do you know what children like in older people? Have you ideas about the way you are going to bring up your children some day? Most of us have, even while we are still in our teens. Such ideas and questions are worth considering. Let us look at them more in detail.

The Children You Know

Now is the time to take an inventory of the children in your life. How many children do you know? Are you in close touch with any babies under one year of age? Do you have a speaking acquaintance with one or more runabouts two or three or four years of age? How many children of elementary-school age do you know by their first names? Have you ever known personally a child genius, a "quiz kid"? Do you know a child with some special handicap: crippled, deaf, sightless, or with a weak heart, perhaps? Have you ever been completely responsible for a little child for any long period of time?

How your answers will differ, even in your own class! Some of you have grown up surrounded with children of all ages and kinds ever since you can remember. There is Ted, for instance. He grew up the oldest of nine children. By the time he was in high school, he knew more about children than many men twice his age. Some of you will have had almost no experience with children yet. Charleen cannot remember her only sister, who died when she was a baby. Her mother has not been well since and must have the house quiet. So Charleen has played alone most of her life. She knows lots of her mother's older friends who come in and out of the house. But she could count on the fingers of one hand the children she really knows.

Brothers and Sisters. Younger brothers and sisters are perhaps your closest contact with children. You get to know a child when you live with him. Sometimes, perhaps, you may wish you did not know him so well. When your kid brother teases you and makes your life miserable, you may wish you had been an only child. These feelings are not uncommon, as you saw back in Units I and II. Fortunately they usually pass. The same boy who can be such a pest on one occasion can be a joy to be with upon another. The important thing is that your understanding of children can be a real help in getting along with brothers and sisters.

Youngsters in the Neighborhood. Some neighborhoods teem with children of all ages. It is all you can do to pedal a bike down the street, what with all the children out at play. Teen-agers differ a great deal in the way they feel and act with these neighborhood youngsters. Some are friendly and really interested in the younger children next door and down the street. Sammy yells, "Hi, kids," and they come running to have a word with him. He has hardly stepped out of the house before he has a cluster of younger boys and girls hanging around him. He always seems to have time for them, even if he gives them no more than a grin, or a wave, or a shouted comment as he passes by. They all adore him.

Other young people find it difficult to know what to say or do with the children of the neighborhood. The children stop and stare as they come by, and they feel embarrassed, and do not know what to say or do. Sometimes they drop their eyes and keep right on going. Sometimes they try to say something, but it never seems quite right. They sense it. And so do the children, apparently. What is the matter? Do you know?

Being a "Sitter." Your generation has brought a new profession into being: "sitting." In the past, when parents wanted to go out for an evening, they got some relative or friend to come in and "mind the baby." This went on for many hundreds of years, until so many young families lived so far away from their folks, and so few had neighbors they knew well enough to "impose upon," that something new had to be added. That something new was the practice of hiring some willing person to come in and "sit" with the children while the parents were out.

Young people of high-school age are in great demand in many communities for baby sitting. Their hours at school allow this service in the late afternoons, in the evenings, and on Saturday. They usually can use the extra money, and so are available. Many mothers like to have alert teen-agers tend their children while they are away. They feel confidence in these young people's willingness to carry out their wishes. They like to feel that such teen-agers understand and like children and get along well with them.

In some communities, teen-age girls (and sometimes boys) have taken regular child-care courses. They have banded together and decided on what is a fair charge for their services, what they are willing to do while sitting, and many other such arrangements. This is sensible indeed. In fact, there would

"The sitter chickened out at 9:15."

be fewer misunderstandings if both sitters and parents had a code to go by. The following items might be jointly considered.

CODE FOR BABY SITTERS AND PARENTS

(Items on Which Some Joint Understanding Is Usually Helpful)

1. *The exact hour at which the sitter is expected to arrive.*
   It is annoying for parents to have to wait for tardy sitters. It is not pleasant for the sitter to hurry to arrive, only to find that the parents have not even begun to get ready to leave.
2. *Just what the parents expect to have done for their children.*
   What do they want done if the child awakens or cries? Is the child to be fed? What? What methods do they approve if the child does not want to do what

the parents have told the sitter he is to do? What is to be done if the child awakens and is afraid? If the child is sick? If there is an accident? If prowlers come?

3. *What do the parents want done besides caring for the child?*
Do they expect the sitter to wash the dishes? Wash out the child's clothing? Clean up the bathroom? Get a meal? Take telephone messages? Such things should be specifically understood.

4. *Just what privileges is the sitter permitted?*
What food may the sitter eat? Is it all right to play the radio? Take a nap? Use the telephone? What about having friends drop by?

5. *What is the rate of pay?*
By the hour or by the evening? Different for week-end evenings than weekday ones? More on special holidays such as New Year's Eve? Extra pay for time after midnight? More when the sitter does work for the family than when nothing extra is expected? What about carfare?

6. *Who will see the sitter home, and how?*
Will some responsible adult drive the sitter home at the end of the evening? If not, what arrangement is to be expected?

7. *What is the sitter to do in an emergency?*
Fire, burglars, severe accidents, unexpected arrival of relatives, an important telephone call? Where can the parents be reached?

What Children Like

You get along better with children if they like you. What can you do to get children to like you? What do children respond to in other people? How can you plan ahead to become the kind of person a child will like?

Little Gifts and Thoughtfulness. Most children like to feel that you have remembered them. They like evidence that you thought of them even before arriving on the scene. Some little children are very open in their demand for such offerings. They rush at you and say, "What did you bring me?" Parents are usually embarrassed by such behavior and discourage it as much as they can, but the hopeful gleam still shines in little eyes, especially if they remember some previous gift. Within reason these expectations are all right, and indulging them will not "spoil" the child, especially if you are wise in the selection of your gift.

"It is not the gift, it is the thought" is especially true for little children. A gift does not have to cost anything to please. It may be a bright-colored pebble for a lad who still has a handful he gathered at the beach last summer. It may be a post card for a little girl's collection. It may be a stick of gum, or a new marble, or perhaps a little ball. It is the fact that you remembered *him* that pleases. If your gift shows, too, that you thought of his special likes and preferences, it is especially enjoyed.

One caution on this matter of gifts is in order. Do not proffer anything of value without being first sure that it is acceptable to the child's parents.

The same is true of candies and other foodstuffs. Parents have definite ideas about what their children may and may not have, and you must reckon with these if you want them to like you, too.

In offering something to a little child still at the stage where everything goes into his mouth, be sure that it is safe. Safe objects have no sharp edges or corners and no poisonous paint. They are waterproof and big enough not to be swallowed.

Children Like Those Their Parents Like. There is something almost uncanny in the way little children can tell how their parents feel about someone. If the person is accepted joyously into the home by the parents, the child soon reflects their attitude. But if one or both of the parents have some question or reservation about the outsider, the child senses it quickly and is often embarrassingly direct about it.

Myrtle had such an experience. She had been taking care of two little children for several evenings while their father visited their mother in the hospital. Everything went beautifully until one night after the mother had come home. Then the little girl, who had always been so friendly, came up to Myrtle and, looking her coldly in the eye, said, "Why don't you go home?" Something had happened to change the whole climate of the situation. It was as if a cold wind had blown through where before all had been sunshine and warmth. Fortunately Myrtle was a big girl and knew that such things happen, especially when there has been illness in a home. She wisely kept quiet about it, but went out of her way to win the mother's friendship. As they became better acquainted, the little girl's feelings changed, and soon she was as affectionate and friendly as ever again.

How could the little girl know how her mother felt so soon? Children learn to recognize such things quickly at a remarkably early age. Even before they learn to talk and to understand words, they can tell how people feel. They watch facial expressions for signs that one of their parents does not like something, or is angry, or glad, or afraid. That is the way children learn. The mother needs to *say* very little. She can shrug when a name is mentioned, and the child realizes that she does not like that person. She may frown or pull her mouth tight and tense, or she may just keep unusually quiet. In a hundred ways she communicates to her child the way she feels. This is the way prejudices are communicated—the many unexplained likes and dislikes children pick up and feel strongly about, often without knowing or even thinking why. What feelings and prejudices do you communicate to children when you are with them?

Being Treated Like Real People. Most of all, children like to be treated like the real flesh-and-blood individuals they are. They do not like to be laughed at or ridiculed, even in fun. Rather they like people who can laugh

Stewart Love from Monkmeyer

Children's play needs vary with their developmental stage. By doing hospital work, a girl can learn how to get along with infants as well as how to care for them.

with them in many little jokes that arise in everyday situations. They like people who really listen to what they are trying to say. They do not like people who talk all the time, even in an attempt to amuse them. They like people who do not talk down to them. They respond to those who accept them as people in their own right. Children like to be liked. They like people who act as if they actually enjoyed them and liked being with them. Children are very much like older people in this respect.

Songs and Stories. Long before a child can understand words, he loves to hear songs and stories. During the first weeks and months of his life little lullabies will often quiet a restless baby more quickly than anything else. Later he begins to enjoy the rhythm of nursery rhymes, and soon to partici-pate in them. Part of the special heritage of little children is the rich collection of nursery rhymes: "Jack and Jill," "Little Bo Peep," "Baa, Baa, Black Sheep," and all the rest, which are enjoyed over and over again. It is interesting to see how often children request the same old familiar tunes, and soon are able to detect the slightest variation from the usual version!

A good collection of songs which children like is a sound investment for anyone who often takes care of children. Especially pleasing to them are songs that can be accompanied by action or pantomime. Here the popular little finger plays come into good service. Becky came into a room where three little three-year-olds were fighting over which would have a small red ball. Without a word to any of them, she sat down near them and began the little finger game, "Here's a ball for baby, big and soft and round." Before she had finished the first sentence, three pairs of eyes were upon her. Three pairs of ears took in every word. Before the first time through, the children were fol-lowing her motions with hesitant efforts to match her gestures. Over and over again the four repeated the game. Each time through the children would look up and smile. One of them would sigh contentedly and say, "Do it again," and so it continued. The fighting mood vanished completely. Three happy children had discovered means of self-expression in the swing and pantomime of the finger play.

Some stories for children seem to live on and on from generation to generation. Fathers and mothers tell them to their children, who grow up and tell them to theirs. Stories such as "Peter Rabbit," "The Three Bears," and "Cinderella" are classics in children's literature. Many children seem not to tire of them, and want them told over and over again. But parents and other storytellers keep trying to provide variety. They can easily do so from the rich collections of children's stories that come out yearly and are part of every good library.

All children enjoy rhymes. Sidewalk play is often punctuated with jingles. Children jump rope and play hopscotch to the rhythm of assorted chants. A new rope jingle is usually welcomed by little girls. Active running games like

"Run, Sheep, Run" and "Hide and Seek," which are taught to the younger by the older children of the neighborhood, are altered from time to time with new variations introduced by interested neighbors.

Children Learn Through Play

"Children play so hard" is a common observation. Children love to play, not because it is easy, but because it is hard. They get bored with things they have mastered and generally want to do things that are challenging. They usually have a tremendous urge to learn about life, about things, about people and ideas, about themselves, and most of all about what they are becoming— more and more grown-up.

Children learn what they need to grow on in various kinds of play. They need to explore their world and find out for themselves the touch, the shape, the weight, and the possibilities of the things around them. They have to find out what makes things work, to take them apart and put them together again in order to learn. They have to act out many roles and try out all sorts of ideas and feelings to learn why people are as they are. They must learn a great deal about themselves and practice hour upon hour the many, many skills whose mastery will make them capable human beings.

Play Is of Many Kinds. It takes many kinds of play experience to build a well-rounded person and to satisfy the fast-growing youngster. Sometimes play is quiet and contemplative. Often it is robust and loud. Sometimes play involves others, but often it is carried out by oneself. At times a child makes something in his play, but at other times he "makes believe." Each of these kinds of play contributes to children's growth: (1) active physical play; (2) quiet manipulative play; (3) creative construction play; (4) make-believe dramatic play; (5) social play with others.

Active physical play is essential to child growth and development. Through active play a child learns to run, to skip, to jump, to climb, to throw and catch a ball, to pull and push and roll things, to ride a scooter and a bike, to skate and fly a kite. His muscles are developed through exercise. He not only must exercise his muscles; he has to train them to do his bidding. Playthings that help children develop physically include push-and-pull toys, wheel toys of all kinds, sports and gym equipment, things to climb on, swings, balls, and plenty of space.

Quiet manipulative play teaches a child how to use his smaller muscles capably. He puts things together and takes them apart. He learns to draw and to paint, to cut and to paste, to model and to sew. Playthings that help children learn fine muscle skills include hobby kits of all kinds, drawing and painting materials, modeling clay, scissors, paste, paper, needles, string, beads, cloth, blocks, nests of cans, boxes, and various kinds of peg boards and toys to be fitted together.

Creative constructive play is seen in many forms of manipulative play as well as in building materials. Blocks of all sizes and shapes are of central importance. Hammer, nails, saws, and other tools for building help the older child make things. Sewing, cooking, baking, and modeling materials interest boys as well as girls in the early years.

Dramatic play is the way children "make-believe" they are someone else whose role in life they are learning. They play house with dolls and house-keeping equipment and so "practice" skills of homemaking. They play school and church and store. They play fire engines and trains and planes and space ships. Thus they act out their interpretations of the world around them and practice the ways adults do things.

Social play with others includes all the group games and sports and activities in which several children play together. Social development is dependent upon a child's learning how to take turns, to share, to take part in and abide by group decisions, to play fair and be a good sport. These things do not come all at once, but through many months and years of participation in group activity.

Guiding Children's Play. Children devise their own play if they have suitable materials available. Guilding children's play involves, essentially, supplying them with the equipment, space, and facilities appropriate to the situation and the development of the individual child.

A tiny baby enjoys watching and grasping bright colorful things—a mobile above his crib, balloons, and fluttery, dangling objects. He likes toys of various textures—rubber, plastic, wood, metal, and soft, cuddly objects to handle and hold.

An infant several months of age likes to play with a cradle gym, to shake a rattle, and to bite a teething ring. By the time he is about a year old he likes blocks, clothes pins, water toys, spoons, pans, and cups, things to shake and pound and fit together.

A toddler is especially pleased with toys to push and pull. He needs, too, things with which he can pound and bang and dig and pour. He is about the world like a young explorer and must literally get into things in order to learn about them and about himself.

Preschool children learn on all sorts of equipment as their world expands around them. Climbing apparatus, push, pull, and pedal toys lead the rest in popularity. Sandbox and wading-pool play are close seconds. Building materials of all kinds; dolls and household equipment for make-believe; clay, crayons, paints, and paper for creative efforts; simple musical instruments such as drums, triangles, and tambourines all have their place in the life of the preschooler.

With school age comes heightened interest in group play, sports, and playground activities with other children. Hobbies and creative interests, such

as collecting all sorts of things, dramatizing various activities, widening his experience with books, and doing construction work, occupy the individual youngster.

Children's play shifts as they mature. Guiding the play of an individual or a group involves providing the materials that will challenge and delight them. Given toys and play materials that meet his needs, the individual child plays well. Recognition of his clues for readiness for more advanced playthings, or a change in pace in the kind of play, makes for a happy growing child with a minimum of adult interference.

Suitable Toys and Playthings. The mechanical toy that amuses Uncle Jim may not interest his nephew. It may be frustrating. It may be boring. It may be dangerous, easily broken, or otherwise quite unsuitable. Suitable playthings for children have the following characteristics:

1. Safe and sanitary—no sharp points or edges, non-poisonous paint or dye, large enough not to be swallowed (nothing smaller than a plum for a little baby), and washable.
2. Durable—will last through normal usage without breaking, will hold a child's interest over a period of time, and can be used in a variety of ways.
3. Appropriate—suited to the child's readiness and interest, geared to his developmental level, focused on his on-going activities and interests.
4. Stimulating—encourages the child's developing abilities, is something he can do something with, opens new areas and avenues for his play.

In general it is the simple multi-purpose toys that are enjoyed most and hold a youngster's interest longest. Blocks, for instance, can be a simple tower for the toddler, and later can become a train or a plane or a castle or a bridge or a garage for his truck and cars. Dolls can be used to cuddle and to comfort, to scold and to nurse back to health, and later to dress and to launder and shampoo and parade and pretend with. Such things are among a child's first loves, and are usually the last to be discarded as the child grows up.

Answering Children's Questions

Children learn in many ways. As they become old enough to talk, they learn by asking questions—all kinds of questions. They ask questions that can be answered quickly and easily, like "Where are we going?" They ask questions that we do not know how to answer, like "What will I be when I grow up?" They ask many questions we find hard to answer, like "Where did I come from?" From the child's point of view, these are all good questions. Any normal growing youngster asks such questions.

Children's Inquiring Minds. Growing is learning. And learning is asking and finding out about things, about people, about oneself. When children ask questions that call for facts that we know, answering them is simply a matter of being patient, of listening, and of giving a clear answer.

When a child asks about things we do not know about, we can bluff by pretending we know, we can put him off, we can dodge his direct inquiry, we can say that we do not know, or we can join forces with him in wondering about the question. Of all the various ways of meeting a child's question, the best is that of accepting the question with interest, and either answering it if we can, or becoming partners with the youngster in the pursuit of an answer. We can look it up together. We can go find someone who might know about the subject. We can say, "That's a good question. Let's see if we can find out more about it."

Children sometimes ask questions that embarrass us. They ask us personal, private questions. They ask about life and death, about men and women, about sex and babies, about how much money we have and how much a man earns, about social status and why some people seem to be "better than others." Such things are not the things we like to discuss. They are the areas of life we do not like to talk about if we can avoid them. Our own questions along these lines have quite probably been dodged when we asked them. Now when children ask them, we reflect the embarrassment we have learned about these topics. Yet from the child's point of view these things have to be understood quite as much as those that we enjoy discussing with him.

Answering Simply and Directly. Children learn a step at a time. When they ask a question, they are not asking for everything that is known about the subject. What they are after is the next step in their understanding that will help them see through to the next, and the next, at some later time.

What a child is after is a simple and direct answer. He asks, "Where are we going?" and you answer, "To Grandma's." That satisfies him and he trots along merrily, aware of his destination without complicating details. So, too, when he asks, "Where did I come from?" he is after the simple fact of his origin. As a little child, he is satisfied with the direct reply, "You grew in your mother." He is not asking for an elaborate recital of biological detail all at once.

Good questions met with good answers lead on to further questioning. A youngster absorbs the answer to one set of questions and grows on to the next level of his understanding. The time comes when he is no longer satisfied with the former answer and presses with another somewhat more sophisticated. Now he asks, "But how did I get in Mother in the first place?" He is answered, "You grew from a tiny seed made by the union of a father and mother cell." Later when he wants to know, "How did I get out?" he is told, "You were

"Want to hear something fantastic? Ask your folks where you came from."

Eldon Dedini and Look magazine

born when you were ready, as all babies are." And so on and on, through the years, one question leads to another—as long as he feels free to ask and confident that he will get a good answer.

When a child's questions are not answered in ways that he can understand, he may stop asking. He learns that it does not do any good to ask some things, so he does not bother any more. This is why dodging children's questions, and giving false or too elaborate replies are discouraging. That is why answering simply, directly, and honestly is the best policy.

Feeling Comfortable Yourself. It helps if you can feel comfortable about the questions children ask. If you are embarrassed, you find it difficult to reply easily and simply; you stammer and hesitate and grope for the right words to use.

One way to become more comfortable in the subjects that you previously have found embarrassing to discuss is to see the child's question from his point of view. If you can sense what he is really asking, you find it easier to answer than if you allow your own feelings to confuse you.

It helps, too, to learn about those things that your child is asking about. Parents find that as their children begin to ask questions about mothers and fathers and babies, it is a good idea to read what has been written for parents about these things. Sometimes they attend parent education classes where their role in their children's education is discussed and where they can exchange ideas with other parents on better ways of handling children's questions.

Feelings are quite as important as facts—more so, sometimes. Therefore, it is important to get over foolish confusions and meet life's questions without embarrassment as often as possible. Nowadays there are special resources to help any young person find out what he or she wants to know.

Special Resources for Answering Questions. Ministers, doctors, teachers, nurses, and other specially qualified persons are often helpful advisers on special questions. Dictionaries, encyclopedias, and children's reference works are particularly valuable in helping children look up facts and figures about well-known things. Special books are available for those hard-to-answer questions. Among these are:

Bro, Marguerite Harmon, *When Children Ask.* New York: Harper & Brothers, 1956. Deals especially with the questions that parents and other adults find hard to answer, with suggestions about the kinds of answers children find most helpful.

Child Study Association of America, *Facts of Life for Children.* New York: Bobbs-Merrill Company, 1954. Includes the answers to give when a child asks about sex, chronologically arranged from children's earliest questions.

Duvall, Evelyn Millis, *Facts of Life and Love for Teen-Agers.* New York: Association Press, 1956. Based upon thousands of questions young people in their teens ask, about what it means to grow up, become men and women, date, fall in love, get married, and have babies.

Eckert, Ralph G., *Sex Attitudes in the Home.* New York: Association Press, 1956. Ways of dealing with everyday family situations so as to develop healthy attitudes in children.

Gruenberg, Sidonie M., *The Wonderful Story of How You Were Born.* New York: Doubleday and Company, 1952. A carefully written book to read to children, or to give to them to read for themselves when they are old enough.

The Kind of Parent You Will Be

What kind of father or mother will you be? It is quite possible that you have already given that question some thought. Perhaps some time when your own parents treated you unfairly, you said to yourself, "When I grow up, I am going to be different." It may be that you especially admire the way some parent you know treats children and have tucked that kind of parenthood away in your memory as a model you would like to follow some day. In hundreds of experiences that you have already had as a child, you have emerged with ideas and feelings about the kind of parent you some day want to be.

Your Goals as a Parent. Your goals as a parent begin to take form long before you are old enough to have children of your own. They may be simply phrased. You may just say to yourself, "I'm going to *be nice* to my children, when I get to be a parent." You may not be very specific about what "being nice" will mean, but you have a strong resolution toward such a goal.

You may already have decided that you are not going to "spoil" your children. Here again, just what it is that "spoils" a child may not be very clear, but your goals and dreams of not over-indulging him are nonetheless firmly fixed.

As you learn more and more about how children grow and what helps them develop well, your conceptions of the kind of parent you want to be may take more definite form and meaning, but still they are apt to be influenced by your own early experiences as a child.

Following or Rejecting Your Parents' Ways. Now that you are in your teens, you are old enough to evaluate your parents' methods of child-rearing. You may look back upon the way they used to punish you. You remember how you used to feel, and you say, "When I get to be a parent, *I'll* never do that to a child." If you feel quite strongly about it, you may so completely reject their methods with you that you make an effort to be just the opposite.

Or you remember fondly the good times you have had with your family. You appreciate what your parents have done with you. You feel warmly happy about them and the methods they followed in bringing you up. You think to yourself, "That's good. This is the way I'm going to have it in my home when I have children."

Our Pledge to Children. Beyond our own personal experiences, wishes, and dreams, is a growing body of knowledge of what all children need for healthy growth. When experts from many fields came together, at the Midcentury White House Conference on Children and Youth, to discuss healthy personality development, they pooled their knowledge and their hopes for children in the following pledge:

TO YOU, our children, who hold within you our most cherished hopes, we the members of the Midcentury White House Conference on Children and Youth, relying on your full response, make this pledge:

From your earliest infancy we will give you our love, so that you may grow with trust in yourself and in others.

We will recognize your worth as a person and we will help you to strengthen your sense of belonging.

We will respect your right to be yourself and at the same time help you to understand the rights of others, so that you may experience co-operative living.

We will help you to develop initiative and imagination, so that you may have the opportunity freely to create.

We will encourage your curiosity and your pride in workmanship, so that you may have the satisfaction that comes from achievement.

We will provide the conditions for wholesome play that will add to your learning, to your social experience, and to your happiness.

We will illustrate by precept and example the value of integrity and the importance of moral courage.

We will encourage you always to seek the truth.

We will provide you with all opportunities possible to develop your own faith in God.

We will open the way for you to enjoy the arts and to use them for deepening your understanding of life.

We will work to rid ourselves of prejudice and discrimination, so that together we may achieve a truly democratic society.

We will work to lift the standard of living and to improve our economic practices, so that you may have the material basis for a full life.

We will provide you with rewarding educational opportunities, so that you may develop your talents and contribute to a better world.

We will protect you against exploitation and undue hazards and help you grow in health and strength.

We will work to conserve and improve family life and, as needed, to provide foster care according to your inherent rights.

We will intensify our search for new knowledge in order to guide you more effectively as you develop your potentialities.

As you grow from child to youth to adult, establishing a family life of your own and accepting larger social responsibilities, we will work with you to improve conditions for all children and youth.

Aware that these promises to you cannot be fully met in a world at war, we ask you to join us in a firm dedication to the building of a world society based on freedom, justice and mutual respect.

SO MAY YOU grow in joy, in faith in God and in man, and in those qualities of vision and of the spirit that will sustain us all and give us new hope for the future.

You Will Still Be You. It may seem incredible to you now, but when your own children come, you will still be quite like yourself as you are now. You will change, of course, between now and then. But not completely. You will still be you when you are a parent. If you have a quick and violent temper now, it is quite possible that you will "fly off the handle" with your children when they annoy you, unless you learn to conquer your temper before then. If you really enjoy children now, you will quite possibly get particular satisfaction from having your own. Marriage and parenthood will help you to mature, but you carry into them the self you have developed through the years that have gone before.

One of the reasons why learning about children is important is that it helps you understand both them and yourself. As you see how children grow up, you often see yourself in them. As you learn about what makes you the way you are, you are often able to mature and to improve in your ways of thinking and feeling and acting. The most encouraging thing about human development is that it can go on and on! You can be a better YOU when you grow up, if you care enough to keep on growing and improving. You will still be you, but a more mature you.

Summary

Getting along with children depends a great deal upon the experience you have had with them. You know children in several contexts. Perhaps you have young brothers and sisters. You may have had close contact with children in your neighborhood and learned to get along easily with them as you grew up. You may have some experience as a "sitter." Because taking care of other people's children is something of a new experience both for teen-agers and for the children's parents, it is suggested that definite understandings about what is expected be arrived at. These may take the form of a code for baby sitters to cover the specific points in question. Knowing what children like is important in getting along with them. In general, children like little gifts and indications that they have been remembered. They like people whom their parents like and learn very easily just who is who in their parents' eyes. They like songs and stories and games and the people who enjoy these with them. They like toys and games, both old and new, to learn from and to grow on. They need to have their questions answered simply and directly as they arise. The kind of parent you will be depends upon your goals as a parent, the way you feel about the way your parents treated you, and the kind of person you are. You will still be *you* as a parent, but, as you learn about how people grow, you will become a more grown-up and a better you.

Suggested Activities

Individual Study

1. List in your notebook the names and ages of each of the children with whom you are personally acquainted. Next to each child's name place his or her outstanding characteristics, with any descriptive anecdotes that seem typical of his behavior and personality. Add to this inventory, as you progress through the unit on children, what further observations you can make of each child you know.
2. Bring to class some simple thing from home that might be used as play material by a child. Tell at what age a child would find it of interest, and what the child might be expected to do with it. What could the child learn from its use?
3. Review for your class one of the pieces of material your church makes available for parents' sex education of their children.
4. Write a paper on "When I have children, I will . . ."
5. Read and report on any of the references listed in your Readings.
6. Observe a child at play, writing down everything he does and says in a five-minute interval. Interpret your observation in terms of his personality and stage of development.

Group Activity

1. Discuss in class the seven points in the "Code for Baby Sitters and Parents," pages 283–84. Is there any point in this code on which it is not necessary to have an understanding between sitter and parents? Are there other points that you would add? What are they? Write your revision of the code on the blackboard for further study.

2. Invite a group of mothers for whom members of your class frequently serve as baby sitters to visit your class and discuss item by item your own revision of a code for baby sitters and parents. Incorporate their suggestions with yours. Mimeograph and distribute it when you feel it is ready.
3. Debate the proposition, "Resolved that children like to be teased." Encourage the debaters to use personal experiences as well as reference materials.
4. Visit a near-by nursery school, kindergarten, or children's library and find out which stories are most popular among children of various ages. Compile a list of stories for children with recommendations of most appropriate ages for each.
5. Assign each of the points in "Pledge to Children" to individuals or committees within the class to elaborate on with examples of how it can be accomplished.

Readings

BRO, MARGUERITE HARMON, *When Children Ask* (New York: Harper & Brothers, 1956). Children can ask most difficult questions from time to time. Mrs. Bro has brought together those that puzzle adults with suggestions that make sense both to little children and to those who are attempting to answer their questions.

FLANDER, JUDY, *Baby-Sitters' Handbook* (Chicago: Science Research Associates, 1952). One of the guides to baby-sitting that covers most of the questions that both sitters and parents are, and should be, concerned about.

GESELL, ARNOLD, et al., *Infant and Child Care in the Culture of Today* (New York: Harper & Brothers, 1953). Appendix C, "Toys, Play Materials and Equipment," has an excellent listing of the toys that are appropriate to children from the first months to the fourth year, stage by stage.

SPOCK, BENJAMIN, *Baby and Child Care* (New York: Pocket Books, Inc., 1957). Pages 304-9, "Play and Outgoingness," by this world-famous pediatrician is a well-written section on the value of play in a child's life and how you may foster it in relating yourself to him.

ULLMAN, FRANCES, *Life with Brothers and Sisters* (Chicago: Science Research Associates, 1952). An understanding treatment of the normal relationships among brothers and sisters, with helpful suggestions for getting along better with these young relatives in your life.

UNITED STATES CHILDREN'S BUREAU, *Home Play and Play Equipment* (Washington, D. C.: U. S. Department of Labor, Publication #238). A practical guide to choosing, making, and using home play materials for children of various ages.

Chapter 16

How Children Grow

Growth is an amazing process. There is nothing quite like it. Feeling yourself grow up is thrilling and satisfying. Watching and helping a child develop is one of the most rewarding experiences there is. It is all so rapid. One day a youngster is tiny and helpless and crying for his food, and the next, so it seems, he is sitting there beside you, big as life, feeding himself. One year he is just a baby, and the next he is a real person with a mind of his own and a genuine place in the family. Knowing what to expect as children grow up, what happens step by step, and how we can help makes all this even more interesting.

Prenatal Beginnings

A child starts as a tiny particle of living matter as small as a grain of fine salt. This little living cell buries itself deep within the mother's body and grows more rapidly than any human ever again grows. If the individual kept on growing at the rate at which he starts, the house would not be big enough to hold him, or the town, or the world! By the time this little embryo is four weeks old, you can already see the beginnings of arms and legs. By three months "he" or "she" (the sex is established at the very beginning) is several inches long and looks very much like a tiny baby, although still less than two ounces in weight. By the time the baby is ready to be born, he weighs six or eight pounds (more or less) and is more than a foot long, and complete down to the last little fingernail.

Life before birth is dramatic in its changes. But it does not require much from the members of the family. As long as the mother keeps herself well, gets enough exercise, sleep, and food of the right kind, the baby will grow on and on. There is *nothing* that the mother can do that will influence the kind of person he or she will be. It is not possible to mark a child before he is born or to determine his character by what the mother does while she is carrying him.

298

What Every Child Starts With. At the moment when the father cell joins the mother cell, conception takes place. As the sperm fertilizes the egg cell, hereditary characteristics of both the mother's and father's family for generations back are blended in the new individual. This results in a unique assortment of traits. Never in all the world could there be quite the same combination again. Nor does any baby ever resemble one parent or the other completely. He may have some characteristics that one or more of his grand-parents had also. He may have hair like his mother's brother, or eyes the color of those of his father's aunt; but he is never "just like" anyone who has ever been before. He may have his father's general body build, but he is not a "chip off the old block" in other ways.

Every child inherits certain tendencies to grow in a particular way. He inherits a tendency to be big and tall, or a tendency to grow slowly and be short or slim. He inherits certain definite characteristics such as eye color and skin color and hair color and texture and most of the other *physical* character-istics. The *kind of person* he becomes is determined later by the way he reacts to and responds to life situations. For instance, a child inherits his red hair, but he grows his own temper. He may inherit a strong chin, but he becomes stub-born or not, depending on the way he is brought up and the way he feels about himself and others. Every child starts as a bundle of tendencies to grow in certain ways. These tendencies are realized or thwarted in actual life situations. This is the reason why knowing about growth and how to help it is so very important.

Watching Babies Grow

If you know some baby intimately, you are very fortunate. Too few young people have a chance to become really acquainted with little babies. The babies pictured in the soap advertisements give you only a sentimental idea of how "sweet" babies are. It takes an honest-to-goodness real infant to teach you what you ought to know about how babies grow during the first months and years of life.

Height and Weight. The simplest measure of the way in which an infant grows is his height and weight. Keeping track of his body length from tip to toe is relatively simple, even if he wiggles. Weighing the baby at regular intervals is routine. A simple homemade chart with spaces for the date, the inches, pounds, and ounces suffices to keep track of the increases in height and weight.

Vision. The way in which the baby's eyes develop is worth noticing. When does he first turn his head toward a light? When is he first able to follow a moving light with his eyes? When does he first seem to notice his own fingers? When does he first seem to recognize a member of the family upon sight? These are just a few of the landmarks to look for in the way a baby's vision develops from blank staring orbs to eyes that focus and really see.

Head and Shoulders. The baby grows from the head downward, so his head and shoulders develop before his legs and feet. Watch and see when he is able to lift his head by himself. When is he first able to hold his head erect without support for a moment or so? When can he keep his head and shoulders up with relative steadiness from a prone position (lying on his stomach)? When can he first sit? When does he begin to crawl? How does he use his hands and arms in his crawling? See if you can notice evidence in the child you are watching that his head and shoulders develop more rapidly at first than do his legs and feet.

Hands and Fingers. Watch the baby's hands. From the first he will be able to clutch your finger held in his hand. After that, see when he is able to pick up a small block (a one-inch cube is about the right size) with his whole hand, and later, with his thumb on the opposite side from his fingers. See at what age he is able to release an object at will. You will know this stage by his interest in picking up and dropping things over and over again. See when he is first able to put his finger on a tiny crumb. Watch for the first time that he is able to get his hands together in the pat-a-cake way. Then see how often he claps his hands after that. You will notice all along that as soon as a child is ready to do a certain thing, he practices that new skill over and over again!

Locomotion. The process of learning to get around is a fascinating one to watch. Some time after the baby begins to sit, you will notice him hitch himself along the floor. Or he may start moving on his hands and knees. Children often move at surprisingly rapid rates by a hitch or crawl method. The day will come when the child pulls himself erect against an upright support. Then watch for the time when he can stand alone. The first steps "holding on" are wobbly and unsure. Then he strides out easily as long as he has a hand to hold to but he totters by himself. With more practice he takes a few steps alone, then more and more, until somewhere in the second year, he is walking fairly well. Learning to run, to skip, to go up and down stairs takes still more months of trial and error and untiring practice, until somewhere between two and four, he gets himself around with assurance.

Learning to Talk. Language development is perhaps the most fascinating of all. At birth the baby can only cry. In a few months he learns to gurgle and make a few sounds. Hour upon hour, he lies and practices these early syllables. By the time he is somewhere around a year old he has discovered that when he makes the *m-m-m-m, mamamama* sounds, his mother responds with especial praise, and so *ma-ma* becomes associated with her. Similarly his early *d-d-d-d, dadadada* sounds become attached to his father as *da-da.*

Young children continually test their playthings for size, weight, shape, workings, and even taste. Such exercise helps develop their minds as well as their muscles.

With help he may have learned to wave bye-bye and perhaps to play so-big and pat-a-cake. After the single words come simple sentences, "me-go-too," "baby-bye-bye," and "baby down" are typical early sentences during the second year. By the time he is three or thereabouts, he is asking simple questions and talking freely. Now his vocabulary grows rapidly, with ever-increasing refinements through the years. Even during the teens he is still learning the right things to say in different situations and practicing the lines he has found rewarding! Being able to use the words learned earlier in childhood is only the foundation for the language development that makes for the scintillating conversation a young person strives to perfect. Talking in front of an audience is a skill that calls for still further practice.

Developmental Tasks from Birth to Maturity [1]

Development does not just happen. Every individual works at his own development as long as he keeps on growing. Watch a little child at play and see how hard he works at it. He is working at his own developmental tasks that are necessary for him to achieve if he is to grow on to the next stage in his development. So it is through life. For every stage of growth there is a series of developmental tasks essential for individual progress.

As we have seen, these developmental tasks start at birth and continue right through the teens and into adulthood. They are the things each person must do if he is to succeed in his development as an individual. When he fails to accomplish his developmental tasks, his progress is delayed. When he succeeds in his developmental tasks, he is pleased and happy, and he grows on to the next stage in his development.

Developmental Tasks of Infancy and Early Childhood (Birth to Thirty Months). A baby is born a helpless little bundle of potentials. By the time he is two and a half years old he is walking and beginning to talk, he is eating and drinking and being a real person in the family. Each of these accomplishments is the result of real effort and lots of practice on the part of the child as he works to achieve the developmental tasks involved. Step by step, the developmental tasks from birth to thirty months are:

1. Achieving physiological equilibrium following birth
   Learning to sleep at appropriate times
   Maintaining a healthful balance of rest and activity

[1] Taken from Evelyn Millis Duvall, *Family Development* (Chicago: J. B. Lippincott Company, 1957), pp. 190–92, 230–32, 262–64, 294–97, from original schemas in: Robert J. Havighurst, *Human Development and Education* (New York: Longmans, Green and Co., 1953); and Evelyn Millis Duvall and Reuben Hill, co-chairmen, *Report of the Committee on the Dynamics of Family Interaction* (Washington, D. C.: National Conference on Family Life, 1948).

2. Learning to take food satisfactorily

   Developing ability to nurse—to suck, swallow, and adjust to nipple

   Learning to take solid foods, to enjoy new textures, tastes, and temperatures, to use cup, spoon, and dishes competently in ways appropriate to his age

3. Learning the know-how and the where-when of elimination

   Finding satisfaction in early eliminative processes

   Recognizing parental pressure and universal practice of control of elimination

   Responding co-operatively and effectively to toilet-training

4. Learning to manage one's body effectively

   Developing co-ordination (eye-hand, hand-mouth, reach, grasp, handle, manipulate, put and take)

   Acquiring skills in locomotion through kicking, creeping, walking, and running

   Gaining assurance and competence in handling oneself in a variety of situations

5. Learning to adjust to other people

   Responding discriminatingly to other's expectations

   Recognizing parental authority and controls

   Learning the do's and don't's of his world

   Reacting positively to both familiar and strange persons within his orbit

6. Learning to love and be loved

   Responding affectionately to others through cuddling, smiling, loving

   Meeting emotional needs through widening spheres and varieties of contact

   Beginning to give spontaneously and trustfully of self

7. Developing systems of communication

   Learning patterns of recognition and response

   Establishing non-verbal, pre-verbal, and verbal communicative systems

   Acquiring basic concepts ("Yes," "No," "Up," "Down," "Come," "Go," "Hot," etc.)

   Mastering basic language fundamentals

8. Learning to express and control feelings

   Developing a sense of trust and confidence in one's world

   Managing feelings of fear and anxiety in healthful ways

   Handling feelings of frustration, disappointment, and anger effectively in accordance with his development

   Moderating demanding attitudes as time goes on

9. Laying foundations for self-awareness
      Seeing oneself as a separate entity
      Exploring rights and privileges of being a person
      Finding personal fulfillment with and without others

Developmental Tasks of Preschool Children (*2½ to 5 years*). From babyhood the preschool child is emerging as a social being who can share with others, who participates as a member of his family, and who is ready for school. His physical growth is slowing down, and many of his body activities are becoming routine. Progress in his emotional and intellectual development is increasingly apparent in his growing ability to express himself, and in his greatly increased acquaintance with his world. The preschool child's chief developmental tasks are outlined below:

1. Settling into healthful daily routines of rest and activity
      Going to bed and accepting need for sleep without a struggle
      Taking his nap or rest, and learning to relax when he is weary
      Enjoying active play in a variety of situations and places
      Becoming increasingly flexible and able to accept changes happily
2. Mastering good eating habits
      Becoming competent in the use of the customary eating utensils
      Accepting new flavors and textures in foods with interest
      Enjoying his food with decreasing incidence of spilling, messing, toying
      Learning the social as well as the sensual pleasures of eating

3. Mastering the basic requirements of toilet training
      Growing in his ability to recognize and indicate the urge for elimination
      Co-operating in the toilet-training program
      Finding satisfaction in acceptable toilet habits
      Achieving flexibility in adapting to varying circumstances
4. Developing the physical skills appropriate to his stage of motor development
      Learning to climb, balance, run, skip, push, pull, throw, and catch through use of large muscles
      Developing manual skills for buttoning, zipping, cutting, drawing, coloring, modeling, and manipulating small objects deftly
      Becoming increasingly independent in his ability to handle himself effectively in a variety of physical situations
5. Becoming a participating member of his family
      Assuming responsibilities within the family happily and effectively
      Learning to give and receive affection and gifts freely within the family

Identifying with parent of the same sex

Developing ability to share his parents with another child and with others generally

Recognizing his family's ways as compared with those of his friends and neighbors

6. Beginning to master his impulses and to conform to others' expectations

Outgrowing the impulsive, urgent outbursts of infancy

Learning to share, take turns, hold his own, and enjoy the companionship of other children, and at times play happily alone

Developing the sympathetic co-operative ways with others that insure his inclusion in groups

Learning appropriate behavior for varying situations (time and place for noise, quiet, messing, nudity, etc.)

7. Developing healthy emotional expressions for a wide variety of experiences

Learning to play out feelings, frustrations, needs, experiences

Learning to postpone and to wait for satisfactions

Expressing momentary hostility and making up readily afterwards

Refining generalized joy or pain into discriminating expressions of pleasure, eagerness, tenderness, affection, sympathy, fear, anxiety, remorse, sorrow, etc.

"Now that I can walk, I'm leaving!"

8. Learning to communicate effectively with an increasing number of people

Developing the vocabulary and ability to talk about a rapidly growing number of things, feelings, experiences, impressions, and curiosities

Learning to listen, take in, follow directions, increase his attention span, and to respond intellectually to situations and to people

Acquiring the social skills needed to get over feelings of shyness, self-consciousness, and awkwardness, and to participate with other people comfortably

9. Developing the ability to handle potentially dangerous situations adequately

Learning to respect and avoid the dangers of fire, traffic, high places, bathing areas, poisons, animals, and the many other potential hazards

Learning to handle himself effectively without undue fear in situations calling for caution (crossing streets, greeting strange dogs, responding to a stranger's offer of a ride, etc.)

Becoming willing to accept help in situations that are beyond him without undue dependence or too-impulsive independence

10. Learning to be an autonomous person with initiative and a conscience of his own

Becoming increasingly responsible for making decisions in ways appropriate to his readiness

Taking initiative for projecting himself into situations and into the future with innovations, experiments, trials, and original achievements

Internalizing the expectancies and demands of his family and culture groups in his developing conscience

Becoming reasonably self-sufficient in accordance with his own make-up and stage of development

11. Laying foundations for understanding the meanings of life

Beginning to understand the origins of life, how the two sexes differ, and who he or she is as a member of his or her sex

Trying to understand the nature of the physical world, what things are, how they work and why, and what they mean to him

Accepting the religious faith of his parents, learning about the nature of God, and the spiritual nature of life

Developmental Tasks of School-Age Boys and Girls. The more insistent of the school-ager's developmental tasks may be introduced by the question:

What is the child in our complex American society called upon to learn during this period? In many areas these learnings are in terms of "continuing," "extending," and "expanding" previous abilities. In others, whole new aspects of life open up.

1. Learning the basic skills required of school children
     Mastering the fundamentals of reading, writing, calculating, and the scientific rational approach to solving problems
     Extending understandings of cause-and-effect relationships
     Developing concepts essential for everyday living
     Continued development in ability to reason and do reflective thinking

2. Mastering the physical skills appropriate to his development
     Learning the games, the sports, and the various roles in activities pursued by children of his age and sex in his community (ride a bike, swim, skate, play ball, row a boat, climb a tree, etc.)
     Developing abilities needed in personal and family living (bathe and dress himself, care for his clothing, make his bed, cook and serve food, clean up after activities, maintain and repair simple household equipment, etc.)

3. Developing meaningful understandings of the use of money
     Finding socially acceptable ways of getting money for what he wants to buy
     Learning how to buy wisely the things he most wants with the money he has, and to stay within his available resources
     Finding the meaning of saving for postponed satisfactions
     Reconciling differences between his wants and his resources, and those of others both poorer and richer than he
     Getting basic orientation into the nature of money in everyday life in the family and in the larger community

4. Becoming an active co-operative member of his family
     Gaining skills in participating in family discussions and decision-making
     Assuming responsibilities within the household with satisfactions in accomplishment and belonging
     Becoming more mature in giving and receiving affection and gifts between himself and his parents, his brothers and sisters, and his relatives within the extended family.
     Learning to enjoy the full resources and facilities available within the family and to take the initiative in enriching them as he becomes able

5. Extending his abilities to relate effectively to others, both peers and adults

    Making progress in his ability to adjust to others

    Learning to stand up for his rights

    Improving his ability both to lead and to follow others

    Mastering simple conventions, rules, customs, courtesies, and standards of his family and groups

    Learning genuinely co-operative roles with others in many situations

    Making and keeping close friends

6. Continuing the learnings involved in handling his feelings and impulses

    Growing in his ability to work through simple frustrations

    Exploring socially acceptable ways of releasing negative emotions effectively

    Becoming more mature in channeling feelings into accepted ways, time, and place

    Gaining skill in sharing his feelings with those who can help (parents, teachers, close friends, scout leaders, etc.)

7. Coming to terms with his or her own sex role both now and as it will become

    Learning what is considered appropriate behavior for boys, for girls, for men, for women, for married people, for parents and grandparents

    Clarifying knowledge about the nature of sex and reproduction

    Adjusting to a changing body in the puberal growth spurt as teen years approach; (accepting the new size and form, function, and potentials of puberal growth)

    Thinking wholesomely ahead to what it will be like to be grown-up

8. Continuing to find himself as a worthy person

    Identifying with his own age and sex in appropriate ways

    Discovering many ways of becoming acceptable as a person, gaining status

    Growing in self-confidence, self-respect, self-control, and self-realization

    Extending the process of establishing his own individuality

9. Relating himself to loyalties beyond the moment and outside himself

    Finding new meanings in religion, in the universe, in the nature of things

    Discovering satisfactions in music, art, drama, nature, and the literature of his culture, appropriate to his age

    Devoting himself to group goals (scouts, boys' and girls' clubs, etc.)

Laying foundations for patriotism, for pride in men's achievements
through history, and for a sense of belonging to the human race

Gaining experience in essential morality in action at home and with
others

Learning and accepting the eternal realities of life—birth, death,
and infinity

Developmental Tasks of Teen-Agers. Each young person must come to
terms with his or her own family situation as he grows up out of it. Whatever
the family strengths and weaknesses, they eventually must be faced and accepted as "the givens" by any young man or woman. Learning to live with
one's family, understanding why parents feel and behave as they do, and
recognizing one's father and mother for the real people they are, are important tasks of all young people in every kind of family. At those points
where families do not meet the pressing needs of youth, other resources
within the community may be tapped by the enterprising youth who does
not demand that his family be everything and do everything for him. The
developmental tasks of teen-agers discussed in Chapter 2 are outlined briefly
below, for review in this context.

1. Accepting one's changing body and learning to use it effectively

    Coming to terms with new size, shape, function, and potential of
    one's maturing body

    Reconciling differences between one's own physique and that of
    age-mates of the same and other sex, as normal variations

    Understanding what puberal changes mean and wholesomely
    anticipating maturity as a man or as a woman

    Caring for one's body in healthful ways that assure its optimum
    development

    Learning to handle oneself skillfully in the variety of recreational,
    social, and family situations that require learned physical skills

2. Achieving a satisfying and socially acceptable masculine or feminine
role

    Learning what it means to be a boy or a girl in one's culture

    Anticipating realistically what will be involved in becoming a man
    or a woman

    Finding oneself within the leeway of sex-role expectations and
    practice allowed by one's family and community

3. Finding oneself as a member of one's own generation in more mature
relations with one's age-mates

    Becoming acceptable as a member of one or more groups of peers

    Making and keeping friends of both sexes

Getting dates and becoming comfortable in dating situations

Getting experience in loving and being loved by one or more members of the opposite sex

Learning how to get along with a wide variety of age-mates in school, neighborhood, and community settings

Developing skills in extending, accepting, and refusing invitations, solving problems and resolving conflicts, making decisions and evaluating experiences with one's peers

4. Achieving emotional independence of parents and other adults

Becoming free of childish dependencies upon one's parents

Developing affections for parents as people

Learning how to be a self-reliant person who is capable of making decisions and running one's own life

Growing through the dependence of childhood and the impulsive independence of adolescence to mature interdependence with others (parents, teachers, and all authority figures, especially)

Learning to be an adult among adults

5. Selecting and preparing for an occupation and economic independence

Seeking counsel and getting specific knowledges about possible fields of work within the limits of real possibilities

Choosing an occupation in line with interests, abilities, and opportunities

Preparing oneself through schooling, specialized training, and personal responsibility to get and hold a position

Getting such try-out or apprenticeship experiences as are possible in the direction of vocational interest

6. Preparing for marriage and family life

Enjoying the responsibilities as well as the privileges of family membership

Developing a positive attitude toward getting married and having a family

Acquiring knowledge about mate selection, marriage, homemaking, and childrearing

Learning to distinguish between infatuation and more lasting forms of love

Developing a mutually satisfying personal relationship with a potential mate through processes of dating, going steady, and effective courtship

Helping a Child Grow Up. You can help a child develop by being with him. As you walk and talk and read, you provide the patterns which he follows. You probably have noticed how quite little children will imitate reading long before they can understand the printed page. They hold the book as they have seen others do, and "read" with the same inflections as they have heard others use, often with the book held upside down! So, too, it is with talking, eating, and everything else.

You help children when you encourage and approve their growth efforts without trying to rush or push them beyond their readiness. When a child feels other people's approval and love about him, he wants to grow and be like them. He will grow up as fast as he can if he is not discouraged by having too much expected of him.

Recognizing What He Is Trying to Do. You are most helpful to children when you see what it is that they are trying to do. Knowing the developmental tasks of each stage helps us anticipate what any given child may be working on at any particular time. Observing a child in a situation and trying to see the episode from his point of view can give real clues as to what he is up to, and what his efforts mean. This is the place where the trained eye can see what escapes the inexperienced observer. The person with some background in child development can spot and appreciate a child's efforts that might be annoying, irritating, or meaningless to the adult who did not have a basis for understanding.

Putting yourself in the child's place and seeing from his viewpoint is helpful to him. When you realize that a child by definition is small—small in experience as well as in size, you are ready to adjust to his perspective. All too often adults see only how the situation affects them, not what it means to the youngster, and thus miss the whole point of his behavior.

Providing What He Needs. You help children accomplish their developmental tasks by providing what they need to grow on. This is generally recognized in things like food and clothes. More often neglected is the fulfillment of the conditions that encourage emotional and social growth. Children need space and materials that they can do things with, as we saw in our discussion of playthings in Chapter 15. Besides sharing the universal needs of all children, each child has also special individual needs because he is himself—with his particular interests, tendencies, and level of development. This is where your awareness of individual differences becomes especially pertinent.

Individual Differences

Every child passes through the same general sequence of stages as he matures. Every youngster faces developmental tasks at every stage of his development. But each child takes as long to complete any given stage of development as is necessary for him to prepare for the next step in his maturation. You can help him most by seeing the real and unique person he is.

"Miss Logan gave us some finger paint today!"

Just because most children do a certain thing about a certain time is no sign that any particular child will. Comparing a real flesh-and-blood child with an imaginary "average" child is neither wise nor fair. It makes far more sense to notice the way in which *he* grows, the pace at which *he* develops, and the progress *he* is making.

Seeing the Child as an Individual. Each child grows at his own rate, and in his own way. These rates of growth are set in the child's inheritance. You can encourage his own best growth by seeing that he gets the food he requires and the chance to develop at his own rate, but beyond that there is little that you or anybody else can do (fortunately) to tamper with his own growth schedule.

Some children are bigger than others at birth. The big ones grow bigger, often faster than the little ones. By the time children are three or four years of age, some four-year-olds may be no larger than other three-year-olds. But it does not matter. The thing that is important is whether any particular child is growing at the rate that is best for him.

So it is with talking and walking and teething, and all the other accomplishments of little children. *When* a child begins to talk or walk or cut his teeth is not especially important. His mother may be very proud if he cuts his teeth earlier than his cousin does, but in the long run, it matters not one bit. The age at which a child begins to talk is no measure of his eventual language ability. Nor is the age at which he walks an indication of his superior intelligence or a future career as a cross-country racer. But the child's sense of being all right is very important. So it is wise *not* to compare children, but rather to accept and enjoy each child as he is, and help him grow and learn and develop at his own best pace.

Success in Developmental Tasks Helps. You help a child most when you see what he is trying to accomplish and do what you can to help him succeed. This does not mean that you do the job for him. In a real way, you cannot accomplish his developmental tasks for him. He must develop for himself, and from early childhood on he senses this. What he needs from others is their encouragement and reassurance that he can do it.

Watch a little child learning to climb steps, or to skip, or to speak. See how many times he repeats the process, and how hard he concentrates on the job he has set for himself. Every once in a while he may look into your face for your reaction. If you are preoccupied, or afraid, or annoyed, he will catch the feeling of distress and be hindered in his job. If he sees pleasure, reassurance, pride, encouragement in your glance, he is motivated to go to his task with even greater zeal. You can observe this response in yourself, too, when you "knock yourself out" pleasing someone you feel really cares how you do!

When an individual succeeds in a task of development, he finds pleasure in his accomplishment and is mobilized for the next stage of his growth. He is happy at his progress and eager to move on to more difficult tasks. He keeps on growing, secure in his own and in others' appraisal that he is doing nicely.

From time to time discouraging elements enter the developmental picture. Just as a child learns to succeed by succeeding, so, too, he must learn to take failure and setbacks from time to time.

Two Steps Ahead and One Back. Children do not always do the very best that they can. Very few of us do, ever. It seems that learning and growing take place in spurts and lapses: two steps ahead and one back. It is this irregularity about a child's growth or performance that often disturbs his family. Suddenly, after walking for weeks, Junior suddenly begins to crawl again. The child who gave up thumbsucking months ago may start in again. The baby who has learned to drink from a cup still wants his milk from a bottle. And so it goes. Little lapses and regressions needlessly worry the too-eager family.

Children tend to slip back to an easier way when they are tired or do not feel well or are unhappy about something. Many "big boys" of six or eight still want a familiar cuddly little toy in bed with them at night. It is at bedtime, when the child is tired, that thumbsucking is apt to crop up again. When a new baby comes into the home or something else happens to make the child feel insecure, he may begin again to wet himself or suck his thumb or refuse to eat nicely. When a child is "coming down with something," he may be cross and less able than usual. In fact, many mothers have found that one way to keep a child happy during illness is to bring out some of the toys that the child *used to enjoy* some months ago. When he does not feel well, his interests and skills are not up to his very best.

As a matter of fact, most learning usually goes by jumps and stops. It starts with the individual's first interest. He tries the new thing. He tries again. He practices hard at it, over and over again. His learning takes place rapidly at first and then tapers off as he gains experience. After a little while, the learning pace levels off and he stays about the same for a time. Something may come along that makes him slip back and be consistently poorer for a while. That is the way it is with many skills—learning to walk or talk or drink out of a cup. It is because little children are learning so many different things so rapidly that we are so often conscious of their tendency to slip back to less than their best at times.

Growing Up and Out

As a child grows up, he grows out. He starts as a snug little circle within his mother. He grows and is born and enlarges his circle to a crib. Soon he has graduated into a play pen and then a real bed. Next he is given the porch to explore. Before long he is a "yard child." He grows some more and is allowed the run of the neighborhood. By the time he goes to school he is getting around in a still wider circle. As a teen-ager he operates in much larger spheres. Soon the highways are his, and then he steps into adulthood, with the whole wide world, or even the universe, to explore!

These widening circles require many types of development. He must learn not only to know how to get around on foot, by bike, by bus, or by car; he must also know how to talk and communicate with others. He must know what people expect of him. He must learn what is good and what is not so good in the eyes of the people of his town and his times. He must learn the way of life of the people with whom he grows up. This takes time, concentration, practice, and a good bit of healthy acting-out of the roles he sees others playing. As the little girl plays with her dolls, she "feels" motherhood. As the boy plays cops or fireman, he "is" a policeman or a fireman. Children play school, they play house, they play out life around them as they see it. Life is indeed a stage and people the players on it, especially as they grow up and out.

Summary

Growth is an amazing process. A child starts as a tiny dot of potentialities. He starts with inherited tendencies from both sides of the family, but he is not a duplicate of anyone who has ever lived before. Knowing what to watch for in a baby's growth helps you understand what is happening. Some things to watch for are changes in height, weight, vision, head and shoulder functioning, hand and finger development, locomotion, and language growth. There are developmental tasks at every stage of childhood and youth. These are the things the child must do if he is to be happy and grow on to the next stage of his development. We help children grow when we see what they are trying to do, provide what they need, and encourage them to develop. There are real individual differences to be accepted and appreciated among children. Growth is rarely smooth, but proceeds two steps ahead and one back through periods of progress and lapses. You grow up and out through the years as you become more and more able to handle yourself as a human being in the company of others.

Suggested Activities

Individual Study

1. Observe a baby over a period of several weeks, making detailed notes at each interval on what the baby can do, his height, weight, teeth, diet, etc. Keep a careful record in your notebook as the basis for a class report on "One Baby's Growth."
2. Compare the items mentioned in "Toys, Play Materials and Equipment," in Gesell et al (see Readings), pages 372–78, with children's growing ability to manipulate objects as found in your observations and readings. Chart these parallels in your notebook.
3. Prepare a book report on Aldrich's *Babies Are Human Beings* (see Readings) with special emphasis on what you think the author means by the title.
4. Talk over some of your childhood memories with some understanding adult in an effort to see how you have matured from your early beginnings.
5. Find an illustration, either in your readings or in your observation of children, of the principle discussed in the section, "Success in Developmental Tasks Helps." Be prepared to describe the situation and to discuss it in class.
6. Prepare an inventory of your own developmental tasks at the present time. List them specifically in your notebook for future reference.

Group Activity

1. Arrange for committees to visit a nursery school, a kindergarten, and a first grade to observe the children's performance and behavior at these three grade levels. Focus the reports to the class in terms of the developmental tasks the children in each stage appear to be working on, as compared with those listed on pages 302–9.
2. Discuss the film, *Preface to a Life* (Castle Films, sound, 28 minutes), in terms of how parents' expectations affect the way a child develops.

3. Show the film, *Your Children's Play* (British Information Service, sound, 21 minutes), and discuss its content in terms of what a child can do at different ages, and the developmental tasks that are implied in the various kinds of behavior.
4. Have committees choose from the listing of developmental tasks ones that they would demonstrate in a series of impromptu skits, or role-playing episodes. Encourage free discussion of each committee's contribution.
5. Suggest that one person become the devil's advocate and insist that "Children have not a care in the world—nothing to do but play all day" as a challenge for the rest of the class to refute, with evidence and examples of children's concentration on their developmental tasks.

Readings

ALDRICH, C. ANDERSON and MARY M., *Babies Are Human Beings* (New York: The Macmillan Company, 1954). One of the modern classics in the field of interpreting infant behavior to those who care for them. A basic book in the field of baby growth and development.

GESELL, ARNOLD, M.D., and ILG, FRANCES L., M.D., *The Child from Five to Ten* (New York: Harper & Brothers, 1946). A step-by-step account of how children develop from their fifth to their tenth birthdays. A good general guide to child development that is most helpful when it is not interpreted too rigidly.

———, *Infant and Child in the Culture of Today* (New York: Harper & Brothers, 1943). This is basically an interpretation of the extensive child development research done through the years at Yale University, with special reference to the understanding and guidance of the little child's growth.

JENKINS, GLADYS GARDNER, SHACTER, HELEN, and BAUER, WILLIAM W., M.D., *These Are Your Children* (Chicago: Scott, Foresman and Company, 1949). This whole book is on child development from the fifth year to adolescence. You will find the front and back pages have an excellent summary of the physical development, characteristic reactions, and special needs of each period from infancy to adolescence.

ROWLAND, LOYD W., et al., *Pierre the Pelican Series* (New Orleans: The Louisiana Association for Mental Health, 1528 Jackson Avenue, 1957). Twenty-eight letters to parents of children from birth through their sixth year about child growth, development, and guidance. Delightfully easy reading, sound material.

SHUEY, REBEKAH M., WOODS, ELIZABETH L., and YOUNG, ESTHER MASON, *Learning About Children* (Chicago: J. B. Lippincott Company, 1958). This book, written especially for young people, serves as a guide to understanding children's development and helping each child attain maturity at his own level. Parts 3, 4, and 5 go through the twelfth year.

SPOCK, BENJAMIN, M.D., *Baby and Child Care* (New York: Pocket Books, 1957). Millions of people have found Dr. Spock's writings about children personally helpful because he knows children intimately and writes so that all who read can understand in ways that are practical, reassuring, and enormously helpful. Put this book in your personal library.

Chapter 17
Caring for Children

Caring for children is a phrase with two meanings, and we mean both of them. We mean taking care of their needs and wants, and we mean being fond of them, too. The two go together. When you care for children in the physical sense of doing things for them, you learn to love and to enjoy them. It works the other way around, too. When you really care for children in the sense of loving them, you are apt to take better care of them and have a greater understanding of how things look from a child's eye view.

Meeting Children's Needs

Little children have real needs that they cannot satisfy by themselves. There are many things that must be done for them throughout the early weeks and months and years of life. Learning what children really need for their best growth and happiness is important for learning how to care for them (in both senses). Review Unit I before continuing with this section.

Keeping Children Comfortable and Safe. A great deal of the care of a little child has to do with keeping him comfortable. The baby is hungry, so you feed him. He is cold, and you cover him. He is too hot, and you remove a blanket. He is wet, and you change him. He needs a bath. He is soothed with a ride in his carriage. Routines are established to satisfy a baby's needs to be made comfortable.

These early routines in caring for a little baby are worth learning. They are fun and give you a sense of knowing what to do when you are around a little youngster. If you have not had the chance to learn how to bathe a baby or keep him happy while his mother is out for a while, it might be worthwhile to look for some good opportunity along these lines now, while you are studying this unit.

As the baby grows big enough to get around, taking care of him means keeping him safe, too. He must be protected from hurting himself. So, you, as a sitter or in whatever capacity you are with him at the moment, must see to it that he does not get hold of such things as knives, scissors, tiny things he might swallow (anything smaller than his fist), pins, forks, any sharp objects which might cut or prick. He has to be kept back from open windows, bodies of water, fire, stoves, electric outlets, and any other danger point. So far as possible, you can try to protect him too from the serious bumps and bruises that come so easily from his early exploration and locomotion.

Feeding Children. Everyone agrees that children should be fed, adequately and regularly. But ideas on what to feed them, and how, and how regularly, change from time to time. Some years ago there was a fad of feeding babies by the clock, quite rigidly. This was hard on babies who were hungry before their scheduled time, and it was hard on their mothers who were supposed to wait, too. Then it became fashionable to feed the baby whenever he cried. But this wasn't satisfactory either, because babies cry for reasons other than hunger. And, rushing about to get him food every time the baby cried wore the mothers out and made them unsure of what to expect. They never could plan on when the next feeding would be. More recently, both of these extremes have given way to a more workable modification in which both mother and baby are satisfied. The most sensible plan seems to be to let the baby be the guide of when he is hungry, and to feed him close to the times when he wants to be fed. Most babies soon want their milk at fairly regular intervals, some every four hours or so through the day, and others a little oftener. Some babies wake up and need a feeding some time after midnight. Others begin to sleep right through the night when they are only a few weeks old. As soon as the baby settles into his own schedule, the family can plan more or less when he will want his next feeding.

Many mothers want to breast-feed their babies and have a sufficient milk supply to meet the need entirely. Other mothers find that their babies are not getting enough by nursing and so they supplement breast-feeding with an occasional bottle. Still other mothers have so little milk, and have so much difficulty getting their babies established in breast-feeding, that they use bottle feedings exclusively. In general it is agreed that breast-feeding is preferred if it is possible. But it is by no means essential. A good formula suited to the needs of the individual baby and fed to him in a warm, loving way is quite adequate.

Modern baby care calls for introducing new foods from time to time as the baby grows. Vitamins, water, fruit juice, and baby cereals all come into his diet very early. They are soon followed by eggs, strained vegetables, meats, and fruits, until by the time the baby is a year old he has a richly varied diet. It is wise to have a baby doctor determine just what a given baby gets, and when.

Weaning from breast or bottle to cup comes along as the baby shows his interest and readiness for the shift. If he has had water from time to time from

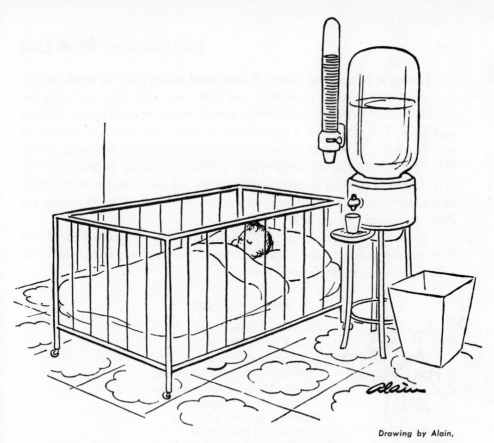

a cup, he learns how to drink from a cup gradually. Then when he has had enough sucking experience, he weans himself with little trouble. Sucking in itself is an important experience in a baby's development. Depriving him of it too early is not wise.

Attitudes toward food are important. A child should enjoy eating. He should not feel that he is pleasing his parents when he eats well. He should eat well because he likes to. This means that food should not be forced upon him. It also implies that new foods should be offered a little at a time along with things he likes, so that gradually he will become accustomed to new flavors and textures. If he spits food out, all right. Wipe him off and remove the offending food for the time being. He may be ready for it in another week or so if an issue is not made of it now. Growing up in a family where people like to eat, where issues are not made over eating, gives a baby a good start in developing healthy, happy feelings about his food.

If a baby gets a good start in his eating habits, food problems are avoided later on. By the time he has all of his teeth, sometime in his third year, he is eating everything at the family table. "Everything" of course does not mean tea, coffee, fried foods, and other hard-to-digest or highly seasoned foods. These may well be avoided throughout his whole childhood.

Loving Is Nourishing, Too. Children need loving quite as much as they need food. Babies who are cuddled and held close while they are being fed grow faster and better than those who have a bottle propped up for them to suck from. This is not just a sentimental old wives' tale, but is supported by sound evidence from careful studies. All along the way children need loving. Warm, close, affectionate contacts with people are essential to growth. There is no danger of spoiling a child by meeting his real needs as they come along, any more than there is a danger of spoiling a rose plant by providing the elements essential for growth!

You need to love children for your own sake, too. As you give them your love, you are nourished and grow yourselves. This warm satisfaction is beautifully expressed in the little poem below.

TWO-AND-A-HALF [1]

Hold him a little longer,
　　Rock him a little more;
Tell him another story,
　　(You've only told him four).
Let him sleep on your shoulder,
　　Rejoice in his happy smile;
He is only two-and-a-half
　　For such a little while!
                          Dorothy Uncle

As long as a person lives, he needs to feel that he is loved. Love expressions shift as people grow, but the basic need remains essentially the same throughout life. At every stage, humans need to feel that they are accepted, understood, and secure within their human circles. A plant withers and dies if it is shut off from air and sunlight. A person shrivels when he seriously feels unloved, unwanted, and insecure. As individuals grow, one of the most important things they learn is how to give and receive affection.

Learning Is Encouraged. Children need to be encouraged to learn and to grow. Deep within each child is a will to grow. If this impetus is given encouragement through opportunities to learn and develop, the child's growth proceeds comfortably. If the child is restrained or discouraged in his growing attempts, he becomes restless, unhappy, and thwarted. Examples are countless. Hold the legs of a vigorously kicking infant and he cries out in anger and distress. Kicking is necessary for his leg development. Keep a year-old baby too long in his playpen when he would be out exploring his universe, and he cries petulantly and lustily for release. Say "no" too often to his efforts to get acquainted with things through touching them, and he rebels or he becomes

[1] Reprinted by permission from *The Christian Home* (July, 1948), Methodist Publishing House, 810 Broadway, Nashville, Tennessee.

discouraged and refuses to try. Children need room and a chance to grow at every stage of their development.

Children need examples of what to do and how to act. Children learn social behavior from being with people. Listening to others talk, they are encouraged to learn how to communicate by talking, too. The behavior of people around him stimulates the little child to become more and more civilized in his responses. Babies brought up by animals, as was the "wolf-child," never really learn how to talk or walk or laugh or do any of the things we consider natural in human beings. Most learnings are present only as potentialities in the baby. They must be developed into realities by constant practice and growth.

Children respond well to encouragement. They like to be praised for their new accomplishments. When they see that you are pleased with the things they are learning to do, they redouble their efforts to do these things even better. They practice them over and over. They look to you for approval, and receiving it, set to work ever more vigorously on the refinement of their new-found abilities and skills. This is a prime factor in good child guidance, for it is in tune with the processes of growth working in the child.

Waiting for Readiness. It does not help to push a child. It is just as frustrating to him to be held back. Meeting a child's needs involves gearing oneself to his readiness for new experiences, new opportunities, and new materials. Expecting too much of a child before he is ready can be especially harmful. You push and he cannot respond as you expect. So, he either ignores your efforts completely, or he tries what you are demanding only to meet with failure. He feels bad because he cannot please you, and senses that he is somehow letting you down. Waiting for his readiness for the next step of development and then giving him the opportunity for it, while encouraging his own efforts and attempts, can be most rewarding for him and for you.

Guiding Children's Growth

Child guidance at its best gives growth a chance. Every child basically wants to grow. He wants to be big. He wants to do what is expected of him if he can. He wants to be loved, and so he tries to please the people around him. Once you learn to have real faith in these growth processes within children, you realize that punishing and "breaking" a child are not sensible. Providing opportunities for experiences in growth and encouraging his efforts to develop at his own pace are the essentials of good guidance.

Good Discipline. Guiding a child's growth does not mean letting him run wild. Not at all. He needs discipline and real guidance as he grows. He needs to learn what he may and may not do. He must gradually become responsible for himself and his behavior. Doing things for him, protecting him from real life experiences, only delays his growth. Punishing his misdeeds is a negative treatment that rarely helps in itself.

Punishing a child, scolding him, merely makes him feel inadequate, "bad," "no good." Punishment may stop him from doing what he is doing at the moment, but it gives him very little help in seeing how he may do better. And even more unfortunately, punishment may take away his faith in himself and his ability to do and to be, just when he needs confidence most. You do not need to be extreme in avoiding punishment at all costs. There may be times when a slap helps a child stop what he may be doing that is harmful. But punishment for punishment's sake is rarely helpful, except in relieving the feelings of the person in charge!

Good discipline allies itself with children's eagerness to grow up. It is founded upon encouragement rather than discouragement. It is based on helping the child learn how to do his best as he becomes ready to try. It recognizes that a child must be ready before he can learn well. He must be ready to learn to walk before he can walk. In a real sense you cannot teach him to walk. He must learn to walk within himself. When his muscles are strong enough, and have practiced enough of the preliminary motions required for walking, when he feels ready to try to walk, he will. So it is with almost everything else the child does. The impetus comes from inside himself. You encourage and guide his own efforts to develop.

The Child's-Eye View. Sound child guidance starts with efforts to understand what the child is trying to do in any situation. When you can get the child's-eye view of a problem, you can help him accomplish his purposes in terms of what is good from your point of view. The world looks different to a little child, because he is little. Children are little in three ways. (1) They are little in size. (2) They are little in experience. (3) They are little in authority.

A little child in a grownups' house is like Tom Thumb in the giant's home. Everything is too big, too tall, too far away. He tries to pull himself up to the table by clutching the tablecloth. This is no crime from his point of view. He is just trying to see. And so it is in many respects through the childhood years. A good house from a child's point of view is arranged somewhat to fit him. There are chairs and a table for him in his size. There are steps up to the bathroom facilities. Hooks for his towels, washcloth, toothbrush, and clothes are low enough for him to reach. He has his things at his level and is shown adult's not-to-be-touched things from time to time to satisfy his growing interest in them. Seeing things from the child's point of view starts with the ability to see things from where he stands; and to bring them close enough to him to make him feel that he belongs, and that they belong to him.

Children are little in experience. It takes a good many years of living to get used to all the wonderful little surprises all around us. In the meantime, children learn by experience. Providing the child with the experiences in learning that he is after is part of seeing things from his point of view. Step by step, as he is ready, must be the rule here.

Children are little in authority. In a clash with adults, children always are inferior. The adults are always right by authority of superior strength and power. Only as they, the adults, see things from the child's subordinate position, and consider his rights in the case, is he given a real chance to have a voice in affairs and to grow at his best. This does not mean that adults do not have rights, too. They do, and are privileged to protect them, even from their children when need be. But as the stronger power, the adult has the responsibility, too, of seeing to it that the child in the situation is not crushed.

What Behavior Means. Behavior speaks. When you know how to translate it, children's behavior can tell you a great deal. You learn to "read" behavior when you try to understand what it means. As soon as you begin to see that what a child does always has a meaning, and that it makes sense to him, you have an attitude that works well. You must see in his behavior not only the aspects that are annoying or frightening from your own point of view, but also what it means to the child. Both are essential to good child guidance.

A child runs out into the street in front of a truck. You swoop down and pick him up without question. From your superior vision, he is in too great danger to deliberate over. Only when he is safe do you take his feelings into account. But suppose he is pulling pans out of the cupboard. The clatter and the disorder may be annoying to the older person. But he is no danger. He is not *trying* to be annoying. Looking at what he is doing from his point of view tells us that he is exploring and "learning" pans. He is finding out about different sizes and weights and textures. He is discovering important things about his world that he must learn somehow. As you see what his behavior means, you keep back the immediate "no-no" from your lips and let him continue his "lesson" in pans.

So it is with most problem behavior. It can be understood both in terms of your fears and hopes for the child, and also in terms of what his behavior means to him. The fourteen common problems in children's behavior, pages 324–27, are given in terms of what they may mean. Only as you understand what the behavior stands for in the child's experience can you choose a wise course of action. In general the treatment listed in column 3 is unwise, because it is negative and does not take into account the meaning of the child's behavior to him.

More constructive methods of handling situations are briefly outlined in the fourth column. They will be helpful only to the extent to which the person

MEETING COMMON PROBLEMS OF CHILDREN [2]

The Child's Problem	It May Mean	So Do NOT	You Might Try Something Like This
He hurts other children.	Troubled feelings, anger.	Punish him harshly. Act angry yourself. Undermine his confidence in your love. Undermine his self-confidence by making him feel his bad behavior means he himself is bad.	Quietly separate the children. Divert his attention. Take away the hurting object, calmly, firmly, always. Teach him that there are some things we just do not do. Help the children play happily together again. Prevent his hurting others by helping him feel loved, by giving him other outlets for feelings.
He destroys things.	An accident. Feelings of helplessness, jealousy, boredom. Wanting attention. Excitement. Exuberance. Curiosity.	Scold, yell, shout. Punish harshly by spanking or hitting him. Tell him he is bad.	Remove the destructible things from child's reach. Provide good place for play. Expect some wear and tear. Substitute something else for what is being destroyed. Expand his world by taking him places, letting him see and explore new areas. Provide things to pound and mess and cut and tear. Teach him what he may and may not do.
He uses bad language	Trying something new. A joke. Imitation. Getting attention. Letting off steam.	Get excited. Act embarrassed or shocked. Scold or punish harshly. Over-emphasize it.	Relax, understand what it means. Calmly tell him to stop. Try rhyming some other word with it for fun, or offer other simple substitutes. Give him healthy outlets for feelings.

Problem	Because	Don't	Do
He won't share.	Too young or too little. Need for experience in owning and sharing.	Snatch from him. Scold or hurt him. Tell him you do not like him. Play favorites in settling dispute.	Help him learn to enjoy sharing. Be sure he has things that are *his*, let him know what it means to own things. Be a fair arbiter in children's squabbles over things. Love him, help him feel secure. Provide experiences as he is ready for them.
He still sucks his thumb (or fingers).	Need for sucking. Need for loving, cuddling, assurance, comforting. Fatigue, hunger, dissatisfaction, boredom.	Force or restrain (no mitts or guards or ties or such). Punish, scold, coax, threaten, bribe.	Provide sucking satisfactions. Give more satisfactions, love, attention, pleasure. Find out what he wants and needs and provide it as best you can. Relax and realize that it rarely lasts and is not serious. See it as a sign that the child is unhappy or dissatisfied at the moment.
He still wets.	He is not ready for training yet. Too early effort to train. Resistance or rebellion. Insecurity. Fear.	Make an issue. Threaten, shame, or punish. Bribe or reward. Insist that he tell you when he should go to the toilet. Tell him you do not love him.	Accept it and him as gracefully as you can. Expect some accidents. Give him your affection freely. Let him know you have confidence that he will do better some day. Help him become independent in other ways and encourage him to grow up.
He masturbates.	Natural exploration. Curiosity. Boredom. Need for love, comfort, and security.	Punish. Shame. Tie his hands. Threaten. Be too anxious about it.	See that he has plenty of interesting things to do. Answer his sex questions freely and frankly. Never fail to love him. Help him make friends.

² Methods Recommended for Common Problems of Children. This outline was inspired by and adapted in part from the series of pamphlets, *Some Special Problems of Children*, by Nina Ridenour and Isabel Johnson, distributed by the New York Committee on Mental Hygiene, 105 East 22 Street, New York 10, N. Y., and the National Committee for Mental Hygiene, 1790 Broadway, New York 19, N. Y.

The Child's Problem	It May Mean	So Do NOT	You Might Try Something Like This
He has fears.	Previous painful times. Strangeness. Need for his parents close by. Feeling unloved or guilty.	Force or reason the child out of his fears. Shame, threaten, or coerce. *Make* him go to or do the feared thing.	Reassure and comfort him. Make the feared place or situation a happy one. Teach him caution for real dangers and hazards. Show him love and comfort. Encourage his efforts to be "big." Help him help himself. Avoid fearful experiences, or prepare him for them.
He steals.	Ignorance of property rights. Unsatisfied needs and hungers. Rebellion. Hostile feelings. Imitation.	Make him feel that he is "bad." Scold or shame. Threaten to withhold love. Take from him something to "make up" for the theft. Humiliate him before others.	Let him own things, get a sense of mine and thine. Help him earn and get what he needs and wants. Be kind, understanding, not too rigid. Provide creative outlets for his interests. Help him make friends.
He lies.	Fear of punishment. Exaggeration. Imagination. Imitation. Attention-seeking.	Preach or prophesy his bad end. Punish or shame or reject. Get upset. Make him apologize.	Relax and try to understand. Give him attention for what he does and is. Provide him with opportunities for enriching his imagination. Help him discover the difference between fact and fancy. Tell him the truth.
He demands attention.	Feels left out, insecure, unloved. Boredom. Interest in you.	Scold or punish. Ignore or isolate him. Ridicule him. Shame him.	Give him a fair measure of attention. Show interest in him as a person. Provide interesting things to do. Share yourself with him.

He gets out of bed.	Curiosity. Interest. Not sleepy. Attention-seeking. Uncomfortable. Seeing what you expect.	Scold or punish. Threaten him. Reward or bribe. Put him to bed as punishment. Tie or restrain him.	Make going to bed a happy time. Read or sing or play with him a little before leaving him in bed. Avoid over-stimulating him at bedtime. See that his needs are met before he goes to bed. Tuck him in bed with evidences of affection. Put him back kindly but firmly. Let him meet any stranger who may be with you when he awakens.
He runs away.	Boredom. Exploration. Independence. Rebellion. Anger.	Make a scene. Cry or make over him. Punish or tie him up. Remove privileges. Unduly restrict.	Find him; find out why he ran away. Provide attractive alternatives within his own yard if possible. Let him know you like him. Let him take real responsibility around his own home. Take him on trips with you. Gradually remove restrictions as he is able to take care of himself.
He won't eat.	Not hungry. Dislikes particular food. Feeling unwell. Trying independence. Getting attention. Imitation.	Force. Make a scene. Punish. Reward. Threaten. Put on an act to divert him.	Be casual and calm; it won't hurt him to miss a meal . . . or two. Introduce new foods only a bit at a time and along with favored foods. Let him rest for now, remove food. Try him later with something else. Help him learn how to feed himself as he shows interest. Make food interesting and attractive. Enjoy food yourself. Let him help prepare food as he shows interest and readiness.

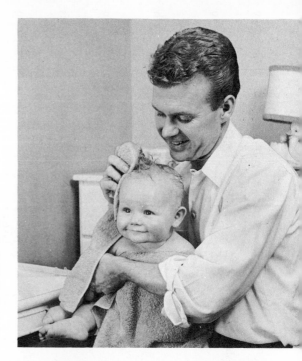

Gerber Baby Foods

More and more fathers today are sharing with their wives the burdens—and pleasures—of child care. Children, father, and mother, too, find that such an arrangement brings new warmth and closeness to their relationships with one another.

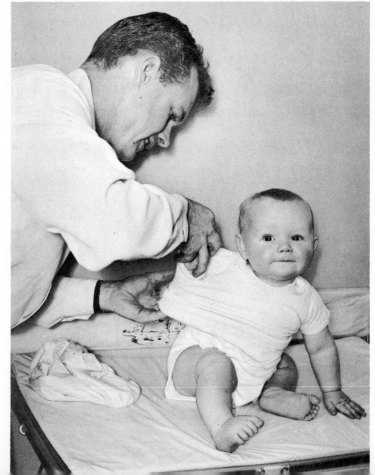

trying to use them understands what the child's behavior means. This is a fascinating quest. No mystery story is half so entrancing as efforts to really understand another person's behavior! It is rewarding, too. As you learn how to understand what children do, and why, you get along better with them. You help them grow, and you become much more deeply acquainted with all other people, too, especially yourselves.

Values in Preschool Experience

Sending a youngster to nursery school or kindergarten can do him worlds of good. It gives him a chance to find himself with other children of his own age. It provides him with experience in group play and group activities impossible in the same way in his family. It offers him a chance to learn to share and to wait his turn and to abide by the decisions of the group. Quite as important, it gives him a feeling that he has work to do, with responsibilities, and rewards and punishments that are accepted as important.

As soon as a little child goes to nursery school or kindergarten, he is confronted with the things that people outside his own family expect of children of his age. He no longer basks in his mother's devotion or his father's adoration. Now he must stand upon his own feet and measure up to what adults and children in his community expect of him. This is an important thing in a person's life, and one that cannot be taken lightly or all at once.

Preparing a Child for Group Experience. The family prepares a child for his first experiences with groups of other children outside his home. When he goes into his first preschool group he must be able to let his mother out of his sight and to stay for reasonable lengths of time with other adults. He should be able to handle his physical needs in ways appropriate for a child of his age. He is making progress in getting along with other people without extreme or continual emotional outbursts. And, he should be eager to learn and able to enjoy a variety of different forms of play and play materials.

No child reaches such a stage of readiness for group experience all at once. Over a period of time he learns to get along without his mother, by being separated from her at intervals while he is growing up. He is given experience in managing his clothing and indicating his needs for attention at home as he shows his readiness. His family provides him with enough opportunity for real play so that he is ready for the play experiences that preschool provides.

The preschool group can help a child grow socially, emotionally, intellectually, and physically. To be ready for what nursery school and kindergarten have to offer, the child must have been prepared at home.

Mother-Teacher Co-operation. When mother and teacher co-operate in planning for the child's welfare, he is fortunate. Mother takes her son or daughter to the preschool and stays with him that first time until he and the teacher feel the time is right for her to leave him. She tells the teacher of his special needs and problems, of his likes and dislikes. She learns from the teacher how he gets along with the other children, what he had to eat while at preschool, and how he responds to the various situations that present themselves to him, in the group.

From time to time teacher and mother confer together about the child's growth. They plan together the next steps and procedures for dealing with the special challenges he presents. They consider his readiness for possible new experiences and together decide when he is ready for more advanced opportunities. As the youngster grows older, he, too, may be brought into these deliberations in three-way decisions that affect him.

The Science and Art of Child Care

There is a great deal of knowledge about how children develop and what is best for them. Recent decades have been marked by outstanding studies of child development. Clinical records of individual children have told us a great deal. Research evidence has been invaluable in helping us predict the timetable of children's growth and the better methods of child care and guidance. But bringing up children is not just a matter of following a set of scientific rules. Its success depends upon the individuals involved.

Flexibility Is Important. Everything we know about child care indicates that it is much more than a science—it is an art. Rigid scheduling is self-defeating. Too-strict adherence to even the best principle may be disastrous. Inflexibility in the care of human beings does more harm than good, especially in fast-moving times like these. So the key to good child care is flexibility, the ability to change, the willingness to see and to do things differently.

The individual matters. As children come to feel that they are important for themselves, they flourish and grow. When a child feels that he is loved and that those who take care of him care what happens to him, he responds to their caring with sturdy growth. He is himself and grows best when he can accept himself and feel that he is accepted by those around him. This means that no two children can be treated exactly alike. For they are different and have to be handled differently, each according to his needs and readiness. The best way to care for children is to be willing to enter into a warm relationship with them, in which you and the children find happy, satisfying ways of living together.

Specialists on the Committee on Home Responsibility of the National Conference on Juvenile Delinquency defined a good home in terms of fourteen universal needs of children. Whether the home be a one-room apartment, a trailer, or a twelve-room house, it is good if it assures the children of certain basic satisfactions listed on page 331.

A GOOD HOME FOR A CHILD

1. He is loved and wanted—and knows it.
2. He is helped to grow up by not having too much or too little done for him.
3. He has some time and some space of his own.
4. He is part of the family, has fun with the family, and belongs to it.
5. His early mistakes and "badness" are understood as a normal part of growing up; he is corrected without being hurt, shamed, or confused.
6. His growing skills—walking, talking, reading, making things—are enjoyed and respected.
7. He plans with the family and is given real ways to help and feel needed throughout childhood.
8. He has freedom that fits his age and his needs; he has responsibilities that fit his age, abilities, and freedom.
9. He can say what he feels and talk things out without being afraid or ashamed; he can learn through mistakes as well as successes. And his parents appreciate his successes rather than dwell upon his failures.
10. As he grows older, he knows his parents are doing the best they can; they know the same about him.
11. He feels his parents care as much about him as they do about his brothers and sisters.
12. The family sticks together and the members help one another.
13. He is moderately and consistently disciplined from infancy, has limits set for his behavior, and is helped to take increasing responsibility for his own actions.
14. He has something to believe in and work for because his parents have lived their ideals and religious faith.

Summary

Caring for children has two meanings: taking care of them and being fond of them. Both are important. Meeting children's needs involves keeping them comfortable and safe, feeding them what they need when they need to be fed, loving them, encouraging their learning, and gearing oneself to their readiness for next steps in development. Guiding children's growth is the basis of good discipline. The child's-eye view is important since children are little in size, in experience, and in authority. Behavior has meanings which can be understood. Methods recommended for solving common problems of children start with trying to understand what the behavior means to the child and continue through avoiding the negative, discouraging reactions that do not help and trying out the constructive suggestions that might help. Nursery school and kindergarten are valuable preschool group experiences for which a child is prepared in his home. Child care is both a science based upon sound child development research and intensive clinical studies and an art in which flexibility is important. The individual child matters in any sound policies of procedures in child care. A good home for a child provides the physical setting and the emotional climate that is good to grow in through the years.

Suggested Activities

Individual Study

1. Write a letter to yourself in which you tell the ways in which you will bring up your children and how they are similar to or different from the ways in which you were reared. Talk it over with your parents or your teacher if you wish. Keep it in your notebook.
2. Write a paper on why some of the old slogans in child rearing no longer are considered good child care: "Spare the rod and spoil the child," "Chip off the old block," "Kill him with kindness," "Children should be seen and not heard," etc.
3. Using the various principles in the detailed outline, "Meeting Common Problems of Children," pages 324–27, work out a similar set of four columns for some other type of problem behavior in a child you know. Check your points with one or more of your reading references such as Baruch, Hymes, listed on page 333, or Spock, page 316.
4. Go over the listing in the section, "A Good Home for a Child," at the end of this chapter, point by point and modify each one as you feel would be necessary to describe "A Good Home for a Teen-Ager." Write a paper on your modifications, justifying them with experience or readings.

Group Activities

1. Discuss the film, *Helping in the Care of Younger Children* (Coronet, sound, 11 minutes) in terms of good and poor ways of recognizing and meeting children's needs.
2. Visit a nursery school or kindergarten and take detailed notes on what group experiences and play materials are available for the preschool children. Ask the teacher to tell your class the chief values of preschool for some of the individual children in her group.
3. Encourage committees within your class to role-play the do's and don't's of one or more of the problems listed in the detailed outline, "Meeting Common Problems of Children," pp. 324–27. Discuss fully, asking why particular methods are or are not recommended.
4. Show the film, *Emotional Health* (McGraw-Hill, New York City). Then discuss the ways in which the boy's childhood problems were related to his health as a young man. Develop a blackboard outline of what happened to him as he grew up.
5. Share the experiences members of the class may have had in learning to like or to dislike certain foods, or in feeling the influence of childhood experiences on later health or illness.

Readings

BARUCH, DOROTHY W., *New Ways in Discipline* (New York: McGraw-Hill Book Company, 1949). A clear statement of newer policies of bringing up children by one of their outstanding exponents. Her *How to Discipline Your Children* (New York: Public Affairs Pamphlets, 1949) is a faithful excerpt from the main thesis of the book.

BRADBURY, DOROTHY E., and AMIDON, EDNA P., *Learning to Care for Children* (New York: Appleton-Century-Crofts, 1943). This book is one of the older ones that still remains a sound and helpful guide to those who care for children and want to promote their development in wholesome comfortable ways. Your library may have it.

DUVALL, EVELYN MILLIS, and HILL, REUBEN, *Being Married* (Boston: D. C. Heath and Company, 1960). Chapter 20, "Bringing Up Your Children," looks at the problem of children acting like brats at the other extreme from being too restricted, and gives practical suggestions for following a middle ground that works between the two extremes.

FAEGRE, MARION L., ANDERSON, JOHN E., and HARRIS, DALE B., *Child Care and Training* (Rev. ed., Minneapolis: University of Minnesota Press, 1958). For thirty years this has been a basic text in child development and care. This eighth edition is up-to-date and attractively written by three outstanding child-development experts.

HYMES, JAMES L., *Enjoy Your Child—Ages 1, 2 and 3* (New York: Public Affairs Pamphlets, 1948). In this small booklet you will find a wealth of good sense about how little children grow and how you can relax and enjoy them step by step through the early years by gearing yourself to their development.

JUSTIN, MARGARET M., and RUST, LUCILE OSBORN, *Today's Home Living* (Chicago: J. B. Lippincott Company, 1953). You probably have this basic text on your classroom or library shelves. If so, look up Units 6 and 7 on understanding and guiding children's normal growth and development.

SMART, MOLLIE and RUSSELL, *Living and Learning with Children* (Boston: Houghton Mifflin Company, 1949). A well-known husband-wife team bring their readers a freshness and vividness of style that makes their sound counsel about ways of dealing with children seem altogether sensible and right.

Growing

VI

How Families Grow and Change
What Families Are For Today
Strengthening American Families

American Families

Chapter 18
How Families Grow and Change

Families develop much as individuals do. Families are started by the original partners—husband and wife. They grow with their children, age as their members grow older, and decline in their later years. All families are in continual processes of change, moving in a series of pulsing tempos and rhythms that change from year to year, day to day, hour to hour.

The Family Life Cycle

There are eight clearly discernible stages in the life cycle through which a family progresses as it grows. The first stage is that of the *beginning family*. It starts with the marriage of the man and his wife and ends as they become aware that their first child is on the way. Usually this is a brief stage of a year or two, more or less. With the birth of the first child the family enters its *childbearing* stage in which it stays until the firstborn child is two and a half years of age. This starts the third stage, that of the *preschool family*, which lasts until the first child enters school. The *school-age family* stage lasts about seven years, from the first child's entrance into school until the beginning of his teen years at thirteen. The *family with teen-agers* is another seven-year stage lasting until the firstborn is twenty years old. These first five stages see the family expanding and growing in size and complexity.

The family begins to contract as it enters the *launching center stage*, which starts when the first child leaves home for work, college, military service, or marriage, and ends with the last child's departure from the family. Then comes the seventh stage, the *family in the middle years*, lasting from the couple's first day in an empty nest up to the time of the husband's retirement. This is typically a long stage of more than a dozen years in twentieth-century America. The final stage of the family life cycle is that of the *aging family*, lasting up to sixteen years, more or less, from the husband's retirement to the death of both members of the original couple.[1]

[1] This eight-stage family life cycle is detailed in Evelyn Millis Duvall, *Family Development* (Chicago: J. B. Lippincott Company, 1957).

337

As the parents' family ages, the children's families are launched to start the family life cycle all over again. Today's men and women usually live to see the children grow up and get married, in an ongoing series of overlapping family life cycles.

Each stage in the family life cycle has its own characteristics that can be predicted and described in general. Each has its own peculiar problems and, special potentialities that can be foreseen and prepared for in the long sweep of the family through time.

The Young Married Couple. Most marriages take place when the members of the couple are in their early twenties. The first baby usually comes when the couple has been married a year or so. This interval gives the husband and wife time for settling down as a couple. Their adjustments to one another are important foundations for their family life. Couples face many problems together during these first few months of marriage, but fortunately they have resources upon which they can draw. Together they learn to act and think and feel as a couple. They learn to work out the many problems of life together in mutually satisfying ways.

During the early marriage stage there is usually an optimistic feeling that everything can be worked out successfully. Both members of the couple are likely to have a determination to succeed in their marriage. They are usually in good health at this stage. Their housing needs are simple, and just for two. Their income is apt to be low, for the young man is just getting started. Their needs for money are considerable, for getting a household established and ready for children is expensive. Many couples find that paying for furniture, a car, and all of the other things that go into the making of a new home seriously drain their resources. That is one of the big reasons why so many young wives work until the children are on the way. A wife's earnings can make up the difference between low income and high costs. The philosophy of life, the habits and the ways of living together that are established in this stage are important both to the couple and their future family.

Childbearing Families. When a husband and wife are expecting a baby, they may feel one of several ways about it. They may both be delighted. They may both wish the baby were not on its way. The husband may be pleased and the wife not. The wife may want it and the husband not. Fortunately most couples want their babies and eagerly begin to anticipate them long before they are born. However a husband and wife may feel about it, they have many new adjustments and problems to face once the baby has arrived.

With the coming of a baby, life is complicated. There are all the new routines of taking care of the baby to be learned and established. The wife takes on the full role of motherhood. The family needs more space for the baby and his equipment. Expenses increase considerably, not only in costs of having the baby but also for the special foods, the extra things, the doctor's services, and the help that is needed from time to time. The social life of the family is quite different from that of the previous stage. The couple can no longer leave home as readily. Nursing and sleeping needs of the infant operate around the clock and tie the mother down close to home. Housework often is simplified to reduce the strain on the mother. Pride and satisfaction in the baby and in their being a family are rewarding experiences for most families at this stage.

Families with Preschool Children. By the time the first baby is ready to go to a nursery school at the age of three or so, there is probably one younger child in the family, and maybe more. Life is more complicated than ever now. Sickness strikes suddenly and unpredictably when children are small. Accidents happen often, and bumps, bruises, falls, cuts, and burns naturally accompany the exploration of normal little children. Children outgrow one set of restrictions and are ready for the next long before the average adult realizes it. Little children advance rapidly from the playpen to the back porch, to the fenced-in yard, and on into the street. It is a lively set of parents who can anticipate the child's ability to take on the next stage and provide opportunities for him as he grows.

There is a feeling of being a family now. The parents have settled into their roles as parents. They are getting used to having children. Their things are not as new and are getting hard usage. They would probably like a larger place to live in, more labor-saving devices, and more help from time to time. Father is working hard trying to make ends meet. Mother is busier than she ever was or will be again. Life is full and active.

Families with School-Age Children. Life thins down at home through the day as the children get into school. The mother has more undisturbed quiet and time in which to get things done at home. The parents are drawn into more and more of the neighborhood affairs as their children get into school. The mother is interested in the local parent-teacher association. The father may be helping equip the playground at the corner. The children of the neighborhood see each other at school and are in and out of each other's houses in play. They get acquainted with others beyond the neighborhood and broaden out as a family.

The family income may be increasing slightly, but costs continue to mount. There is a great deal of wear and tear on the house and its furnishings. Children run in and out of the house in bursts of activities with their playmates. Laundry and cleaning are heavy and constant. Repairs seem never to be done. Tasks now are shared as all members of the family help with the food preparation, the dishwashing and drying, the cleaning up, and most of the other jobs around the home. The parents feel very much needed and wanted. The children are finding themselves in their own world. There are many satisfactions in this stage of family life.

When a family has expanded over several generations, gatherings of this kind help build up a sense of continuity and belonging in each individual member, young and old.

Families with Teen-Agers. You know this stage in the family life cycle. You are in it in your own family right now. It is probably one of the stormiest periods of all. Considerable conflict between the generations is to be expected at this stage. Teen-agers are growing up and out and are in the process of emancipating themselves from their childhood dependency upon their parents. This takes time and is rarely easy. Parents, too, are learning new ways as they face life without the constant tasks of parenthood upon them.

Expenses are high at this time. The social life of the teen-ager is important, and it requires clothing, transportation, and entertaining costs far above those of younger children. Parents and children may have many decisions to make as to which needs are most imperative. Fortunately the family council works well now that the children are old enough to reason and hold their own in family discussions. The work of the home is often shared, too. Husband and wife are free to take up recreation as a couple because their children are off so much with their friends of their age.

Stepping out as a middle-aged couple sometimes has to be encouraged by teen-age children, who can be of great help in bringing their parents up to date. Some parents need to be introduced again to the full life of the larger community that they may have skipped when their children were young. Mother may again take up interests that she dropped some years ago. Or she may go back to work to help augment the family income. Father is beginning to slow down a bit physically, but must keep up the pace of his earnings since they are so urgently needed. There is never a dull moment in the interaction of the teen-age family. In many ways it is one of the most exciting and stimulating stages of all.

Families as Launching Centers. When a ship is completed, it is launched into the water, where it makes its way on its own. When children grow up, they, too, are launched by their families into the wider seas of adult participation. Young adults leave home for further education or for jobs or to get married. Soon they will be on their own. But, for the moment, they and their parents are busy with the many details of finding and preparing for a job, or choosing a college, or planning a wedding. New vistas open up for the whole family as it explores these horizons.

Expenses are now so heavy that the family may have to draw upon its savings to see a daughter through her marriage or a son through college. The parents may be facing new health problems as they reach middle age. They find that they are not quite as active as they once were. Still they are not yet ready to retire. The woman especially is apt to have a deep reservoir of vital energy that is no longer needed in her home. She faces real problems in finding herself as a person in recreational, vocational, or other activities that will prove really satisfying. Her husband is still busy making ends meet. Her children are getting out into lives of their own. She must make some major readjustments to life if she is to let her children go without clinging to them.

Families in the Middle Years. After the last child has grown up and left home, the couple is left in an empty nest. This may be very satisfying and something of a relief after the burdensome childrearing years. Or it may be a period of great loneliness for those who have not made their readjustments as a couple successfully. However they feel about it, they will find that their expenses are now much lower than they have been in years. But the furniture is worn out and the place looks shabby. Many couples use the first part of the empty-nest period for remodeling and refurnishing their home. The place is too big for just the two of them and so they may take in roomers, or move to a smaller place, or make over the upstairs for a married son or daughter. Their savings are apt to be depleted. They must now recoup and prepare for their old age.

Aging Families. In some families the empty-nest period is very short. Parents have hardly let the youngest child go before the children of their eldest begin to arrive. Grandparents often find their new role richly rewarding. They may find a real place for themselves helping the overworked parents and enjoying the new babies.

Some couples in their later years are responsible for others besides themselves. There may be aged parents to look after and provide for. Other relatives may need a home, which is now available. Grandchildren may come for a few days or a few years. In times of housing shortages and highly mobile families such responsibilities of couples whose own children have grown up have become increasingly common.

As a couple grows older, the husband retires from active work. Then the couple's income is greatly reduced. Its expenses are low, though there may be illness and a need for personal help and service. The husband and wife may have to adjust to living with their married children and to being dependent.

Widowhood is the final phase of the family. Normally the woman survives the man by more than a dozen years (about sixteen according to census estimates). She may live on alone. She may go to live with one of her grown children. She may share a home with another older woman, she may remarry, or she may enter a home for older folks. Each of these possibilities has its problems and its privileges. None is a complete solution for the woman who has lived out her active years in a family.

How different is the family in each of these stages! No one is like any of the others. In each stage and phase the family members must make new adjustments, learn new roles, and find satisfactions in the new possibilities. The changes in families through the years are real and universal.

Family Developmental Tasks Through the Years

Individuals have their personal developmental tasks at every stage of life. Each family member works at achieving his or her developmental tasks as a person throughout the years. While children and teen-agers are fulfilling their growth responsibilities, their parents and grandparents, sisters and brothers, are all striving to accomplish their developmental tasks.

Paralleling the developmental tasks of individual family members are the family developmental tasks of the family as a whole. Each family faces certain inevitable responsibilities necessary for its survival, continuation, and growth. These are the requisites for development that must be accomplished by the family at every stage of its life. Nine family developmental tasks described in *Family Development* are: (1) establishing and maintaining a home; (2) establishing and maintaining mutually acceptable systems for obtaining and spending money; (3) establishing and maintaining mutually satisfying patterns of who does what and who is accountable to whom; (4) establishing and maintaining a continuity of mutually fulfilling sex relationships; (5) establishing and maintaining ways of getting through to each other intellectually and emotionally; (6) establishing and maintaining workable relationships with relatives; (7) establishing and maintaining ways of interacting with friends, associates, and community organizations; (8) bearing and rearing children; and finally (9) establishing and maintaining a workable philosophy of life.

Housing Through the Family Cycle. The family requires a different kind of home when it has a houseful of children than will be needed when the aging couple faces retirement. In general, the husband and wife start out with simple housing facilities that they can afford when they are first married, and go into more commodious quarters when their children begin to arrive. It is during the early years of marriage that they move most often, as the young husband-father changes jobs and moves to better himself vocationally. When children reach school age, the family may move to the suburbs for the advantages of play space and educational facilities. As the children grow up and leave home, the mother and father may move into a smaller place located near their central interests as a married couple in the empty nest. With retirement, there may be further changes in their housing to fit their current interests and needs. Wherever home is for the family, it must be established and maintained as one of the central family developmental tasks.

Getting and Spending Money. If a family is to survive and thrive, it must have adequate ways of getting and spending money. Customarily, when a young couple marries, its costs are high and its income is lower than it will be when the husband becomes established in his vocation. It is not unusual for the wife to work until the first baby arrives. Then she usually drops out of the labor force, not to return until after the children are reared. Husband and wife devise ways of budgeting the family income to meet the needs of the family. These needs swell as the family grows until, during the teen-age and launching-center years, there are heavy financial outlays to get the children well prepared for life ahead. The mother often returns to work at this point to help provide the many things the family can use so well during its peak years. As the children grow up and leave home, there is a period of recovery, when the financial pressures are off and the family exchequer gets a breather. With retirement, the aging family gets along on its own combination of savings, annuities, pensions, and social security. During the later years medical, hospitalization, and nursing costs tend to increase, while income is relatively low. Then responsibility for aging family members may have to be shared with other younger, more affluent relatives. Getting and spending the family income is a continuing challenge throughout the life cycle of the family.

Who Does What, When, and How. A third developmental task of families is establishing ways of dividing responsibilities among its members. As the roles of men and women change through time, traditional definitions of what is expected of husbands and wives, fathers and mothers, are challenged. Many a woman is at work outside as well as inside her home. Many a man is at home doing household chores his father and grandfather never would have dreamed of doing. Early in marriage the young husband and wife have to work out some mutually acceptable division of responsibility that takes into account their own situations, their work loads inside and outside the family, their strength and health, and their feelings and attitudes about themselves and each other. These divisions of responsibility change as children come, putting their extra physical burdens on the young mother and the additional pressure for breadwinning on the young husband. As children grow old enough to help, they are taken into the team in greater or lesser degrees depending upon the family's definition of the role of its children.

Who accounts to whom differs among families and shifts from stage to stage within a given family. Each family decides this for itself, adopting a system that is mutually agreed upon and understood by the various family members. Changes from authoritarian family life to more democratic families is taking place in the United States, making it necessary for families to work out consciously what makes sense to their members, rather than to rely blindly on what their ancestors always did as a matter of course. This increases the complexity of the developmental task of deciding who does what and who is accountable to whom. It provides an ongoing challenge for the family at every stage of its life.

Communication Through the Family Life Cycle. If a family is to have a sense of togetherness, communication systems must be established and maintained through the years. Husband and wife establish some form of intercommunication during their dating and courtship days. After they marry, this communication system bears the additional burdens of household strains and stresses at the same time that both members of the pair are intent upon learning what it means to be married. As children come, the husband and wife take on new roles as parents that neither has played before. At the very time that husband and wife are busy laying down new lines of communication between each other, they both must learn how to understand their babies' behavior and how to get through to their young children with the love and security so important for their growth. The children grow and learn to talk and behave in a multitude of ways that have to be shared and communicated to be most meaningful. Strains come with the teen years as young people pull away from earlier close communication with their parents in favor of more intimate sharing with friends of their own age. Even so, much still must be mutually understood as each generation tries to get through to the other.

In the empty-nest phase the middle-aged husband and wife have to find each other again as sweethearts. This may not be an easy task for them after they have submerged themselves in their roles as parents for twenty years or more. They may even have to revise their modes of addressing one another— from "Mother" and "Father" to terms more approprate to their new status.

Some families never quite master the task of establishing true communication. Their members hear each other's words, but they miss the tune—the emotional "music" of what things mean to one another. Other families share their most intimate thoughts and dreams with one another in a rich harmony of communication that makes life full and deeply meaningful.

Relatives as Part of the Family Circle. Relatives are part of family living. As soon as two people marry, they find they have three families—"His," "Hers," and "Theirs." His parents become her father-in-law and mother-in-law. Her family becomes his in-laws. There are family holidays to plan and celebrate together, family troubles and crises to be met and faced together, visiting and entertaining relatives from the larger family circle, giving and receiving gifts, writing letters and telephoning each other in a web of interaction that is truly part of larger family living.

Some couples start married life with a chip-on-the-shoulder attitude toward each other's families. He says, "I'm not marrying her family; I'm marrying HER." She thinks, "As soon as we are able, we'll move just as far away from his family as we can." These thoughts of avoiding all contact with relatives are rarely very realistic; nor are they helpful. There should come a time in every family when the members of the larger family circle come to terms with their relationship and work out satisfactory ways of recognizing and dealing with each other.

Family rituals add a dimension of depth to family living that means a great deal to many people. The occasional all-family get-together, the special anniversary celebration, the rallying of the whole family to attend a graduation or a wedding, have meanings that often the lone orphan truly envies. One of the developmental tasks of the family as a whole is developing pleasantly satisfying tie-ins with other relatives so that a sense of family belonging results.

Being Geared to Community Life. No family lives to itself alone. Each family lives out its life within the larger community of which it is a part. The couple starts by joining a church, joining some clubs and organizations of mutual interest, and participating in the causes that make sense to both husband and wife. As their children come, they go through a "nesting period" when they are not as active in the larger community as they once were. Baby sitters are hard to find, so the young parents find more of their interests with their own children at home. As children get into school, they take their parents with them to parent-teacher meetings, neighborhood affairs, and wider areas of community life.

When grown children marry, they bring their parents intimately in touch with still other facets of life outside themselves for a while until, in the later years, there is a struggle between the desire to withdraw and the need to continue active participation—the conflict between "Why not?" and "Why bother?" Studies show abundantly that the older adult who remains geared to life within the community is happier and better adjusted than the lone, inactive man or woman. Being geared to community life is an important function of family living throughout the family life cycle.

Bearing and Rearing Children. This is an important family developmental task. Most couples want children. These days more families than ever are having children because they want them. Learning what it means to have children, learning how to care for them, to rear them, and to let them go as they become adult is a series of tasks that every father and mother must accomplish.

Few parents are prepared for their jobs as parents. You do not need a license to become a mother or a father. You have to know how to drive a car before you can get a driver's license. But you can have any number of children whether or not you know how to raise them effectively. Men and women who have not had courses in child care before they marry may take child care courses after their children arrive. They may read books about child development, consult their children's doctor about child growth, and learn their jobs as parents as their children grow from one stage to another.

No matter how much you know about child training, the task of bearing and rearing your own children is a never-ending challenge. What is best to do for the child, for the family, for the present, and for the future is not

"What did you do in school today?" Children of nine and ten chatter readily about their classmates, whom they expect their parents to know by first name.

Fujihira from Monkmeyer

easy to determine in most situations. Husband and wife may not see eye to eye about the ways of dealing with their children. They may desire one way of life intellectually, and be driven emotionally toward another because of the way they were brought up. Bearing and rearing children is not a simple sequence of tricks and devices. It involves coming to terms with oneself and with life's deepest and most important values.

Building a Family Philosophy of Life. Every family must discover the values that have meaning for itself if it is to have a sense of direction. These family goals and values differ among families, and they shift from one stage of the family life cycle to the next. One family is self-centered and selfish in its personal ambitions. Another is tied into a life of service beyond itself. One family is intent upon immediate gains, another is working for long-term goals. Early in the family life cycle the young husband and wife tend to be absorbed in getting their own home established and their house furnished. As children come, their attention shifts to the values inherent in their developing sons and daughters. When the children have grown up and gone from home, the middle-aged husband and wife come face to face with their lives as a couple with a future to carve out together that has real meaning for them both. The aging family sees beyond the years in a mood of philosophical inquiry and a quickening interest in religion that reflects its own inner searchings at every stage of its life cycle.

No one else can accomplish these developmental tasks for any given family. Their achievement is essential for the future of each family. With success in any developmental task, the family is happy and succeeds in its future tasks along the same line. With partial success or failure, there is disappointment and difficulty in future related developmental tasks. As long as a family continues, it struggles with the accomplishment of its business of living as a family. Out of this ongoing job of living comes the satisfaction of tasks undertaken and completed. This is of the nature of life—for the family as for the individual.

Seasonal Variations in Family Life

In most families in the United States there are observable changes in family activities around the calendar. Life shifts gears as the family moves out of one season and into the next. What the family does, and how, differs from season to season.

Families in Spring. All across the country families shake themselves loose from winter activities as spring comes. Spring is a period of activity, of bursts of energy, of the family mobilizing itself in tune with the shift in the climate.

Family Life in Summer. Summer is a time of many possibilities for American families. School is out. Men have vacations. The whole family can take a trip, or visit relatives, or be visited, or go camping, or settle down for more leisurely living at home.

Family Activities in Autumn. As soon as Labor Day is over, most families with school-age children find themselves back in fall routines, as school starts again. There is a general settling down into regular routines and schedules that continues on into the winter.

Family Living in Winter. Winter living in the family is dependent upon the climate in which the family lives. In the northern part of the United States family life is punctuated by episodes of snow-shoveling, traffic tie-ups, and winter sports. In more clement climates through the South, life goes on much as usual with only an occasional storm.

Weekly Rhythms

Within the stages of development and seasonal variations of family life, are the weekly rhythms in which the pace shifts in regularly recurrent ways.

Monday Through Friday Routines. Most families have established routines which they follow fairly regularly week after week. Father goes to work at the same hour and returns about the same time each day. Children have regular hours at school. Meals are served at about the same times. Mother plans her work through the week around the others' projected schedules. Now that the five-day week is relatively well established in America, most families find that their activities from Monday through Friday are fairly predictable according to a definite pattern.

Saturday Is Special. There is no school on Saturday. Father is home from work at least half the day. Almost anything can happen on Saturday. Teen-agers may be off early to a part-time job. The children may sleep late, or they may be up early for an all-day excursion. Saturday is the big shopping day in many families. They pile into the family car and drive it to the shopping center, where they purchase supplies for the coming week. Saturday sales in stores encourage this practice.

Saturday may be a day of play in a week of work. Special sports events are scheduled then. Family outings are planned for the weekend. Little trips, special projects, entertaining, and recreation generally find their place in the Saturday program.

Family Sundays. Sunday is a special day, but in a different way from Saturday, in most homes. Most stores are closed. Shopping or part-time jobs are unlikely. Typically, in many communities, the family has breakfast a little later (and a little fancier) than usual and after reading the Sunday paper, goes to Sunday school and church. Then comes Sunday dinner which, in most homes, is heavier and more festive than any other meal of the week. After the dishes are done, the mother and father may take a little nap. The whole family may go for a ride. This is the time for calling upon relatives and close friends. Home again in the early evening perhaps, to watch television, the family has a light supper and a leisurely evening ahead. Older children may be out for young peoples' meetings or casual recreation in the early evening. And so Sunday, America's day of rest, draws to a close.

Daily Tempos

Tempos change throughout every day of family living. You cannot talk about family life as though it were the same around the clock. Its mood and rhythms change from hour to hour.

The Morning Rush. The typical family gets under way in the morning with a rush. In the space of an hour or two every member of the family must wash and dress and eat his or her breakfast, collect the day's equipment, and be on his way. Getting each member into and out of the bathroom takes some tight scheduling in most homes. Breakfast is apt to be a hurried meal. Children often have a last-minute hunt for rubbers, books, and other school paraphernalia. Father may have mislaid his papers. Friends call to walk to school with the children, or to ride to town with the father. By the time the family is on its way, the mother is ready to relax with a second cup of coffee, unless she, too, is off to work.

Morning and Afternoon Pause. From the time the last member of the family has left the house until the first one returns home in the afternoon, home is a rather quiet place. Except while the children are small (a relatively few years for the average family) this midday pause is one in which there is no one home except the mother and the dog. In fact, the mother herself is very possibly out working, shopping, calling, or attending meetings. Fewer and fewer families eat lunch together at home as families did when most people lived on farms. Now the family members are scattered and eat where they are, the children at school, the father at or near his work. Even the mother often lunches out, as part of her larger community work. If we were to chart the activities of the average family around the clock, the late morning and early afternoon would be a slow, empty time with very little interaction between family members.

Late Afternoon Hustle. Late afternoon is a busy time in most families. Children return home from school, change their clothes for play, bring their friends by for a snack, practice their music, and perhaps get started on their homework. Father comes home and may try to get a little gardening or household repairing done before the evening meal. There is apt to be a great deal of telephoning, especially in families where there are older children. Last-minute shopping is quickly done and the evening meal prepared with more or less co-operation by various members of the family. The late afternoon is rarely a quiet period. It is filled with activity and a great deal of family interaction.

"Supper will be ready in about ten pages."

Pause for the Evening Meal. As the family gathers for dinner (or supper as it is often called), attention is focused on its members. Outside pressures are at a minimum. Reports of the day are exchanged. Father may tell an amusing episode from his day. Children may share their successes and their feelings about school. Comments and feelings shared often teach important lessons about other people and help build a philosophy of life. A lot happens during the family meals besides the eating of food.

Evening Variables. Families spend their evenings in many ways. Sometimes they stay quietly at home. Then there may be friction over personal privacy, noise and quiet, and the use of common facilities. Father may want to read, while Mother wants music. The children may have to study, while an older member wants the television on, or vice versa. Even quiet evenings at home are not always noiseless!

The family may be out for the evening, with a "sitter" taking care of the younger children. One or more of the members may go out, leaving the others in. Friends and relatives may be entertained. Old friends and relatives may be treated as "members of the family." More formal entertaining is in order when there is an important dinner guest, when a boy friend calls, or when some family member is giving a party.

Differences Among Families

In a sense, the "typical" family does not exist. Every family has its own characteristic ways of doing things, its own pace, its own peculiar programs and routines. Families differ by the section of the country in which they live, the cultural group to which they belong, their place in the community, their developmental stage, their size, and their general make-up.

Different people in the same family move at different paces and follow varying tempos. These differences between the timing of family members may cause friction. Within the family individual differences can be accepted and adjusted to to the extent to which that family values the freedom of the person. Certain whole-family policies may be adhered to by all family members for the good of the family as a whole. So it is with families in our society. Each is free. Yet each jointly functions with other families for the common good.

Summary

Families grow and change through time. Typically, each family passes through eight stages of the family life cycle: (1) beginning families as married couples; (2) childbearing families with the coming of the firstborn; (3) families with preschool children; (4) families with school children; (5) families with teen-agers; (6) families as launching centers; (7) families in the middle years; and (8) aging families. Each stage of the family life cycle has its own problems and potentialities. Every family faces certain inevitable family developmental tasks that must be accomplished if the family is to continue to grow. Family developmental tasks may be seen through the family life cycle in establishing and maintaining a home, getting and spending money, determining who does what and who is accountable to whom, working through mutually satisfying systems of emotional, sexual, and intellectual communication, relating to relatives, participating in the larger community, bearing and rearing children, and building a workable philosophy of life. There are recognizable seasonal variations, weekly rhythms, and daily tempos as family life pulses through predictable variations of activity around the clock and calendar. Individual differences in families are ever present in a free society as each develops in its own way.

Suggested Activities

Individual Study

1. Write a paper on the family developmental tasks your own family now is attempting to accomplish, following the general outline of family developmental tasks in your text. Deal with each family developmental task individually, considering what helps and what hampers your family's effective achievement of the particular task under consideration. Give recommendations of what might help these family developmental tasks be more successful.

2. Review Bossard and Boll, *Ritual in Family Living,* especially looking for the contribution rituals make to family life. Illustrate your review with examples from your own family experience.

3. Make a pie-shaped chart showing the schedule of a recent day in your family, by time taken for the various family activities in the home around the clock. Compare your chart with those of others in your class. How is it different? How similar? Why?

4. Make a calendar of your family's activities for the year, listing month by month the special things the family does. Include birthdays, anniversaries, celebrations, holidays, etc. Copy it in your notebook with appropriate illustrations.

5. Jot down everything you remember about what was said around your dinner table last night. Include both the "good" and the "not so good" things. Ask yourself what the members of your family were learning in these interchanges. Write yourself a little reminder of ways in which you can improve these family learnings by what you do or say at the family table.

6. In your notebook make a column of the names of ten families you know well. Opposite each family's name place the stage in the family life cycle that that family is now in according to the schema in your text. With each stage placement, note why you have placed that particular family at that stage of the family life cycle. See if your teacher agrees with your classification.

Group Activity

1. Present a group review of *Family Development* (see Readings), in which the leader is assigned the general conceptual framework of family development and the members of the group assume responsibility for each of the stages of the family life cycle as presented in the book. Use the blackboard and mimeographed outlines as helps in presenting sections of the material. Allow time for some class discussion.

2. Conduct a class discussion of the family developmental tasks of the teen-age family, using the general outline from the text, elaborated with examples from the personal experience of members of the class.
3. Debate the question, "Are Families with Teen-Agers at the Most Stormy Stage of Family Life?"
4. Take a trip to parts of the community where families at various stages of the family life cycle live—for instance, housing developments catering to families with young children, apartments for couples without children, homes for aging family members. Encourage class members to note the special characteristics of each of these areas in terms of the developmental stage of family life they represent.
5. Pantomime various stages, seasons, rhythms, and tempos of family life in a game of charades in your class, having the rest of the class guess the family episodes portrayed.
6. Poll your class on the things that they find irksome in the typical Saturday jobs to be done around home. Consider ways in which such tasks can be done more satisfactorily for everybody concerned. Write a class memorandum of ways in which you can improve your Saturdays at home.
7. Discuss why there is no such thing as a "typical family" in America.
8. Discuss the film, *Make Way for Tomorrow* (New York University Film Library), with special attention to the grandmother's feelings and adjustment. This film is adapted from the book, *The Years Are So Long*, by Josephine Lawrence, which may be reviewed in place of the film showing.

Readings

BACMEISTER, RHODA W., *Growing Together* (New York: Appleton-Century-Crofts, 1947). A highly readable book about how family members grow up together as their families grow and change through the years. The first sentence starts, "A family is a growing thing, not only because the people who compose it grow, but also because the family as an organized group changes and grows."

BOSSARD, JAMES H. S., and BOLL, ELEANOR S., *Ritual in Family Living* (Philadelphia: University of Pennsylvania Press, 1950). This contemporary study of the rituals and routines of family living will interest all but the most immature student. See especially Chapter 7, "Family Ritual and Family Cycle."

CAVAN, RUTH SHONLE, *The American Family* (New York: Thomas Y. Crowell Company, 1953). Part Three, "The Cycle of Family Life," takes you from your teen years in the family through to the later years of married life in several hundred pages of well-documented text of interest to the scholarly student.

DUVALL, EVELYN MILLIS, *Family Development* (Chicago: J. B. Lippincott Company, 1957). This book is devoted entirely to the ways in which families grow and change as they develop over time. Here you will find elaborated the developmental tasks of each member of the family and of the family as a whole through the entire family life cycle.

ENGLISH, O. SPURGEON, M.D., and FOSTER, CONSTANCE J., *Fathers Are Parents, Too* (New York: G. P. Putnam's Sons, 1951). A wise and understanding psychiatrist focuses on what it means to be the father of the family from the time the first baby is expected until he finds himself a grandfather about to go around the cycle again.

SMART, MOLLIE STEVENS and RUSSELL COOK, *Living in Families* (Boston: Houghton Mifflin Company, 1958). An able husband-wife team vividly describes the cycle of family life in their Chapter 16, an easily read chapter that gives you the gist of the concept of developing families and how you can use it to make yours a better home.

Chapter 19

What Families Are For Today

There are certain universal purposes that families of all times share. The right for a man and woman to live together, have children, and bring them up as they will have been the central reasons for family life through the ages. For the individual family this means keeping the family members *safe* (from intruders, dangers, threats), *well* (prevention of sickness, recovery from illness, maintaining health through food, rest, care), and *in tune* with their times (able to use their resources and to gear themselves to life around them).

How Families Have Changed

Family life always reflects the times. Far back in the dawn of history, families lived in caves and foraged for a living. The discovery of fire meant protection from the cold. The development of agriculture meant that families could settle down and not have to keep on the move searching for new food supplies. The development of modern industry has brought far-reaching changes in family life which we are just beginning to understand.

Family life in the last several generations has changed more drastically and more rapidly than ever before in the history of man. We are still part of a gigantic transition period from one way of life to another. With widespread industrialization, families began to cluster around cities (urbanization). These two processes of industrialization and urbanization have brought with them many other changes that are all part of the great movement from a simple, stable type of family to a complex, unstable family unit. In order to see these shifts more closely, let us see just how families have moved in the last two or three generations.

From Rural to Urban. Not nearly so many of us live on farms today as did in our grandfather's time. In 1890 almost two-thirds of our families (64 per cent) lived in rural areas. Now only about 10 per cent of our households are still on farms. This means that the vast majority of our families live in cities and small towns and that relatively few of us keep close to the soil as did our forebears. Even those who still live in small communities are "citified" in their speech, their thinking, and their interests, thanks to the telephone, the movies, the radio, television, and the automobile.

From Large to Small. Big families used to be very common. It once was usual for as many as eight or ten or more children to grow up in the same family. With them and their father and mother frequently lived an unmarried aunt, a grandfather or grandmother, and sometimes other relatives. Today's family is small by comparison. The birth rate rises because (1) there are more marriages; (2) more couples have children; (3) fewer families have only one child; and (4) most families have two or three children today.[1]

From the Making to the Buying of Things. Just a few generations ago, families were very busy making things. Our great-grandmothers worked from dawn to dark spinning, weaving, sewing, knitting, gardening, cooking, canning, preserving, baking, churning, and doing many other manufacturing jobs. Making all the goods essential and desirable for family members today is big business and no longer the job of the family. Today's family is freed from the drudgery of making its own butter. Modern dairies make it more uniformly and economically than our grandmother ever could. Few of us bake our own bread. Modern bakeries have bread and pastry making down to a fine science. So it is with much that we need to eat and wear and have for our comfort at home. This is one reason why families have shrunk in size. There no longer are so many tasks to keep many hands at work. Your aunt Cora is no longer needed to help quilt and make apple butter and vegetable soup. Even children are no longer an economic asset! Today's children in cities cannot earn their way in their families as children once could when there were so many things to be made and raised and processed. Business has moved out of the family and into the larger community.

From Fixed to Mobile. Today's families are "on the go." They do not "stay put" as they used to do. In the years between 1940 and 1960 practically ten million families moved from one place to another in the United States during every single year! That is quite a contrast to the way our grandfathers lived in the same house, on the same farm for several generations. We are no longer rooted to the soil. Our families are smaller and easier to move. Our jobs shift, and so must we. We have fast and efficient transportation. We have been uprooted, too, by the two World Wars and the economic changes of recent decades.

From Stable to Unstable. Families no longer stay together the way they used to do. Children marry and move across the continent, instead of onto

---

[1] Interdepartmental Committee on Children and Youth, *Children in a Changing World* (Washington, D. C.: Golden Anniversary White House Conference on Children and Youth, 1960), Chart 3.

the farm next door, as once was the case. A husband and father may take a job miles away from his home and see his family only occasionally. A wife and mother may work outside the home, away from her family for hours or days at a time.

More serious than these temporary separations are the more permanent disruptions of family life seen in divorce, desertion, and annulments. From 1860 on our divorce and annulment rate increased steadily decade by decade to an all-time high in 1946, at the close of World War II. Since then it has been declining, but it is still higher than at any time before 1940, as is clear from the chart below:

DIVORCES AND ANNULMENTS IN THE UNITED STATES [2]

Rate per 1,000 Existing Marriages

1860	1.2	1900	4.0	1940	8.7
1870	1.5	1910	4.5	1946	18.2
1880	2.2	1920	7.7	1950	10.2
1890	3.0	1930	7.4	1956	9.3

There are many reasons why families no longer stay together as they once did. The most significant of these factors is social change. It looks as though we have not yet learned to build strong families that can withstand the stresses and strains of our times. We must know much more about these modern families of ours. And we need to know how to build new foundations for marriage and family life in our times.

From Scarcity to Abundance. Modern American families have more wealth, power, and resources than any families have ever had in the whole history of mankind. Our grandparents and their ancestors in frontier days had to do with very little. They saved every scrap for possible use later. String and paper, household fat and drippings, bits of cloth and all sorts of old clothing, furnishings, and equipment were saved year after year and handed down in the family for generations.

Ours are problems of plenty rather than of scarcity. Our economy is based upon a planned obsolescence in which the new model automobile, washer, suit, or packaged food makes the old familiar product out of date, often long before it is used up or worn out. New forms of energy, new products, new resources present themselves in amazing array to modern man. Somehow modern man and wife must pick and choose, from a welter of possibilities, the way of life and the possessions that are best for them.

[2] Paul H. Jacobson, *American Marriage and Divorce* (New York: Holt, Rinehart and Winston, Inc., 1959), p. 90. The 1956 figure is provisional.

In just a few generations our families have shifted from being units of production to being units of consumption. Most of us need help in learning how to be wise consumers. Individually and as citizens our welfare depends upon how well our families learn to live in abundance in a world that has had all too little experience with this particular problem.

Families as Working Democracies

Families used to be controlled by the head of the house, usually the father. Children were to be seen and not heard. They had little to say in family decisions. The authority of the father was absolute and not to be questioned. Today some families are organized around much more democratic principles. Each person in the family is recognized as having rights as a member of the family.

Authoritarian Ways No Longer Fit. Fathers and mothers no longer lay down the law for children to obey in many American homes. Their authority has so diminished that, if they try to bring up their children as they were raised, their children rebel. Family councils and joint decisions are being widely accepted. Of course not all, or even most, families are truly democratic yet, but the trend toward democratic controls is clear.

Family Members Play Flexible Roles. There used to be no question about what was woman's work and what was man's work in the family. When a woman married, she slipped into a role of domesticity as definite as her apron. Her work was in the home with her children and the multitude of housekeeping jobs to be done. The man was the wage-earner and provider. He rarely helped in the home. His wife even more rarely was employed outside. Today all that is changed. Men increasingly help with the children, the dishes, and other homemaking tasks. In many homes man and wife share both the earning and spending, the inside and the outside tasks. Few jobs are now classified rigidly as either for men or for women. Men, women, and children now tend to follow their own individual inclinations and talents with far more freedom than was granted their ancestors.

Families as Laboratories of Freedom

When grandmother was a girl, there was a long list of things that no nice girl would ever do. Today girls (and boys) are much less rigidly bound by restrictions. The neighborhood supervises people less than it used to. In the days of the horse and buggy, a couple on a date could never get so far away from home that they could not be recognized. If the neighbors were not quite sure who the couple were, they could always spot the horse! Then a person knew that he was expected to behave as a member of his family, church, and community should.

"Go on in and read your paper, you won't disturb them."

The Wall Street Journal

Today two young people start out for a good time in an automobile, and in a few minutes they can be so far away from their neighborhood and the people who know them that for all practical purposes they are unknown. What they do is up to them. Since there are few definite rules as to exactly what is right and what is wrong, their freedom is apt to be confusing and indefinite.

Freedom with Responsibility. If individuals are to be free, they must learn to assume responsibility for themselves and for their situations wherever they are. This is true in all situations. The little child can be given as much freedom as he can be responsible for at that time. The older child, the teen-ager, the adult, face inevitable responsibilities as they become more and more free.

Families in a democracy encourage their members to care for themselves, to grow in their ability to assume real responsibility, and to use as much freedom as they can be responsible for at any given time.

Although many characteristics of family life have changed in modern times, playing piggy-back is still a favorite pastime for fathers and young children. For a few minutes the little boy glimpses a world that is usually far "over his head."

Such freedom differs widely from license, which is irresponsible behavior without regard for consequences. Children who are really free have learned to use their freedom for the promotion of their own welfare without hurting others. This begins very early in childhood and is a thread that runs through the lifetime of a mature democratic person. It is rooted in the basic learnings found in joint planning, mutual responsibilities, and shared privileges within the family.

Learning to Be Free. As people mature, they have to learn how to be free. Freedom is not something that can be given to an individual. It is earned through increasing ability to assume the responsibility that freedom requires. Families are the natural laboratories of freedom since they provide the earliest training ground for the human personality first, and continue to shape it over the longest period of time, in situations where freedom and responsibility operate most fully. Therefore, one of the chief functions of families in a freedom-loving culture like ours is to help family members learn how to live in freedom.

Families at Home in the World

Yesterday's families were isolated. Before the days of modern communication, radios, hourly news services, air travel, and all the rest, the family was dependent upon the party line and the local newspaper for its knowledge of what was happening to other people. Interests were largely bounded by people whom the family knew personally. What happened to other people around the world was of relatively little concern to families even a few generations ago. They were more provincial in those days than we ever will be again.

Families Live in More of the World Today. Today the world flows into our homes every time we turn on a radio. We know more about millions of people whom we shall never see than our grandfather did about his own cousin in the next county. Members of our families have traveled all over the world and lived near all sorts of people. The map of the world is no longer an impersonal page in a geography book, but a living, pulsing, personal experience to most of us. Today's families live in a great deal more of the world than was possible for those of yesterday. We are increasingly at home in the world, recognizing our interdependence, seeing events with broader sights, and living with larger awareness.

Caring About What Happens. When the plight of millions of families around the world is made known to us every day through radio, television, newspaper, and personal travel, we cannot help being aware of what is happening. Standing for human rights and values is a learned reaction to the inequalities among men. We Americans pride ourselves on helping the underdog. We spend billions of our national income and resources to help less privileged nations around the earth. It is in our families that children learn to care about what happens to other people. The self-centered, selfish family inculcates selfish attitudes in its children; while the selfless, sensitive, world-minded family teaches its children to care about others, to stand for human dignity, and to fight injustice wherever it occurs. These are vital family functions in a world threatened by the convulsions of social changes and conflicting philosophies.

Family Functions in Our Democracy

Back in Great-Grandmother's time the functions of the family were clear. The baking, cooking, preserving, and gardening were essential for family survival. Spinning, knitting, weaving, and sewing were imperative if family members were to be clothed. The mother and father were absorbed in the making of the *things* the family needed. Children and the "extras" of the family—the Aunt Lindas and the Cousin Jims—helped, too, as they could. The family stayed put and remained together through tight bonds of economic necessity.

Modern industrialization and urbanization of life have removed these family functions centered around things. *We are now in the process of moving to a type of family life that functions primarily for the development of persons*, rather than the production of things. This is a gigantic step to take in just a couple of generations. It is resulting in many confusions, as does any rapid move. As the functions of family life in our kind of modern democracy are better understood, we will settle down in new ways of family living.

The chief function of our families is the development of strong, sturdy, wholesome persons, capable of withstanding the stresses and strains of modern life, and able to make a constructive contribution to their times. This is imperative if our democracy is to survive. No other institution can fulfill this function as can the family.

Encouraging Individual Development. A democracy rests upon its faith in the individual. Families are in the best position to encourage and develop individual growth. They can have confidence in growth. They can encourage personal talents and inclinations, provide opportunities for special aptitudes, and accept individual differences. The democratic family encourages persons to grow at their own rates, along the lines indicated by their own needs and interests. Traditional roles of men and women, boys and girls, children and adults, give way to the rights and privileges of the person in the family. The father can don an apron without losing his masculinity. The mother may work at those things that are best for her and her family without being bound to custom. A boy may paint without being a sissy. A girl may play ball without being a tomboy. Respect for personality is the number one criterion of successful functioning of a family in a democracy.

Providing for Personal Security. The family is the base line of security for its members. It is their place of refuge to which they can retire from the stresses and strains of complicated modern living. Home is where a person can be natural and pour out his experiences and his feelings in the presence of people who care. It is in the family that problems are discussed, troubles aired and confusions cleared. As the family interprets life situations and encourages its members in them, personal security is assured.

You belong to your family more truly than to any other group. No matter what you do, you are still theirs, and they are yours. You cannot stray so far away that you do not still belong to them. You count for more in your family than in any other association. As long as you live, you will be someone special to your parents, your brothers, your sisters, grandparents, and other relatives. No one can ever take your particular place with them. It is this intimate sense of family ties within you that helps keep you feeling secure.

Families are important to personal security because they provide that precious sense of belonging that all persons need. When contacts with other people are brief and impersonal, as they are so often today, it becomes more important than ever that the need to feel related should be satisfied at home. Personal security is rooted in the warm soil of family living.

Teaching the Tools of Our Times. Families encourage the use of the fundamental tools and inventions upon which our culture rests. Children should be taught the use of money through graduated experiences in earning, spending, and planning for its future use. Members of the family (without too much regard for sex or chronological age) should be encouraged to develop skills in handling the physical equipment of our times; the care and driving of the automobile, the use of the electrical equipment, the telephone, modern plumbing, and all the rest.

Upon families rests the task of teaching their members the use of language through reading, critical radio listening, stimulating discussion, acquaintance with the major points of view, the big ideas, and the attitudes that underlie our culture.

Science as seen in health, sex education, mental hygiene, marital happiness, family satisfactions, and personal growth, as well as in its more technological forms, is a challenge for the family seeking its true place in a democratic society. Only as persons grow up in homes which promote growth through the application of sound insights, can we hope to realize our full destiny.

Fostering Brotherhood. It is in the family that we learn to live with differences in a constructive way. The family generates the first racial and religious attitudes. As the family fosters tolerance, brotherhood, and co-operation among people, so these attitudes spread outward to the neighborhood, the community, the world. One World is seen first in the family that lives out new ways of appreciation and interdependence in its daily life. As families become more and more sensitive to peoples everywhere, they open wide their doors for the rest of the world to stream through. Such are the families alive to the challenges of democratic living.

Building Dynamic Patterns of Peace. Peace begins at home because that is where most wars start. Peace in this sense is not the absence of conflict, but rather the resolving of conflicts constructively. Families in a democracy are normally laboratories in which conflicts arise, are met, and worked through, so that a stronger, sounder relationship emerges than existed before. The cross-currents of conflicting values, struggles for supremacy, and emotional honesty with one another, provide rich opportunities for families to learn the ways of peace.

The dictatorial father lays down the law, and the children obey. The democratic father listens as well as speaks. He lives both *with* and *for* his family. He prefers a little hectic interchange to peace at any price. The dominating mother who was "always right" gives way today to the woman who can dare to admit being wrong, who can learn with her children and her husband to live through intricate day-by-day problems that would have nonplused her grandmother.

There are times when family relationships get out of hand. The family that takes an intelligent accepting attitude toward expert help in time of

By making bedtime a happy time for his little sister, a teen-ager helps establish a warm and loving relationship between himself and the younger child.

Campbell Hays

trouble is teaching a valuable lesson. Emotional problems need attention as much as physical ones. Yet many people refuse to seek professional help for an ailing parent-child or husband-wife relationship. When our families can accept guidance in such problems without embarrassment, as they accept the help of the dentist or the medical doctor, we will be close to the attitude that is fundamental to our peace everywhere.

Growing Strong People and Families

As our families move out of the traditional forms and functions that operated in Great-Grandmother's day, into the new ways that are needed today there is confusion, bewilderment, and disruption. Our hope for family stability lies in education that will clarify the place of the family in modern society and strengthen its role in democratic living. This means adequate marriage and family research. When we invest billions of dollars in atomic research, we might keep social research at least within sight. We need sound knowledge about personality development, marriage, and family life in all of its aspects on which to base a strong program for family stability.

As you will see in Chapter 20, there are imperatives for family-life education today at all age levels. None of us was trained for our role in the family. Families that support programs of education for family living in the schools, the churches, and the communities are performing essential functions. It is out of families that much of the family-life movement has come during the past several decades. Such a past augurs well for the future.

Summary

Families have always had basic purposes. Specific family functions change as families do. Families have changed drastically in the recent past due to the social change brought about by industrialization and urbanization. Some of these changes are (1) from rural to urban; (2) from large to small; (3) from the making to the buying of things; (4) from fixed to mobile; (5) from stable to unstable; (6) from authoritarian to democratic; (7) from rigid to flexible; (8) from definite standards to indefinite freedoms; (9) from provincial to world-minded. Family functions today no longer center as much in the making of things as they do in the development of persons.

Seven family functions in a democracy like ours are to: (1) encourage individual development; (2) provide for personal security; (3) promote freedom with responsibility; (4) foster easy mastery of the tools of our culture; (5) nurture sensitivity to and concern for others; (6) provide constructive opportunities for building dynamic peace; (7) strengthen the family itself. These functions are a challenge to all of us today.

Suggested Activities

Individual Study

1. Review either of the books, *The Late George Apley*, or *Life With Father*, contrasting the type of family authority represented with the kind of controls operating in families with which you are personally acquainted. Write a short paper on these contrasting family types for your class notebook.

2. Copy the following into your notebook and match each of the changes listed with an appropriate illustration.

HOW FAMILIES ARE CHANGING WITH SOCIAL CHANGE

(Do not write in this book.)

Family Change	Illustration
1. From rural to urban	1. More and bigger cities today
2. From large to small	2.
3. From the homemade to the store-bought	3.
4. From fixed to mobile	4.
5. From stable to unstable	5.
6. From authoritarian to democratic	6.
7. From rigid to flexible roles	7.
8. From definite standards to new freedoms	8.
9. From provincial to world-minded	9.

3. Give a book report on Frederick Lewis Allen's *Only Yesterday*, or *The Big Change*, by the same author. Stress those changes most closely touching family life.

4. Write a paper on "Freedom and Responsibility," including what this means in child-rearing, in husband-wife relationships, and in the family circle. Illustrate with episodes and experiences known to you.

5. Make a personal survey of what your church is doing in family-life education and summarize your findings with relevant materials in your class notebook.

Group Activity

1. On the blackboard, make a column of things no nice girl would do in Great-Grandmother's day. List another column of definite "Do's and Don't's" for girls today. Copy the lists into your notebook as a basis for your further thinking about our changing standards.

2. Outline the family functions discussed in two or more references in your listed Readings. List on the blackboard under the the author's name. Discuss.

3. Act out a scene from your great-grandmother's family life and a parallel one from your home showing some of the ways in which families have changed. Discuss the purposes of each type of family for its time.
4. Send to United Nations headquarters in New York City, to the nearest office of the American Association of United Nations, or to UNESCO for materials on underdeveloped countries around the world. Discuss family attitudes about these conditions in your class.
5. Send a class delegation to confer with your Superintendent of Schools, Board of Education, or Public Schools Curriculum Committee to find out what is being done in the schools of your community in family-life education at the various grade levels from kindergarten through public high school or junior college. Report and discuss in class.

Readings

ALLEN, FREDERICK LEWIS, *The Big Change* (New York: Harper & Brothers, 1952). A fascinating account of the way in which America transformed itself from 1900 to 1950, that serves as a vivid background for the social changes that have so greatly affected marriage and family life through the past several generations.

DUVALL, EVELYN MILLIS, *Family Development* (Chicago: J. B. Lippincott Company, 1957). Part I, "Growing Families in Changing Times," has several chapters of interest to the mature student. We suggest especially Chapter 2, "Family Functions Reflect Social Change," and Chapter 3, "Changing Patterns in Childrearing."

DUVALL, EVELYN MILLIS, and HILL, REUBEN, *When You Marry* (Boston: D. C. Heath and Company, 1953). Chapter 20, "Marriage Isn't What It Used to Be," traces the social changes in the twentieth century that have had a direct impact on marriage and family life, with charts and data to indicate the extent and meaning of recent shifts in the nature of American marriage.

LANDIS, PAUL H., *Your Marriage and Family Living* (New York: McGraw-Hill Book Company, 1954). Section One, "What Marriage and Family Mean Today," has three chapters of special interest: (1) "Why We Need Marriage and the Family"; (2) "The Family—Yesterday and Today"; and (3) "The New Meaning of Marriage and the Family."

MOORE, BERNICE M., and LEAHY, DOROTHY M., *You and Your Family* (Boston: D. C. Heath and Company, 1953). Chapter 17, "Family Life Has Changed," has a section on how the modern family came about, another on why the old-fashioned family could last, and concludes with a treatment of the way the roles of family members have changed.

OGBURN, WILLIAM F., and NIMKOFF, MEYER F., *Technology and the Changing Family* (Boston: Houghton Mifflin Company, 1955). Two of America's outstanding students of social change have written a clear well-documented statement on the various ways in which modern technology has changed the American family and what that means for modern family functioning. A basic background work for the mature student and his teacher.

Chapter 20

Strengthening American Families

Families carry America's burdens. Families bear and rear America's children, teach them American ways, and send them forth as citizens, soldiers, workers, and parents—the men and women of the future. Families are proving grounds for all the professions. Doctors, nurses, and medical research workers depend upon families to put their recommendations into action. Nutrition experts' work counts little unless it is correctly translated into family food habits. Ministers, priests, and church workers depend on families to give religion a place in the daily lives of their members. Law enforcement officers, crime prevention experts, and even the judge on the bench must count upon families to do the major job of maintaining law and order.

When economic depression strikes, families are the first to feel the pinch. When inflation spirals, families are the first hit. When war comes, families are directly involved. When disaster of any kind occurs, families suffer the first and the most lasting losses. Illness, accidents, epidemics, and death all strike families, where they hurt most. Emotional upheaval, marital rifts, mental illness, and family disruption hit close to the heart of the home. America's families are vulnerable to all the adverse forces of twentieth-century living.

Family Troubles and Crises

Every family carries its own peculiar brand of trouble. Many an inexperienced family member may wonder why his family has suffered. Many a sensitive teen-ager may feel that his family is in trouble more than others. Many a person caught in the midst of a family crisis may feel that somehow something is the matter with his family, or it wouldn't be so afflicted. Yet, family crises are universal. No family lives for long without suffering some loss, having difficulty assimilating some new addition, or risking a loss of face of some kind.

368

Losing Family Members. The most obviously painful family crisis is the loss of one of its members. A baby dies before, during, or after birth and the family mourns its loss. A beloved husband or wife is lost. An older relative—father, mother, grandparent, or other aging member of the family has a fatal accident or illness. A family member is hospitalized and is lost to the family circle for the duration of his or her stay in the institution. Family members are separated in wartime, in times of industrial expansion, and periodically in any occupational shift.

When a family loses a member, neighbors and friends express their sympathy. Funeral and memorial services mark the loss appropriately for all to see. The family gradually recovers its equilibrium in its own way and goes on without the absent member. Family adjustments must be made, as the roles of the absent member are assumed by those still in the family. These things are not easy, but they can be done with the support of those who know and care. The thing that helps most is the general recognition of the nature of the loss.

Assimilating New Family Members. Add a new member to a family and there is supposed to be rejoicing. Yet, the addition of another individual to a family can be a genuine crisis. An unplanned and unwanted pregnancy is a real problem that must somehow be faced and worked through in the family with little knowledge or help from the outside world. The coming of a new stepmother or stepfather can be rough on the family as a whole as well as on one or more of the individual family members. The arrival of a foster child or an adopted son or daughter can be a crisis for a time, and perhaps indefinitely disturbing. The return of a long absent family member—the father after years away or a run-away son—may be a dubious joy after the family has reknit itself tightly over the long separation.

The coming of an aging family member to make his, or more often her, home with the family has its critical aspects. The family is expected to be delighted that Grandma or Great Aunt Kate has come to live with them. But the pleasure is diluted by all the shifts and changes that must be made to accommodate the newcomer. Three generations sharing the same home are bound to see things differently. Aging relatives may adore the children but find them noisy and distracting. The children may be pleased with the gifts and services that their resident relatives shower upon them but at the same time irked by efforts at control and by the new demands that older family members make upon them. Parents, caught in the middle, have to play buffer roles in two-way interpretations from crisis to crisis within the family.

Facing Shame and Disgrace. Hardest of all family crises is that of saving face when some family member discredits the family. A boy runs away and his family covers up for him. An unmarried girl gets pregnant and her family shares her disgrace. A husband or wife "runs around" and the community buzzes with the whispers about it. A relative is taken to prison and the rest of the family bears the brunt of the shame. Suicide within the family brings not only a sense of disgrace, but a burden of guilt as to "What could have driven him to do it?" Divorce, separation, desertion have somehow to be "explained" to outsiders who consider the break-up of a family a disgrace or a disaster.

All of these crises, and more, are not uncommon among American families. At some time or other most families have to mobilize themselves to face, accept, and cope with one or more family crises. One reason for this is found in the sequence of hazards that greet the family throughout its entire life cycle.

Meeting Hazards Through the Family Life Cycle

Every stage of family life has its challenges and hazards. The forces that threaten a family at one stage of its life must somehow be met and dealt with at that stage, for with the next stage of family life come other hazards peculiar to it. This sequence of hazards by stages of family life is summarized briefly in the sections that follow.

Attending religious services together gives parents and children a chance to renew and strengthen their sense of emotional and spiritual unity from week to week.

Louise Van der Meid

Hazards of Beginning Families. Young married couples face so many difficult hazards in the first year of marriage it is a wonder that so many marriages survive. Marriages of persons from different cultural, economic, social, religious, and racial groups bring the problems of learning to live with difference within the intimacy of everyday family interaction. Marriages of young people whose education is not yet completed, who are not vocationally established, whose military service is still ahead of them, and who are not mature enough to assume such complex responsibilities are particularly risky, as evidenced by the high percentage of very young marriages that break up in divorce, separation, or annulment.

The beginning family has many expenses to meet on a relatively low income. It is under pressure to establish and equip a home, to "keep up with the Joneses" by getting a car and a television set and a variety of equipment that taxes its income to the limit. This leads to installment-buying abuses, to pressures upon both husband and wife, and to a philosophy of materialism that is a poor start for worthy family living.

Not knowing what to expect in marriage is the greatest hazard of the beginning family. The romantic illusion has spread so many misconceptions and fictions about love and marriage that many a couple struggles to discover meaningful realities as distinct from fallacious stereotypes. A good example is the mother-in-law taboo that keeps many a young married pair from effectively utilizing the resources represented by the two mothers who upon their children's marriage suddenly become discredited as mothers-in-law.

Childbearing Challenges. The hazards of childbearing begin before the baby is born. Some couples who want children face disappointment because of sterility. Other couples have unwanted or unplanned children that are hard to accept. All childbearing couples must work through the fears and uncertainties of pregnancy and learn how to become parents in the process of having children. The high costs of medical and hospital care come at the very time when the family income is sharply curtailed by the woman's quitting her job to have her baby.

Housing problems for families with small children, the high cost of infant clothing and care, and the sense of being tied down by little children are a triple threat to the young family-in-the-making. What to expect of oneself as a parent, of one's parents and grandparents, and most of all of the little newcomer himself is learned only gradually in action within the family.

Childrearing Challenges. An ever-present challenge in childrearing families is that of parents' inability to predict, understand, and meet children's needs. Spotting physical deficiencies, emotional tangles, and mental illness is as important as it is difficult for parents. The high incidence of illness and accidents among young children presents their families with one hurdle after another in keeping children happy and well.

Through the years when children are being reared, the family grows in size and activity. Its needs are great both for physical facilities and for becoming an active part of the community.

Launching Teen-Agers from Home. Families with teen-agers face the double challenge of making things pleasant for young people at home at the very time that they are readying themselves to leave for lives of their own. The hazards are so great this stage that some families do not pass the hurdles without getting hurt. Some adolescents run away, are truant from school, and get into trouble, with each other and with the police. Other young people are confused about what is expected of them as boys and girls, men and women. Many are baffled about what occupation to choose and train for, when to get their military service out of the way, whether to get married and get things settled or to wait until they are more truly ready.

Families face their peak expenses when they are launching their sons and daughters into advanced schooling, vocational establishment, and marriage. Parents' emotional costs are high too, as they worry about the difficulties young people face as they enter the complex world of the twentieth century. They have done the best they can, and yet somehow it never seems to be enough. They want their children to make good marriages and find happiness in homes of their own, but these are the areas that are hardest to discuss, as

"There's a feeding station in *here* that could use some attention too!"

pointed out in Unit II. During the teen years both parents and their young people need the help of resources outside the family to complete successfully the job of launching the younger generation on its adult journey.

The Contracting Family's Challenges. As children grow up and leave home, the family enters its long shrinking phase, ending with the mother and father in their "empty nest" facing old age and retirement. The needs and problems of these stages are unique in each family's history. They are very real and often urgent, yet they have received but scant attention so far.

Proposals for Strengthening American Families

There is general agreement that present-day American families can be strengthened by programs designed to meet their needs and to assist them in their complex modern functions. The proposals that have been most heartily endorsed by national organizations with a central interest in family welfare are in the areas of (1) housing; (2) social security; (3) legal reforms; (4) human relations; (5) education for family living; (6) marriage and family counseling; and (7) family research.

Housing America's Families. The population of the United States is ballooning upward. During the latter 1950's there were in the neighborhood of four million babies born every year. The estimates are that during the latter 1960's there will be close to five million babies born every year. By the 1970's America will average six million babies each year—all to grow up, get married, and have children of their own some twenty to thirty years afterwards—starting still another upward thrust in the population curve.

Where are all of these people going to live? Keeping up with a rapidly expanding population is a major challenge of this century. Housing is an ever-growing problem at a time when our standards of living call for better homes and ways of living for all American families.

Although experts and family members agree upon our need for adequate housing, there is no effective method that is generally accepted for accomplishing this tremendous task. Construction costs continue discouragingly high. Building codes protect the workers and some businesses, but they increase the building costs. Prefabrication and mass-assembly methods are discouraged by labor unions. Real estate interests oppose governmentally subsidized housing developments. While all of these countroversies go on, many families may be inadequately housed. The arrangements families make in shoehorning in with their relatives or living in trailers and basements cannot be called real solutions.

Projects that attempt to provide adequate modern dwellings at moderate cost for large numbers of families should be encouraged. Some of these are initiated by the national government, others by community groups, still others by insurance companies, banks, and real estate operators. The problem of housing is too critical to deny. Families can no longer band together as they once used to and take turns helping each other build their homes. Modern solutions must be found for present-day housing problems.

Social Security. There is general agreement that dependent individuals should be a responsibility of the entire community, not just of their own families. Aid to Dependent Children is a program that protects America's children from neglect through inadequate parental support. Unemployment insurance protects the working man and his family during the time he is laid off from his work. Old-age and survivor's assistance programs safeguard the aging family member from having to be dependent upon other family members. These are just three of the programs within the net of social security America provides for all families.

If America's families are to be strong, there must be a base line below which no family can fall in its daily living. This means far-reaching programs of health, welfare, assured income, and basic services necessary for maintaining an adequate standard of living. Steps already taken in this direction show promise. The job is yet to be finished if the United States is to realize the tremendous potentialities that lie in her greatest resource—the American family.

Legal Reforms. You do not need to be a lawyer to realize that social changes affecting families have greatly outdistanced changes in the legal systems set up to protect them. Present laws of marriage, divorce, adoption, and inheritance are confused and out of date. What is legal in one state is not recognized in others. A man divorced and remarried in one state may be a bigamist across the state line. Similar confusion in the laws between the states brings needless heartache to thousands of families caught in legal tangles in all sorts of family questions. Judges and lawyers sense these problems, but recognize, too, how hard it is to change our laws. It will take a great deal of public concern and pressure to bring about the legal reforms so urgently needed.

Human Relations Programs. America is great because of her differences. This country is made up of people from all over the world. Here the races and the nationalities mingle as citizens of a free society. Yet there are inequalities, misunderstandings, and tensions between the various ethnic and racial groups that present an ever-present challenge to an emergent democracy.

Inequalities emerge in any group situation where some people get in first and stake out their claims to what is available. Go to summer camp, and you find that the first campers to arrive "corner" the best coat hangers, the most desirable locations, and leave what is left to the late-comers. On a larger scale this is what happened in the settling of the United States. Those who came first had their pick of the resources at hand. They developed what they found into the richest nation on earth. Those who came more recently

The shared adventures and discoveries of a family vacation often blaze a pleasant trail of memories. These build a mutual understanding which lasts a lifetime.

to these shores started at the bottom of the economic and social ladder. They settled in the less desirable locations, took the more menial jobs and only after years of struggle achieved anything near the status won by previous generations of "old Americans."

Human relations programs are of service in helping all citizens understand the social forces that play upon all mankind. People of every group can learn to see who they are, where they have come from, where they are going, and where they fit into the larger society. All men everywhere can come to see the essential likenesses of mankind and increasingly to feel a sense of universal brotherhood in which each person is a member of the greater human family.

Education for Family Living. Families have shown considerable ingenuity in meeting their needs for education in the arts and skills of family living. Early in our history the older taught the younger in a system of formal and informal apprenticeship. Daughters learned from their mothers what was expected of them as housewives and mothers and how to do the many things that made up homemaking then. Sons learned from fathers on down through the years. Only when family life differs greatly from one generation to another does this kind of family teaching in family living prove inadequate. Now new knowledge, new insights, and new functions in family life necessitate new methods of education for family living.

Parents today band together in child study groups and parent education meetings, while young people meet in group sessions on dating, courtship, and preparations for marriage problems. Hundreds of universities and colleges in the United States offer courses in some phase of marriage and family living, while public schools from kindergarten through junior college are rapidly increasing their offerings of courses in these fields. Community groups such as the YMCA, the YMHA, the YWCA, churches, women's clubs, and social organizations, offer informal programs in family life education for their constituencies, often with trained leadership and far-reaching influence.

Adequate professional training for the many people who wield influence among families (doctors, nurses, ministers, social workers, librarians, teachers, and community leaders) is now recognized as important for the sound development of family life education. As the training of such workers improves, all families benefit greatly.

Progress in selecting, training, and certifying those who spend full time in family life education is also to be encouraged. Leaders in this field have been self-appointed and educated according to their own sense of need. Full professional training for persons in the family field is now developing. Nothing less will satisfy the rapidly growing demands of millions of family members.

Marriage and Family Counseling. People always have talked over their troubles with someone. It used to be Aunt Clarissa or Grandmother. Now it may be a marriage and family counselor. In a society that changes as rapidly as ours, with as many new developments as there are now, trained counselors are especially necessary.

When a girl is having trouble with her friend, when a boy is worried about his parents, when a mother is upset about her children, or a husband is having trouble with his wife, the difficulty can often be worked out in the family. But sometimes it cannot. Sometimes it becomes worse with time. Situations that seem hopeless to the people involved often can be ironed out with the help of a skillful counselor.

Suitable training for counselors is imperative. Universities offer some work in this field for professional persons. The National Council on Family

Relations has a National Committee on Marriage and Family Counseling, which, in co-operation with the American Association of Marriage Counselors, has set standards for professional practice and a basic curriculum for training qualified counselors. Families themselves can help this movement directly by inquiring into the training and adequacy of the persons who practice in this field in their neighborhoods. Quacks, charlatans, and emotional pirates who prey upon human misery for a fee must be discouraged.

Basic Family Research. Research in marriage and family living is basic. By now, you who have read this book know how helpful sound data can be in answering serious questions about love, marriage, family life, and child-rearing. You must realize too, how many areas there are in which all you can do is to identify the problems and speculate about what would help. Too often you do not have facts to help you.

Research studies in this field have as much promise as they do in technological development. As a nation, we spend millions of dollars annually in research and development of the automobile. Other millions go into the development of the radio, telephone, and household equipment. All these investments have paid for themselves in the great advances they have made possible and in the time and money they have saved. So it can be with research in the family field, as soon as enough resources, enough well-trained social-science research workers, and enough public interest and support are available.

HOME IS THE HUB OF PROGRESS [1]

The homemaker is the primary agent of health care and much of the credit for our improving health, the reduction of disease and early death is due to the increasing knowledge and skills of homemakers.

Likewise, if there is to be any effective program for mental health, as distinguished from diagnosis and treatment of mental illness, it cannot be provided by psychiatrists, psychologists, social workers or clinics, however important their services and their guidance may be. The development and maintenance of healthy personalities capable of living productively, finding fulfillment and continuing to mature is the unique function of the home and family.

It is in the personal relationships of husband and wife, parents and children, brothers and sisters, that our personalities develop and find expression. The family alone can provide the emotional climate, the reassuring feeling of belonging, the psychological "vitamins" of love and affection for living and for renewal of our strength necessary to healthy, maturing personalities and an effective social order.

Thus in the incessant activities of baby care and childrearing, of socializing and cultivating the child and the adolescent, the family is the unique agent for inducting each generation into our symbolic cultural world of meanings and values, feelings and aspirations.

Today we have an immense body of new knowledge and understanding, of new techniques and methods, of penetrating insights and awareness for improving

[1] Excerpts from a statement made by Lawrence K. Frank at the National Conference on Women in the Defense Decade, September 27, 1951, mimeographed materials.

human living, for better health care, for advancing and maintaining mental health, for finding the fulfillments that men and women seek in marriage, family living, and parenthood. The translation of this new knowledge and understanding into all the daily living habits in homes and family practices is an enormous task because it calls for revision of so many of our long-accepted beliefs and practices and such far-reaching reorientation in many of our traditional ideas and expectations.

What Makes Family Living Good? What is a good family like? How do you recognize a family that is doing its job well? Which are the strongest families? What are American families doing that make them good—for their members, and for the country as a whole? When a group of key family life leaders met together at the first National Conference on Family Life, in Washington, D. C., they agreed upon a fourteen-point definition of good family living. These are the qualities that make a family good.[2]

1. It provides a stable base for the development of its members.
2. It transmits the cultural heritage to oncoming generations.
3. It cultivates the deeper, more intimate aspects of living.
4. It interprets life's experiences to its members.
5. It assures the physical and mental health of its members.
6. It encourages the expression of human personality.
7. It serves as a "choosing agency" among many ways of life.
8. It encourages the wholesome expression of love impulses.
9. It protects the human reproductive function.
10. It is a haven—a place where "if you have to go, they have to take you in."
11. It offers a place where individuals may make mistakes within an atmosphere of protection.
12. It practices interdependence rather than competition.
13. It stands for the enjoyment and the fulfillment of life.
14. It lives for something more than the moment and for causes beyond itself.

You Can Improve Your Family. When you were younger, you probably complained when things did not go to suit you. If something was to be changed, you tended to feel that the job belonged to someone else. As you mature, you yourself can accept the responsibility of changing what can be improved. As an adult, you assume the obligation of taking whatever you were dealt by life and making it better if you can. This goes for all that you have and are, including your family.

You can make your family better than it is. You will have to know how to do it. You will need to study and find out what its problems are and how they can best be solved. Families can be improved by the people who live in

[2] Adapted from *Unique Values of Family Life*, Group No. 5, National Conference on Family Life, Washington, D. C., May 5–8, 1948.

them. The family you build some day can be better than the one which your parents developed. It should be. You have had better opportunities than your parents enjoyed.

✓Good families don't just happen. They grow good with the love-in-action of every one of their members. They become strong through mobilizing their resources to meet their challenges. They become good to live in as every member cares for every other member and communicates his feelings, loyalty, affection, and confidence. Would you like to live in such a home? If so, part of the job of making it so is up to you. Your family living is yours to develop, both now and in the home that you some day will establish.

✓Summary

Families bear America's burdens. They are the first hit by national crises, and the most vulnerable to the recurrent troubles, stresses, and strains in today's world. Family crises are faced in losing family members, assimilating new family members, and facing shame and disgrace as a family. Hazards have to be met at every stage of the family life cycle. What these barriers to family success are is seen throughout the lifetime of the family. Programs for strengthening American families include the areas of: (1) housing; (2) social security; (3) legal reforms; (4) human relations; (5) education for family living; (6) marriage and family counseling; and (7) family research. Homes are the hub of progress in which all that is centrally important is focused. There is general agreement on what makes family living good in terms of what it does with and for its members within the larger society. Teen-agers emerging into adult responsibilities can find ways of improving their families— both now and for the years to come.

Suggested Activities

Individual Study

1. Prepare a book report on Earl L. Koos, *Families in Trouble* (New York: King's Crown Press, 1946), and be prepared to present some of the central findings of this classic study to the other members of your class.
2. Select one stage of the family life cycle and elaborate the hazards inherent to it and the services and resources that might be recommended for it, illustrating and documenting fully.
3. Write an essay around one of the fourteen points in the section in this chapter on "What Makes Family Living Good."
4. Review recent issues of the journal of the National Council on Family Relations, *Marriage and Family Living*, for reports of programs in education for family living, marriage and family counseling, and basic family

research. Report your findings in a paper outlining your observations of current trends in efforts to strengthen family life.

5. Write a letter to yourself to be opened upon the birth of your first child, reminding yourself of all you want to do and be as a parent.
6. Write a short statement on how you and your friends could improve your own recreational opportunities. Keep it in your notebook until you can act upon it.

Group Activity

1. Write to state and national agencies with central interests in family life for materials describing their programs, purposes, and offerings. Collect and exhibit these materials in an all-class "Family Life Fair."
2. Invite a school administrator or member of your Board of Education to address your class on the current status of family life education in the total curriculum. Have questions ready for this visit and be prepared to contribute to a discussion of the topic.
3. Take a field trip to your local office for Aid to Dependent Children, to talk with the workers who administer the program about who applies, why some children need such support, and what is done for them.
4. Visit a new housing development in your area to discover the types of dwelling units being constructed, for families of what size, in what income brackets, and whether these units are to be for sale or rent. Find out how soon the units are going on the market and what the prospects are for their attaining full occupancy.
5. On your class blackboards copy off the section, "Services Needed to Help Families Meet Present-Day Challenges and Hazards," from *Family Development* (Chicago: J. B. Lippincott, 1957, pp. 495–510). Discuss each stage of the family life cycle, using double columns, one for its hazards and one for its challenges. Add items that come out of class discussion. Document and illustrate from the family situations known to members of the class.
6. Consider ways that your class might help ease the load of young families in the childbearing stage of life in your neighborhood by such collective services as (a) training and scheduling baby-sitters; (b) volunteering for supervision of small groups of children at the playground; (c) other services that seem needed and for which members of your class might become competent. Prepare a memorandum for neighborhood distribution on the recommendations most likely to emerge as possible service programs.
7. Follow the same procedure as in Number 6, focusing on the needs of older persons in your community. What do they need that your class might help supply?

Readings

DUVALL, EVELYN MILLIS, *Family Development* (Chicago: J. B. Lippincott Company, 1957). This entire book is written around the tasks families face as they develop and what helps families grow strong and good. You will find a detailed outline, "Services Needed to Help Families Meet Present-Day Challenges and Hazards," pp. 495–510.

FORCE, ELIZABETH S., *Your Family Today and Tomorrow* (New York: Harcourt, Brace and Company, 1955). Unit 6, "Outside the Family Circle," has three relevant chapters: 22, "Houses Divided" on the problems of marriage failure and broken homes; 23, on the family's friends (school, religious groups, professional services); and 24, on the family's foes. See especially the parallel outline of friends and foes of family living, pp. 380–84.

KOOS, EARL LOMON, *Families in Trouble* (New York: King's Crown Press, 1946). A classic modern study of the troubles actual families in one city block had within a given period of time, with data on how the families reacted to their crises, what they did about them, and how they finally weathered them, with many implications for improving family living.

MOORE, BERNICE MILBURN, and LEAHY, DOROTHY M., *You and Your Family* (Boston: D. C. Heath and Company, 1953). Chapter 18, "The Family Faces the Future," deals with such problems as divorce, housing, juvenile delinquency, poverty, and unhappiness in families, with suggestions on where hope may be found for the future of the family.

SMART, MOLLIE STEVENS and RUSSELL COOK, *Living in Families* (Boston: Houghton Mifflin Company, 1958). Unit Five, "Family Living in a Changing World," consists of two chapters—the first, "Families Live in Communities," with emphasis on how each affects the other as they both change; the second, on "Today's Families Link Past and Future," showing the strengths that today's families have.

Appendix A

Sources of Films and Filmstrips [1]

Aetna Casualty and Surety Company, Public Education Department, 151 Farmington Avenue, Hartford 15, Connecticut (and affiliates)

Association Films, Inc., Broad at Elm, Ridgefield, New Jersey

Brandon Films, Inc., 200 West 57 Street, New York 19, New York

British Information Services, obtainable through Contemporary Films, Inc., 13 East 37 Street, New York 16, New York

Campus Film Productions, 14 East 43 Street, New York 22, New York

Cathedral Films, obtainable through Association Films

Contemporary Films, Inc., 13 East 37 Street, New York 16, New York

Cornell University Film Library, College of Agriculture, Ithaca, New York

Coronet Instructional Films, 65 East South Water Street, Chicago 1, Illinois

Educators' Guide to Free Films, Educators' Progress Service, Randolph, Wisconsin

Encyclopedia Britannica Films, Inc., Public Relations Department, 1150 Wilmette Avenue, Wilmette, Illinois

Films, Inc., 1150 Central Avenue, Wilmette, Illinois

Filmstrip House, 347 Madison Avenue, New York 17, New York

Household Finance Corporation, Prudential Plaza, Chicago 1, Illinois

Human Relations Aids, 1790 Broadway, New York 19, New York

The Institute of Life Insurance, Educational Division, 488 Madison Avenue, New York 22, New York

International Film Bureau, Inc., 57 East Jackson Boulevard, Chicago 4, Illinois

Kimberly-Clark Corporation, Educational Department, Neenah, Wisconsin

Life Filmstrips, 9 Rockefeller Plaza, New York 20, New York

McGraw-Hill Book Company, Text-Film Department, 330 West 42 Street, New York 36, New York

Mental Health Film Board, 13 East 37 Street, New York, New York

Mental Health Materials Center, Inc., 1790 Broadway, New York 19, New York

---

[1] State universities frequently have film services available to schools in their states. Write for a catalogue of films and filmstrips available through yours.

Methodist Publishing House, Box 871, Nashville, Tennessee

Metropolitan School Study Council, 525 West 120 Street, New York 27, New York

National Association for Mental Health, 13 East 37 Street, New York 16, New York; or 10 Columbus Circle, New York 19, New York

National Education Association, Department of Audio-Visual Instruction, 1201 16 Street, N.W., Washington 6, D. C.

National Film Board of Canada, Box 6100, Montreal 3, Quebec, Canada; or Suite 658, International Building, 630 Fifth Avenue, New York 20, New York; or Suite 1412, Garland Building, 111 North Wabash Avenue, Chicago 2, Illinois

New York State Department of Commerce Films, 40 Howard Street, Albany, New York

New York State Department of Health, Film Library, 26 Washington Place, New York 3, New York

New York State Teachers Association, 152 Washington Avenue, Albany, New York

Personal Products Corporation, Milltown, New Jersey

Pix Film Service, 34 East Putnam Avenue, Greenwich, Connecticut

Syracuse University Film Library, Collendale at Lancaster, Syracuse, New York

State Department of Mental Hygiene, 217 Lark Street, Albany 10, New York

United States Department of Agriculture, films available through United World Films

United World Films, Inc., 1445 Park Avenue, New York 29, New York (and regional offices)

H. W. Wilson Company, 950–972 University Avenue, New York 52, New York

Appendix B

Sources of Pamphlets [1]

A. Caswell Ellis Memorial Collection, c/o Austin Public Library, Box 1145, Austin, Texas

Alcoholics Anonymous Publishing, Inc., Box 459, Grand Central Annex, New York 17, New York

American Association on Mental Deficiency, Box 96, Willimantic, Connecticut

American Institute of Family Relations, 5287 Sunset Boulevard, Los Angeles 27, California

American Medical Association, Bureau of Health Education, 535 North Dearborn Street, Chicago 10, Illinois

American Social Health Association, 1790 Broadway, New York 19, New York

Anti-Defamation League of B'nai B'rith, 515 Madison Avenue, Suite 300, New York 22, New York

Association for Childhood Education, International, 1200 Fifteenth Street, N.W., Washington 5, D. C.

The Association for Family Living, 32 West Randolph Street, Suite 1818, Chicago 1, Illinois

Association Press, 291 Broadway, New York 7, New York

Brethren Publishing House, 22 South State Street, Elgin, Illinois

Child Welfare League of America, Inc., 345 East 46 Street, New York 17, New York

Children's Bureau, United States Department of Labor, Washington 25, D. C.

The Connecticut Mutual Life Insurance Company, Hartford, Connecticut

Division of Christian Education, Department of Adult Work and Family Life, Room 805, 14 Beacon Street, Boston 8, Massachusetts

Educators' Progress Service, Randolph, Wisconsin

Emerson Books, Inc., 251 West 19 Street, New York 11, New York

Family Service Association of America, 215 Park Avenue South, New York 3, New York

---

[1] State extension services and departments of health and education often have helpful pamphlets on child care and family life.

Good Housekeeping Bulletin Service, 57 Street at 8 Avenue, New York 19, New York

Group for Advancement of Psychiatry, 1790 Broadway, New York 19, New York

Hogg Foundation for Mental Health, Mailing Division, University of Texas, Austin, Texas

Household Finance Corporation, Prudential Plaza, Chicago 1, Illinois

Institute of Life Insurance, Educational Division, 488 Madison Avenue, New York 22, New York

John Hancock Mutual Life Insurance Company, Health Education Service, 200 Berkeley Street, Boston 17, Massachusetts

The Kansas City Social Hygiene Society, Inc., 1020 McGee Street, Room 401, Kansas City 6, Missouri

Kimberly-Clark Corporation, Educational Department, Neenah, Wisconsin

Ladies' Home Journal, The Curtis Publishing Company, Independence Square, Philadelphia 5, Pennsylvania

Licensed Beverages Industries, Inc., 155 East 44 Street, New York 17, New York

Louisiana Association for Mental Health, 1528 Jackson Avenue, New Orleans 13, Louisiana

The Macmillan Company, 60 Fifth Avenue, New York 11, New York

McGraw-Hill Book Company, 330 West 42 Street, New York 36, New York

Mental Health Materials Center, 1790 Broadway, New York 19, New York

Michigan Council of Churches, Division of Christian Education, P. O. Box 206, 205 West Saginaw, Lansing 33, Michigan

Minneapolis Public Schools, 807 N.E. Broadway, Minneapolis 13, Minnesota

Minnesota Education Association, 2429 University Avenue, St. Paul 14, Minnesota

National Association for Mental Health, 10 Columbus Circle, New York 19, New York

National Association for Retarded Children, 99 University Place, New York 3, New York

National Committee for Mental Hygiene, 10 Columbus Circle, New York 19, New York

National Committee on Alcoholic Hygiene, Inc., 490 Peachtree Street, N.E., Suite 243, Atlanta 8, Georgia

National Congress of Parents and Teachers, 700 North Rush Street, Chicago 11, Illinois

National Council of Churches, Department of Family Life, 475 Riverside Drive, New York 27, New York

National Council on Alcoholism, Suite 564, New York Academy of Medicine Building, 2 East 103 Street, New York 29, New York

National Council on Family Relations, 1219 University Avenue, S.E., Minneapolis 14, Minnesota

National Institute of Mental Health, Bethesda 14, Maryland

National Society for Crippled Children and Adults, 11 South LaSalle Street, Chicago 3, Illinois

North Carolina Agricultural Extension Service, North Carolina State College, Raleigh, North Carolina

Personal Products Corporation, Milltown, New Jersey

Public Affairs Committee, 22 East 38 Street, New York 16, New York

Science Research Associates, 57 West Grand Avenue, Chicago 10, Illinois

Service Department, Board of Education, The Methodist Church, P. O. Box 871, Nashville 2, Tennessee

State Department of Mental Health, 410 East 5 Street, Austin, Texas

State University of Iowa, Publications Department, Iowa City, Iowa

The Superintendent of Documents, Government Printing Office, Washington 25, D. C.

Texas Association for Mental Health, 2410 San Antonio, Austin, Texas

United States Government Printing Office, Washington 25, D. C.

Yale Center of Alcoholic Studies, Publications Division, 52 Hillhouse Avenue, New Haven, Connecticut

Appendix C

About You

STUDENT QUESTIONNAIRE [1]

(*Do not write in this book.*)

Age ————————
Grade ————————
Boy ————————
Girl ————————

Following are some questions about kinds of things you do at home, some of your likes and dislikes, and your problems in personal and home living. Will you please copy this list and, on your paper, put a check in the blank at the right of the question which best describes you and your feelings. This information will help in improving your junior-high home-living program.

Part I

Following is a list of home activities. Will you read carefully, copy on a separate sheet, and check on your paper in the column to the right whether you do these activities "often" (which means about every day), "sometimes," or "never."

	Often	Sometimes	Never
1. Set the table	——	——	——
2. Clear the table after meals	——	——	——
3. Wash the dishes	——	——	——
4. Help wash the dishes	——	——	——
5. Get breakfast for the family	——	——	——
6. Help get breakfast	——	——	——
7. Get lunch for the family	——	——	——
8. Help get lunch	——	——	——
9. Help pack lunch	——	——	——
10. Get the dinner for the family	——	——	——
11. Help get dinner	——	——	——
12. Help buy groceries	——	——	——
13. Wash woodwork	——	——	——

[1] Circulated at the Family Life Education Workshop sponsored by the Canadian Home Economics Association, Sackville, New Brunswick, July, 1958.

		Often	Sometimes	Never
14.	Wash windows	___	___	___
15.	Wash and wax floors	___	___	___
16.	Clean the bathroom	___	___	___
17.	Run the vacuum cleaner	___	___	___
18.	Dust furniture	___	___	___
19.	Take care of my room	___	___	___
20.	Make my own bed	___	___	___
21.	Help with family laundry	___	___	___
22.	Clean and rearrange cupboards	___	___	___
23.	Wash out my own socks and underwear	___	___	___
24.	Wash my own sweaters	___	___	___
25.	Polish my own shoes	___	___	___
26.	Press my own clothes	___	___	___
27.	Iron my own clothes	___	___	___
28.	Make some of my own clothes	___	___	___
29.	Help make some of my own clothes	___	___	___
30.	Sew on the sewing machine	___	___	___
31.	Sew by hand	___	___	___
32.	Buy some of my own clothes	___	___	___
33.	Help buy some of my own clothes	___	___	___
34.	Mend my own clothes	___	___	___
35.	Wash my own hair	___	___	___
36.	Take care of younger brothers and/or sisters	___	___	___
37.	Baby-sit with other children	___	___	___
38.	Play with younger brothers and sisters	___	___	___
39.	Plan and carry out parties for friends	___	___	___
40.	Help plan and carry out parties for friends	___	___	___
41.	Help with family picnics	___	___	___
42.	Help take care of older people in the home	___	___	___
43.	Help with family parties	___	___	___
44.	Care for pets	___	___	___
45.	Help care for the yard or lawn	___	___	___
46.	Dispose of trash	___	___	___
47.	Arrange flowers for the home	___	___	___
48.	Help arrange flowers for the home	___	___	___
49.	Sweep the sidewalks	___	___	___
50.	Help label and arrange things in the medicine cabinet	___	___	___
51.	Help when someone is ill in my home	___	___	___
52.	Earn some of my own money	___	___	___

Part II

Most of us like to do some things better than others.

1. What things do I *like* to do *best* with my family? (list)

2. What things do I *dislike most* to do with my family? (list)

3. What things do I *like* to do *best* in helping at home? (list)

4. What things do I *dislike most* to do in helping at home? (list)

5. What do I *like* to do *best* with my friends? (list)

6. What do I *dislike most* to do with my friends? (list)

Part III

What problems are troubling you? Following is a list of problems which some high-school pupils have had. Will you please copy this list, and, on your paper, check in the blank to the right if you feel troubled about any of these things.

With Myself—

1. How to have nice-looking hair   _____
2. What to do about pimples   _____
3. Perspiration odors   _____
4. Poor posture   _____
5. Biting nails   _____

6. Rough skin   _____
7. Too few nice clothes   _____
8. How to care for clothes   _____
9. How to be better-looking   _____
10. Often feel shy and bashful   _____

11. Too short for my age _____
12. Too tall for my age _____
13. Overweight _____
14. Underweight _____
15. Wish I were older _____

16. Clumsiness _____
17. Being careless _____
18. Losing my temper _____
19. Being stubborn _____
20. Hurting people's feelings _____

21. Trying to stop a bad habit _____
22. Worry too much _____
23. Being nervous _____
24. Not being serious enough _____
25. Giving in to temptations _____

26. Awkward in meeting people _____
27. Wanting to be more like other people _____
28. Feeling nobody understands me _____
29. Not eating the right food _____
30. Often not hungry for my meals _____

31. Feel tired a lot _____
32. Wanting more information about sex matters _____
33. Knowing how to act wherever I am _____
34. How to have a more pleasing personality _____
35. Not enough time to do everything _____

With My Friends—

36. Slow in making friends _____
37. Wishing people liked me better _____
38. Girls don't seem to like me _____
39. Boys don't seem to like me _____
40. How to keep friends _____

41. How to quit being friends without hurting feelings _____
42. Disliking someone _____
43. Someone disliking me _____
44. Going out with the opposite sex _____
45. Dating _____

46. Not knowing how to make a date _____
47. Not knowing what to do on a date _____
48. No place to entertain friends _____
49. How to give a party _____
50. Trouble in keeping a conversation going _____

51. Learning how to dance   ————
52. What to do for fun with friends   ————
53. Feelings too easily hurt   ————
54. Picking the wrong kind of friends   ————
55. What to do if someone gets angry with me ————

56. No one to tell my troubles to   ————
57. Suitable gifts for friends   ————
58. How to make gifts which will not cost much ————

With My Family—

59. How to ask parents for money   ————
60. Mother scolds me too much   ————

61. Father scolds me too much   ————
62. Parents show favorites   ————
63. Parents won't let me do the things I want to do ————
64. Parents don't like my friends   ————
65. Parents away from home too much   ————

66. Being treated like a small child at home ————
67. Parents do not trust me   ————
68. Parents old-fashioned in their ideas   ————
69. Unable to talk things over with parents   ————
70. Talking back to parents   ————

71. Getting along with mother   ————
72. Getting along with father   ————
73. Getting along with older brothers and/or sisters ————
74. Getting along with younger brothers and/or sisters ————
75. Getting along with grandparents, or others living in my home ————

76. What to do for fun with my family   ————
77. How to be more pleasant and co-operative with my family ————
78. Why my family is different from other families ————

List on your paper other problems which you have:

With myself—

With my friends—

With my family—

Index

(Page references in italics refer to illustrations and tables)

of child in family, 8–10; reciprocal needs of youth and, 94–96; rejection of children by, 12; selection of clothes by, 83–84; setting goals, 293–294; strict, 84–85, 84; subjects difficult to discuss with, 101–104, *102, 103*; teen-agers and, 28–30, 80–85, 89–91, 101–117; teen-agers need, 85–87; teen-agers' view of "parent problem," 29, 80–85, *81, 82*; treating teen-agers like children, 82–83; "understanding" by, *81*; what they expect of teen-agers, 91–94; working-class, 14, 92–93
Parent-youth code, 108–112
Parent-youth relationships, 28–30, 89–91, 109
Parties, parent-youth code, 109
Part-time jobs, *24*
Patience, of parents and teen-agers, 95–96
Peace, families build patterns of, 261–263, 364–365
Personal attractiveness, 25
Personality: body physique and temperament, 6; check test for growth, 40; definition, 146; effect of sex differences on, 4–5; feelings about being born a boy or girl, 4–5; individual differences, 6–8, *7*; influences affecting, 3; inherited traits, 6–8; of identical twins, *7*; of marriage partners, 218; special abilities and talents, 6; types, 10
Personality development: abilities and interests, 11–12; community and, 13–15; conception of self, 13; cultural and social pressures, 34–35; developmental tasks of teen-agers, 22–34; evaluating progress, 56; family influence, 10; going steady may cause it to be one-sided, 187–188; good families grow good people, 71–72; good physical health needed, 55–56; growing independence, 12–13; how to take failure, 66–69; identical twins, 11; intellectual maturity and, 55; knowing and understanding self, 54–56; need for love and affection, 63–65; needs as a growing person, 60–63; of children, 294–295; philosophy of life and, 15; position in family, 8–10; requirements for growth, 60; self-confidence, 11–12; social status and, 14–15; White House Conference on, 294–295; willingness to improve, 56
Petting, 102
Philosophical maturity, 52–54
"Philosophy Four" (poem), 41
Philosophy of life, 15, 52; family living and, 347; starts in childhood, 53
Physical development: changes during adolescence, 24–25; personality development and, 6; teen-agers, 19–22, 35
Physical maturity, 42; individual differences, 21

Physical needs, 60–63
Pimples, treating, 21
Plant, James, 60
Play: guiding, 289–290; kinds of, 288–289; learning through, 288–290; toys and playthings, 290
Poise, development of, 175; ease in meeting strangers, 49
Polls, of high-school students, 80
Popularity: changes in time, 158–159; clothes not everything, 145–146; definition, 145; factors causing, *159*; friendship and, 145–160; girl everyone likes, *147*; ideal boy and girl, 26; looks, 146; personality and, 146–147
Population trends, 373
Praise, need for, 64
"Prayer, The" (poem), 33–34
Preschool: developmental tasks, 304–306; family life and, 339; mother-teacher cooperation, 329–330; preparing child for, 329
Prescott, Daniel, 60
Pride: in family, 138; injured, 9; of parents, 87, 93
Privacy: need for, 138; teen-agers' desire for, 80; time for being alone, enjoyment of, 49–50, 80
Problem-solving: approaches, 44, 107–108, *110–111*; direct attack, 69; getting through to each other, 107–108; making stepping stones out of stumbling blocks, 69; patterns for, *110–111*
Projection, as a defense mechanism, 68
Puberty, cycle of: changes during, 20–21; definition, 36; individual differences, 21; velocity of growth, 19, 20
Punishing children, 322
Purchases, family, 130–132, 268–269
Purdue Opinion Panel, 29, 80, 82, 101, 174, 182, 231

Quarrels: between children, 133; constructive techniques, 261–263
Questions of children, answering, 290–293

Rationalization, 69
Readiness for learning, 321
Records, household, 131
Recreation: definition, 115; family, 115–116; married couples, 249; values in family fun, 115
Regional differences, 14–15, 355–358
Regression, 66–67
Rejection, feelings of, 12
Relationships: acceptance of others, 25–28, 156; family, 28–30, 87–88, 121–139, 345; speaking well of others, 156–157; teen-agers', with parents, 79–98. *See also* Grandparents

INDEX OF FOOTNOTE REFERENCES